W9-BEH-291

The Ray Dream Handbook

Second Edition

The Ray Dream Handbook

Second Edition

Edited by

John W. Sledd

CHARLES RIVER MEDIA, INC.
Rockland, Massachusetts

Publisher: David F. Pallai
Executive Editor: Jenifer Niles
Production: Reuben Kantor
Cover Design: John W. Sledd & Monty Lewis
Printer: InterCity Press

CHARLES RIVER MEDIA, INC.
P.O. Box 417
403 VFW Drive
Rockland, Massachusetts 02370
781-871-4184
781-871-4376 (FAX)
chrivmedia@aol.com
http://www.charlesriver.com

This book is printed on acid-free paper.

The Ray Dream Handbook
Edited By John W. Sledd
    ISBN 1-886801-36-3
    Printed in the United States of America

98 99 00 01 02 7 6 5 4 3 2 Second edition

CHARLES RIVER MEDIA titles are available for site license or bulk purchase by
institutions, user groups, corporations, etc. For additional information, please contact
the Special Sales Department at (781) 871-4184.

DEDICATION

To Janel, my wonderfully amazing wife, for putting up with me, in general; and for putting up with yet another seemingly endless period of time when her husband was virtually invisible (and when visible, often grouchy).

— JWS

Contents

Foreword

Ever since the beginning of the *Ray Dream* saga (back in the days when *Ray Dream* was the company and *Designer* was the product), its users have been among the most creative and innovative artists in the world of 3D. *Ray Dream's* creators have always been impressed by the work and successes which have come from such innovation and have worked very hard to provide these artists with new and better tools to aid and augment the creation of their masterpieces.

The above facts haven't changed one bit over the years, and the book you are holding in your hands is testament to that fact. The first edition of this book was brought to you by many of these artistic innovators and was a wonderful tool in the effort to educate members of the digital (and even some of the traditional) art community on the wonders of 3D illustration and animation. I think you'll find this second edition takes that even a couple of steps further. The current version of Ray *Dream Studio* is more powerful than anyone ever "dreamed" when *Designer* first shipped thanks to the hard work of the Ray Dream Team; the third-party developers who work just as hard to provide you with additional Ray Dream tools to add to your artistic toolbox; and thanks to you, the users, whose imagination and suggestions have been responsible for much of this power. This book does a great job of uncovering much of this new power with new contributions from artists using many of the new features, as well as maintaining the tradition of the first edition by showing you how to utilize the power *Ray Dream* has been known for over the years.

Whether you use *Ray Dream Studio* to create your own personal images and animations, or whether you rely on it for your livelihood, you will certainly benefit from the experience of those whose contributions grace these pages. While this book may not turn you into an award-winning artist overnight, it will help to streamline the technical and creative processes which will inevitably take a few degrees out of that steep learning curve 3D is known for. By design, *Ray Dream Studio* already makes the climb considerably easier, but partnered up with the *Ray Dream Handbook*, the trip is little more than a mild incline. 3D has an ever-changing face. New products, new techniques and new expectations are constantly emerging, so even if you've already made the initial climb, you will find a good deal of useful, production-enhancing and inspiring knowledge to apply to your future projects and to help you stay camped at the summit.

Furthermore, we at MetaCreations want to know what you're doing with our tools. Please don't hesitate to keep us up-to-date by sending us pieces of your work and by participating in the various contests we have from time to time. If you are a developer — whether you're a weekend warrior or a professional software king — we encourage you to take a look at Ray Dream's API. We'd love to work with you on the next RDS Extension.

Lastly, we want you to know that we are as committed to providing you with the tools (and the knowledge to use them) as you are to the art itself, which is why we're so excited about our role in providing you with another edition of this book. Good luck with your endeavors and enjoy the book.

Mark Zimmer
Chief Technology Officer
MetaCreations

Acknowledgments

This second edition of the Ray Dream Handbook is the product of oodles of diligent hard work left over from the first edition. It also contains a good bit of new information which was needed to bring everything up to date with RDS 5.0, and to provide some additional goodies to those who have dog-eared and otherwise destroyed their first edition copies.

I'd like to begin by thanking Craig Patchett for setting the stage. This edition had a good solid foundation to build upon thanks to his effort and trials with the first one. I'd like to thank the contributors of the first book, especially Mr. Steve McArdle, whose talent and contributions were outdone only by the amount of bad luck he had trying to get his copy of the book. Many great thanks also to those who have donated their time, once again, to share their discoveries since last time and to those who are newcomers to the Ray Dream Handbook hall of fame.

These people make this book the success it is so please take the time to read a little bit about them in the Contributor Directory section in the back of the book. All of the information you need to let them know how much you appreciate their efforts is located there. Please be sure to make plenty of references to their apparent genius, generosity, vision, and overall genetic superiority. It'll make them feel good to have a groupie or two slobbering at their feet. Many thanks to them all.

I'd also like to thank my publisher, Dave Pallai and Executive Editor, Jenifer Niles for showing a great deal of patience and compassion during some of the trials and tribulations my family faced throughout this project. As a matter of fact, Janel and I both thank you.

It simply wouldn't be proper to have an acknowledgment page without thanking my family and friends for putting up with, and supporting, yet another book. Mom, Dad, Grandma, Gran'dad, Connie, John, Joe Bob (I mean, Robert), Terry, Kathy, Helen, Ellsworth, Rick, Dennis, John C., Walt,

Scott, Cecilia, Aureliano, Tony, Gayle, Keith L., and MarioÉthank you all for the patience and support.

I would also like to extend a big "warm fuzzy" thank you to the *Ray Dream Studio* people themselves (past and present); Pierre Berkaloff, Pascal Belloncle, John Stockholm, Yann Corno, Eric Graham, Greg Mitchell, Logan Roots, Emil Valkov, Joshua Van Abrahams, Eric Brayet, Joel Derrienic, Thomas Ripoche, Damien Saint-Macary, Gray Norton, Michael Cinque, Curt Hironaka, Randy Hollingsworth, Joe Grover, Steve Yatson, Jonathan Trachtenberg, Stephanie Arvizu, Jason Green and Teri Campbell. Thanks to some of them for their assistance in making this book a reality, and some simply for creating this marvelous piece of software that brings us all so much enjoyment (not to mention the occasional smattering of frustration) — and some of them for a little bit of both.

Many additional thanks to God and Jesus for being the recipients of the late night panic-chants of: "Please God . . . let me finish this book. Oh Jesus, let me finish this book. Oh God, PLEASE let me finish this book. Lord, I'll never <insert favorite sin here> again, if you just please let me finish this book." Thanks for listening.

Thanks also to the creators of "South Park" for providing me with many needed chortles and yuks during the process.

Lastly, I'd like to thank you readers out there for making this book such a success at the box office. I hope it helps make reaching those 3D goals just a little bit easier.

To everyone mentioned, above and to anyone I may have errantly left out, THANK YOU!

— John W. Sledd

About the Editor

John W. Sledd is a freelance illustrator/animator (and sometimes author) residing deep in the mountains of Front Royal, Virginia, where he enjoys throwing dirt clods and hunting the elusive snipe (for those of you unfamiliar with snipe hunting, don't worry — nobody gets hurt. Cold maybe, but not hurt.)

His work appears in and on magazines, books, collectible card games, computer games, CD-ROMs and many other vehicles where high-tech, science fiction, futuristic, businesslike or sometimes just-plain-silly imagery is needed to tell a tale or sell a ware.

About The CD-Rom

The CD-ROM included with this book provides Scene, Texture, AVI, QuickTime, and Shader files from the book for you to practice with. It also includes demo textures and movies from the ArtBeats collections for you to use in your own projects.

The files are set up for all the chapters that contain the tutorials. Please note that not all chapters have these files.

The Data Folder on the CD contains samples from Hash's standard.

What is this "Data Folder" stuff? I have also included a *read_me* for the CD-ROM that explains that some chapters do not have accompanying files.

System Requirements

Ray Dream Studio 5.0 (I took out 4.0 here because the scene and shader files are not backwards compatible)

PC
486 Pentium or Pentium Pro-based PC
Minimum of 16 megs of RAM (24+ recommended)
Windows 95 or Windows NT
Minimum of 40 megs of Hard drive space
Color display
Windows compatible graphics card with minimum of 256 colors
CD-ROM drive (does it have to have a 32 bit driver?)

PowerMac
PowerMac or compatible running system 7.0 later
Minimum of 20 megs of available RAM (24+ recommended)
40 megs of Hard drive space
CD-ROM Drive
Color display

Installation

Insert the CD into the appropriate drive. Select the folder you wish to open. Most all files can be displayed and/or edited using only Ray Dream Studio but some of the files may require additional programs to edit or view based on their file type (e.g. Adobe Illustrator/Photoshop or similar paint/drawing applications).

For problems with the CD please contact us at chrivmedia@aol.com or 781-871-4184.

The Adventure Begins...Again

Welcome to the second edition of the *Ray Dream Handbook*, the premier guide to getting the most out of Ray Dream Studio, Ray Dream 3D and CorelDream. The following pages are filled with knowledge gleaned from Ray Dream masters with years of experience who have generously offered to share their expertise. The tips and techniques you'll learn from them will help you to become a better 3D artist/designer.

The objective of the first edition of this book was to go beyond simply teaching you some new skills; it was also designed to inspire you in your 3D projects and help you to make them more adventures than chores. I'm sticking with that intention this time around too, hence the first part of the title of this chapter hasn't changed a bit.

I added the ". . . Again" to the end of the chapter title not only because this is a second edition, but also because we're working with an entirely new application. Ray Dream Studio 5.0 may look the same on the outside, but on the inside it's a screamin', vertex-pullin', animatin' animal of a 3D application.

WHAT'S NEW

This edition of the Ray Dream Handbook contains many new tips and techniques not present in the first edition. For starters, this second edition has been completely updated for Ray Dream Studio 5, so all screenshots and commands have been updated to correspond with the new version. In addition to the updates, many features were added in version 5 and we've covered several of those too. And if that wasn't enough, we added a bunch of great techniques that don't necessarily require version 5 but are simply good tips and techniques in general.

You'll find new tips and techniques in the following areas:

- Using the Mesh Form Modeler
- Using Links and Inverse Kinematics
- Using RDS 5 with Detailer
- Using Extensions like Four Elements, BoneBender, HotLips and FaceShifter
- Tips and Tricks for using deformers, fountain primitives, shaders and plug-ins in ways you may not have thought of before.
- A great tip for aiming cameras and lights
- Getting a Radiosity look
- Using Global Mix shader components
- Animating Master Groups

- A great "flying logo" tutorial
- Shockwaves, Lightning and Smoke
- Using RealVR
- Three new Featured Artists

PLUS many Scene, Texture, AVI, Quicktime and Shader files are included on the Accompanying CD-ROM.

The hope is that as you go through this book you'll learn more than just which button to push and when. I hope you will learn how to tame this animal and express your creativity more freely without being limited by not knowing how to get something done. Please look at this book as more than just pages of directions. Don't just punch in the numbers in these tutorials. Try to get a feel for why the creator chose this way or that way to do something. Think about ways that might be better, or at least different, ways to achieve the same results. Once you understand the ifs and whys, you'll be well on your way to being able to solve your own problems as they arise; and may quite possibly come up with the next brilliant tip or technique. This is the Zen of Ray Dream Studio.

Section One: Getting the Most from This Book

This section answers some of the basic questions you may have about the book and how you can best benefit from it. It will tell you what hardware and software you need and what level of experience is required.

Section Two: Overview of the Ray Dream Handbook

This book is divided up into three basic parts. This section will tell you what each part is about, how each part is laid out, and generally where you need to go to find a particular type of information.

SECTION ONE: GETTING THE MOST FROM THIS BOOK

Creating good 3D art can be one of the most intimidating tasks an artist can face . . . even for a pro. Good 3D requires skills in sculpture, painting, photography, lighting and, although you may not think about it right away, good organizational skills as well. If you're planning on making this stuff move, you've got to be versed in direction and motion theory too (thus adding a fourth dimension to your 3D work). This isn't exactly a walk in the park, but once you get the hang of it, your results can be extremely rewarding. There's nothing quite like looking at a wonderful piece that's full of life and energy and thinking to yourself, "I made this." This book is here to help you get to that point.

The *Ray Dream Handbook* can be distinguished from other 3D graphics books because it is the first book to focus exclusively on Ray Dream software and it also draws from the combined experience of more than 20 top Ray Dream artists rather than the limited experience of one or two. Therefore you can use it to skip right past a good bit of the learning curve normally associated with 3D software, and get right to the fun part: translating your ideas into 3D images, which, as far as I'm concerned, is why we're all here.

WHAT IS THIS BOOK ABOUT?

The *Ray Dream Handbook* is about getting the most from your Ray Dream software: plain and simple. Top Ray Dream artists will share with you the tips and techniques they use to create the images you've seen time and time again and wondered: "How did they do that?" You'll learn how to apply these tips and techniques to your own images and use them not only to get some really cool visual effects, but also to make the whole process of creating a 3D image or animation a lot easier and faster. You'll also learn how to develop a 3D thought process that will let you approach any model or scene and know exactly what you need to do in order to build it in Ray Dream. Finally, you'll get a chance to go behind the scenes with several Ray Dream artists and see how they create their images.

WHAT SOFTWARE AND HARDWARE DO I NEED?

You can use the *Ray Dream Handbook* with any computer that will run Ray Dream Studio, Ray Dream 3D or CorelDream. The Macintosh and Windows versions of the software share the same interface and are functionally identical, so the tips, techniques and concepts presented in the book are applicable to either version. In fact, you may notice that some of the screen shots in the book are from the Windows version while others are from the Macintosh version. The only major difference is in how shortcut key commands are accessed; Windows uses the **Ctrl** key while the Macintosh uses the **Command** key. To accommodate this, shortcut commands are referenced in the book using **Command/Ctrl**. In the case of modifier keys, **Option** on the Mac is equivalent to **Alt** on the PC. So you'll see these key conventions listed as **Option/Alt** where appropriate.

With respect to software, you will, of course, need a copy of Ray Dream Studio, Ray Dream 3D or CorelDream. I recommend that you use at least version 5.0 (applicable to RDS and RD3D only) since that's the version we base this edition on. Many of the tips and techniques will work with older versions, but version 5 contains so many cool new goodies that it's virtually a sin not to upgrade. For the sake of consistency, I use the term *Ray Dream Studio* or *RDS* (that's what all we extremely cool people call Ray Dream Studio) throughout the book when referring to the software.

You'll also find references to other software programs in the book, especially image editing, video composition and illustration software (for instance, Photoshop, Painter, Premiere, Illustrator or CorelDRAW). Although there are several tips and techniques that rely on the use of such programs, most notably in the postproduction chapter, the vast majority of information in the book requires Ray Dream Studio alone.

HOW MUCH EXPERIENCE DO I NEED?

While the *Ray Dream Handbook* is designed to be used by beginners and experts alike, I must assume that you are familiar with the basic workings of Ray Dream Studio, have gone through the tutorials, and have at least browsed through the other parts of the manual. In particular, make sure you have a basic understanding of how to use the **Perspective** and **Modeling** windows and how to create and edit a simple shader. This will make it a lot easier to get the most out of the book, although you may still be able to follow along without it.

The most important thing is to approach the book with a desire to learn and a willingness to experiment. These two things are the key to turning both this book and Ray Dream Studio itself into the adventure they were designed to be. This book will not turn you into a 3D pro all by itself— 3D requires a lot of work and a lot of exploration. We can help you over some of the humps but climbing the rest of the mountain is ultimately your responsibility.

HOW SHOULD I USE THIS BOOK?

If you're already at least somewhat familiar with Ray Dream Studio, then this book is designed so you can sit down in front of your computer with RDS running, and read it from cover to cover. There are several other approaches you might prefer to take, however, depending on your level of experience with Ray Dream Studio and with 3D graphics in general; and depending, of course, on what you want to do right now! For example, you may have already built a spaceship but you're unsure how to create a good shader for it. Well then, just skip to Chapter 9 and look for something that will get you started.

Beginner

Start out by reading the next chapter, "Thinking in 3D," which gives a good overview of how to approach the 3D process in general and with respect to Ray Dream Studio (this is *very* important). Make sure you've gone through the tutorials in the Ray Dream Studio user manual to get acquainted with the basics. That's what it's there for. Use this book as a supplement to the user manual as you learn the program, and then let it become a reference and resource guide as you start delving into more advanced techniques and features.

Intermediate

Intermediate users will also find Chapter 2 useful. Use it to hone the thought process that you've already started to develop, and also to give you some new ideas as to how Ray Dream Studio's tools can be used. You can then browse through the tips and techniques chapters for those areas of the program where you would like to strengthen your level of expertise, or for when you're looking for that special doodad or effect. At some point, take a look at Chapter 16 to get a feel for how some of the top Ray Dream artists approach their projects.

Advanced

If you're already a Ray Dream Studio expert, you're holding an excellent reference and resource guide that I hope will quickly become dog-eared. Browse through the tips and techniques chapters for new ideas, use Chapter 16 to compare strategies with some of your peers, and see how your own thought process compares with that in Chapter 2. Regardless of how much experience you have, you'll be able to use this book to make the 3D design process even smoother and to fuel your creative engine.

SECTION TWO: OVERVIEW OF THE RAY DREAM HANDBOOK

The remaining chapters in the *Ray Dream Handbook* can be broken down into three distinct parts that are designed to be somewhat sequential. You can, however, read through them in any order you like.

PART ONE: CHAPTER 2

The first part of the book is only one chapter long, but is probably as important as the rest of the chapters combined. It explains how to think in 3D, or how to approach any 3D project and start thinking about it in the same terms that Ray Dream Studio does. Once you have the ability to do this, you can communicate your ideas to Ray Dream Studio in its own language rather than struggling to interpret everything for the program one step at a time.

Even if you've already had some experience with 3D graphics, avoid the temptation to skip over this chapter. Not only does the information in the chapter make Ray Dream Studio a lot easier to use, it also offers insights into some of the program's capabilities that you may not know about.

PART TWO: CHAPTERS 3 TO 16

This part of the book contains specific tips and techniques for getting the most out of Ray Dream Studio and for creating some unique effects. (Tips are more advice-oriented, while techniques are more hands-on.) All were selected by the contributing artists based on their ability to make the 3D design process easier, to add to a scene's realism or effectiveness, or to push Ray Dream Studio to new limits. In other words, you'll find a little of everything, but it will all be useful.

The chapters in this part are arranged so that they follow the typical creative process involved in creating a 3D image or animation: modeling, lighting, composition, shaders, animation, rendering, postproduction, special effects and Ray Dream and the Internet. (While shading may seem out of place in this sequence, both lighting and composition will affect the way shaders appear, and should therefore be taken care of before you create and apply your shaders.) If you're working on a particular project, you may want to browse through each chapter in this part for ideas as you move through each stage of development in your project.

PART THREE: CHAPTER 17

Like the first part, the third part of the book is only one chapter, but it offers a unique and valuable behind-the-scenes look at how several top Ray Dream artists approach the design process. From concept to completion, you'll see how these artists develop a project and you'll have an opportunity to learn from their techniques and experience. You'll also be able to see how some of your favorite images were put together.

GETTING YOUR HANDS DIRTY

Regardless of how you decide to approach this book, get your hands dirty as quickly as possible. The information on these pages is meant to be *used*. Sit down in front of your computer, start up Ray Dream Studio, and start experimenting. The more you do so, the quicker you'll learn.

You'll become a better Ray Dream artist by reading this book. You'll become a much better one by applying it. Have fun and enjoy the adventure!

2

Thinking
in 3D

I t should come as no surprise to you that we live in a three-dimensional world. (If it does then this book will be that much more enjoyable!) Everything around us has height, width and depth. We take this for granted when communicating in any visual medium, but since the Renaissance artists have struggled to add the third dimension to their work. Only relatively recently have computers made the transition into 3D graphics, but the match is perfect. Computers are so powerful and so precise that their capabilities are ideally suited to dealing with the complexities of 3D. Add a program like Ray Dream Studio, and your imagination is the only thing standing between you and incredible 3D creations.

While I did mention that the 3D design process can be intimidating, I didn't say it was impossible. As a matter of fact, it gets much easier as you get better acquainted with how your tools work and, most importantly, how *you* work. One of the most valuable techniques you can use to streamline your work flow is planning ahead. This chapter will teach you how to think in 3D, how to develop the thought processes necessary to analyze any 3D project, and how to prepare the best approach for completing the project smoothly. Consider it essential basic training — kind of like boot camp, but you don't have to get up early.

Section One: The Modeling Thought Process
Success in modeling depends on how well you can see the object you're trying to model in terms of how Ray Dream Studio will see it. The modeling thought process involves analyzing each object to determine the best way to reproduce it using Ray Dream Studio's modeling tools.

Section Two: The Lighting Thought Process
Lighting plays a big role in setting the mood of a scene by enhancing the depth effect and colors of the objects in it. The lighting thought process will help you understand the different types of lighting and the effect they have on a scene, and will make it easier to determine what type of lighting you need.

Section Three: The Shading Thought Process
Shaders define how real your scene looks and can make a simple object look stunning or a complex object look mediocre. The shading thought process will help you understand how to use Ray Dream Studio's powerful shaders to get just the effect you're looking for.

Section Four: The Composition Thought Process
When all the other elements of your scene are in place, composition and camera positioning ultimately make the difference between taking a snapshot and

creating a work of art. The composition thought process involves learning how to present your scene in the most artistic way.

Section Five: The Animation Thought Process

Animation literally brings your scene to life, and brings all of the associated complexities with it. The animation thought process helps you break down an animation into manageable parts, understand the different elements involved, and choose the best approach for your particular needs.

SECTION ONE: THE MODELING THOUGHT PROCESS

The first step in 3D design is to create, or model, the objects that will appear in your image. This process can seem overwhelming at first, and if you're working with complex objects it's often difficult even to know where to start. The solution is to gain a basic understanding of the modeling process and learn how to think ahead when planning your scene. You'll then start to see the world around you in a whole new way that will make recreating it on your computer much easier.

MAKE THINGS SIMPLE

The key to the modeling process is to realize that every complex object can be broken down into simple objects and that these simple objects can then be broken down into simple shapes (some more simple than others). Think about it. Simple objects such as an egg, a football, a pencil, a lightbulb, a bottle and a wineglass are all based on a circle. The only difference between them in terms of shape is how that circle is manipulated in each of the three dimensions.

Ray Dream Studio allows you not only to stretch or pull the circle (or any other shape) in any of the three dimensions, but also to manipulate each of the dimensions to distort the results. For example, look closely at a wineglass. First look at it sideways and then from the top. From the side it looks like a letter U sitting on top of an inverted T. From the top it looks like a series of circles. What if you could take a circle and stretch it into a cylinder, but along the way adjust the shape of the edges so they conformed to the side view of the wineglass? You would then have a pretty good copy of the wineglass, made from a simple circle. (See Figure 2.1.)

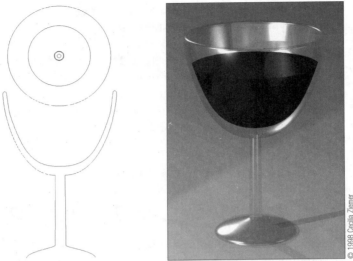

FIGURE **2.1**   *Look at the top and side of a wineglass and you can see that it is built from a simple circle that has been extruded along a particular shape.*

Call this circle a *2D primitive*, meaning it is a primitive shape compared to a more complex one. Spin the circle around its center and you have a sphere, which we'll call a *3D primitive*. Now think along the same lines for other 2D primitives. A square spun around its center becomes a cylinder and a triangle becomes a cone. You can also create a cylinder by adding depth to a circle and you can create a cube by adding depth to a square. These 2D and 3D primitives are the basic objects that can be combined and manipulated to create more complex ones.

Most of the objects around you are built from 2D and 3D primitives in one respect or another, as is easy to see with simple objects like the wineglass. But what about a more complex object, such as your hand? If you look at your hand carefully, you'll notice that your fingers are basically made up of three cylinders connected by spheres (your knuckles and your fingertips). Your thumb is much the same. The palm of your hand is essentially a flattened sphere. Of course, simple spheres and cylinders will never look exactly like a human hand, but they will form a very good foundation upon which you can build, as you can see from Figure 2.2.

When you start to look at objects in terms of 3D primitives, you will never look at anything in quite the same way again. People will become a series of spheres, cylinders and cones walking down the street, bicycles will suddenly become an intricate arrangement of cylinders (a wheel is nothing more than a flat cylinder with a hole in it), and your faithful pet will be transformed into a weird and wonderful combination of shapes and objects. Most importantly,

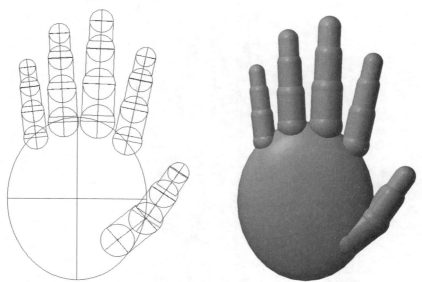

FIGURE **2.2** *While 3D primitives such as cylinders and spheres aren't enough to build a perfect replica of complex objects, they form the basic building blocks for most objects.*

you will have taken the first step in the modeling thought process and will be ready to make the leap to creating 3D objects on your computer.

ORIENT YOURSELF

Sculptors start with a block of marble and gradually take away from it until they get the shape they are looking for (reduction). Ray Dream Studio's Free Form and Mesh Form Modelers in most cases use the opposite method (additive) to create objects. You can create a model by subtraction, using Boolean tools, but it's seldom the best alternative.

The Free Form modeler is based on an extrusion method that is defined by successive profiles in all three dimensions. The Mesh Form modeler also works in a similar fashion but adds the extra control of being able to edit the individual vertices and polygon faces of your objects. (This is a lot easier to use than it sounds!) In the real world we refer to the three dimensions as width, depth and height, but on the computer we use mathematical traditions and refer to them as the X, Y and Z axes. Understanding how these axes work is the second key to mastering the modeling process.

Like the axes on a graph, each of the X, Y and Z axes has a positive and negative direction. The X axis, which corresponds to width, moves from right

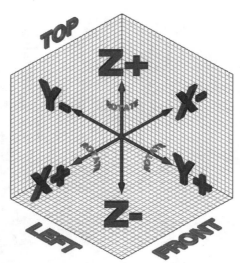

FIGURE *Understanding how Ray Dream Studio represents 3D*
2.3 *space is essential to the modeling process.*

to left as you look at the front of an object. The Z axis, which measures height, moves from bottom to top. The Y axis, which measures depth, moves from back to front. Figure 2.3 shows these relationships.

On a graph, you can refer to any point using coordinates, which measure the distance from each of the axes to that point. For example, (2, 3) would refer to the point two units to the right on the horizontal axis and three units up on the vertical axis. The same is true in 3D space, which is really nothing more than a 3D graph. The coordinates (10, 5, 12), for example, refer to the point 10 units to the left on the X axis, five units forward on the Y axis, and 12 units up on the Z axis. (Coordinates are always given in X, Y, Z order.) The point 10 units to the right on the X axis would be expressed as (–10, 5, 12). This may be a little confusing at first, since you would expect a negative X coordinate to be on the left, but you'll get used to it quickly. All distances are measured from the origin, or (0, 0, 0), which is the point where the three axes cross.

Rotation also plays a large role in the modeling process (not to mention most other aspects of scene setup and animation). Ray Dream Studio also has it's own little way of working with rotation. Instead of working on a full 360° rotational scheme, RDS works on a negative and positive relationship just as its X, Y, Z coordinates do. The rotational values of 1° to 180° are normal, but once you hit 180°, RDS flips over to the dark side, and you start counting down from –179° to –1°. Similar to the X axis, the positive rotational numbers run to the left — or *counterclockwise,* a more appropriate explanation of rotation. For example, a rotation of 90° would rotate the object ¹/₄ of a full rotation counterclockwise, but a rotation of 270° would actually be −90° in Ray Dream Studio and would be a rotation of 1/4 of a turn clockwise. Figure 2.4 is a chart I drew up for myself a while back as a reference tool for easy rotational values. Looking at it should clear up any of the confusion I've just created. The word *Rotate* in Figure 2.3 illustrates how an object rotates on an axis. For example, an object rotated on the Z axis would spin around the Z axis in the same way Rotate is oriented on the Z axis in Figure 2.3.

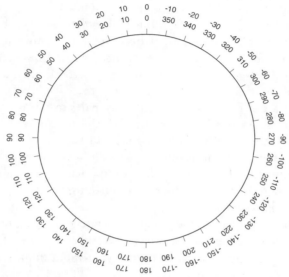

FIGURE **2.4** *Here's a quick reference chart for converting real-world rotational values to Ray Dream Studio rotational values.*

Once you understand the coordinate system and how objects behave in this coordinate system, you're well on your way to thinking in 3D. This transformation of thought not only will make you more aware of the objects and the space around you, but will also allow you to understand how Ray Dream Studio interprets your 3D input. As soon as you understand what Ray Dream Studio expects from you, you have the beginning of the perfect relationship for 3D creation.

PLAN AHEAD

The modeling thought process you've been developing throughout this section makes it easy to plan ahead. Figure out what you want to build, and break it down into simpler components. Use Ray Dream Studio's ability to open multiple **Modeling** and **Perspective** windows to build each component separately, and then bring them together as you complete them. (See Chapter 3, "Modeling Tips," and Chapter 4, "Modeling Techniques," for several ways to make sure all the different components align properly with each other when you bring them together.) This method of modeling results in a much less cluttered working environment and makes it easier to select and manipulate each component.

For example, modeling a car may seem like a complex and intimidating task at first glance (see Figure 2.5) but if you plan ahead and focus on it part by part, as we discussed earlier, it becomes much more manageable. You might start by focusing on a wheel, which is much less complex than an entire car. (See Figure 2.6.) Then focus on a gas tank, then a headlight, then a seat, and in no time you will have created the parts that you can assemble into a complex car. Don't be afraid to group parts to form subassemblies during this process. As a matter of fact, I heartily recommend it. A wheel, for example, may be made of a tire, a rim, and several cylinders, spokes and bolts. Once assembled and grouped, however, a whole wheel is much easier to manipulate than all of its individual components. It can also be easily hidden from view to make redraws faster by making the group invisible instead of each individual part.

Figure 2.7 shows part of the grouping hierarchy for the wheel in Figure 2.6. Notice how some of the subassemblies have subassemblies of their own. Not only does this make sense in terms of how your mind thinks, it also makes it a lot easier to work with complex objects.

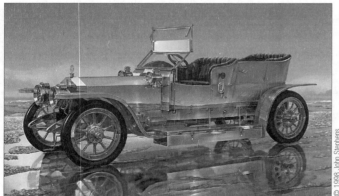

FIGURE
2.5   *A complex object such as a car may seem like an impossible modeling task unless you break it down into parts.*

FIGURE
2.6   *A wheel is a lot easier to model than an entire car.*

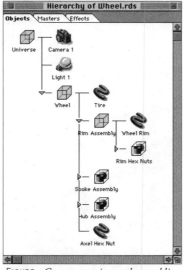

FIGURE
2.7
Group parts into subassemblies to make things easier to manage.

BE EFFICIENT

Ray Dream Studio includes many features that help you work efficiently. Many of these features aren't even available in the higher-end (read "much more expensive") 3D packages. For the modeling process, these features include master objects, master groups and duplication. Understanding these features and making them part of the modeling thought process will make a dramatic difference in the amount of time you spend modeling.

Master objects and groups let you create an object or group and then make copies (or instances) of it that are tied to the original (or master) in terms of their characteristics. For example, you would probably want to make your wheel a master group and then make three more instances to use as the other wheels of your car. Any changes you made to the master group would then be made automatically to all four wheels.

Ray Dream Studio's duplication features also allow you to automatically repeat a series of position, orientation and resize operations when creating instances. In the example of the wheel in Figure 2.6, one spoke was created and then used as a master object. The **Duplicate** command was used to create a new instance of the spoke, and the new spoke was rotated into position. With the new spoke still selected, the **Duplicate** command was then used 12 more

© 1998 John Stephens

FIGURE *Thanks to Ray Dream Studio's modeling features, these 10*
2.8 *objects become a complex wheel with just a few mouse clicks.*

times to create and position each of the other 12 spokes automatically. The same technique was used for the bolt heads. You can also find a more complex example of this command in the "Modeling Techniques" chapter.

The best thing about using Ray Dream Studio's master objects, master groups and duplication features is demonstrated by Figure 2.8. The 10 objects shown are the only objects that we needed to create in order to make all four wheels of the car in Figure 2.5. This is why learning and applying the modeling thought process is so important in terms of saving you time and building confidence in your modeling abilities.

LEARN HOW TO MOVE

Manipulating the components of an object or scene in 3D space can be difficult at first but only takes a little practice to master. Moving an object can be especially problematic because your computer's mouse or trackball can move only in two-dimensional space. The solution is to learn how to work with Ray Dream Studio's XY, YZ and XZ planes (each plane is named after the two axes that lie on it) in conjunction with its powerful alignment tools.

Figure 2.9 shows Ray Dream Studio's **Perspective** window with all three planes turned on. (Clicking on a plane in the **Display Planes** tool will turn that plane on or off.) An outline of your object's bounding box is projected onto each of the planes, and these outlines can be moved or manipulated using the mouse. This gives you precise control over an object while still allowing real-time feedback from the object itself. If you have to manipulate an object

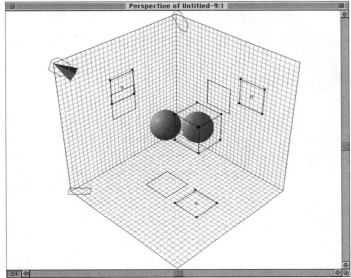

FIGURE **2.9** *Manipulating the projections onto the three working planes is the best way to move an object directly.*

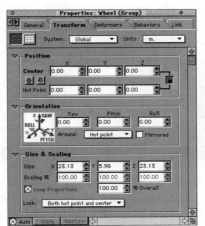

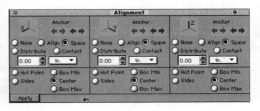

FIGURE **2.10** *Ray Dream Studio's **Transform** tab and **Alignment** palettes are the key to manipulating and moving objects with any degree of precision.*

directly (as opposed to using the **Transform** tab in the **Properties** palette), this is the way to do it. You can then use the **Transform** tab to fine-tune the object's position, orientation and size. (See Figure 2.10.)

Once you have an object positioned where you want it, you can then use Ray Dream Studio's **Alignment** palette (see Figure 2.10) to position other objects relative to it. If you haven't already familiarized yourself with this palette, do so as quickly as possible. It allows for fast and precise positioning of multiple objects relative to each other and is another great time-saver.

SUMMARY

You may have noticed that this section has touched on virtually every aspect of the modeling process except for the modeling tools themselves. While there's no question that mastering these tools is an essential part of mastering the modeling process, it's a relatively minor part of the modeling thought process. Understanding what each tool and each modeling method can do is obviously important when determining how to create a specific object, but the modeling thought process is focused primarily on determining how to break an object down into its basic components and then determining the most efficient way to put them back together again. You will, however, find plenty of tips and techniques on how to use the modeling tools in the "Modeling Tips" and "Modeling Techniques" chapters of this book, and you should also brush up on the modeling chapters in the *Ray Dream Studio User Guide*.

We hope this section has shown you that, with the right mental approach (and Ray Dream Studio's tools), the modeling process becomes very manageable, even with projects you might otherwise have thought twice about pursuing.

— STEVE MCARDLE, CRAIG PATCHETT & JOHN W. SLEDD

SECTION TWO: THE LIGHTING THOUGHT PROCESS

Some consider lighting to be the most integral part of any scene composition, since light is what allows us to see the scene. You can walk into the most beautifully decorated room in the world, but if it's the middle of the night and all the lights are turned off, the room's beauty is lost. The presence of lighting alone is not enough to make the most of a scene, however. The way in which you position and control the lighting has a tremendous effect on the way the viewer will see and perceive the objects in your scene and the scene as a whole. (As anyone who has taken a flash picture in a dark room can attest.)

This principle is just as true in Ray Dream Studio as it is in the real world. No matter how spectacular the objects you create or how brilliant your shaders are, without proper lighting your scene will never live up to its

FIGURE **2.11** *Improper lighting can make even the most well-crafted scene fall flat.*

FIGURE **2.12** *Proper lighting makes a big difference in how a scene appears and how it is perceived by the viewer.*

potential. (See Figures 2.11 and 2.12 for examples.) When you begin a project, you should already be thinking about what type of lighting you are going to use. Even though Ray Dream Studio makes it easy to change your lighting setup at will, knowing what type of lighting you will be using is often helpful in determining how to construct your objects and build their shaders. In some cases it can even save you some work. (See the section on "Using Gels and Gobos.")

BASIC LIGHTING TYPES

You can use two basic types of lighting when composing a scene: environment lighting (sometimes referred to as natural lighting) and effects lighting. Each type makes its own contribution to the scene and, ideally, works in conjunction with the other to make a coordinated visual statement. Understanding how and when to use each is the key to the lighting thought process.

Environment Lighting

Environment lighting is important for setting the general mood of the scene and, properly used, will help stimulate specific emotions in the viewer. For example, soft, warm environment lighting can elicit a sense of calm, comfort and serenity. Cool, harsh lighting, on the other hand, will elicit a sense of apprehension, sterility and unease. You can even mix the two to create a feeling of confusion and anxiety. The "Setting the Mood" section has more on this, but for now, realize that even this most basic form of lighting will have a significant effect on your scene.

Effects Lighting

Effects lighting is important for directing and moving the viewer's eye by bringing attention to certain areas of the scene. A soft-edged spotlight on a single object with low ambient light settings, for example, isolates that object and directs the viewer's attention to it. You can control the viewer's eye this way and lead him around your scene. Effects lighting also encompasses a variety of special effects that you can add to your scene, from light passing through a stained glass window to simulated neon glows, laser effects and explosions. (See "Special Effects Lighting" for some examples.)

Balancing Environment and Effects Lighting

The mixing and balancing of environment and effects lighting is very important to the production of a well-rounded, visually interesting and thought-provoking image. Oversaturation of a scene with either lighting type can deaden the dynamics of that scene. A scene that has several spotlights, for example, tends to lessen the effect of the individual spotlights and takes away from their intent of isolating a particular object. (See Figures 2.13 and 2.14 for examples.)

A good analogy for this would be walking into the electronics section of a department store and seeing a wall of televisions. If only one of them is on, you will focus on it immediately. If two are on, your focus will tend to move back and forth between them. If all of them are on, however, you will experience visual overload and will either pick one at random or run away and not bother looking back. This is what can happen with too much movement and/or too many focal points created via poorly thought-out lighting in your scene. The resulting visual confusion may result in the viewer losing interest in your image . . . and we can't let that happen, now can we?

© 1998 Steve McArdle

FIGURE **2.13** *A scene with too many focal points can lead to visual overload or confusion.*

FIGURE **2.14** *The appropriate use of effects lighting draws the eye to a specific point or object in the image.*

Of course, there are times when overpowering the viewer may be exactly what you want to do. As the artist, you have the ability to create the terms by which the viewer looks at your image and, in some circumstances, visual overload may be exactly what you want. Just keep in mind that most of the time people do not like to be completely controlled by an image, but would rather be allowed to move through the image at their own pace.

SETTING THE MOOD

More than any other visual element, lighting has the ability to create a sense of mood in a scene. Mood is one of the factors in an image that allows you to stir particular emotions in the viewer. It is here that you are able to direct and manipulate how the viewer feels about the imagery within your scene and to elicit the emotions you want her to feel. There are two primary aspects of lighting that allow you to do this.

Color

With the exception of brightly colored spotlights, the color of the lighting in a scene is something that a lot of people never think about. Yet color plays a dominant role in defining mood. A soft, warm light (a light that moves toward the reds, yellows and browns of the color wheel) usually invokes feelings of heat, calm and ease. Cool light (light that moves toward the blues and greens of the color wheel), on the other hand, is more apt to invoke a feeling of cold, unease and harshness. Contrasting colors (those that appear opposite each other on the color wheel) can create a sense of tension, while complementary colors (those that appear close to each other) tend to create a sense of harmony.

Shadows

Shadows are another significant way in which lighting adds to a scene's mood. Dark, contrasty shadows tend to set a forbidding tone or add a sense of harshness to the scene. Longer, softer shadows can give a scene a more inviting or romantic feel, while minimal shadows or a lack of shadows altogether can create a sense of sterility. (See Figures 2.15 and 2.16.)

To get an idea of just how much impact shadows can have on a scene, study your favorite movie and notice how shadows are used to set or enhance the mood in each scene. (The effect is usually more dramatic in older movies from the 1940s and 1950s.)

FIGURE **2.15** *Harsh, contrasty shadows can add a sense of foreboding to a scene and have a dramatic effect on mood.*

FIGURE **2.16** *Softer shadows set a more romantic and inviting mood, while minimal shadows add a sense of sterility.*

Manipulating Mood

An understanding of how color and shadows work allows you as the artist to play with the rules and manipulate them to create the precise effect you want to have on the viewer. Mixing a "happy" object with cool lighting and hard shadows, for example, can confuse the emotions that a viewer might feel and make him look at the object with unease, even though the object itself would normally invoke happy feelings. A scene with a doll in a room with stark blue and white lighting will take on a sterile feel with a lack of emotion, while the same doll in a room with slightly orange and yellow-white soft lighting will result in a scene that is warmer, calmer and happier.

The more you understand how lighting can affect mood, and the more you integrate this knowledge into your 3D thought process, the more powerful your 3D imagery will become. We encourage you to delve deeper into this topic and the topic of lighting in general by looking for photography or fine art books that cover mood and lighting in more detail.

SPECIAL EFFECTS LIGHTING

Special effects lighting encompasses a variety of techniques by which lighting is used in ways that go above and beyond environmental and conventional effects lighting. In general, whereas environmental and effects lighting merely contribute to the overall effect of the scene, special effects lighting is often an integral element in the scene — it plays a specific role rather than merely standing on the sidelines. As such, consideration of when and where to use special effects lighting becomes a very important part of the overall 3D thought process.

Visible Lights

The recent addition of the 3D Light Pack and Pro Lens Effects filters as standard equipment in Ray Dream Studio gives you a wide range of control over your lights and their visible qualities. The Glow channel (added in version 4 of RDS) of your Shader Editor also adds to your arsenal of visible light tools. While the Glow channel is not lighting in the true sense, since it does not actually emit or project light, it can be used to simulate the appearance of an object glowing from an internal light source. This is valuable when you don't actually need illumination or for when the addition of lights to achieve a desired effect would be undesirable or impossible. For example, if you were modeling a skyscraper or a space station, it would make much more sense to use the Glow channel for your windows than to put individual lights into a couple of thousand individually modeled windows. The Glow channel is also very useful for illuminated objects that aren't easily created with real lights, such as LED displays, fires or CRTs. As an example of this, create a free-form bulb-shaped object and give it an off-white glow through its shader properties. Place a bulb light very close to the object (or inside if you're using transparency or if you turn off your light's or object's shadows) to create the effect of light coming from the object. This same technique can be used for other light sources as well, and several examples are given in the "Lighting Techniques" chapter. If a more pronounced, visible light effect is desired, a filter might suit the situation well. (See Figure 2.17.)

If you're using version 4.x.x of RDS (without Rayflect, Inc.'s 3D Light Pack), you can also use the Glow channel in conjunction with a little shader trickery to

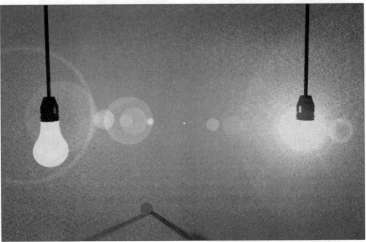

FIGURE 2.17 *The Glow channel can be used to create the illusion of a visible light bulb (left). Adding a Lens Flare from the Pro Lens Pack filters (right) provides the same effect but in a different way and with a different feel.*

create realistic visible light beams. The step-by-step technique for accomplishing this is given in the "Lighting Techniques" chapter, so make sure you include it as part of your lighting thought process. If you're using version 5.0, you should know by now (because I told you only a few paragraphs back) that the 3D Light Pack is now a standard option, and visible shafts of light are only a couple of clicks away. Visible light beams can really add to your work, especially when you're working with fog or underwater scenes. (See Figures 2.18 and 2.19 for examples.) There may be times — even if you have version 5.0 — when you'll want to use the old-school recipe for visible light cones, so don't dismiss it.

FIGURE **2.18** *The Glow channel can be used in combination with the Transparency channel for visible light beam effects.*

FIGURE **2.19** *The 3D Light Pack filter is often your best option for visible light beam effects because it will automatically calculate 3D shadows.*

Science Fiction Effects

Neither the Glow channel nor special effects lighting is limited to imitating traditional light sources. If you ever venture into science fiction scenes, you'll inevitably run into the need to create a laser effect. The Glow channel and the Transparency channel work together nicely to create several different kinds of laser effects, as demonstrated in Figure 2.20. See if you can figure out on your own how this effect was done, then turn to the "Lighting Techniques" chapter to see if you were right.

© 1998 Steve McArdle

FIGURE *Science fiction scenes are yet another place where the Glow*
2.20 *channel can be used for special effects.*

You can also use the Glow channel to imitate other special effects . . . such as explosions! See the "Special Effects" chapter for many other techniques, several of which make great use of the Glow channel.

Using Gels and Gobos

We've already discussed the importance of shadows in a scene, and it's obvious that each object you place in a scene will cast its own shadow. There are times, however, when you will want to add shadows to a scene that come from objects that don't appear in the scene. In real life, for example, an outdoor scene may include shadows from the sunlight filtering through trees, even though those trees aren't part of the scene. Similarly, an indoor scene may include shadows cast from a nearby window that is out of the picture frame.

Ray Dream Studio gives you a very easy way to add additional shadows to a scene without having to create additional objects and significantly increase rendering time. Using gels, you can attach an image to a light source and create the effect of the light source shining through the image, thereby projecting it

FIGURE
2.21
Gels can add detail and realism to a scene without requiring much additional effort.

onto the scene. Figure 2.21 shows an example of how using a gel can dramatically change the look of your scene without a lot of extra work on your part. (See Figure 2.36 for an example of the same scene without a gel.)

There might be times, however, when you would want to create a gobo instead of a gel. A *gobo*, in the real world, is simply a piece of cardboard or plastic with shapes cut out of it. This object is then placed in front of a light to cast specific shadows. It's essentially the same thing in the virtual world of 3D, except that you use a model to create your shadows. Why would you want to use a gobo instead of a gel? Well, I can think of two reasons. One would be when you want more control over your shadows than Ray Dream Studio's Gel function allows. Currently there is no way to adjust how large your shadow area is without moving the light back and forth. With a gobo, however, you can simply change the position of the gobo to make your shadows fall more precisely where you would like them. The second reason is when you want your shadows animated but simply don't have the means to create a movie that fits your needs, or when you may want more control over the way the shadows are animated than a gel would easily offer. (See Figure 2.22 for an example of a gobo.) Personally, I'd rather use a gel, but you should be aware of the gobo option.

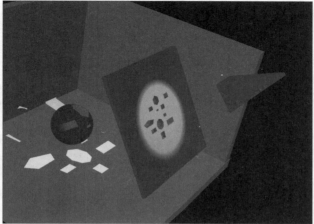

FIGURE **2.22** *Gobos sometimes come in more handy than gels. You can animate the gobo directly in RDS and you can also determine how the shadow strikes the object simply by moving the gobo back and forth.*

DRAMATIC LIGHTING

Dramatic lighting is lighting that helps bring contrast or conflict to the scene, thereby adding dramatic value. One of the keys to dramatic lighting is to rely on cast light from a spot or bulb light to place emphasis on the scene. Because of this, it is a good idea to lower the ambient light setting, which allows you to add more contrast to a scene. The lower the ambient light, the greater the contrast between the background and the lit object, thus increasing its dramatic presence. Figures 2.23 and 2.24 demonstrate this.

Bear in mind, as you develop your lighting thought process, that ambient light not only plays an important role in dramatic lighting, it is also an essential part of setting the mood (especially since it has a strong effect on shadows) and in setting the time of day for both outdoor scenes and many indoor scenes. Make sure you take it into consideration on all these levels as you develop your scene.

Dramatic lighting is achieved primarily through the use of spotlights or strategically placed bulb lights. The intention is to lead the viewer through your scene based on the lighting, and spot lighting does this well by illuminating specific areas. Making something a focal point in a scene in this way increases its dramatic presence through isolation and the creation of a sense of space.

FIGURE 2.23 *Low ambient light can set the time of day for a scene and also enables you to use more dramatic lighting.*

FIGURE 2.24 *High ambient light makes it difficult to create much contrast in a scene, reducing the potential for drama.*

FIGURE 2.25 *Dramatic lighting creates contrast and directs the viewer's eye through the scene*

Giving an object its own space helps push everything into another space and contributes to the scene's sense of depth. (Figure 2.25 shows an example of this, along with Figure 2.14 and several other images scattered throughout this chapter and the rest of the book.) Accomplishing this sense of depth involves both dramatic lighting and proper composition, which we'll discuss later in the chapter.

SUMMARY

As you can see, the lighting process plays a very important role in determining not only how your scene appears but also how it is perceived by the viewer. It should therefore be an integral part of the 3D thought process. As you develop in your mind or on paper what you are striving for in a scene, make sure you have a good grasp of how lighting can contribute, not only in terms of how it can reveal your scene and set the mood, but also in terms of what additional special effects elements it can add to the scene. By knowing what resources are available to you and how they work (a recurring theme throughout the 3D thought process) you will be better able to draw from them and have more control over your scene.

— *Steve McArdle, Craig Patchett & John W. Sledd*

SECTION THREE: THE SHADING THOUGHT PROCESS

While lighting allows you to see an object, shaders are what Ray Dream Studio uses to define how the object looks. The only difference between a plastic cylinder and a tree trunk, as far as Ray Dream Studio is concerned, is the shader that has been applied to it. Therefore it's important that you learn to take full advantage of the incredible versatility the program's shaders give you. You'll be amazed at what you can create once you get the hang of it.

The basic components of Ray Dream Studio's shader are impressive in themselves, giving you extensive control over an object's appearance. Manipulating the Color, Highlight, Shininess, Bump, Reflection, Transparency, Refraction and Glow channels gives you the ability to create almost any type of surface you can imagine. In particular, the Operators and Functions of the shaders allow you to create rich and complex looks. It is here that you can start to categorize shaders into two different types: simple and complex.

SIMPLE SHADERS DEFINED

Simple shaders are shaders that use only one component or operation in a channel. For example, a chrome shader with gray in the Color channel, a high value in the Highlight and Shininess channels, no Bump, a mid- to high value in the Reflection channel, and no Transparency, Refraction or Glow comprises a simple shader. This is not to say that it doesn't create dynamic or complex

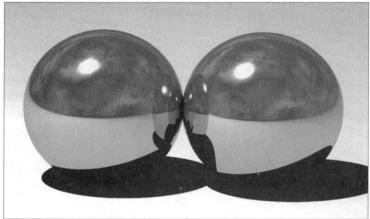

FIGURE **2.26** *A simple shader can produce complex results, as this chrome shader illustrates.*

results (as you can see from Figure 2.26); it just means that it is simple in its components. Simple shaders are often the easiest way to quickly achieve the basic look you want. If you limit yourself to simple shaders, however, then you are only brushing the surface of Ray Dream Studio's capabilities.

COMPLEX SHADERS DEFINED

Complex shaders are shaders that go beyond simple shaders by using operator trees and multiple function levels in one or more channels. For example, if you wanted to create a marble shader, you could go into the Color channel and mix two colors using the Marble function. This may look satisfactory at first glance, but it is very superficial. (Figure 2.27 shows an example of a marble shader created this way.)

If you look at real marble closely, you'll notice that it is comprised of several different tones, with different-sized veins at different depths in the marble. Unlike the basic marble shader I've just described, real marble doesn't just show its surface; it shows about an eighth of an inch inside itself. To simulate this effect, you can build colors and veins on top of each other using nested operators and functions in the Color channel of your marble shader. Instead of mixing two colors with a Marble function, mix two Marble functions that use slightly different color combinations. This will result in different veins overlapping each other, thereby simulating different depths and giving a much more realistic effect. Compare Figure 2.28 with Figure 2.27 and notice how much more realistic

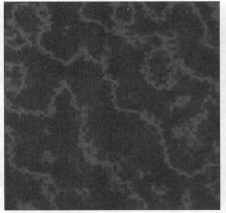

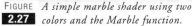

FIGURE **2.27** *A simple marble shader using two colors and the Marble function.*

FIGURE **2.28** *A complex marble shader mixing two Marble functions.*

Figure 2.28 appears. (A recipe for a complex marble shader can be found in the "Shader Recipes and Techniques" chapter.)

Make sure you experiment with your shaders as you build them. You are not restricted just to mixing colors as you build your shader trees. You can add, subtract and multiply colors and subshaders to get different effects. Build your shader trees as deep as you want, but don't overdo it; overlapping too many things on top of each other will eventually create a muddy effect and you'll lose the subtle colors and textures that add a sense of realism. Also bear in mind that the more complex your shader, the longer it will take to render the final image.

TEXTURE MAPS

Often when you want a particular look, it's easiest to use a texture map to get the effect you want. If you're not careful in your planning, however, texture maps can offer unexpected pitfalls that procedural textures (textures made using only RDSs components) do not.

Texture Map Shortcomings

First, in order to be effective, texture maps have to be tilable (assuming you want to use them to cover a large surface) or large enough to cover the entire object being shaded. Second, they have to be created at a high-enough resolution that they will not stretch and pixelate or lose detail. For example, suppose you are using a texture map on an extruded rectangle that is to be used as the floor in your scene. Often what happens is that when the camera is far away from the floor, the texture map

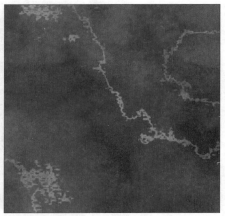

FIGURE **2.29** *Texture maps will pixelate if their resolution isn't high enough.*

FIGURE **2.30** *This close-up of Figure 2.28 shows the unlimited detail of procedural shaders.*

looks fine, but as you get closer to the texture map, you start to encounter an effect called *pixelation*. The larger the rendered image, the more apparent the pixelation becomes. Figure 2.29 shows an example of what pixelation look like.

How do you avoid this? Knowing the size of your final rendered image is a start. If you're rendering an image at 1600 × 1600 pixels and you want to use a texture map that will take up half the image, you need to make sure the texture map is at least 800 × 800 pixels. If you're tiling it four times, then it only needs to be 200 × 200 pixels. You get the idea.

By using Operators and Functions (RDS's shader components) instead of texture maps, you don't have to worry about scale. Because Operators and Functions are mathematically generated, they can be scaled as large or as small as necessary without any loss of detail. (See Figure 2.30, which is a close-up of the bottom-left corner of Figure 2.28.) You also have the ability to make subtle or drastic changes to an operator- or function-based shader simply by adjusting a slider or inputting a value. Texture maps don't offer this flexibility.

All of this is not to say that texture maps don't have their place — quite the opposite. There are times when texture maps are the only way to go. Suppose, for example, that you wanted to make a 3D happy face. This would be an impossible task using procedural shaders but a simple one using a texture map. Figure 2.31 shows just how easy it is. The same is also true of text, of course; the only way to add text to the surface of your object is through a texture map.

There will also be times when you want a specific texture with full realism. For example, if you wanted to create a tabletop made out of a specific type of wood, it would probably be better to use a scan of the wood itself rather than trying to create it using shader functions. It should also be noted that texture maps can often render faster due to the fact that RDS does not have to make

FIGURE   *Sometimes texture maps are the only way to go. This happy-face shader*
2.31   *could not have been created any other way.*

the same number of calculations as it does for a complex shader built solely from procedurals.

Using Texture Maps

If you do decide to use texture maps, you're then faced with the challenge of creating a texture map that will look right when it's applied to your object. This is easy if your object is simple, but more complex objects become more challenging. Part of the problem is that textures wrap around an object in 3D. Therefore you have to think in 3D when trying to create the right type of texture map.

The first step to thinking your way through the texture-mapping process is to make sure that you understand all the mapping modes so you can pick the one that best suits your needs. (Mapping modes are accessible via the **Mapping Mode** tab in the **Properties** palette.) If you're creating a building that is straight on to the viewer, for example, use the Box Mapping mode and select only the side that is facing you. If you're creating a building where you can see all sides but not the bottom or the roof, use the cylindrical mapping method. (If you can't see the top or bottom, why bother trying to map textures there?) By understanding how the Mapping Modes work (which I encourage you to do by picking a few different types of objects and then applying the same texture to each of them using all four Mapping Modes), you'll be ahead of the game in terms of successfully working with texture maps.

You'll find some specific techniques to help you work with texture maps in the "Shading Recipes and Techniques" chapter. One of the most important things to consider during the shader thought process is whether an object will be best served by a procedural-based shader, a texture-map-based shader, or a combination of the two. The ability to combine procedurals and texture maps is another one of RDS's features that stands out in the crowd of 3D applications.

SHADER FUNCTIONS

The shader functions are the core of Ray Dream Studio's abilities to manipulate an object's surface attributes. It is essential that you understand what each of the functions can do if you want to be able to create specific shader effects. Trying to approach the shader process without understanding the functions first would be like trying to speak a foreign language without knowing the vocabulary.

Once you have a basic understanding of what each function is capable of, you can then start to think about how to use those capabilities to create the properties of the shader you are trying to build. You'll be surprised at how much easier shaders become once you have the basics mastered.

The functions are broken up into two main categories: Pattern Functions and Natural Functions. Third-party developers may create shader components for Ray Dream Studio which may or may not fall under the Functions menu in the shader editor, but they will most likely be functions nonetheless. For instance, Rayflect, Inc.'s Four Elements extension includes a few new shader functions, but they appear as Four Elements Shaders instead of under the Function menus; they are functions just the same. To keep it simple, we're going to cover the shader functions that come right out of the box with Ray Dream Studio 5.0, starting with the Pattern Functions and working our way through the Natural Functions.

Formula

The Formula function is a new addition to Ray Dream Studio 5 and allows you to input mathematical equations which translate into color or grayscale images. Figure 2.32 shows what happened when I loaded the default shader function formula and started tweaking around with it. This is a power-user feature and may be over many users' heads (it certainly makes me wish I'd paid more attention in math class). Since some knowledge of higher math and/or programming is recommended for use of this function, this option is great for the weekend programmer who doesn't want to commit to writing full-blown extensions or for the average user who just happens to remember how to use the left side of her brain.

The possibilities for customizing RDS via these formulas are very exciting (the Formula option is also available for behaviors, deformers, backgrounds, gels,

FIGURE
2.32
This picture is only a sample of the possibilities available with the new Formula function.

primitives and more). No need to fret if you aren't a math wiz, though, I expect there to be a surge in formula availability on users' Web sites and in other forums.

Checkers

The Checkers function is a useful function that can be combined nicely with other operators and functions. As a simple example, you can use the Checkers function with the Mix operator and two complex subshaders to get striking effects. One of the traditional 3D creations is a chessboard. Using the Checkers function and the Mix operator to combine two complex marble subshaders results in a very effective and beautiful marble chessboard, as shown in Figure 2.33. Using this idea in other channels, or with something other than two marbles (for instance, metals and woods), can provide you with very different

© 1998 Steve McArdle

FIGURE
2.33
The most obvious use for the Checkers function is to create a grid effect, as demonstrated by this chessboard.

© 1998 Steve McArdle

FIGURE
2.34 *The Checkers function can also be used for striped patterns, as shown in this multicolored beach ball.*

and interesting results. (See Cecilia Ziemer's brick shader in Chapter 9, Shader Recipes and Techniques.)

You don't need to use both vertices with the Checkers function. Mixing different colors using only the horizontal setting, for example, is an easy way of creating a multicolored striped beach ball such as the one shown in Figure 2.34 (the recipe for this can be found in Chapter 9, Shader Recipes and Techniques.)

Wires

The Wires function is a wonderful function too, not only for its more obvious uses, but even more so for its less obvious applications. For example, if you check the **Grayscale** option in the Wires function box, your wires will become smooth transitions from one color to another, rather than sharp lines. This opens up some interesting possibilities. (See Figure 2.35.)

Understanding how this gradient works opens up a lot of possibilities for smooth transitions between colors, textures, bumps, highlights, reflections and so forth. (See the visible light beam technique in the "Shader Recipes and Techniques" chapter for a unique application.) It's also a great example of how understanding the shader functions expands the tools you have available to you and makes the creation process so much easier.

Using Checkers and Wires Together

Using the Checkers and Wires functions together can enhance the usefulness of each. If you think back to the chessboard example, you can see how easy it would

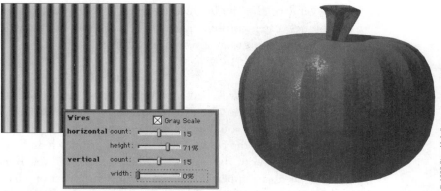

FIGURE **2.35** *The Wires function can be used to create grayscale bands, which were used in the Bump channel to create this pumpkin. (Try the Color channel for a watermelon.)*

be to use the Wires function to add grout between the squares and create a bump map to turn the chessboard into a ceramic-tiled floor. Figure 2.36 shows an example of this, using one shader to turn a simple extruded square into a complex three-dimensional surface. You can use this same technique to create wooden shingles, brick walls and more with just a little imagination and experimentation.

FIGURE **2.36** *This ceramic-tiled floor was created using a combination of Checkers and Wires.*

Several of the shader recipes given in Chapter 9, Shader Recipes and Techniques, use a combination of Checkers and Wires, which will provide a good starting point to give you ideas.

Gradient

The Gradient function is best used when you want a smooth transition between colors or other components. If, for example, you want a sphere to blend from blue to yellow, you would create a mix in the Color channel with the color blue in the left branch, the color yellow in the right branch and a Gradient function as the mixer. You can also use the Gradient function in the Transparency channel to make an object appear to fade in, or in the Reflection channel to simulate a blending from wet to dry. The **Turbulence** slider in the **Gradient function** control panel mixes up the smooth transition to give it more of a cloudy, organic blend. Figure 2.37 shows three spheres. The first sphere's shader uses a mix in the Color channel with a Checker function in the left branch, a Cellular function in the right branch and a Gradient function as the mixer. Notice how the Checkers blend into the Cellular look. The middle sphere uses exactly the same shader, except that I dragged the Gradient mixer into the Reflection channel as well. Notice that the bottom of the sphere is very reflective but the reflective properties fade out towards the top. The sphere on the far right has the same shader as the first sphere, but with the Gradient function copied into the Transparency channel. As a result, the sphere fades in from the bottom to the top.

FIGURE 2.37   *These three spheres illustrate some of the uses for the Gradient function.*

Psychedelic

The Psychedelic Function is another wonderful function that simulates waves and swirls of differing levels and blends. Although it's in the Pattern

Functions category, it can also be used to generate some very creepy organic looks. Using this function, you can generate smooth blends from color to color or function to function, or any combination of the above. The Psychedelic function is best used as a mixer in the color channel and/or all by itself in the Bump channel. It's also very good for a hypnotic effect. By animating the phase, the rings will undulate along in a very ... ahem ... psychedelic fashion. Figure 2.38 shows a cartoon character hypnotized by the Psychedelic function.

Now that we're done with the Pattern functions, let's move on to the Natural functions.

FIGURE **2.38** *The Psychedelic function is great for many effects. Among them is the standard hypnotized look.*

Wood

The Wood function is a great function that, despite its name, is not limited to creating wood textures. Granted, using complex subshaders mixed with a Wood function can give you convincing wood textures, as Figure 2.39 demonstrates. Just make sure you follow the same guidelines mentioned at the beginning of this section regarding complex marble shaders, that is, keep in mind that not all woods are simply undulating grains moving through a colored fiber. Some woods have several types of colored grains, and the fiber these grains move through is patchy. Play with different sizes of grains and don't be afraid to mix in weak Spots or Marbles functions to help with the

FIGURE   *By using layered Wood functions you can create reasonably realistic wood surfaces that*
2.39 *work well in a variety of situations.*

color toning of the wood. (See Chapter 9, Shader Recipes and Techniques, for an example.)

Because the Wood function creates smooth transitions between its sub-shaders, it can be used to create interesting wandering gradients and color transitions. Wood functions used in the Bump channel can be especially useful, creating a range of effects from strange textures to water waves and ripples. (See the "Shader Recipes and Techniques" chapter for a water shader technique.)

If you use your imagination, you can really have some fun with this. Imagine a sphere, for example, that is mostly transparent, with some Refraction and a rippled water Bump channel created with the Wood function. Position the sphere so it is floating above the ground, and you have a wonderfully surreal, gravity-defying water globule. (See Figure 2.40.) You could animate the Bump channel and add a rippling water effect to the sphere. The result? A cool science fiction effect that is ridiculously easy to create and will really make people take notice. (When using a Bump channel for any transparent object, by the way, create the Bump channel before you create the Transparency channel. This makes it easier to preview the effect the Bump channel will have on the object.)

The Wood function can be combined with other Wood functions through operators. If the Wood functions have different directions and centers, you can get interesting cross-hatchings and ripples. By increasing the

Perturbation and Undulation settings, you can push this function past all sense of normalcy to create alien, reptilian and other effects. (See Figure 2.41 for an example.) Try it in the Glow channel as well as the Color channel for some really wild results.

FIGURE 2.40 *The Wood function is not limited to creating wood surfaces, as this Bump channel example clearly shows.*

FIGURE 2.41 *The only difference between these two images is a single, complex, multichannel Wood shader.*

Marble

The Marble function is another versatile shader function and is great for marbles, woods, clouds, Bumps, and much more. The Marble function is actually quite similar to the Wood function in the effects it creates, with the most noticeable difference being the way it dithers the edges of the veins instead of blending them smoothly. The more you increase the Vein Blending setting, the more pronounced this effect becomes. It's especially useful for creating a cloudy effect, as can be seen in Figure 2.42. You can also see this effect in the Marble examples used earlier in the complex shader section.

Marble is another function that works well in a combination of channels. Figure 2.43 is an excellent example, showing how a single complex shader applied to a smooth surface can create what at first glance seems to be a modeling nightmare. In fact, the Marble function was used in different ways in the Color, Highlight, Shininess, Bump and Transparency channels to create this

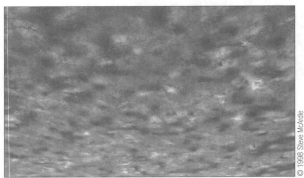

FIGURE **2.42**   *The Marble function is just as versatile as the Wood function, as you can see from this cloud shader.*

FIGURE **2.43**   *The Marble function was used in several channels of one shader to create this complex rust effect.*

very realistic rusted-metal effect. (The recipe appears in Chapter 9, Shader Recipes and Techniques.)

Spots

If you look closely at almost any surface, you'll notice that nothing is perfectly smooth or has a perfectly consistent color. Computers, however, have a tendency to make everything as uniform as possible. The Spots function makes it easy to maintain a sense of randomness and is an essential tool for making your shaders more realistic.

The Spots function is interesting for several reasons. First, it doesn't create spots so much as it does random splotches — a type of visual noise. These splotches can be small enough to create a random noise effect, or large enough to create noticeable patterns. This makes them perfect for use in the Color and Bump channels. For example, Figure 2.44 shows two different ways the Spots function was used in the ceramic tile image in Figure 2.36. From left to right, Spots were used to create a dirty stucco effect for the wall, and to mix two different Bump maps (one created using Spots) to create a textured plaster effect for the vase. (They were also used to add a little visual noise to the plant leaves.) The resulting shaders look a lot more realistic than they would have otherwise.

Once you understand how Spots work, you'll think of a variety of uses for them, including several types of special effects. For example, the snow on a television screen is made up of little squares randomly jumping across the screen. You can achieve the same kind of effect with the Spots function by mixing grays

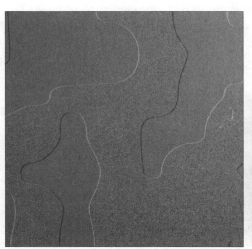
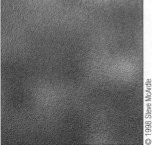

© 1998 Steve McArdle

FIGURE **2.44** *Spots were used in the ceramic tile scene in Figure 2.36 to create a dirty stucco effect for the wall (left) and to create a textured plaster look for the vase.*

FIGURE **2.45** *Use of the Spots function in different channels, such as Color and Glow, can create interesting effects.*

and whites in the Color channel, using a relatively small spot size and a high smoothing level (75% or greater). Apply this same shader to the Glow channel, and the effect is complete. (See Figure 2.45.)

You'll learn several more examples of how to use the Spots function in Chapter 9, Shader Recipes and Techniques.

Cellular

The Cellular function works in the same way as the other functions described. It creates a transition between white and black but uses a very organic pattern with a structure similar to cells viewed under a microscope. The Cellular function comes with several different cell types which can be used to create any effect from reptilian skins to rocks to ocean waves to gooshy, fleshy textures. This function is most similar to the Spots function but, in my opinion, is infinitely more flexible and is a staple function in my own shader toolbox. Take a look at Figure 2.46 for some examples. In the first picture, different Cellular

FIGURE **2.46** *Just a few of the possibilities available when using the Cellular shader function.*

functions were used in the dino's Color and Bump channels to give different areas of the scales a different color. In the second picture, the same Cellular function was used for the Color and the Bump so that they matched up to make the perfect rocky texture. In the third image, one Cellular function was used in the Bump channel.

USING CHANNELS

You've already seen several examples throughout this section showing how shader functions can be used in any of Ray Dream Studio's shader channels. The Color and Bump channels are the ones you will use most often, but don't neglect the others, especially the Transparency channel, which can be used as a very powerful modeling tool. Figure 2.47 for example, shows a complex mesh shader that was created simply by placing a texture map in the Color and Transparency channels. (Other examples appear in Chapter 9, Shader Recipes and Techniques.) If you don't include the possibility of using this technique as part of your shader thought process, you'll end up wasting a lot of time modeling objects that don't need to be modeled.

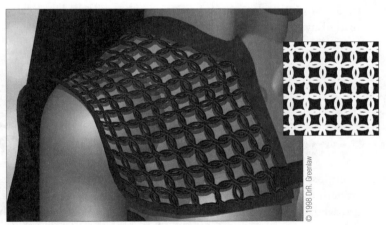

© 1998 DrR. Greenlaw

FIGURE   *This complex mesh object was created using a texture*
2.47   *map in the Color and Transparency (right) channels.*

Determining which channels to use for your shader is an important part of the shader thought process. Make sure you understand what qualities each channel contributes to a shader, and then think carefully about whether or not the shader you're trying to create has any of those qualities. If so, ask yourself how those qualities appear in the shader, and then set to work to recreate that appearance using the shader functions and operators. Wherever possible, have a real-world example in front of you to study.

SUMMARY

By now it should be clear that there are two keys to the shader thought process. The first is to make sure you know your tools and their capabilities. Experiment with each shader function, playing with the different settings to see what effect they have. (Switching to **Flat Preview** mode will help during this process.) This is the best way to learn the intricacies of any of the shader functions and will make it a lot easier for you to choose the appropriate functions when it comes time to create a specific effect. In particular, see what happens when you set each slider at or close to its extremes; this is where the functions are most likely to behave in ways you might not expect. Also make sure you understand the capabilities of each shader channel.

The second key is to think ahead and analyze the characteristics of the surface you're trying to create. Break it down in terms of each shader channel and then break down each channel in terms of the capabilities of each shader function. Once you've done that, even the most complex surfaces can be thought of in terms of simple components that can easily be duplicated and combined using Ray Dream Studio's shader tools.

— *STEVE MCARDLE CRAIG PATCHETT & JOHN W. SLEDD*

SECTION FOUR: THE COMPOSITION THOUGHT PROCESS

Composition may be one of the hardest design elements to master, because it's something that we tend to take for granted. As both image creators and viewers, we have a tendency to focus on the object itself, and not how it relates to its environment. Part of the problem is that as human beings we don't see things in a nice little frame. Instead, our peripheral vision gives us an almost 180-degree viewing environment, something that is impossible to replicate on a flat monitor screen. Because of this limitation in transition from sight to screen, we must be aware of how object placement, emphasis, viewing angle and scene coordination affect how an image or scene is viewed. This, then, needs to become an integral part of our thought process when we begin to create a 3D scene.

OBJECT PLACEMENT

There are several conventions when it comes to composition, all of which have rules of exception. Probably the most important convention, and the one that's easiest to work with, is object placement.

A governing rule when determining how to place an object within your scene is to try to avoid any centrally located objects. For example, if you have a scene of a table with a lamp on it, you should try not to place the lamp right in the center of the image. Instead, it would be better to place it slightly off to the left or right and/or up or down, as shown in Figure 2.48.

© 1998 Steve McArdle

FIGURE **2.48** *Centered objects create a static, confrontational look, whereas off-center positioning is more dynamic and offers more options for the rest of the scene.*

There are several reasons to place objects off center. First, a centered object divides the picture plane in half, thereby limiting your composition options for the rest of your scene and creating a very static look. It also presents a confrontational situation, with you as the viewer versus it as the object. Finally, it limits your horizontal viewing range, because you become locked into looking at the dead center of the image. There are times, of course, where one or more of these things may be just what you're after. You might want an object to be confrontational, or to pull the viewer's eye to the center of the image. In that case, go ahead and use a centrally placed object. As mentioned before, there are always exceptions to the rules.

Object placement involves all three dimensions, of course, and determining how close each object is to the camera is a big part of determining how your scene will appear. Objects that are cluttered together at the same distance from the camera won't be as effective in setting your scene as those that are arranged in a way that adds some depth to the scene. (Unless, of course, they're together for a reason.) How close an object is to the camera is also important in defining your scene's emphasis, which is the next element of scene composition.

EMPHASIS

Emphasis in a scene can be created through several different methods. Proximity to the camera is one, as discussed briefly above. Lighting is another. Imagine a singer on stage. The lights go down and a spotlight appears on him or her. It is very difficult for you as a viewer to drag your eyes away from the singer, since extreme emphasis is being placed on him or her by the spotlight. In a 3D scene this is equally true. Lowering the ambient lighting and allowing spotlights (dramatic) or bulb lights (less dramatic) to highlight certain objects places emphasis on those objects and draws your attention to them. Figure 2.49 shows an example of this principle. (Notice how the emphasis has been enhanced by moving the can closer to the camera and away from the other objects in the scene.)

FIGURE 2.49　*Moving an object closer to the camera and careful use of lighting are two ways of adding emphasis to a scene.*

© 1998 Steve McArdle

Movement, or potential for movement, can also place emphasis on certain areas of a scene. For example, think of a dinner-table scene with knives, forks, plates and glasses. Everything is sitting as expected on the table, with the exception of one fork, teetering at the edge with the potential to fall off. There are no lights pointing you to this fork, it is no larger than the other objects in the scene, nor is it a different color. The only thing that distinguishes it from the other elements of the scene is that it has the potential to fall. It is the tension and suspense of whether or not the fork will fall that will place emphasis on it.

Creating tension and suspense can work in many areas of a scene, from something falling to something about to break under the weight of something else. It is a fun and visually interesting way to add emphasis to objects within a scene. Figure 2.50 shows how you can enhance it with lighting for an even stronger effect. (Notice also how your eye is drawn through the scene.)

© 1998 Steve McArdle

FIGURE *Emphasis can also be created*
2.50 *through tension and lighting.*

There are several other ways you can create emphasis in a scene, including the use of size, color, texture and anything else that creates a contrast between the object or objects you want to emphasize and the rest of the scene. While proximity to camera and lighting may be the most obvious choices, make sure you take all your choices into consideration during the composition thought process. Each can be very powerful in different situations. (Have you ever seen the image of a red rose in the middle of a field of white flowers?)

VIEWING ANGLE

As an artist, you have complete control over your scene, including the angle or angles (in the case of an animation) from which it is viewed. Choosing the right viewing angle is an essential part of making your scene more interesting and dynamic.

© 1998 Steve McArdle

FIGURE **2.51** *An eye-level view of a scene is only one possibility.*

Three terms that are often heard when referring to viewing angles are eye-level view, bird's-eye view and worm's-eye view (sometimes referred to as frog's-eye or mouse's-eye view). Eye-level view is the way we're used to seeing things and probably the most common way of presenting a scene due to its familiarity. Figure 2.51 shows a scene viewed from eye level. It's interesting, but lacks something.

The other two views are ones that we usually don't see in everyday life but which can provide an interesting and fresh look at a scene or object. A bird's-eye view is one taken from above the scene looking down on it, while a worm's-eye view is one taken from below the scene looking up at it. While such views are often difficult or impossible to achieve in real life, in Ray Dream Studio they are as simple as repositioning the camera. More importantly, they do much more to the scene than simply give the viewer a sense of being above or below it. Used properly, they can add a sense of excitement and interest.

Understanding how the different views affect the way a scene is interpreted by the viewer is as simple as examining the way we talk. To "look up" to someone is to impart them with a sense of importance, to "look down" on someone is to diminish their importance, and to "see eye to eye" is to consider them your equal. So it is with the way you view a scene. Figure 2.52 shows how a bird's-eye

© 1998 Steve McArdle

FIGURE **2.52** *Looking down on a scene takes away from its sense of importance, while looking up does just the opposite.*

view and a worm's-eye view each give not only a different perspective, but a completely different dramatic feel to the scene shown in Figure 2.51.

As you can see, deciding how to view your scene is a very important part of the composition thought process. If the context of your scene doesn't call for a particular view (for example, it's to illustrate part of a story where the hero is perched high above the ground and looks down to survey the surroundings), try several and see which one best fits the mood you're trying to convey. Try different variations on each view as well. The view from high above a scene is very different from the one from just above eye level.

SCENE COORDINATION/DIALOG

Usually a scene contains several elements. Even the most sparse scene such as a planet in space has the planet, stars in the background, a light source and possibly elements such as nebulae and galaxies. Regardless of how many elements there may be, they all need to be coordinated so they work together to complete the composition. Elements that don't work together in some way will detract from your scene, and the scene will lose impact regardless of how detailed and complex the individual elements are.

© 1998 Steve McArdle

FIGURE **2.53** *A well-coordinated scene speaks a strong, unified visual message.*

Figure 2.53 shows an example of a well-coordinated scene. Notice how each element adds to the others without detracting from the composition. Notice also how your eye is guided around the scene, and how lighting and view have been used to enhance the image.

If you want to make your scenes truly effective as a form of visual communication, their elements also need to affect each other in some way in order to produce a compositional dialog. For example, something that is beautiful and shiny could be placed in direct contrast to something that is ugly and dull to emphasize their differences. Two clichéd but effective examples are a rose growing up an old, rusted, iron fence, or a dove flying over a war-torn land. Such contrasts are often referred to as *dialog*, because the elements have a relationship to one another in such a way that this relationship speaks to the viewer. The viewer, in turn, interacts with the scene by projecting onto it ideas, biases and opinions that are stirred by what the image is communicating both visually and emotionally. (See Figure 2.54 for an example.)

Accomplishing this sense of dialog is a skill that must be developed, and there are several art books devoted to it. You would do well to pick one up and read through it. You can also benefit by studying those images (whether 3D or otherwise) that speak to you, and thinking about why they do so.

© 1998 Steve McArdle

FIGURE
2.54
The ideal scene conducts a dialog with the viewer.

SUMMARY

Any image is a form of communication, and the level of communication fluctuates in terms of how much the artist wants to say or not say. Because of this, it is important that what you want to say is being projected through your work and not being lost because of composition problems. Good composition provides visual interest and is important consciously and subconsciously in how an image is viewed and perceived. Don't overlook this very important part of the 3D process — make sure it's part of your thought process.

— *STEVE MCARDLE & CRAIG PATCHETT*

SECTION FIVE: THE ANIMATION THOUGHT PROCESS

The models have been completed, the lighting is in place, the texture maps have been applied, and the composition is perfect. The last step, if you choose to take it, is to add a fourth dimension to your project — time. Time is what allows you to turn a still image into an animation.

A traditional animation project typically has a staff of hundreds. Dozens of artists, choreographers and directors are needed to complete the most simple cartoon. With Ray Dream Studio, it's all up to you and your computer. This is why planning ahead and understanding the thought process involved is especially important when it comes to animation.

PLAN AHEAD

More than any other part of the 3D process, animation requires that you plan ahead. An animation consists of anywhere from several to dozens of events, many of which occur at the same time. Even if you could keep track of them all in your head, it's much easier to plan everything out on paper first before you start moving things around in Ray Dream Studio.

There are three basic elements to planning an animation: a story script, a storyboard and an animation script. Ideally you'll use all three, but at the very least you should try to put together a story script and an animation script.

Story Script

A story script is simply a written description of your animation. Try to get all the basic ideas down and then string them together into a logical stream of events. Since the script is primarily for your own benefit (unless you have to present it to a client), don't worry as much about making it readable as you do about making it flow. Remember also that an animation is a form of communication. If you don't succeed in communicating your message, then it doesn't matter how cool the animation looks.

In the process of putting together your story script, you should also spend some time watching as much television and as many movies and commercials as you can stomach. Watch to see how camera angles are used, how the camera and objects move relative to each other, and how the speed of their movement affects everything. In other words, study camera and movement techniques so you can borrow from them when you create your animation. There are some basic concepts to fuel your thought process later in this section, but you might want to pick up some books on cinematography and study them as well.

Once your research is complete, write your script. As you put down the story, try to weave into it descriptions of camera motion and model direction and speed. Be clear when you write down the sequence of events in your animation, so that you or someone else working with you understands the action.

Storyboard

With your story script in hand, start to break down your story into the major scenes. Then, using your story script as a guide, try to draw the major events in the scene. The level of detail (and quality, for that matter) is entirely up to you, but try and be as precise as you can.

The idea of each individual storyboard is to illustrate all of the important sequences or changes in the scene. For example, if you plan to have a spaceship zoom by the camera, try to give a good idea of how the ship will move through space, how the camera will track the ship, and where it should be placed in the scene. If you find it hard to draw a particular detail (such as speed, general lighting conditions or the presence of fog) then write it in a caption beneath your drawing. You should also include timing information in this caption (that is, how many seconds or frames into the animation does this storyboard occur?). Figure 2.55 gives one example of how a storyboard for a scene might look.

With that said, I realize that programs like Ray Dream Studio often make it possible to whip up a rough animation in less time than it takes to sit down and sketch out a storyboard. If that's easier for you to do, then by all means do it. But make sure you start out with some visual idea of what it is you're aiming for. At the very least, I draw a quick sketch of camera position, model movement and other relevant details before I move into the animation process. (See Figure 2.56.) It may take more time up front, but it will definitely save time in the long run.

00:00:00 Four distant ships head towards the camera, which is stationary. The larger ship is out front, followed by three smaller vessels.

00:01:28 The ships zoom closer to the camera, the camera tracks the larger lead ship which appears to be fleeing from the smaller vessels.

00:04:15 The lead ship speeds past the camera and the camera pans to follow it. The ship banks 20° and a large planet starts to appear in the lower left of the screen.

00:07:02 The large ship speeds off towards the planet and levels off again. The three smaller ships come back into view. The planet begins to fill the screen.

© 1996 Craig Lyn

FIGURE **2.55** *A storyboard takes time to create but is an excellent way of visualizing the flow of your animation before you sit down to create it.*

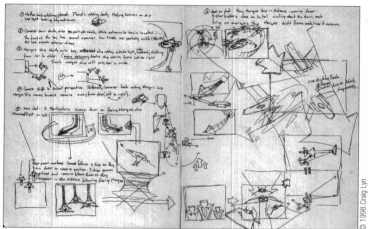

FIGURE
2.56
A storyboard can be as informal as you want it to be, as long as it is useful in planning out your animation.

Animation Script

The animation script is essentially a handwritten version of Ray Dream Studio's **Time Line** window. You use it to translate your storyboard into key events before sitting down and actually creating those events on the computer. (Figure 2.57 shows a sample template that could be used for creating an animation script.)

Why bother with this step? While Ray Dream Studio makes it easy to add, remove or manipulate key events once you've created them, it's a lot easier to

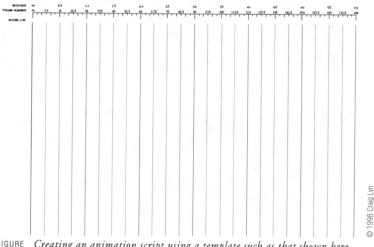

FIGURE
2.57
Creating an animation script using a template such as that shown here will save you time when you set up your time line in Ray Dream Studio.

move them around on paper while you're still deciding exactly how the sequence of events should flow. Once you've completed this process you can then quickly transfer the animation script to Ray Dream Studio's time line and make any final adjustments after you've had a chance to see a rough version of the animation.

KEY EVENTS

Key events, which were mentioned briefly above, are the most important concept you need to grasp with respect to the animation process. In fact, the key event is what makes animation logistically feasible.

In traditional cel-based animation, a lead artist (also known as a *keyman*) would draw the most important parts of the action, which became known as *keyframes*. The keyframes would then be handed over to hundreds of artists who would draw the frames between the keyframes, a process referred to as *tweening*.

With Ray Dream Studio, the exact same process takes place, with a slight twist. You take the role of the lead artist and are responsible for creating the key events (the 3D equivalent of keyframes), while Ray Dream Studio takes care of all the tweening necessary to generate the action between those events. This saves you a tremendous amount of work, as is demonstrated by Figure 2.58. These three frames are from the beginning, middle and end of a complex, four-second, 61-frame animation sequence that was created using just seven key events, only two of which were used for the flower bloom. (If you're curious as to how the flower was animated, you'll find the technique in the "Animation Techniques" chapter.)

What defines a key event? Any time anything in your animation starts to change, stops changing or starts changing in a different way, there needs to be a key event. This covers any type of change, including motion, size, shape, shading, lighting, camera lens and so on. The *Ray Dream Studio User Guide* covers key events in more detail; if you haven't already gone through the

| 00:00:00 | Frame 1 | 00:02:00 | Frame 31 | 00:04:00 | Frame 61 |

© 1998 Cecilia Ziemer

FIGURE **2.58** *These three frames show the power of key events: This complex, four-second, 61-frame animation sequence was created using only seven key events.*

tutorials in it, you should do so. Key events form the foundation for the entire animation thought process.

INVERSE KINEMATICS

Animating a simple, one-piece object is easy. Animating complex objects, especially any type of jointed object or character, is one of the most challenging tasks in 3D and is next to impossible without Inverse Kinematics or IK (a feature of Ray Dream Studio). *IK* refers to intelligent links between the different parts of a model. Constraints can be placed on these links so that they stay within a specific range of motion. IK's capabilities, for example, allow you to drag a character's foot with your mouse and have the calf, thigh and hip follow along automatically. As a less complex example, they also allow you to drag a doorknob and have the attached door swing open on its hinges.

Hierarchy

As you can infer from the above examples, IK's usefulness is dependent on your models having a hierarchical structure. In the case of animating a character's leg, for example, you need to define the hierarchy for the legs so that the foot is dependent on the calf, which is in turn dependent on the thigh, which is in turn dependent on the hip. These relationships between the different objects that make up the leg are referred to as *parent-child* relationships. In other words, the foot would be considered the child of the calf, which is the parent of the foot.

This hierarchy isn't limited to characters. Consider an airplane, which consists of a fuselage, propeller, landing gear and wheels. You would want to set up a hierarchy so that the fuselage is the parent of the propeller and landing gear, and the landing gear is the parent of the wheels. (See Figure 2.59.)

The logic behind setting up a hierarchy is simple and can be illustrated using the airplane example. The fuselage is the main parent because everything

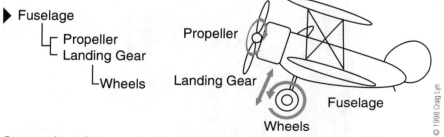

▶ Fuselage
    └┌ Propeller
       └ Landing Gear
         └ Wheels

© 1998 Craig Lyn

FIGURE **2.59** *A hierarchy is set up based on the dependency relationships between each object in a model and the other objects in that model.*

else is dependent on it. The propeller is a child of the fuselage because it has to travel wherever the fuselage goes, as does the landing gear. Both the propeller and the landing gear also have to be animated separately from the rest of the model, but their animation will be relative to the fuselage. The wheels are a child of the landing gear because they are attached to the landing gear and have to go wherever it goes. (When the landing gear retracts into the fuselage, the wheels need to go with it.) At the same time, the wheels need to be able to rotate independently of the rest of the airplane but relative to the landing gear. These dependency relationships define the model's hierarchy.

Links

Once the parent-child relationships and the resulting hierarchy are established, you need to define how each child can move relative to its parent. Even though the propeller, as a child of the fuselage, will automatically follow the fuselage when it moves, for example, you want to limit the propeller's movement relative to the fuselage to a spinning action. (You don't want it to be able to move forward and backward.) Ray Dream Studio handles this using links.

Three basic types of links are available in Ray Dream Studio. A Lock link locks the child to the parent and prevents any movement of the child independent of the parent. A Slider link allows you to constrain movement on each of the X, Y and Z axes. An Axis link allows the child to be rotated around the parent object on one of the three axes. Both the Slider and Axis links allow you to limit movement to a specified range. You can also specify custom combinations of the Slider and Axis links, as shown in Figure 2.60.

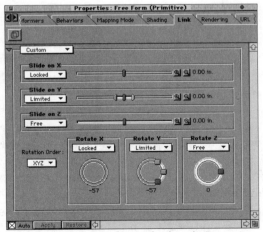

FIGURE   *Ray Dream Studio's **Link** tab in the **Properties***
2.60   *palette let's you specify exactly how each child*
          object can be moved relative to its parent.

Experiment with links to get the hang of them and also make sure you look at the appropriate section in the *Ray Dream Studio User Guide* if you haven't already done so. Links are an important part of the animation thought process, and it's well worth taking the time to understand them. You will also find a tutorial or two on setting up and using links in Chapter 12, Animation Techniques.

BASIC ANIMATION TECHNIQUES

While IK, links and key events make it easy to create complex motion, there are several basic animation techniques you'll need to learn and keep in mind if you want to create realistic motion. They are especially important to include in the animation thought process if you will be doing character animation.

Many of these techniques were developed (and all were perfected) at Walt Disney Studios back in the 1930s and 1940s. If you'd like to explore them in more detail and pick up some additional Disney animation theory and technique, pick up a copy of *Disney Animation: The Illusion of Life* by Frank Thomas and Ollie Johnston (two of Disney's original animators). It's a fascinating study of Disney animation from an animator's perspective, and everything in it is just as applicable to 3D animation as it is to traditional animation.

Anticipation

Action doesn't just start — there are usually a few movements that lead up to the primary action. If something is being shot out of a cannon, for example, it would be boring to see a cannon sitting there and then a puff of smoke emerging from it. If you think in terms of cartoons, the cannon usually swells first and then spits out a cannonball as it returns to its regular shape. The same principle is true of a character. If someone is going to jump into the air, he crouches down first before springing away. (See frames 1, 11 and 15 in Figure 2.61.)

Exaggeration

Exaggeration is a tool for drawing attention to a particular action, as any street mime will tell you. To use the cannon example again, if the base of the cannon swelled only slightly before spitting out the ball, it wouldn't be very interesting. On the other hand, if the cannon swelled to almost-bursting and then stretched out after spitting the ball before returning to normal, the action would be much more exciting.

The amount of exaggeration you want to use depends, of course, on the effect you're after. In Figure 2.61, notice how each part of the jumping sequence involves exaggeration, creating a cartoonish effect.

© 1998 Johnathan Banta

FIGURE
2.61
These frames, from an animation of a character jumping, demonstrate anticipation, exaggeration, overlapping action, squash and stretch, and follow-through.

Overlapping Action

The world does not operate on a sequential timetable; everything starts and stops at different intervals. Try to overlap your motion so the action looks more natural. Take a walking character for example. As its foot starts to travel forward, the calf and then the thigh start to rise. Finally the hip swings forward as well. In Figure 2.61, notice how several things are happening at once as the character prepares to jump. The character crouches down, its arms move down and back, and its eyes close. Although this is done in a cartoonish way, the resulting animation is a lot more realistic than if the character had crouched first, then moved its arms, then closed its eyes.

If you want your animations to look smooth and realistic, avoid the temptation to move one thing and then another. Keep in mind, however, that you would move one thing and then the other while you're setting up the animation. That's one of the beauties of 3D. You can make sure the crouch is right, then you can go back and tweak the arms over the same period of time. This layering-of-motion technique is not unlike the layering of models and textures and lighting. Breaking an animation down into little bite-sized motions can make the job much less daunting. By working one gesture at a time it is possible to create a complex action scene before you even realize you've started.

Squash and Stretch

As soft objects move, they become distorted because of inertia. Take a rubber ball, for example; as it bounces on the ground it squashes slightly. As it rebounds, it elongates itself in the direction that it is traveling before returning to a circular shape. (Ray Dream Studio's Stretch deformer makes it easy to add these distortions.) In animation, this phenomenon can be applied to any object or character, and is known as *squash and stretch*.

Used properly, squash and stretch not only add significantly to the realism of an animation, they also make it easier to exaggerate motion. For an example, take a look at frames 11, 15, 19, 22, and 26 in Figure 2.61. The character squashes as it crouches down, stretches as it jumps, returns to normal at the peak of the jump, stretches again while falling, then squashes when it lands. The effect is exaggerated in this example, but even subtle amounts of squash and stretch are very helpful in adding to the realism of an animation.

Follow-Through

The laws of physics dictate that every action has an equal and opposite reaction. If a cannon fires a cannonball, it's going to roll backwards a little bit. If a car comes to a screeching stop, it's going to shimmy from side to side before it comes to rest. You can see an example of this in frames 22, 26, 29, 34, and 38 of Figure 2.61 as the character bounces slightly when it lands. The result is more realistic than if the character had simply gone from frame 22 to frame 38.

Inertia should always be accounted for as well. An object doesn't just come to a complete standstill after cruising along (unless it happens to crash into a brick wall). It decelerates first. Nor does it suddenly switch from standing still to moving at a high speed. It accelerates first. This is where Ray Dream Studio's Bezier Tweener and Ease-In/Out controls become important. Make sure you understand them and use them.

BASIC CAMERA MOVEMENTS

There is more to animation than animating the objects themselves; camera movement also plays a big part in an animation. There are three basic camera movements that you should learn before moving your way up to the really fancy stuff. Add them to your animation thought process and, once you get them down, try variations on the same theme.

Zoom In

The first type of camera movement is a simple zoom in, and is perhaps the most basic camera movement to use and learn. Position the camera a distance away from the subject and then gently zoom in. Once you're satisfied with the speed of the zoom, another variation is to try slowly rotating the camera around the object while zooming in.

Model Fly-By

For moving objects, a staple camera movement is a model fly-by with the camera in a stationary position. The camera should be placed fairly close to the motion path of the moving object. Set the camera to track or point at the object. You can use one of three variations for the camera placement, each of which has a different effect. These variations are illustrated in Figure 2.62.

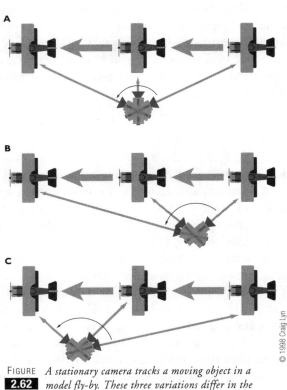

© 1998 Craig Lyn

FIGURE **2.62** *A stationary camera tracks a moving object in a model fly-by. These three variations differ in the placement of the camera.*

In Figure 2.62A the camera is positioned midway between where the plane starts in the sequence and where it finishes. The viewer will see the plane grow larger and then fly by and grow smaller. The action will flow smoothly and evenly with no surprises for the viewer.

In Figure 2.62B the camera is positioned closer to the plane at the beginning of the sequence. With this setup, the action starts abruptly as the plane flies past early in the shot. This will grab the viewer's attention immediately and direct it toward the plane's destination. A good idea is to have an interesting background or model for the airplane to fly toward in the later part of the animation, shifting the viewer's attention toward the background model. This would then make a good transition to a clip featuring a close-up of the background model.

In Figure 2.62C the camera is positioned near the end of the plane's path, which has the effect of gradually drawing the viewer's attention toward the plane. This is a good way to bring or introduce a model into a scene. With the model slowly growing in size and separating itself from the background, the viewer is gradually brought in to the action.

You can do several variations on this simple model fly-by. It's a good idea to try things such as banking the wings of the plane as it approaches the camera, or making the motion path incline slowly upward or downward. Remember always to think in three dimensions instead of two. Let your motion paths and the actions of your models take full advantage of 3D space wherever possible.

Camera Dolly

An alternative to the fly-by is the dolly. In movie production, a camera has to be fairly steady and level when it is tracking a moving object, especially when the camera itself is moving. To accomplish this, cinematographers use a dolly, which is basically a camera on wheels that is placed on top of a pair of tracks. In 3D we don't need to go to all that effort, but we do want to try to recreate the same results a dolly would give us.

There are three basic types of dolly movement that can be used to track a moving object. These are illustrated in Figure 2.63. The first type of dolly movement is shown in Figure 2.63A and has the camera moving evenly alongside the model as the model travels along. The results are fairly predictable, and this type of shot is good for showing detail in the model or for showing action that is taking place on or within the model. In Figure 2.63B the camera has a higher speed than the model, and eventually passes it. This type of shot is great for showing the viewer more of the front end of the model. In Figure 2.63C the camera moves slower than the object and eventually falls behind.

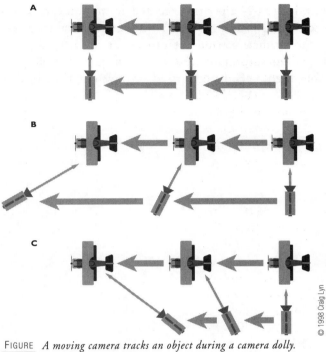

© 1998 Craig Lyn

FIGURE
2.63
*A moving camera tracks an object during a camera dolly.
These variations differ in the speed of the camera relative to
the object.*

For obvious reasons, this type of camera footage is good for showing the back
end of the model.

SUMMARY

The key to the animation thought process is realizing that animation adds a
fourth dimension to your scenes. The extra dimension is time, which means
that your scenes are no longer static images, but can change as time progresses.
Ray Dream Studio allows you to animate a wide variety of things in your
scene, but the primary ones to be concerned with are the objects in your scene
and the camera through which those objects are viewed. By changing either or
both of these elements over time, you can communicate far more with your
scene than you ever could with a single image.

Along with this increase in communication potential comes a dramatic increase in the number of ways you can interfere with your scene's

communication — a poorly executed animation can be less effective than a well-executed still image. That's why it's essential that you understand and apply the animation thought process at the very beginning of a project. The extra work you put in up front will pay off well in the finished product. You might even find yourself saving some time in the process.

— *CRAIG LYN*

CHAPTER

3

Modeling
Tips

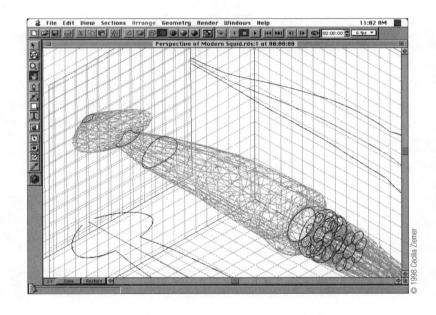

Modeling is where the art of 3D design begins — just think of the modeling window as a blank canvas, and you'll be in the right frame of mind to begin crafting your masterpiece. But no matter which 3D software package you use, you're still going to go through a learning curve as you get used to the modeler(s). Drawing three-dimensional objects on a two-dimensional screen is a process that takes a little getting used to, no matter what the approach.

Fortunately, Ray Dream Studio has two of the easiest to use and most powerful modelers available, and it doesn't take much effort to become skilled at using them — especially if you know a few special tips to make things even easier. The tips in this chapter come from a wide variety of artists who use Ray Dream Studio on a daily basis and who have figured out the best ways to get things done quickly. All of your favorite Ray Dream models were created using at least one of these tips and, in most cases, several.

By taking advantage of these tips and using them with your own modeling efforts, you'll create models faster and with less effort. You'll also discover ways to do things that you may not have realized you could do at all, and you'll prevent yourself from making some all-too-common mistakes.

BUILD MODELS IN SEPARATE FILES

When a scene starts to get complex, try building each model in a separate file. As you complete each model, select it in the **Hierarchy** window of the model file and drag it into either the **Perspective** window or **Hierarchy** window in the main illustration file. This saves redrawing time and also allows you to experiment with different models without affecting the whole scene.

— *TONY JONES*

MODEL IN LAYERS

Another way to speed up the modeling process is to build your scene in layers, keeping visible only the parts of a model that you're working on at any given time. This lets you reduce screen clutter and speeds redraw time.

The process for creating layers is easy. Once you have completed an object or group of objects, make it invisible by selecting the object or group and then selecting **Object Invisible** from the **View** menu. The group will disappear from the **Perspective** window but will still be visible in the **Hierarchy** window. You can reverse the process by selecting the group in the **Hierarchy** window and then selecting **Object Visible** from the **View** menu. Be aware though that invisible objects do not render, so make sure you make them visible before starting the rendering process . . . unless, of course, you don't want them to render.

Complicated scenes can make managing multiple visible and invisible objects a chore. A quick way around this is to make a group called *Invisible Objects*, and then drag each object you want to make invisible into this group. The objects won't become invisible when you put them in the group, even if you've already made the group invisible, but if you select the group and then choose **Object Invisible** from the **View** menu, the visible objects within the group will be made invisible. If you then add more objects to the group and want to make them invisible, simply select the group in the **Hierarchy** window and choose **Object Invisible** again. The beauty of this technique comes at rendering time, when you need to make all of your invisible objects visible. Since you've made only the group invisible, the only thing you need to do to make everything in it visible is to select the group and choose **Object Visible** from the **View** menu. All objects within the invisible group will become visible.

— *Craig Lyn & John W. Sledd*

USE MULTIPLE PERSPECTIVE WINDOWS

It's impossible to get a complete look at a three-dimensional object using only one view. A car, for example, looks completely different from the side than it does from the front. And while Ray Dream Studio's perspective view is a good way to get an overall look at your model, you'll probably find yourself switching back and forth between several different views to make sure your objects look just the way you want them to and are positioned precisely where they need to be.

You can make life easier on yourself by taking advantage of Ray Dream Studio's ability to have more than one perspective window open at a time. By creating several perspective windows with different views, you can quickly see how your model is shaping up.

To add a new perspective window, just select **New Perspective** from the **Windows** menu (or type **Command/Ctrl-7**). The **New Perspective Window** dialog box will appear, as shown in Figure 3.1. Make sure the **Create New Camera** option is selected, and then select a camera position from the **Camera Position** popup menu on the right. You'll find it helpful to select **Isometric** from the **Camera Parameters** popup menu as well, for reasons we'll get into later in Chapter 7, "Camera Tips and Techniques." Click on **OK** and a new Perspective window will appear.

Each Perspective window you create can be configured with its own working plane and preview mode settings. For the sake of speed, you may want to have your main Perspective window use the **Preview** or **Better Preview** mode

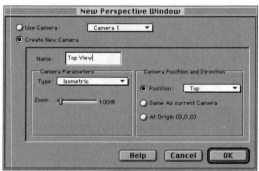

FIGURE *The **New Perspective Window** dialog box, accessible*
3.1 *from the **Windows** menu.*

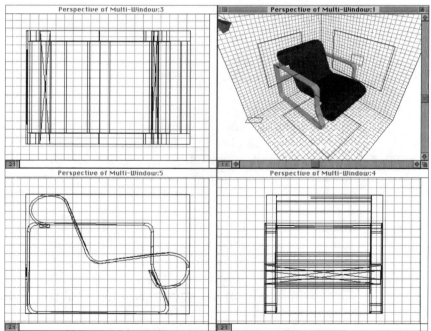

FIGURE *Multiple perspective windows showing top, reference, front and side views*
3.2 *and using different preview modes.*

and the rest use **Wireframe** mode. This will give you a good look at your model without slowing everything down.

Once you've created your additional windows, resize and arrange them on your screen so they make visual sense. (You may also need to zoom your new cameras in or out, depending on the size of your model.) Figure 3.2 shows one possible arrangement using (clockwise from upper left) top, reference, front and side views. Notice how easy this makes it to check the shape of the model with just a glance.

The last thing you need to do when setting up a custom workspace like this is to save it so you can access it again later. Ray Dream Studio lets you save any workspace arrangement, and then you can switch to it quickly at any time from the menu bar. Just choose **Workspace** from the **Windows** menu and select **Save Current**. The **Save Workspace** dialog box will appear. (See Figure 3.3.) Give your new workspace a name and click on **OK**. It will now appear in the **Workspace** popup menu.

— TONY JONES

FIGURE *The Save Workspace dialog box.*
3.3

MODEL FROM DIFFERENT PERSPECTIVES

If you followed the tutorial in the *Ray Dream Studio User Guide,* you already know how to make the process of editing cross sections easier by switching to the **Drawing Plane** view. You can also make editing the sweep path and scaling envelope easier by switching to the top or left views. Once in the modeling window, choose **Preset Position** from the **View** menu and select **Top** (**Command/Ctrl-8**) or **Left** (**Command/Ctrl-4**). (See Figures 3.4 and 3.5.) If you aren't using this tip already, you'll be surprised at how much easier it makes the modeling process.

— CECILIA ZIEMER

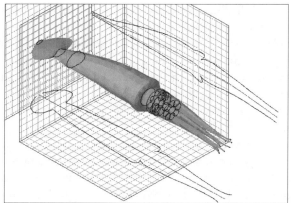

FIGURE 3.4   *A normal perspective view of the modeling window.*

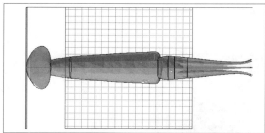

FIGURE 3.5   *A top view of the modeling window, which makes it easier to see and edit the scaling envelope.*

USE THE TRANSFORM TAB

Although it may seem easy to move, place and rotate your models using the standard Ray Dream Studio tools, they quickly become frustrating if you're trying to achieve any degree of precision. Instead, spend some time learning how to use the **Properties** palette, and keep it open at all times. Do rough positioning of your models using the standard tools if you must, but use the numerical **Position** fields in the **Transform** tab of the **Properties** palette for all the fine-tuning. (Figures 3.6 and 3.7 show examples.) You'll find it especially useful for rotation once you become comfortable with it.

This tip may seem daunting at first, but you'll find that it's not that hard to master and will help you move through the modeling process quite a bit faster than you would without it.

— *TONY JONES & VICTOR WONG*

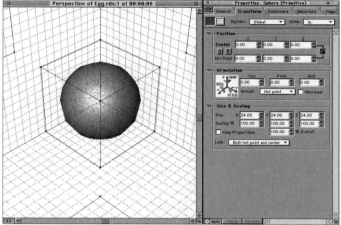

FIGURE **3.6** *Numerical fields of the **Properties** palette's **Transform** tab and*

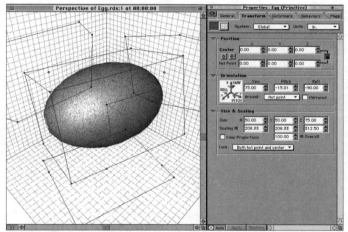

FIGURE **3.7** *Numerical fields of the **Properties** palette's **Transform** tab and associated model after directly modifying name (in the **General** tab), rotation and size using **Numerical Properties**.*

SHOW AXIS INFORMATION

You may have noticed that the screen shots for the previous tip included **Axis Indicators** (the three axis lines in the middle of the sphere and egg). When you're using the **Transform** tab of the **Properties** palette to rotate objects, **Axis Indicators** make it much easier to determine which axis needs to be rotated

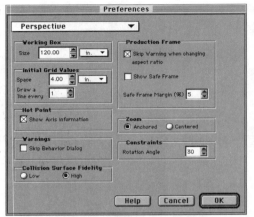

FIGURE   *The **Preferences** dialog box showing perspective*
3.8   *preferences with **Show Axis Information** selected.*

and by how much. They are color coded to match the orientation axes in the
Numerical Properties dialog box.

To turn the **Axis Indicators** on, select **Preferences** from the **File** menu to
open the **Preferences** dialog box. Select **Perspective** from the popup menu in
the upper left, click on **Show Axis Information** at the lower left, then click on
OK. (See Figure 3.8.)

Keep in mind that the **Axis Indicators** for an object will not appear until
the object is selected.

— *CRAIG PATCHETT*

MEMORIZE KEYBOARD SHORTCUTS

As enticing as it may be to navigate through Ray Dream Studio using your
mouse, this is a program that makes it worth the time to learn as many keyboard shortcuts as you can. This is especially true, of course, for the commands
you use most often. (The preset views are good ones to start with.) It may only
take five seconds or so to pull down a menu and make a selection, but when
you're doing it hundreds of times a day, it quickly adds up.

— *TONY JONES*

DON'T MAKE MORE OBJECTS THAN NECESSARY

Complex objects don't always have to be as complex as they seem. Before you
decide to break an object down into individual parts, look to see whether or not

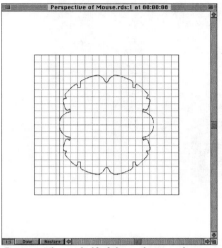

FIGURE **3.9** *The top half of this scaling envelope was created in Illustrator and imported into RDS with the **Extrusion Envelope > Symmetrical in Plane** option selected.*

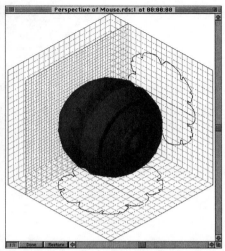

FIGURE **3.10** *A complex joint structure created as one object using a creative scaling envelope.*

the object could be modeled as one piece instead ofusing a complex scaling envelope. (The scaling envelope is a powerful tool that is well worth your time to master. You'll see examples of its use throughout this chapter and Chapter 4.)

In the example shown in Figures 3.9 and 3.10, a path was created in Adobe Illustrator and imported into Ray Dream Studio to form the top half of the scaling envelope. The **Symmetrical in Plane** option (**Geometry Menu > Extrusion Envelope > Symmetrical in Plane**) was selected to mirror the path at the bottom of the envelope. The result is a complex object that would have taken a lot more time to model with multiple parts, and one that will render faster as well.

— JOHNATHAN BANTA

USE BUMP MAPPING AS A MODELING TOOL

You should already consider bump mapping to be a way to add texture to your models. But it can also be used as a modeling tool. The baseball shown in Figure 3.11 is one example. It's entirely possible to use Free Form objects to create the seam and stitches on the baseball if you have plenty of time to spare. But a better solution is to use the bump map shown in Figure 3.12.

FIGURE 3.11   *An example of how to use bump mapping as a modeling tool. The seams and stitches were created using a bump map.*

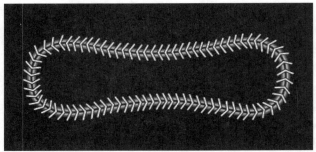

FIGURE 3.12   *The bump map used for Figure 3.11.*

The only drawback to this technique is that the bump map doesn't alter the geometry of a model, and the illusion usually falls apart around the edges (notice that the edges of the ball are flat where the seam is instead of raised). Chances are, however, that in most scenes no one will notice (did you?) and the amount of time you save will be well worth the trade-off.

— *CRAIG LYN & GRAY NORTON*

SELECT OBJECTS IN THE HIERARCHY WINDOW

If you're building a complex scene with multiple objects, you may find it challenging at times to select the right object in the **Perspective** window.

(This is especially true if you're modeling in layers using invisible objects.) Instead, click on the object in the **Hierarchy** window to select it. If you've given descriptive names to each object, this approach is faster and a lot less frustrating than trying to get a clear shot at a particular object in the **Perspective** window.

— *TONY JONES*

NAME OBJECTS AND GROUPS DESCRIPTIVELY

When creating and grouping objects, use straightforward naming conventions and try not to be obscure. Use names that describe what the object is in a way that you, and everyone else who works with you, can easily understand. (See Figure 3.13.) This may sound like common sense, but it's easy to get lazy and use the default **Free Form 1** and **Sphere 2** names. As your scene gets more complex, this makes it harder to select the right object from the Hierarchy window and also makes it more difficult when you or someone else has to animate or apply shaders to a scene.

— *CRAIG LYN*

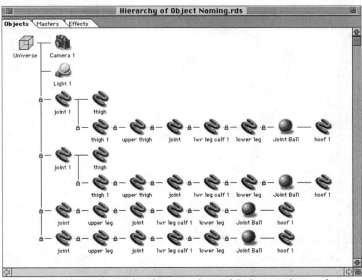

FIGURE **3.13** *The Hierarchy window for a complex model, showing the use of descriptive names.*

BREAK COMPLEX MODELS INTO SIMPLE OBJECTS

There is almost always more than one way to build a model, and part of the modeling process involves determining which approach to use. Part of this decision depends on whether or not you have enough time to work with Ray Dream Studio's more advanced modeling features. If you're on a tight deadline, the best approach may be to ignore the "Don't Make More Objects Than Necessary" tip, and instead break your model down into simple objects and then group them together to make something more complex. (If time is not an issue then you'll find other approaches in Chapter 4 that take advantage of such Ray Dream Studio features as complex scaling envelopes and shape numbering.)

The example shown in Figure 3.14 takes a complex windshield assembly for a vintage Rolls Royce and breaks it down into cylinders and some simple free-form objects. Notice how these objects have been grouped into subassemblies that can then be selected and worked on easily.

— *JOHN STEPHENS, TONY JONES & CHRISTIAN NAKATA*

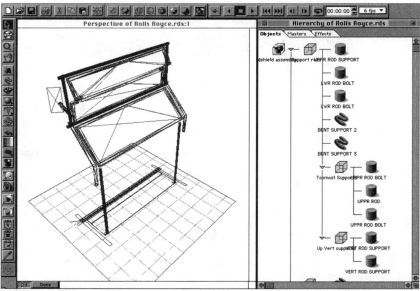

FIGURE   *A complex windshield assembly broken down into groups of simple objects.*
3.14

ROUND YOUR EDGES

In the mathematical world, an edge is a very precise, one-dimensional line. In the real world, you'll never come across such a thing. All edges have some depth to them, some degree of curvature no matter how small. Look around you and see for yourself.

For this reason, "imperfect" rounded edges can make a big difference between realistic models and ones that look like they came out of a computer. Even a tiny amount of curvature on an edge will add subtle highlights and other visual clues that give it a real-world look. (See Figure 3.15 for a simple example.)

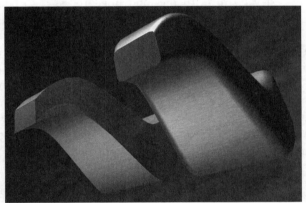

FIGURE *The object on the right uses rounded edges to give it a less* **3.15** *computer-generated look than the object on the left.*

Adding rounded edges to your models is usually as simple as adding a few additional points to the edges of your cross sections and scaling envelopes. You'll be surprised at how much of a difference it can make in the look of your finished piece, though.

— *JOHNATHAN BANTA*

SAVE OFTEN

It's easy to get so wrapped up in the modeling process that you forget to save your budding masterpiece. Unfortunately, it's just as easy for your computer to suddenly decide to take an unscheduled break and take everything you've just worked on with it. It has happened to every 3D artist, and is especially frustrating when it happens in the middle of the creative process or at the end of a long creative session (the two most likely times, by the way), so get into the habit of saving your work on a regular basis.

— TONY JONES

LEARN FROM OTHERS

One of the best ways to learn the modeling process is to take other people's models apart and see how they put them together. Fortunately, the Ray Dream Studio CD-ROM comes with a large variety of models from the modeling experts at Viewpoint Datalabs. Any one of these models is a learning experience waiting to happen. (See Figure 3.16.)

Pick a model that looks interesting, and use the **Hierarchy** window to see how the different parts are organized and broken down into smaller objects. Then open the modeling window to study different parts of the model and see how the modeler used cross sections, scaling envelopes and sweep paths to shape the model. You'll end up with a ton of ideas and a

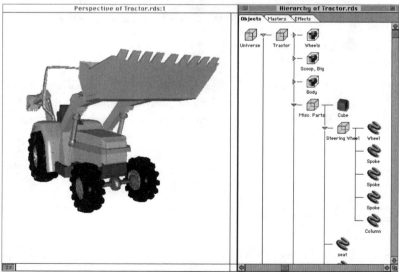

FIGURE *The models that come on the Ray Dream Studio CD-ROM are great resources*
3.16 *for studying modeling techniques.*

much better understanding of the modeling process than you could ever get from just reading the manual.

— CRAIG PATCHETT

DON'T OVERMODEL

Think about what really needs to be in your scene. For example, don't model a background if you can get away with using a scanned image. A background can also be composited later in postproduction, which is another time-saver.

Also consider whether the backs of your models will ever be seen. If you're doing a shot of a house and you never see the back of it, there's no point in creating walls or windows for the rear of the building. Visualize your scene in advance and determine what does and doesn't need to be included. You'll end up saving both modeling and rendering time.

— CRAIG LYN

KEEP CAPS LOCK ON

If you prefer to move objects around by dragging their projections in the **Perspective** window, then you know that it's easy to grab the hot point and move it instead of the object accidentally. There's an easy way to avoid this problem, and although it is mentioned somewhere deep in the *Ray Dream Studio User Guide*, it's easy to miss: When the **Caps Lock** key is down, dragging the hot point will move the object with it, keeping the position of the hot point relative to the object intact. So keep **Caps Lock** on while you're moving objects, and you'll never misplace another hot point again.

— TONY JONES

BUILD YOUR SCENE IN WIREFRAME MODE

Take advantage of the speed that **Wireframe** preview mode offers while you're building and positioning your models. (See Figure 3.17.) **Preview** and **Better Preview** modes will just end up wasting valuable time until your models are

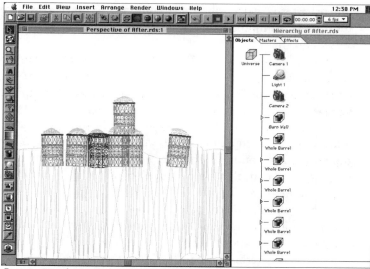

FIGURE **3.17**　*Wireframe mode is fast and accurate, which makes it perfect for building and positioning models.*

complete and at least roughly positioned, because lighting and shading aren't generally important during the modeling phase. **Wireframe** mode may not be as pretty as these other two modes, but the time it will save you is well worth the trade-off. Try it and see for yourself.

— TONY JONES

USE WIREFRAME MODE TO FIND TROUBLE SPOTS

If you're having trouble with the way a particular model looks, try switching to **Wireframe** preview mode in the **Modeling** window. You'll find that this makes it a lot easier to spot problem areas, because it gives you a quick glance at cross sections and the way they are connected to each other.

— TONY JONES

USE REAL-WORLD CROSS SECTIONS

One of the most difficult tasks in 3D modeling is trying to create accurate cross sections for your models, especially when you're trying to model something that exists in real life. You can make your job a lot easier by using cross sections from the actual objects themselves. There are several ways to do this.

If you're modeling an object that is reasonably small (rocks, model airplanes and so on), you can take pieces of flexible wire and wrap them around the contour of the object at key areas (both widthwise and lengthwise). Scan each piece of wire and then use a drawing program such as Adobe Illustrator to trace over the outline. Import these outlines into Ray Dream Studio as cross sections and scaling envelopes, and viola! You just saved yourself hours of work and frustration.

An easier method, although it's not always an option, is to find blueprints of the object you're trying to model. (See Figure 3.18.) Scan the blueprint into your computer and use it as a template in your drawing program to create the cross sections. Whichever method you use, you'll create more accurate models in less time.

— *CRAIG LYN & JOHN STEPHENS*

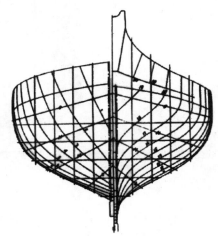

FIGURE **3.18** *Blueprints make excellent templates for creating cross sections.*

ADD POINTS FOR MORE ACCURATE COMPOUNDS

Compound objects can be very powerful modeling tools, but they don't always behave as you would expect them to. Often, when objects are combined as a

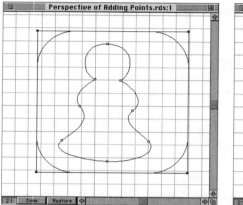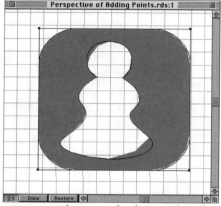

FIGURE
3.19
The two objects on the left were combined as a compound to create the object on the right. Notice how the compound cuts into the original.

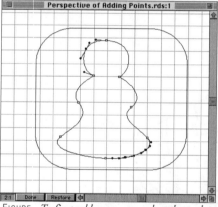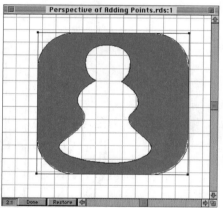

FIGURE
3.20
To fix problem compounds, release the compound and add additional points to the original objects at the problem areas, as shown here.

compound, the compound does not accurately follow the shape of the original objects. See Figure 3.19 for an example.

To clean up problem compounds, first note where the problem areas are, and then release the compound by selecting it and selecting **Break Apart Compound** from the **Arrange** menu. Now add one or two additional points near the problem areas to the object that is not being followed, and compound the objects again. (See Figure 3.20.) Repeat the process if necessary.

You can also minimize compounding problems by ungrouping objects before compounding.

— *VIEWPOINT DATALABS*

USE FREE FORM CUBES AND CYLINDERS

Although you would expect a cube primitive to behave the same way as an extruded square, it doesn't when it comes to shaders. Cube primitives have a tendency to be somewhat unpredictable when it's time to apply a shader, as do cylinder primitives. (See Figure 3.21 for an example.) Changing the shader mapping mode can help overcome these problems, but your best bet is to use **Free Form** objects for both cubes and cylinders by extruding a square or a circle.

— *VIEWPOINT DATALABS*

FIGURE *Shaders behave differently on primitives (left) than they do on*
3.21 *Free Form objects. (The shader is an 8 × 8 checker pattern.)*

BUILD TO SCALE IN THE MODELING BOX

Another way to make shaders more predictable is to build your models to scale in the **Modeling Box** rather than resizing them in the **Perspective** window. Use the grid in the **Modeling Box** to make sure your models are the appropriate sizes relative to each other (for example, a model that is twice as large as another model should be built twice as large in the **Modeling Box**). This will ensure that your shaders will also be scaled appropriately when applied to the models.

— *TONY JONES*

USE A DRAWING PROGRAM

Since most of the modeling process is spent manipulating 2D shapes (cross sections, scaling envelopes and sweep paths), consider partnering Ray Dream

Studio with a dedicated drawing program such as Adobe Illustrator or CorelDRAW. You'll gain additional tools, including text manipulation, and greater precision to make modeling easier, and you can import your creations directly into the **Modeling Box** in Ray Dream Studio. (Illustrator, .CGM, .WMF and .CDR file formats are supported).

— *CRAIG LYN*

USE ISOMETRIC CAMERAS FOR POSITIONING

Unless you're building a scene out of objects with flat surfaces at right angles to each other, positioning your objects with precise relationships to each other can be an exasperating experience. This is partly due to the fact that the standard camera, called a *Conical* camera, views your scene as you would — with perspective. Distant objects appear smaller, and parallel lines converge toward an invisible vanishing point on the horizon. While this results in a natural-looking image, it also makes it difficult to position objects accurately in your scene.

Fortunately, Ray Dream Studio provides a second type of camera called an *Isometric* camera. Viewed through an Isometric camera, same-sized objects appear the same size no matter how far away from the camera they are, and parallel lines remain parallel as they move away from the camera.

For an example of how this can be useful, see Figures 3.22 and 3.23. Figure 3.22 shows three spheres of identical size viewed through a Conical camera. Knowing that they're the same size, you can tell that the sphere on the left is farthest from the camera and the sphere on the right is closest. It looks as though the sphere on the left is tucked slightly behind the middle sphere, and the sphere on the right is moved slightly away from the middle sphere. The spheres' projections on the grid behind them show that this isn't the case, but it's still impossible to tell exactly how they line up.

If you switch to an Isometric camera (select **Camera Properties** from the **Windows** menu and then select **Isometric** from the **Type** popup menu in the **Camera Properties** palette) you can immediately see that the spheres are spaced evenly *from this angle*. (Notice the direct relationship between the spheres and their projections now.) This is why the Isometric camera makes the positioning of objects so much easier.

When using either type of camera, make sure you check two perpendicular views (that is, left and top, left and front, front and top and so on) to get the whole picture. A single view will show you only two dimensions. You must look at two perpendicular views to see all three dimensions. Figure 3.23 alone,

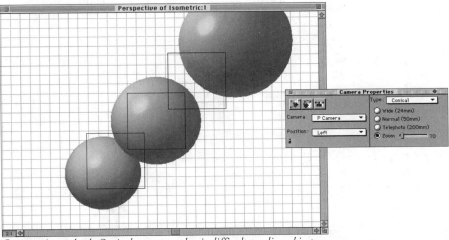

FIGURE **3.22** *A standard, Conical camera makes it difficult to align objects by eye.*

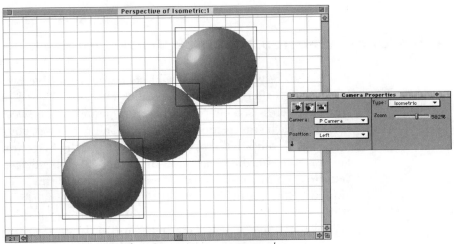

FIGURE **3.23** *The same view with an Isometric camera removes the perspective and makes it easy to see the alignment.*

for example, makes it look as though the spheres are touching. Figure 3.24 is a top view of the same scene, and shows that there is actually some space between the spheres. You can also see the front-to-back relationship again. (Figure 3.23, in case you're wondering, is the view looking from the bottom of Figure 3.24 toward the top.)

— *VICTOR WONG & CRAIG LYN*

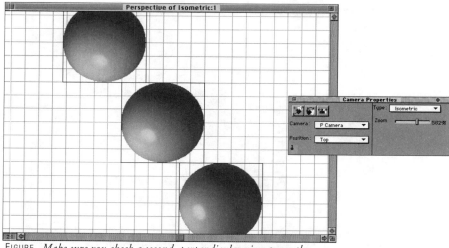

FIGURE *Make sure you check a second, perpendicular view to see the*
3.24 *alignment in all three dimensions.*

ADD A CROSS SECTION FOR EACH VERTEX POINT

You can make your Free Form objects more predictable by adding additional cross sections after you create the scaling envelope. A good rule of thumb is to create one cross section for each vertex point on the sweep path or scaling envelope. Each cross section must correspond to a vertex point.

To add additional cross sections, first use the **Selection** tool to click on the last point on the sweep path or scaling envelope. Select **Create** from the **Sections** menu to add a cross section at that point. (You may run into unpredictable results if you skip this step.) Count the number of vertex points between the first and last point, then click on the first cross section to make it active. Finally, select **Create Multiple** from the **Sections** menu and type the number of vertex points between the first and last point into the dialog box. Click on **OK**, and the additional cross sections will automatically be added at each vertex point. See Figures 3.25 and 3.26 for an example.

You can also add cross sections as you add points to your sweep path by holding down the **Option/Alt** key while clicking with the **Add Point** tool. It's easier, however, to finish your sweep path (and scaling envelope) first and then follow the steps just outlined.

— JOHNATHAN BANTA

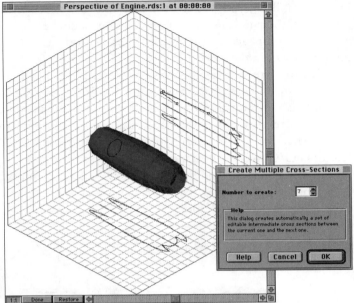

FIGURE **3.25** *Add a cross section at the end of the sweep path, then cross sections for each remaining vertex point . . .*

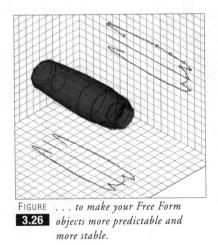

FIGURE **3.26** *. . . to make your Free Form objects more predictable and more stable.*

REALIGN YOUR AXES

It's often easier to position and rotate objects if their axes are realigned. For example, the easiest way to model a wineglass is with it lying on its side. To make it stand up, you would then have to rotate it 90 degrees on the X axis. Realigning the axes would let all the rotation values be zero when the wineglass was standing up, making it much easier to work with the wineglass as you position it within the scene.

To illustrate how do do this, Figure 3.27 shows a more complicated example using a cube that has been rotated 30 degrees on each axis. You can see the axis indicator in the middle of the cube. We now want to realign the cube's axes so that this is the cube's normal orientation. To do this, simply select the cube and then select **Group** from the **Arrange** menu (**Command/Ctrl-G**). As strange as it may seem to create a group from one object, you'll notice that the group's axes are in the default position after doing so (see Figure 3.28). Now whenever you want to position or rotate the cube, select the group instead.

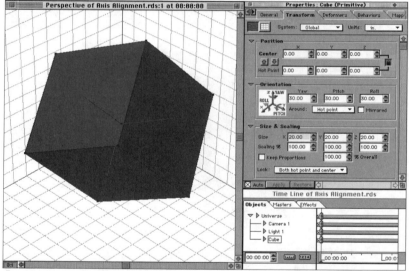

FIGURE *We want to realign the axes for this cube so that this is its default orientation*
3.27 *(that is, its* **Yaw**, **Pitch** *and* **Roll** *settings are all zero).*

Once you get the hang of this tip, you'll find quite a few places where it comes in handy, especially when you're working with a complex scene that contains a lot of different objects. You can also apply this tip to groups (that is, group a group).

— *STEPHANIE ARVIZU*

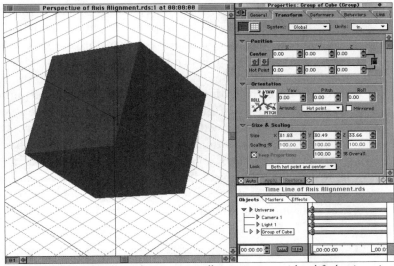

FIGURE **3.28** *Selecting the cube and grouping it will create a group with a default orientation. Notice the change in the axis indicator and the **Yaw**, **Pitch** and **Roll** settings.*

WORKING WITH THE WORKING BOX

One of the most flexible tools in Ray Dream Studio is the Working Box, yet many see this box as a limiting factor in their work. Keep in mind that the Working Box is an object just like every other object in your scene. It can be moved, resized, rotated and sent anywhere in the universe you want. It does not define the boundaries of your universe; it simply makes it easier for you to manage it.

Take some time to play around with the Working Box and its controls. To select the Working Box, **Command/Ctrl-click** on it. Now see how many operations you can perform on it with RDS's various tools. Keep in mind that the Working Box's movement is constrained by its own settings, which can get confusing, but as I've said, it's just like any other object.

Learning how to use the Working Box properly can really help when you're arranging large scenes or models.

— JOHN W. SLEDD

START MESH FORM MODELS OFF IN THE FREE FORM MODELER

The Mesh Form modeler is a powerful modeler in and of itself, but the Free Form modeler has some very powerful features that you might find yourself wishing you had in the Mesh Form modeler. Since the Mesh Form modeler is new, you might feel more comfortable using the Free Form. This is not a problem, though. You can create the basic shape of your desired object in the Free Form modeler and then reopen it in the Mesh Form modeler by selecting your Free Form object in the Perspective window and choosing **Jump In Another Modeler** from the **Edit** menu. Select the **Mesh Form modeler** from your **Available Modelers** list and click on **OK**. Now you have a good basic foundation to begin tweaking with the new vertex-level tools.

Another important thing to notice in the **Jump In Another Modeler** dialogue box is the little checkbox about half-way down. The checkbox says **If conversion, apply deformers on object.** This is an amazing addition which allows the effects of a deformer to be applied to the actual mesh of your object. This is a very powerful modeling tool that will open up wonderful new techniques in the future.

— *JOHN W. SLEDD*

BRINGING IT ALL TOGETHER: PROJECT PEGASUS

Many of you will recognize the illustration in Figure 3.29. Whether it was in your Fractal Design direct-mail pieces, on the cover of your *Ray Dream Animator User Guide,* riding the splash screen of Ray Dream Studio 4, or in any number of software catalogs out there, you should have seen this piece by

FIGURE   *Mark Jenkins' Pegasus*
3.29

now. If, in fact, you've been in a cave for the past year, I'll let you in on the secret. It is the incredible rendition of the Ray Dream Animator Pegasus by Mark Jenkins of the Rucker Design Group.

This piece illustrates many of the tips outlined in this chapter. It illustrates the idea of breaking complex objects into simple shapes. It illustrates what rounding edges can do for your piece. And it illustrates how forethought and planning can bring everything together.

The Pegasus piece is truly an astounding (and somewhat intimidating) work, but in closing this chapter we are quickly going to cover how Mark built it from the ground up. Notice that the winged equine didn't simply jump onto the screen. It took a great deal of forethought and preparation before Ray Dream Studio was even opened. A model of this complexity may seem an arduous task at first, but once you notice that it's built out of many simple shapes, the road to the masterpiece becomes just a little less frightening. Let's take a look.

In Figures 3.30 and 3.31, Mark sketched out the simple ideas that he wanted to incorporate into the Pegasus model. As you can see, he was pretty detailed, all the way down to the joints and trim details. He even made some notes as to what type of modeling to use. This made it easy for him to decide which approach to take before he even started. This meant he didn't waste any time trying one technique before deciding that he needed another approach and having to start all over. Although this does happen often, it's best if you can keep these problems to a minimum, and forethought is the best prevention.

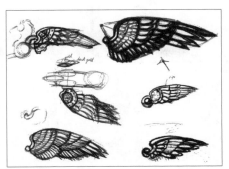

3.30

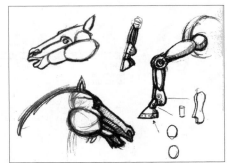

3.31

In Figure 3.32, Mark draws a 2D view of the Pegasus head and mane. This illustrator artwork will be used to create the cross sections in RDS's Free Form modeler.

Figure 3.33 shows the cross section for the mane being separated out into a separate Illustrator file to be saved and then imported into RDS's Free Form

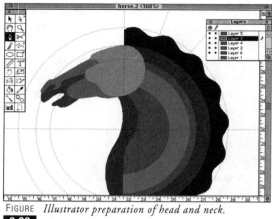

FIGURE
3.32
Illustrator preparation of head and neck.

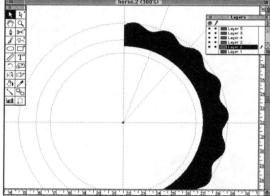

FIGURE
3.33
The mane cross section in Illustrator.

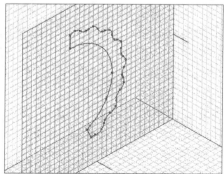

FIGURE
3.34
The mane cross section imported into the modeling window.

modeler. Figure 3.34 shows the imported Illustrator mane in RDS's **Free Form** modeling window. Mark adjusted the extrusion path as necessary to get the overall shape of the mane and then repeated the same steps for the other pieces of the neck. Figures 3.35 and 3.36 show how the separate objects come together to form something we begin to recognize.

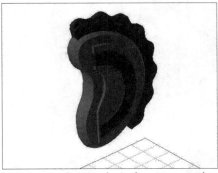

FIGURE **3.35** *Overlapping shapes form composited neck.*

FIGURE **3.36** *Full composited head.*

Mark continued to create, import and position objects, such as the feather in Figure 3.37, and arrange them to build Pegasus' other necessary parts. Figures 3.39 and 3.39 show the finished Pegasus model in the **Perspective** window. As you can see, the entire model is built of cleverly positioned and well-thought-out simple shapes.

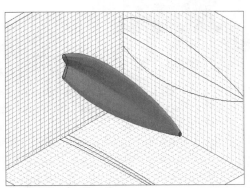

FIGURE **3.37** *Feather Free Form.*

The point here is that no project is impossible if you put your mind to it. Think of everything as a collection of smaller parts instead of one big,

FIGURE *Full Pegasus frontal view.*
3.38

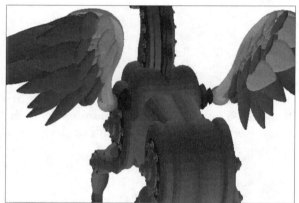

FIGURE *Full Pegasus back view.*
3.39

complex, impossible whole. Good art lies just as much in your mental approach to a project as it does in your actual skills and abilities to implement them.

The above techniques can be used to create virtually anything your twisted mind can conjure up.

— *MARK JENKINS*

4

Modeling
Techniques

Sometimes the best way to learn is by example, and that's certainly true for the modeling process. Each of the techniques in this chapter offers an example of (and a mini-tutorial on) a different aspect of modeling. Even though you may not be working on models that match the examples, each technique was selected for inclusion because it develops concepts that can be applied to a variety of projects. By the time you finish reading through this chapter, you will have learned some key modeling skills that will help you develop your models faster and with greater accuracy.

MODELING ROCKS

While you may not have an immediate need for a rock model (see Figure 4.1), the process for creating one can be adapted to many other organic objects, and is also a good exercise in working with Free Form objects. Once you've mastered this technique, which is easy to do, you'll be well on your way to enhancing the realism of all your Ray Dream Studio projects.

FIGURE *Richard's rock modeling technique and his rock shader*
4.1 *technique work together for surprisingly realistic results.*

Step One

Create a new Free Form object by choosing **Free Form** from the **Insert** menu. The **Modeling** window will appear. Using the **Pen** tool, draw a random-looking cross section, as shown in Figure 4.2. This will serve as the foundation for your rock. The precise shape of this cross section isn't really important, but it should be close to the shape you want your rock to have. Now center the cross section by choosing **Center** from the **Sections** menu.

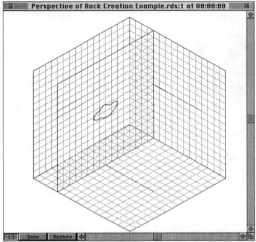

Perspective of Rock Creation Example.rds:1 at 00:00:00

FIGURE 4.2 *The first step to creating a rock is to draw a rough cross section in the modeling window.*

Step Two

Group the cross section by selecting it and choosing **Group** from the **Arrange** menu. Resize the cross section until it is very small by choosing **Scale** from the **Geometry** menu and entering a value of 1% in both the horizontal and vertical fields. This will serve as one end of your rock.

Step Three

Now we'll start building the rock's shape. Choose **Extrusion Envelope** from the **Geometry** menu and select **Symmetrical** from the menu that appears. Click on either of the path description planes to activate it, and use the **Pen** tool to draw a multipoint envelope that defines the basic shape of the rock. Figure 4.3 shows one possibility. Don't worry about the position of your extrusion path when you start to draw with the Pen tool. The second point of the path will be redefined by your first click.

Don't make the envelope too smooth unless you're planning to create a beach stone or pebble. Some of the points in your shape may be rounded, but some should also be at least slightly sharp and jagged (that is, corner points) to lend some variety and realism to the rock. You might find it useful to have a real rock handy to serve as a model, especially if you're looking for a particular effect. Reality is always a good reference model!

Step Four

The next step is to create a more natural, asymmetrical shape for your rock. To do this, you need to be able to work with each of the four scaling envelopes

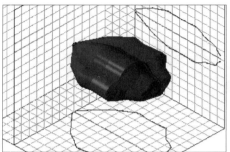

FIGURE **4.3** *The second step is to group and resize the cross section then draw a rough scaling envelope using* **Symmetry.**

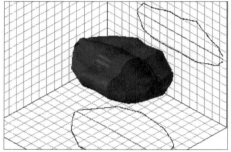

FIGURE **4.4** *Once the basic shape is defined, switch to Free mode and create a more random shape.*

individually. Choose **Extrusion Envelope** from the **Geometry** menu and select **Free** from the menu that appears. Rework each of the scaling envelopes to create a more realistic shape. (See Figure 4.4.)

Step Five

Now that you have your basic rock shape, the next step is to add additional cross sections so you can tweak the surface of the rock and create a more random look. First, select the beginning cross section of your rock and choose **Ungroup** from the **Arrange** menu. Now select the end point of your extrusion path and choose **Create** from the **Sections** menu to add a cross section at the very end. (See Figure 4.5.) This will prevent RDS from giving you a big, funky cross section shape when you create multiple sections in the next part of this step. (Feel free to move on to the next paragraph without adding this end cross section — if for no other reason, just to see what happens.)

Now choose **Create Multiple** from the **Sections** menu. (See Figure 4.6.) The number of cross sections you create will depend on the amount of detail you want to add to the rock, but eight to ten is usually enough.

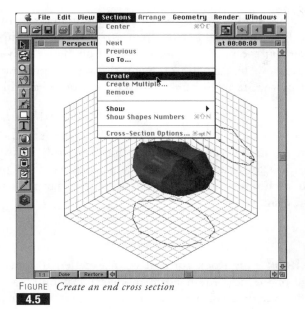

FIGURE *Create an end cross section*
4.5

FIGURE *Multiple cross sections*
4.6 *give you more control*
over surface shape.

Once the cross sections have been created, select and modify each one slightly by pulling points and modifying their handles to create bumps and depressions that change from one section to the next. (See Figure 4.7.) Try to rid the rock surface of too many continuous bumps and valleys that run the length of the rock. You might also try slightly rotating a cross section (with **Twist Surface** off) and, if necessary, add an additional cross section or two. It also might help you keep things organized if you choose **Show>Current** from the **Sections** menu, so that you see only the cross section you're currently working on.

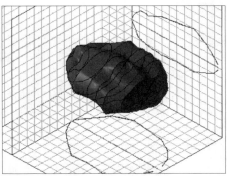

FIGURE *Select and modify each cross section to add*
4.7 *some randomness to the rock's surface.*

The objective of this step is to add some randomness to the rock; if one cross section has a depression at one point, try adding a bump at the corresponding point in the next cross section. Turn on **Better Preview** every now and then to see how things look. You might also want to preview the rock from different perspectives to make sure you haven't overlooked anything.

Step Six

The last step is to apply a shader to your rock, which is as important as the modeling process itself if you want your rock to look truly realistic. (You'll find several techniques for creating rock and marble shaders in Chapter 9, "Shader Recipes and Techniques.") Placing your rock in a natural setting will also enhance its realism.

— *RICHARD BUCCI*

⇨ **Editor's Note:** This Rock tutorial is an excellent opportunity to take advantage of the new Mesh Form modeler's capabilities. When you are done with your Free Form rock, click on *Done* in the *Modeling* window to return to the *Perspective* window. Now duplicate your rock free form and move the duplicate out and away from the original. With the duplicate selected, choose *Jump In Another Modeler* from the *Edit* menu. Choose the *Mesh Form Modeler* from the *Choose Another Modeler* dialogue box and click on *OK*. (See Figure 4.8.) Now you can tweak each vertex and use the *Sphere of Attraction* tool to randomize the surface of your rock. (See Figure 4.9.)

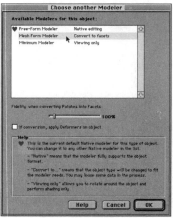

FIGURE **4.8** *For additional randomization, convert your rock to a mesh form.*

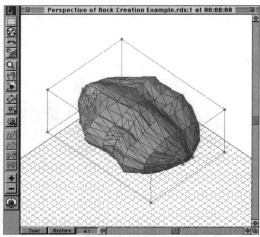

FIGURE **4.9** *Use the Sphere of Attraction tool to adjust the surface of the rock.*

CREATING WRINKLES

Wrinkles add realism to a variety of different models, such as sandstone, fabrics, skin and so on. While they may, at first, seem complicated to create, this technique shows you how to take advantage of a minor quirk in Ray Dream Studio that will do most of the work for you. The results will look as if you've slaved away for hours over your model, as the models in Figure 4.10 demonstrate. (Only you need to know the truth!)

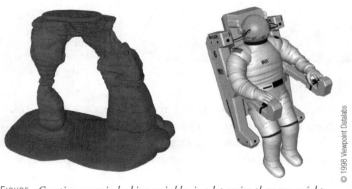

FIGURE *Creating organic-looking wrinkles is a lot easier than you might*
4.10 *think, if you take advantage of this technique.*

© 1998 Viewpoint Datalabs

Step One

The first step is to create a basic object to add wrinkles to. Create a new Free Form object by choosing **Free Form** from the **Insert** menu. The **Modeling** window will appear. Using the **Pen** tool, create a cross section shape. It can be as simple or as complex as you like, depending on what you want the final object to look like. Choose **Center** from the **Sections** menu to center your cross section. Choose **Create** from the **Sections** menu to add an additional cross section to the end of the extrusion, as shown in Figure 4.11.

Step Two

The next step is to add a few curves to the extrusion path, which is what will prompt Ray Dream Studio to generate the wrinkles in Step Three. First, choose **Extrusion Method** from the **Geometry** menu and select **Pipeline** to switch to Pipeline mode. Next, select the extrusion path on the right drawing plane using the **Selection** tool. Using the **Convert Point** tool, drag out the handles of both end points on the extrusion path to add some shape to the path. You can also use the **Selection** tool to move the end points up or down to

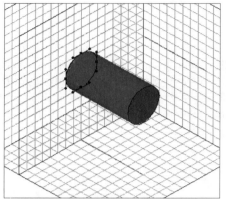

FIGURE
4.11 *The first step to creating organic wrinkles is to extrude a basic cross section in the Free Form modeler.*

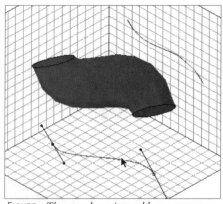

FIGURE
4.12 *The second step is to add some curves to the extrusion path. The more pronounced the curves, the deeper the wrinkles.*

enhance the path. When you've finished, repeat this process with the extrusion path on the bottom drawing plane.

See Figure 4.12 for an example of what you might end up with. The exact shape isn't as important as the curviness of the extrusion path.

Step Three

The next step is to create an envelope and add some cross sections as final preparation for adding the wrinkles. Choose **Extrusion Envelope** from the **Geometry** menu and select **Free** to create the envelope. Create the cross sections by choosing **Create Multiple** from the **Sections** menu. Three to five cross sections are usually enough, depending on the length of your object. Figure 4.13 shows an example of the object at this point.

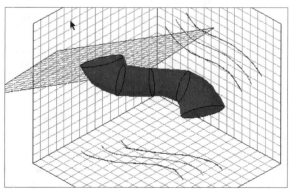

FIGURE
4.13 *The last step before creating the wrinkles themselves is to add a scaling envelope and some additional cross sections.*

Step Four

Now you're ready to create the wrinkles by using the **Add Point** tool to add a large number of points (as many points as you want wrinkles) along the scaling envelope, as shown in Figure 4.14. Ray Dream Studio will then begin to create a wrinkled look for you.

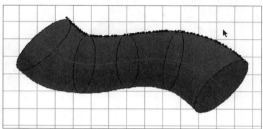

FIGURE **4.14** *The wrinkles are created simply by adding points to the scaling envelopes where you want wrinkles to appear.*

If you look closely at the scaling envelope after adding the points, you'll see that each point adds a tiny jagged edge to the envelope (see Figure 4.15), which is what creates the wrinkled look. You can see the effect of these edges on the object's surface in Figure 4.16.

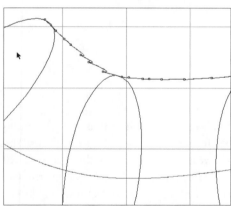

FIGURE **4.15** *A close-up look at the scaling envelope shows tiny jagged edges where the additional points have been added.*

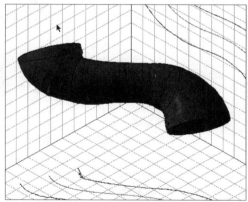

FIGURE **4.16** *The effect of the jagged edges on the shaded object is to create subtle wrinkles along the surface of the object.*

Step Five

The last step is to use the **Convert Point** tool to tweak the handles on individual points to get the exact look you want. (See Figure 4.17.) You can also mod-

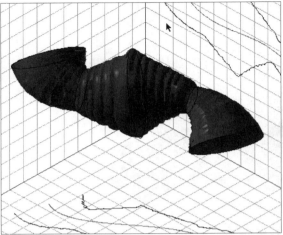

FIGURE *The last step is to tweak the handles on the points to*
4.17 *enhance the effect and to customize the scaling envelope.*

ify the scaling envelope and cross sections at this point to customize the shape
of your object. This step will take a lot of trial and error (remember that you
can undo using **Command/Ctrl-Z**) if you want a specific look, but it's well
worth the effort, as you can see by the sample images at the beginning of this
technique.

— *VIEWPOINT DATALABS*

CREATING A SHAPE WITHIN A SHAPE

There are many times when you need to create an object that will fit snugly
within another object. (See Figure 4.18 for an example.) At first glance this
may appear to be a daunting task, since you need to match the shape of the
second object precisely to the inside of the first; and you need to align the two
objects just as precisely. Fortunately, there's a very simple technique you can
use that makes Ray Dream Studio do all the work for you.

Step One

We'll use wine in a wineglass for this example, but the technique can be
applied to virtually any shape (multishape torused objects work especially
well). The first step is to select the object you want to work with, and choose
Duplicate from the **Edit** menu to create a new instance of the object. Double-

FIGURE *Creating an object (wine) to*
4.18 *fit perfectly within another*
object (glass) is easy.

click on the new instance to jump into it and open it's **Modeling** window.
When you double-click on the object, you'll get a dialogue giving you the
option to either **Create New Master** or **Edit Master**. You want to choose
Create New Master. You're going to modify this copy of your original object to
create the new object. Figure 4.19 shows a basic wineglass in the **Modeling**
window, which we'll work with as an example.

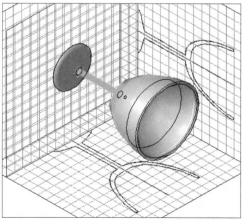

FIGURE *The first step is to create a duplicate of the*
4.19 *original object and jump into it.*

⇨ **Editor's Note:** Before you begin, it's a good idea to rename this master object. After a while it would get confusing having Glass 1, Glass 2, Glass 3 and so on. Let's name this object "Wine." Since you have the object open in the *Modeling* window, the *Masters* tab in the *Hierarchy* window should be activated. To change the name of the current object, select it in the *Masters* tab window and hold down the mouse button (not too hard though — mouse oppression is against the law in many states). This will bring a dialogue to the front, allowing you to change the name. As I said before, let's call it "Wine." I know, I know, I'm being redundant, but we don't want you to miss anything.

You can also change the name of the master object while in the *Perspective* window. Simply activate the *Masters* tab, select the object you wish to rename and then press the *Return* key. This will bring the same dialogue box to the front.

Anyway, enough of that naming drivel. Let's get on with it, shall we?

Step Two

Type **Command/Ctrl-4** to switch to a left view of the object, so you can work with the scaling envelope more easily. You may also want to turn off the preview. Using the **Selection** tool, click on the scaling envelope so you can see the points on the envelope. (See Figure 4.20.) In the next step you'll be deleting the points you don't need, so it's helpful to see where they are.

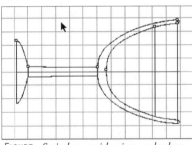

FIGURE **4.20** *Switch to a side view and select the scaling envelope so you can see where the points are.*

Step Three

Using the **Delete Point** tool, click on each of the points that will not be touching the inserted object. (Figures 4.21 and 4.22 illustrate this process.) The basic idea is that you want to use only the part of the shape of the original object that is shared by the inserted object. When you've finished, you'll be left with the part of your inserted object that touches the original object. You

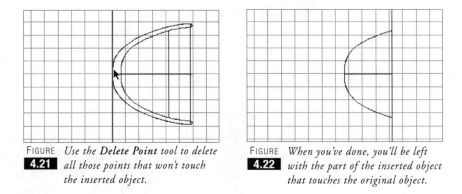

FIGURE 4.21 *Use the **Delete Point** tool to delete all those points that won't touch the inserted object.*

FIGURE 4.22 *When you've done, you'll be left with the part of the inserted object that touches the original object.*

could also do it the other way around, and start by creating the inserted object then building the surrounding object. In the case of the wine in our example, we're left with the entire shape we need. Depending on what you're creating, you may use the results of this step as your starting point and build the rest of your object from it. If you do, make sure you don't change or move this part of the object, or you will lose your perfect fit.

Also note that in our example a cross section was built into the original wineglass at the point where the top of the wine would be. This cross section and its corresponding points automatically defined the top of the wine when we deleted the other points. By planning ahead when you build your objects, you can make this technique go more smoothly by adding cross sections and points at strategic places.

Step Four

If you want your new object to be a solid shape, you'll probably need this extra step. Switch back to **Reference** view by typing **Command/Ctrl-0**. Select each cross section in the **Modeling** window and select **Cross Section Options** from the **Sections** menu. Click on **Fill Cross Section** in the dialog box that appears, then click on **OK** to fill the cross section. (See Figure 4.23.)

This is also a good time to apply a shader to your new object while it's out in the open and unobscured by the original object. Figure 4.23 shows the filled and shaded wine ready to be placed in the glass. (Incidentally, the modeling window is a great place to apply a shader for several reasons. See Chapter 9, "Shader Recipes and Techniques," for more details.)

Step Five

The last step is to place your new object in the original object and align it properly. You'll be pleasantly surprised to learn that this is as simple as clicking the **Done** button at the bottom left of the **Modeling** window. As long as you haven't

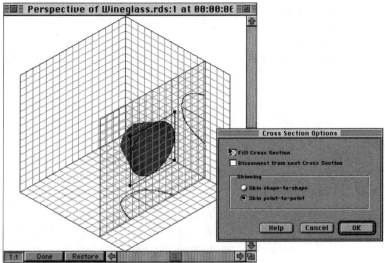

FIGURE   *Select the Fill Cross Section option in the Cross*
4.23   *Section Options dialog box to make a solid shape.*

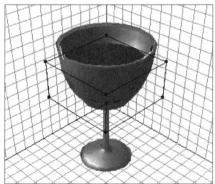

FIGURE   *As long as you haven't moved any of*
4.24   *the original points, your two objects*
will be aligned when you click Done.

moved any of the original points or cross sections in your new object, Ray Dream Studio will remember how the points were positioned relative to the original object and will align the two objects automatically, as shown in Figure 4.24.

Other Uses

Once you understand how this technique works, you'll quickly realize that it can easily be adapted to a variety of alignment problems. It's great, for example, in situations where complex objects need to touch each other at a particular point, even if they share only a single surface point. In general, you'll find this technique useful for any situation where different objects need to have a specific spatial relationship with each other. You'll be surprised at how often it comes in handy and how much time it will save you in the process. Have fun with it.

— CECILIA ZIEMER

EASY SPIRAL STAIRCASE

What 3D artist completes a career without at least one call for a spiral staircase? The spiral staircase, while seemingly a daunting task, is made easy in the following steps.

Figure 4.25 is a good example of a spiral staircase in action. The actual rendering took about 12 hours. Rendering time is in direct proportion to the complexity of the scene, as well as the resolution chosen. The stairs were assigned a silver surface to reflect the people. Notice how, in the wireframe version, crude mannequins were made in 3D for placement. Lighting was accomplished with 10 lights strategically placed. A photograph of the girl was later pasted into the boat.

FIGURE *The finished illustration and accompanying wireframe.*
4.25

Step One

Create the first tread for the stairs by choosing **Free Form** from the **Insert** menu. When the **Modeling** window appears, choose the **Rectangle** tool and draw a cross section with the desired proportions. Center the cross section by choosing **Center** from the **Sections** menu, then choose **Cross Section Options** from the **Sections** menu, select the **Skin point-to-point** option, and click **OK**. You should have something similar to Figure 4.26.

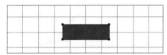

FIGURE **4.26**   *Create the first tread's cross section.*

Step Two

Extrude your tread a bit to give it some width, as shown in Figure 4.27. Make your tread about twice as long as you really want it (I'll show you why in a moment). The far end will be the outside of the staircase, and the closest end will be the center of the spiral. Now choose **Create** from the sections menu to add a cross section to the end of the tread.

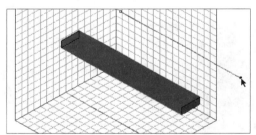

FIGURE **4.27**   *Extrude the tread and add a cross section to the end.*

Step Three

Now select the end cross section and scale it down to 1% horizontally by choosing **Scale** from the **Geometry** menu and typing **1** in the **Horizontal** field. (See Figure 4.28.)

Step Four

Figure 4.29 shows another section being defined — a middle section. This is actually going to be the end of the stair tread, as will be seen in the next picture (and this is why I told you to make the tread about twice as long as you wanted it to

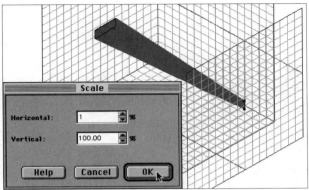

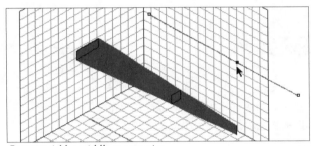

FIGURE   *Scale the end cross section to 1%.*
4.28

FIGURE   *Add a middle cross section.*
4.29

be). To define that cross section, simply choose the **Add Point** tool and **Option-Click** on the extrusion path at about the midway point. It's OK to eyeball it.

Step Five

Now choose the **Delete Point** tool and delete the end cross section by clicking on it's corresponding point on the extrusion path. We now have something that is recognizable as a stair tread. (See Figure 4.30.) It is the shape we will use to build the spiral. But first, though, you need to select that middle shape, choose **Cross Section Options** from the **Section** menu, and fill that cross section. Since it was originally in the middle of the shape, it was not filled by default. When we deleted the end cross section, we were left with an open middle cross section . . . well, until we just filled it, of course. Now click on **Done** to exit the modeler.

Step Six

Every object created in Ray Dream Studio has a *hot point* which locates that object in space. Normally it is in the center of the object. However, we have

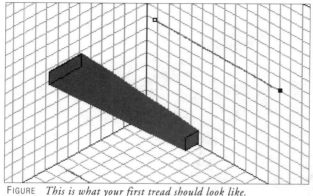

FIGURE
4.30
This is what your first tread should look like.

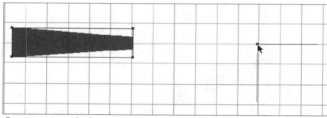

FIGURE
4.31
Move the hot point.

the option of moving the hot point to another place. In Figure 4.31 we are looking straight down on the stair tread (**Command/Ctrl-8**). Shift-drag the hot point of your tread off to the right, which will be the imaginary center of the spiral staircase. The distance between the inside edge and the center point should be roughly the same as the width of the object itself. Make sure you don't have your Caps Lock down, or you'll move the entire object by dragging on it's hot point. This is often desirable, but not now.

Step Seven

Now comes the fun part. Choose the **Wireframe Preview** mode and then select the tread object with the **Selection** tool. Choose **Duplicate** from the **Edit** menu. This creates a duplicate of your object in the same space as your current object. While still in the top view, select the **2D Rotation** tool and click and drag on the upper left-hand corner of your tread object. The object will rotate around it's hot point. Use the wireframe as a gauge as to when to stop dragging. You should match up the inside corners of your treads as shown in Figure 4.32.

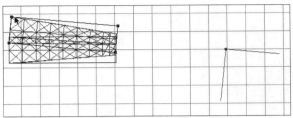

FIGURE *Match up the corners of your treads.*
4.32

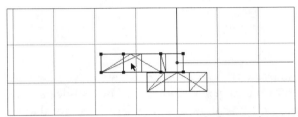

FIGURE *Drag the second tread to stack on the first tread.*
4.33

Now, while the second tread object is still selected, change your view to show the scene from the back (**Command/Ctrl-3**). Select the second tread object with the **Selection** tool and shift-drag it up so that it is stacked on top of the first tread object. (See Figure 4.33.)

What you have just done is to set up a little "script" for RDS's Duplicate function to follow. With the second tread object still selected, choose **Duplicate** from the **Edit** menu (or just use **Command/Ctrl-D**), and watch a third tread appear, perfectly aligned with the second. Just repeat this over and over, and you'll see successive treads form, each with the same rotational and placement increments set by the first pair. (See Figure 4.34.) Just keep hitting **Command/Ctrl-D** until you have your full spiral staircase.

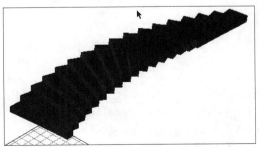

FIGURE *Multiple duplications make up a finished*
4.34 *section of stairs.*

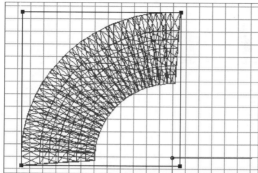

FIGURE *Make a group of stairs.*
4.35

If your **staircase** is supposed to be really big, you may find it easier simply to duplicate treads until you've constructed one 90-degree section of your staircase, and group them as shown in Figure 4.35. Notice that the hot point must be repositioned at the lower right corner of the box.

Step Eight

This new one-piece unit is easily duplicated, rotated 90 degrees, and elevated to fit on top of the first unit just as we did with the first two treads. In Figure 4.36 we have a side view of two stair groups. We can either further combine these two groups and duplicate that new grouping, or keep hitting the **Duplicate** command just as we did with the first set of treads. In no time at all, an elaborate spiral staircase like the one in Figure 4.37 can be created.

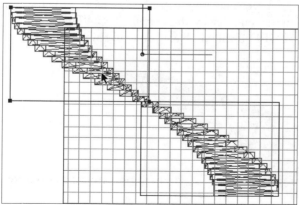

FIGURE *Combine stair groups.*
4.36

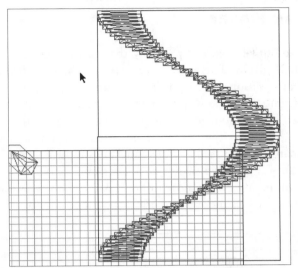

FIGURE *A spiraling staircase.*
4.37

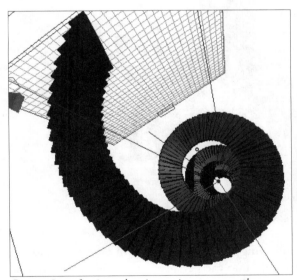

FIGURE *Lots of stairs and an interesting camera angle.*
4.38

Figure 4.38 shows what a bunch of stairs and an interesting camera angle can do for the imagination.

— *JOHN STEPHENS & JOHN W. SLEDD*

MODELING THE HUMAN FIGURE

Modeling the human figure is probably the most ambitious task an artist can tackle in RD3D/RDS. There are as many ways to approach the subject in 3D as there are in traditional art forms like painting and sculpting. The model Fox Paw demonstrates just one way to create a human figure model, but the basic concepts used in this model can be applied to creating to other characters.

Figure 4.39 shows the complete model in preview and rendered form. Note how many objects used in this model are simple geometrics — the key to its realism can be attributed mainly to a few clever shader tricks. In the following steps I will highlight the more difficult parts. Once you understand those, the easier parts, such as the legs and arms, should be a snap.

FIGURE *Fox Paw preview and rendered.*
4.39

© 1998 D.R. Greenlaw

For the following steps, each Free Form object is created either by dragging the **Free Form** icon into the **Perspective** or **Hierarchy** windows, or by choosing **Free Form** from the **Insert** menu. It's your choice.

Step One

Let's start with the head. Figure 4.40 shows the basic skull object I like to use for many of my characters. It's made from three simple cross sections. These cross sections can be created either in Ray Dream Studio or in a 2D drawing application such as Adobe Illustrator.

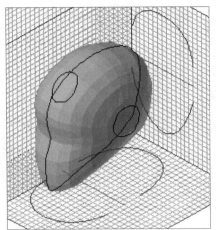

FIGURE *The basic head shape.*

4.40

⇨ **Note:** Envelopes, in many cases, are not necessary. To smooth the shape between cross sections, handles can be drawn out from the center point of the sweep path. In this instance, however, I wound up wanting to give Fox Paw a narrower chin, so using envelopes became necessary. Note that the basic shape of the object has not been affected by the envelopes; only the bottom "chin" portion is affected. This was accomplished by slightly adjusting the side view envelope using the *Free* option. Further "modeling" can be accomplished through shader effects. Fox Paw's cheeks, for example, were enhanced by applying *Paint Shapes* to the head using the *3D Paint Brush* in the *Airbrush* mode.

Step Two
Figure 4.41 shows the basic nose. You can add details to the head like the eyes, ears, nose and lips, if you wish. The nose is a very simple Free Form object using only two cross sections with free envelopes.

Step Three
Eyes can be simple orbs but, as Figure 4.42 shows, Fox Paw's eyes are fairly complicated. Each eye is made from four parts which can be repositioned — eyeball, upper and lower lids, and an eyelashes object. The eyelids can open and close, and the eyeball can be freely rotated for added realism. The eyelash object is a flattened ring with a transparency mask to define individual lashes.

Step Four
Figure 4.43 illustrates how the neck is built in the **Free Form** modeler. Notice again how this object is built using relatively simple shapes.

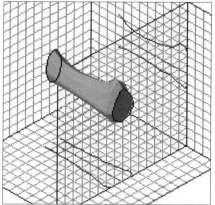

FIGURE
4.41
The nose Free Form.

FIGURE
4.42
The eyes have it.

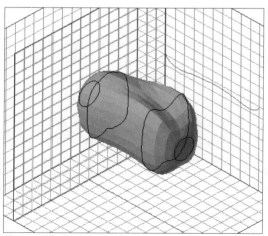

FIGURE
4.43
The neck.

Step Five

The chest. For some reason, I've found the human chest most difficult to model using RD3D/RDS's **Free Form** modeler. Figure 4.44 shows a basic chest object, again made with a few simple cross sections. Although this chest is made for a female character, slight modifications make it appropriate for male characters. Like Fox Paw's cheeks, details like abdominal and pectoral muscles, ribs and even the belly button can be added using **Paint Shapes** or the **3D Paint Brush**. Figure 4.45 shows a way to add extra detail to an object by simply placing another object within it. For Fox Paw's collarbone, I modeled one collarbone in the **Free Form** modeler, duplicated and rotated it to form a second collarbone, and then grouped the pair. I then placed this group slightly embedded in Fox Paw's chest, so that this group of objects actually appears to be part of the chest object.

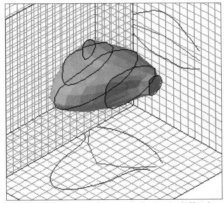

FIGURE **4.44** *The chest, for me, is the most difficult part to model.*

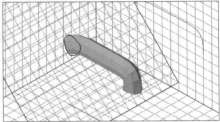

FIGURE **4.45** *The collarbone adds realistic detail.*

Step Six

Now come the arms. Figures 4.46 and 4.47 show how I created Fox Paw's arm and forearm. The good thing about arms and legs is that you only have to make one of each. Once you get it right, a simple **Duplicate with symmetry** from the **Edit** menu will create the arm or leg for the other side.

Step Seven

The hand: for models viewed at a distance, small details like fingers and toes may not be necessary (don't model more than you need). My character, Fox Paw, will be used in some fairly detailed renderings and animations, so it was necessary to spend time with such details. Figure 4.48 shows the hand model made from five master objects. Since the finger models were all basically similar in structure, it made sense to use duplicates to conserve RAM and disk

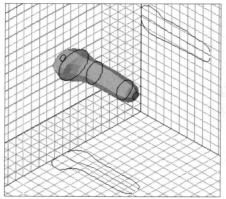

FIGURE **4.46** *Fox Paw's arm.*

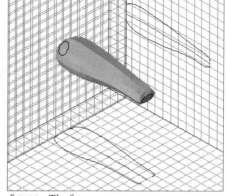

FIGURE **4.47** *The forearm.*

FIGURE **4.48** *The hand is built of several Free Form instances.*

space. The finger joints were individually resized as instances in the **Perspective** window rather than in the modeler. Altering the segments in the modeler would have either altered all instances or created a new master.

Step Eight

Figure 4.49 shows Fox Paw's pelvis. Again, simple shapes are used to form a crucial piece of the object. After all, without a pelvis, her legs would fall right over.

Body Perspective

Figure 4.50 is the completed model shown at the standard perspective view. To make the model easier to position and pose, you can link the individual body parts in a logical hierarchy. After linking the body parts, drag the hot points to appropriate coordinates — for example, the hot point for the head object should be at the base of the skull; the hot point for the forearm would be at the elbow.

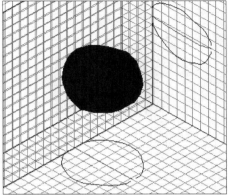

FIGURE *The pelvis.*
4.49

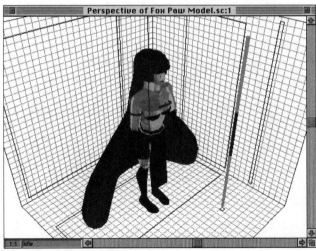

FIGURE *Fox Paw in full model form.*
4.50

➪ **Short note:** A key feature for character modeling in Ray Dream Studio is *Inverse Kinematics* (IK). This feature allows you to link objects so that child objects have an influence on parent objects up the chain. For example, if an arm model used IK, moving the hand object toward the shoulder may bend the arm at the elbow.

However, it's important not to get carried away with applying this feature. IK was used in Fox Paw at the major joints like the elbows, shoulders, hips and knees, but was not used in the hands and finger joints. Using IK in the fingers

FIGURE *Final rendered image.*
4.51

would actually make it more difficult to pose Fox Paw, because any slight repositioning of a finger joint would affect the entire arm. Of course, if your model was just a hand, instead of an entire body, it might then make sense to use IK on the finger joints.

Figure 4.51 shows the completed model, posed and rendered.

— *D.R. GREENLAW*

MODELING A LEAF

Here we learn how to make a basic (monocot) leaf.

Step One

Create a Free Form object in the main perspective by dragging the **Free Form** tool icon into the **Perspective** or **Hierarchy** windows, or by choosing **Free Form** from the **Insert** Menu.

Create the base of your leaf, or the cross section of the stem which will become the midrib (see Figure 4.52), on the **drawing plane**, and use the **Center** command under the **Sections** menu.

⇨ **Editor's Note:** You might want to draw the cross section bigger and then scale it down before continuing with Step Two. In recreating this file, I drew the cross section at about the size shown in Figure 4.52 and then scaled the cross section down to 25% so that it was closer in size to Figure 4.53.

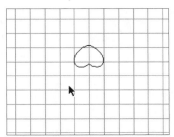

FIGURE *The first leaf cross section.*
4.52

Step Two

Create the shape of the leaf by choosing **Extrusion Envelope>Symmetrical in Plane** from the **Geometry** menu. Then, by drawing the top view and the side view using your **Point** tools, you define the shape of the leaf. (See Figure 4.53.)

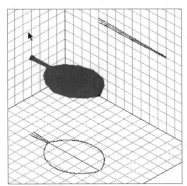

FIGURE *Adjusting the leaf envelope.*
4.53

Step Three

Then you must define the "waviness," or the liquidity versus the rigidness of the object. Use the side view of the object, add Bezier curves to the middle line, the one which determines the extrusion path, and pull down slightly. This will make the leaf look more lifelike, adding a pseudo-gravity effect. (See Figure 4.54.)

Step Four

This step requires a third-party program which can be used to generate two-dimensional images rather than three-dimensional environments (for example, Adobe Photoshop, MetaCreations Painter and so on). First, save the model you are working on, and either quit RDS, or (if you have enough memory) open

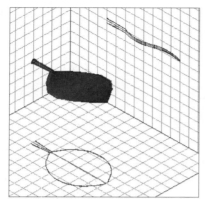

FIGURE **4.54** *Adding some natural deformations.*

up the other application and leave RDS in the background. This is where you will create your leaf's grayscale bump map. You want to draw all of the primary veins of your leaf in black against a dark gray background. That will limit the amount of height that the veins are able to achieve. After that, you should invert the image (if your application does not support this, then you can do it in RDS's shader editor), and then save it in a directory that is easy to remember, with a filename that is easy to remember. See Figure 4.55 for an example of the finished bump map.

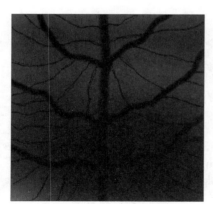

FIGURE **4.55** *The leaf's bump map.*

Step Five

Now quit the 2D application you are working in, and open up RDS, along with the model you were working on. You will now make the shader for your leaf.

These are the ideal (yet simplistic — this is only a basic demonstration) values to use for our model to make it look realistic.

Color	(RGB values of color picker) Red = 34, Green = 149, Blue = 0
Highlight	(value) 38%
Shininess	(value) 50%
Bump	This is where you import the 2D image you've just made (invert it if you haven't already) and tile it once horizontally and twice vertically. To import the texture map, click on the **Bump** tab of the **Shader Editor**. Choose **Texture Map** from the Shader Editor's **Insert** menu and then navigate to the bump map you created or to the "Veins" map supplied on the CD-ROM.
Reflection	(value) 0%
Transparency	(value) 2%
Refraction	(value) 0%
Glow	(default black)

Now apply the shader to the object. (See Figure 4.56.)

⇨ **Note:** It is wise when applying a shader to hold the mouse button down on the *Apply* button, which reveals a popup menu, and select *Apply all channels*. This will prevent your object from combining certain elements of your previous shader with the new shader.

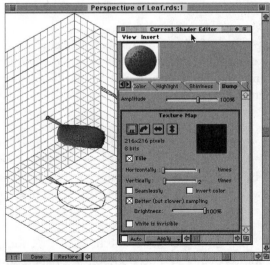

FIGURE *Applying the shader.*
4.56

FIGURE **4.57** *Finally, a sample plant.*

Step Six

Duplicate the leaf as many times as needed for your plant, and position the leaves as desired. (See Figure 4.57.) This is a very basic leaf project, but by using these steps as building blocks you'll be creating more complex foliage before you know it.

— AARON PUTNAM

INSTANT GAZEBO

This basic example uses circles as cross section elements and a compound object to hollow the dome. The method is close to infinitely adaptable; you can build very complex objects with it, adding one cross section at a time and renumbering when necessary.

Step One

Start this project by creating a Free Form object. By now you should know the routine, but we'll do it again just for fun. Create the Free Form object in the main perspective by dragging the **Free Form** tool icon into the **Perspective** or **Hierarchy** windows or by choosing **Free Form** from the **Insert** Menu.

Step Two

Using the **Ellipse** Tool, draw a circle on the first cross section plane. From the menu, choose **Sections>Center** and **Sections>Show Shape Numbers**. While the circle shape is selected, choose **Copy** and then **Paste** from the **Edit** menu. This will paste an exact duplicate of your circle shape on top of the first one. Now click to the side to deselect the circles (both are selected at this point) and then click on the circles again to choose the top one. Now choose **Scale** from the **Geometry** menu and enter 75% in both the horizontal and vertical fields. Choose **Arrange>Combine as Compound**. This is shape 1. You will now create two more cross sections on the Sweep Path. Create the first new cross section (cross section 2) by **option-clicking** in the middle of the extrusion path with the **Add Point** tool. Then create the second new cross section (cross section 3) by clicking on the last point of the extrusion path with the **Selection** tool and choosing **Create** from the **Sections** menu. Cross section 2 is a "place marker"; you will work on cross section 3. (See Figure 4.58 for what your model should look like at this point.)

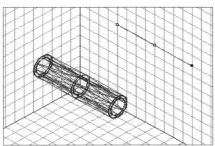

FIGURE *Let's begin at the beginning.*
4.58

Step Three

Go to cross section 3. Shift-drag a corner of shape 1 to the size you want the bottom of your dome to be. Between the outside and inside lines of shape 1, add circles for pillars. Add the top and bottom circles first, and group the two circles, being careful not to add shape 1 to the group. You can then copy and paste this group as you did in Step One. Don't forget to deselect the groups, then reselect the top group, choose **Geometry>Rotate**, and enter 45° clockwise. Repeat this until you get a total of eight columns (you'll have to do your own math if you want more or fewer columns for your own gazebo). When the pillar circles are in place, ungroup everything (except shape 1, of course). Renumber the small circles sequentially (see Figure 4.59) clockwise; this will come in handy in the next step.

Step Four

Create two more cross sections using the **Pen** tool, and use the **Sections>Create** command on section 4. (See Figure 4.60.) What you now have may look rather confusing, so let's clear it up by going to the **Sections** menu and choosing **Show>Current**. This will make things a little easier to deal with.

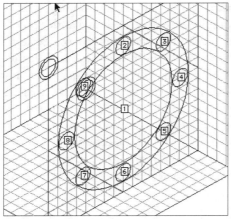

FIGURE   *The beginnings of the columns emerge.*
4.59

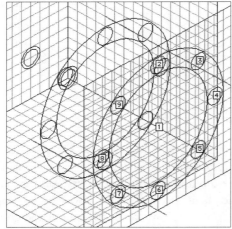

FIGURE   *Create two more cross sections.*
4.60

Go to cross section 4, select shape 1 and choose **Arrange>Break Apart Compound**. Deselect the large circle and delete the smaller circle. If you enable **Wireframe preview**, you'll notice that your object has become a mess of crossed shapes. (See Figure 4.61.) Don't panic! It's an easy fix. Turn off the preview again and renumber the small circles to correspond to the numbering in the previous cross section (this is why we numbered them sequentially and clockwise in the first place), then give the large circle a number just a bit higher than your last small circle. By my calculations, this number should be **10**. (See Figure 4.62.)

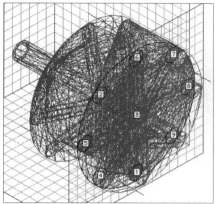

FIGURE *This mess is easily fixed.*
4.61

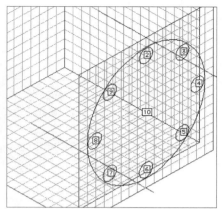

FIGURE *Renumbering more shapes.*
4.62

Now if you turn on **Preview (fast)**, you'll see we're starting to make some definite progress. (See Figure 4.63.)

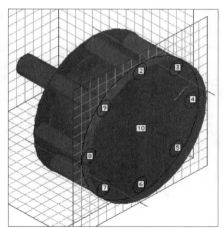

FIGURE *Making progress.*
4.63

Step Five

Our gazebo is getting a tad big for it's britches at this point, so let's choose **View>Modeling Box Size**, change it from **32** to **64**, and leave the **Scale object with Modeling Box** option unchecked. From the menu, choose **Geometry>Extrusion Envelope>Symmetrical**. You should have something close to Figure 4.64.

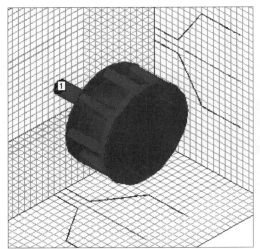

FIGURE *The gazebo ready to be sculpted.*
4.64

Step Six

Now you're ready to get down to business. First, let's position this gazebo in the modeling box a little better. Type **Command/Ctrl-4** to go to the **Left** pre-set view, select the extrusion path and reposition as in Figure 4.65. Now select the first shape and scale it to 10% by using **Geometry>Scale** and entering **10%** in both fields. Further sculpt the overall shape of the gazebo by adding a couple of points to the end of the extrusion path, and by sculpting the envelope paths, mold your gazebo into a shape similar to Figure 4.66. Go back to the **Left** view and add a few points to the envelope to get something like what you see in Figure 4.67. Add a couple of creative shaders, and presto . . . instant gazebo. (See Figure 4.68.)

— *CECILIA ZIEMER*

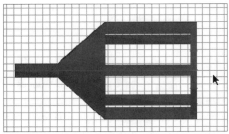

FIGURE *Reposition the gazebo.*
4.65

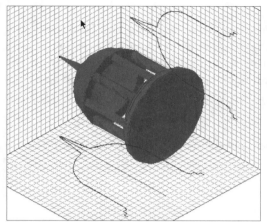

FIGURE *Let's add some curves.*
4.66

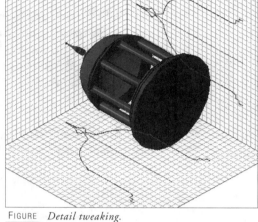

FIGURE *Detail tweaking.*
4.67

FIGURE *Your finished gazebo*
4.68

SHAPE CORRESPONDENCE TREE

Trees might seem pretty difficult to do but thanks to the Free Form modeler, they aren't quite so bad.

Step One

Let's begin by creating a Free Form object by dragging the **Free Form** icon into the **Perspective** or **Hierarchy** window or by choosing **Free Form** from the **Insert** menu. Select **Pipeline** as your **Extrusion Method** from the **Geometry** menu. Show shape numbers and current cross section from the **Sections** menu.

Step Two

Using the **Ellipse** tool, make three slightly overlapping ovals on the first cross section plane. (See Figure 4.69.)

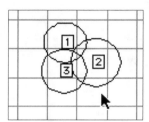

FIGURE *Base of the trunk.*
4.69

Step Three

Create a cross section close to cross section 1. There's no need to worry about being precise here. Just **option-click** on the extrusion path with the **Add Point** tool a little bit in front of your original cross section. (See Figure 4.70.)

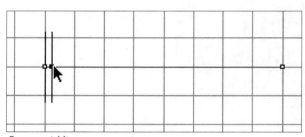

FIGURE *Adding a cross section.*
4.70

Step Four

Go to the new cross section 2. In the drawing plane, select the ovals and move them closer together. (See Figure 4.71.) Again, don't worry about being precise. We're making a tree here — they come in all shapes and sizes.

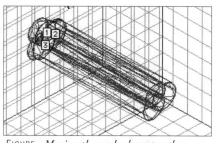

FIGURE **4.71** *Moving the ovals closer together.*   FIGURE **4.72** *Create the end cross section.*

Step Five

Select the end point of the sweep path and create a cross section (select the end point with the **Selection** tool and choose **Create** from the **Section** menu). This sweeps the shapes in cross section 2 to the end of the path. (See Figure 4.72.)

Step Six

Go to cross section 3. Resize each oval so they're a little smaller, moving them if necessary to keep them overlapping. The shape numbers should read 1,2,3. Choose **Select All**, then **Copy** and then **Paste** from the **Edit** menu. The visible shape numbers will read 4,5,6. The shape numbers 1,2,3 are underneath. (See Figure 4.73.)

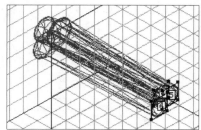

FIGURE **4.73** *Resize, copy and paste.*

Step Seven

Select the end point of the sweep path. With the **Pen** tool, add a new point at a distance somewhat shorter than the length between cross sections 2 and 3. Create another cross section by selecting **Create** under the **Section** menu. (See Figure 4.74.) This copies all the shapes from the last cross section to the current cross section.

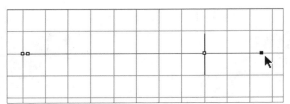

FIGURE *Adding the end point and a cross section.*
4.74

Step Eight

Go to cross section 4. In the cross section plane, you will see shape numbers 4,5,6. Select shape 4 (or any shape for that matter) and drag it a short distance away. (See Figure 4.75.) Select shape 1 (revealed by dragging 4 off its number) and drag it close to the same distance away but at a different angle. (See Figure 4.76.) Do the same for the other shapes, keeping the shape generally radial. (See Figure 4.77.) This is the first set of branches.

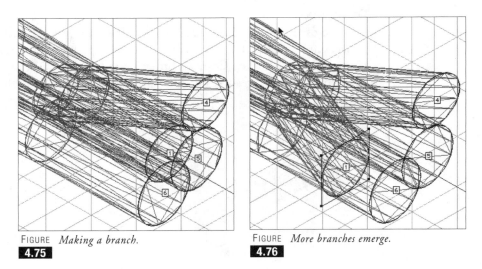

FIGURE *Making a branch.*
4.75

FIGURE *More branches emerge.*
4.76

Step Nine

Resize each of the ovals smaller so that they taper. Choose **Select All**, then **Copy** and then **Paste** from the **Edit** menu just like before. The highest shape number should now be 12. (See Figure 4.78.) What you have been doing here with all of the copying and pasting is doubling the number of shapes with each successive cross section. This is what keeps your branches looking like branches as they get longer, because it essentially anchors the ends of the next set of branches before they spread out, and keeps the branches coming from the same sources.

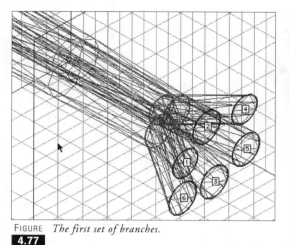

FIGURE *The first set of branches.*
4.77

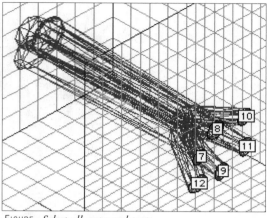

FIGURE *Select all, copy and paste.*
4.78

Step Ten

Select the end point of the sweep path. With the **Pen** tool, add a new point at a distance somewhat shorter than the length between cross sections 3 and 4. Create another cross section. This is essentially the same as Step Seven.

Step Eleven

In the cross section plane, repeat the steps you performed in the previous cross section plane. Spread the ends of the branches out, resize them, then choose **Select All, Copy** and **Paste**. (See Figure 4.79.) Then add another point to the end of the sweep path. Continue this series of steps until your tree looks as you

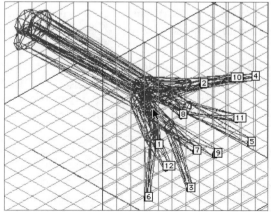

FIGURE *Sizing ovals even smaller forms the ends of the*
4.79 *branches.*

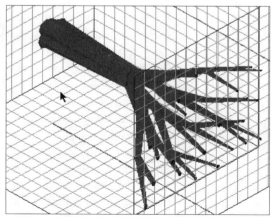

FIGURE *Keep spreading out, resizing, copying and pasting*
4.80 *until your tree looks like a tree should look.*

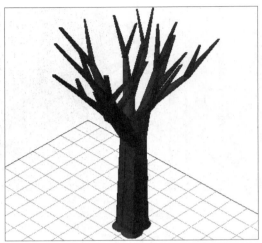

FIGURE *Behold the finished tree.*
4.81

want it to. If you do everything right, you should have a tree similar to the one in Figure 4.80.

Add a groovy bark shader, and you've got yerself a convincing tree. (See Figure 4.81.)

— CECILIA ZIEMER

MODELING COMPLEX SURFACES WITH SUPERMESH

Ray Dream Studio provides very powerful free form and mesh form modeling tools for creating objects. However, many objects still aren't so easy to create . . . even with such power.

SuperMesh is an extension for Ray Dream Studio that provides a completely different way to model complex objects. Starting from a grayscale image created in your favorite paint program, SuperMesh creates an array of triangles where the height of each triangle vertex is related to the brightness of pixels in the grayscale image.

The brighter the pixel, the greater the Z value SuperMesh will use for that vertex. The resulting mesh object can be used directly, or can be wrapped around a cylinder or sphere. You can control how many times the grayscale image is sampled in the X and Y directions, which controls the coarseness of the mesh.

Figure 4.82 shows a Kabuki mask modeled with SuperMesh. Notice that the mask is partially curved into a cylinder shape and texture mapped.

FIGURE **4.82** *A complex object modeled with the SuperMesh extension.*

FIGURE **4.83** *The grayscale image used to create the Kabuki mask.*

Modeling this mask using the Free Form modeler would require a lot of patience. Using SuperMesh, the mask can be modeled in just a few minutes.

Step One

The first step in creating any SuperMesh object is to create a grayscale image that represents the height of the object at each point. Figure 4.83 shows the 244 × 274 pixel grayscale image used to create the mask. This is an 8-bit image, so it contains gray values from 0 (black) to 255 (white).

The highest points of the mask (like the nose) will use large values, and the lowest points (the sides of the mask) will use the smallest values. SuperMesh uses the pixel value 0 to indicate triangles that should be removed, so we'll use black (pixel value 0) to color the background outside the area of the mask itself.

Any paint application can be used to create these grayscale images, but Adobe Photoshop has some airbrush tools that are particularly useful. The Photoshop airbrush can be set to darken or lighten, which for us makes the surface lower or higher, respectively.

To make the mask image, first create a new grayscale image, and clear the entire background to black using the Photoshop **Fill** tool.

Next, using the **Airbrush** tool set to **20%** pressure and mode set to **lighten**, draw just the left half of the face. Using the **Marquee** tool, select the left half of the face, and flip it horizontally to ensure that the right half of the face is exactly a mirror image of the left.

For the best-looking geometry, it's a good idea to blur the geometry image a little. Three pixels of **Gaussian Blur** is about right for most images. Choose the **Blur** item from the **Filter** menu, and slide right to select **Gaussian Blur....** Make the blur radius **3.0** pixels, and blur the entire image.

Figure 4.84 shows the resulting grayscale image. Save a copy of this image as MASKGEOM.PSD, but don't close Photoshop yet. We'll need it to create a nice texture map for coloring the mask.

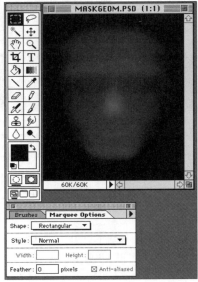

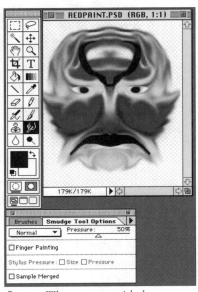

FIGURE **4.84** *The Photoshop Airbrush tool can quickly make a smooth grayscale image, which will give you smooth changes in geometry.*

FIGURE **4.85** *When you start with the grayscale image used to control geometry, the texture map for color will line up perfectly.*

Step Two

The next step is to create the texture map used to color the Kabuki mask. Choose **RGB Color** from the **Mode** menu to change the type of the image from grayscale to color. Using the **Airbrush** tool again, paint over the left half of the image with appropriate colors (you can find a book from your local library as a source for Kabuki mask ideas). Mirror the left half of the face, using the same method you used to mirror the geometry above, and save the file as REDPAINT.PSD. The final texture map is shown in Figure 4.85.

Step Three

The next step is to create the SuperMesh object itself, using the grayscale image from Step One. In Ray Dream Studio, choose **New** from the **File** menu to create a new scene. Use the default lighting and leave the background black. If you want to do image compositing later with Photoshop, a solid black background will make it easier to select just the mask part of the image.

Click on the **SuperMesh** icon on the toolbar and drag it to the **Perspective** window to create a SuperMesh object. Set the parameters in the **Options** dialog box as shown in Figure 4.86. To set the image used for geometry, click on the **floppy disk** icon, and specify the file MASKGEOM.PSD that we created in Step One. This part of the dialog box works the same as the shader dialog does, so it should be familiar to you.

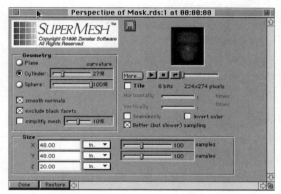

FIGURE *Set SuperMesh parameters exactly as shown. The*
4.86 *X and Y scale values control the overall size, while the Z scale value controls the depth of the mask.*

Use the **Transform** tab in the **Properties** palette to rotate the mask so you can see it better by changing the **PITCH** to **90** degrees. Use the camera controls (**pan, dolly, zoom**) to move the camera to a pleasing location. The resulting SuperMesh object is shown in Figure 4.87.

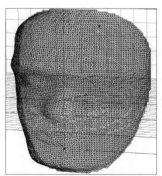

FIGURE *SuperMesh objects can*
4.87 *be positioned within the scene like any other Ray Dream Studio primitive.*

We turned on **Exclude black facets** to get rid of any triangles where all three vertices had a grayscale image value of zero. If we didn't check this box, we'd get something like the object shown in Figure 4.88.

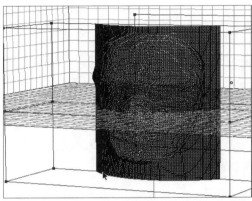

FIGURE **4.88** *If **Exclude black facets** is not checked, the black background also generates triangles for the mesh.*

Step Four

The next step is to create a shader that uses the REDPAINT.PSD file, and apply it to the SuperMesh object. Using the **Shader** browser, create a texture using the REDPAINT.PSD file as the Color portion of the shader, as shown in Figure 4.89.

FIGURE **4.89** *The REDPAINT.PSD shader looks nice on this mask. You can use any Ray Dream Studio shader on your SuperMesh objects.*

The Photoshop **Smudge** tool is great for smoothing out the edges of color. Notice that it's OK to color outside the mask boundaries here. All the triangles outside the mask area will be excluded anyway.

Select the mask geometry in the **Perspective** window (click on it once), and apply the shader to it.

Step Five

So far, the resolution on the SuperMesh object has been pretty high so that we could give you a good idea of what is going on. To get the best performance for positioning the camera and mesh objects, you might want to use the **Simplify Mesh** option in the SuperMesh dialog box to change to the final mesh resolution. Double-click on the SuperMesh object to reopen the **SuperMesh** dialog. Check the **Simplify Mesh** box, as shown in Figure 4.90.

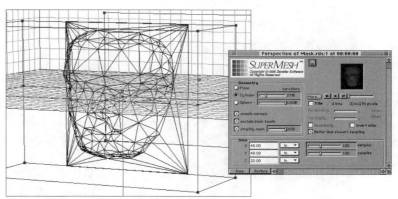

FIGURE **4.90** *Turn on **Simplify Mesh** to reduce the number of triangles it takes to create your object.*

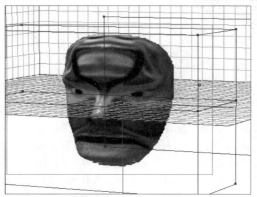

FIGURE **4.91** *The finished mask.*

This will decrease the number of triangles used to make up your image, without reducing the overall quality.

Click on the **Better Preview** mode icon to preview your object. (See Figure 4.91.)

— MICHAEL POGUE

DEFORMING THE CAN

Believe it or not, one of your best tools for creating used distressed objects is the deformer. With deformers you can add just that little bit of "turbulence" to an otherwise perfect-looking object. Here we have a nice, brand-new, paint can. (See Figure 4.92.) Let's start by putting a bend in the lid.

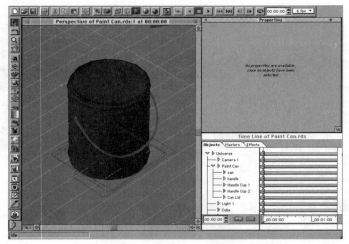

FIGURE
4.92   *Our nice, new can is about to get a couple of years and a lot of abuse added to its age.*

Step One

The first object that we are going to start with is the lid object. Select the lid and bring up the **Properties** palette under the **Windows** menu. Click the **Deformer** tab, select **Bend and Twist** from the drop-down list, and make sure that the **X axis** option is selected. Set the **Bend** to **20¡**, the **Bend Axis** to **39°** and the **Twist Size** to **76%**. (See Figure 4.93.) This will give the object the dented, been-around-the-block look that we are after. Take a look at your lid. You may have to move the lid slightly to make sure that it aligns properly with the can object. (See Figure 4.94.) At this point, save your file.

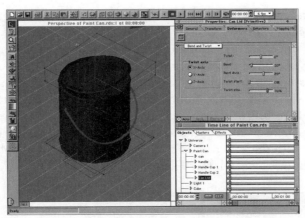

FIGURE *Adding the bend to the lid.*
4.93

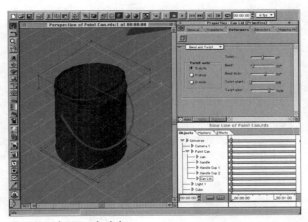

FIGURE *Aligning the lid.*
4.94

This is important, because we will now decide how to achieve the next effect we are after.

Step Two

Before continuing, make absolutely sure that the can is aligned the way you want it, and that all the items are grouped properly. The grouping of the objects is very important, because we will use a deformer to deform this entire group in one motion. Remember that you can apply only one deformer per object. By applying the deformer to the lid object, and then to the whole can group, of which the lid is a part, we can deform the lid one way and deform the can another. The importance of this is that it effectively allows us to layer deformers, and it provides a way for us to keep objects aligned even when they are being deformed.

Select the can group. Bring up the **Properties** palette again and select the **Deformer** tab. Select the **Bend and Twist** deformer for the whole group. Click the **Z axis** option (actually, it's most likely selected by default) so that the deformer will affect the can through its height. Set **Twist** to **–18¡**, **Bend** to **23**, **Bend Angle** to **0**, **Twist Start** to **0**, and **Twist Size** to **100**. (See Figure 4.95.) This will achieve a believable bend and subtle "crunch" in the object. If you are not happy with this effect, go back and use the **Direct Manipulation** option to tweak the values by hand. (See Figure 4.96.) With this option selected, you can

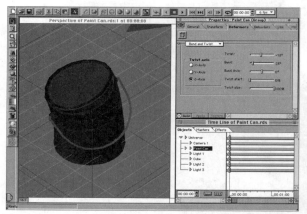

FIGURE **4.95** *Putting the bend to the whole can . . . lid too.*

FIGURE **4.96** *Try the **Direct Manipulation** controls.*

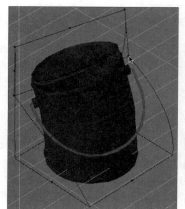

FIGURE **4.97** *Twist and bend to your heart's content . . . and in real time too.*

FIGURE **4.98** *A can even the most discerning of banged-up-junk collectors would relish.*

click on the deformation box that surrounds the object and by pulling or pushing on the various handles, you can add all of the bending or twisting you like to any axis without having to deal with those silly numbers. See Figure 4.97 for a sample. Many of RDS's deformers support this Wireframe control option.

Well, the can is all but done. Add some clever shading, and you'll have a rusty, banged-up can that any rusty, banged-up can collector would be proud to own. (See Figure 4.98.)

— *Robert Lominski*

CREATURE HEADS IN THE MESH FORM MODELER

The Mesh Form modeler is a wonderful addition to the RDS modeling arsenal. It is now possible easily to create objects that used to require either tons of patience and workarounds in the Free Form modeler, or the vertex-level editing power of another application. These other applications always yielded limited results due to the fact that you couldn't use some of RDS's advanced mapping modes on the imported objects. Now that we have a native Mesh Form modeler, we have the power to command our models at the most basic level — the vertex.

I devised the following tutorial to walk you through the creation of a creature head. Not any specific creature head mind you, just the generic creature head. It can be an alien, a monster, whatever you like (this one closely resembles a dinosaur), but it'll give you a good lesson in vertex modeling. You can use the same techniques to create human heads, animal heads, rocks, whatever you like. Figure 4.99 is what you should wind up with.

FIGURE *A friendly dino.*
4.99

Step One

Let's start by inserting a Mesh Form. Choose **Insert>Mesh Form** from the menu.

Step Two

I'm going to take the same cross section or Rib-based approach that I'd use if I were in the Free Form modeler, so let's go to the Left view by choosing **View>Preset Position>Left**, where we'll use the **Polyline** tool to draw the first cross section, which will be the midsection of our creature's skull. (See Figure 4.100.)

At first the Polyline tool may seem limiting since you can only draw straight lines, but this is just another advantage to the Mesh Form modeler. You can quickly sketch out your cross sections and save the fine-tuning for later.

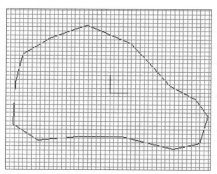

FIGURE **4.100** *Draw out the basic outline of your creature's head.*

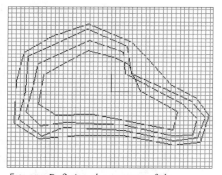

FIGURE **4.101** *Defining the contours of the creature's head.*

Step Three

Continue to draw the internal cross sections of your creature as though you were defining the various levels of the face from the inside out. Three more cross sections should be plenty. Your model should look something like Figure 4.101. Here's a helpful hint: having the same number of points on each shape and having them relative to each other will make a mesh that is easier to understand.

Step Four

Now you need to go to the Reference Preset position (**View>Preset Position>Reference**) to position your Ribs. Select the innermost Rib and double-click on one of the vertexes. This will select the entire shape. You'll know that the shape is selected because it will have a bounding box. If the shape does not have a bounding box, or if only a vertex or line segment is selected, then you must try again until you get the entire shape selected. Once you have the entire shape selected, tap your **left arrow key** 15 times. The arrow keys move the selected object relative to the currently highlighted drawing plane. Since the bottom plane is the active one (or should be), tapping the left arrow key moves your shape toward the left.

Step Five

Now repeat Step Four on the remaining Ribs while decreasing the number of times you tap the left arrow key each time. For example, select the next Rib and click the **left arrow key** 12 times instead of 15. Then select the next Rib and click the key nine times. Repeat until each Rib is spaced similar to those in Figure 4.102.

Don't forget that you can navigate around in the Mesh Form modeler by using your keypad. This can make positioning of the shapes much easier.

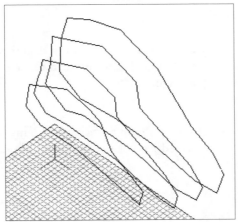

FIGURE *Spacing out the head cross sections.*
4.102

Step Six

 When you've arranged your points the way you like, choose **Select All** from the **Edit** menu. Now go to the **Selection** menu and choose **Loft**. This will create a skin that covers the Ribs of your creature's head. Feel free to choose **Preview (fast)** from the View menu. This will make it a little easier to discern that this is half of your creature's head, and also to make the necessary selections for the next few steps much easier.

Step Seven

Now go to the preset Front view (**View>Preset Position>Front**) and select the entire model by double-clicking. Now center your half-head in the drawing plane. (See Figure 4.103.)

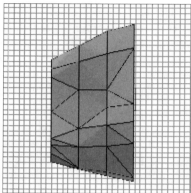

FIGURE   *Lofted and centered half-head.*
4.103

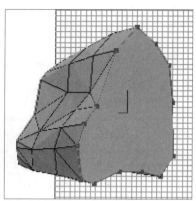

FIGURE   *Select the innermost shape.*
4.104

Step Eight

Using your keyboard's keypad, rotate the model around so that you are looking at the inside of the half-face. Using the **Selection** tool, select the shape that makes up that inner side. (See Figure 4.104.)

Step Nine

Now choose **View>Send Drawing Plane to>Selection**. This will send the current drawing plane to the selected part of the model, which just happens to be the middle of the head.

Step Ten

Double-click on the selected shape to select the entire model, and choose **Duplicate with Symmetry** from the **Edit** menu. The **Duplicate with Symmetry** command relies on the current active drawing plane for it's information as to where to place the duplicate. Since we sent the drawing plane to the outside edge of the model, the duplication yields a perfectly aligned and mirrored copy of the original half-face. (See Figure 4.105.)

Step Eleven

Again choose **Select All** from the **Edit** menu and choose **Boolean Operation** from the **PolyMesh** menu. If you have your **Auto Apply** checkbox checked in the **Object Properties** palette, this should result in a teeny little part of your model (if anything at all) being left on the screen. Don't panic, though; we'll fix it.

Step Twelve

If it's not already open, open the **Object Properties** palette, select the **Action Modifiers** tab and then click on the **Union** radio button. (See Figure 4.106.) If

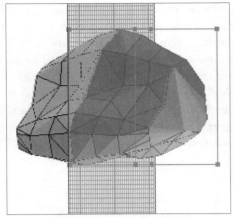

FIGURE **4.105** *The Duplicate with Symmetry command creates the other half of the creature's head.*

FIGURE **4.106** *Select Union to combine the two halves into a whole head.*

you don't have Auto Apply enabled, click on the **Apply** button in the **Object Properties** palette to complete the operation. Take a moment to pan around your creation using the numeric keypad.

Step Thirteen

Your creature's head should look pretty good as it is, but if you're looking for a little higher triangle count, just select the entire model again and choose **Subdivide** from the **Selection** menu. Now we have a wonderfully smooth, organic, creature's head. (See Figure 4.107.)

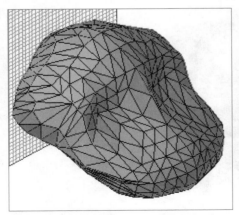

FIGURE **4.107** *The subdivided geometry of the head.*

You may find that certain areas don't smooth enough with the Subdivide command but that running it again will divide the already adequately smoothed areas even further, which would make the model unwieldy (note that you should never have too many triangles, but just enough to get the desired look — any more just eats up RAM and CPU juice). This isn't a problem at all with RDS's Mesh Form modeler. If certain areas need to be subdivided, simply select the vertices that need the extra triangles and run the **Subdivide** command again. Only the selected areas will be smoothed.

Add a nice texture map, and you have a creature everyone's sure to love.

— *JOHN W. SLEDD*

EDITING A MESH FORM MODEL

So you turn that last creature's head in to your Art Director, and she says, "You call that a creature? I wanted a mean, evil creature that might chew off the heads of fluffy bunnies, not Bernard the cuddly dragon-boy!"

So you open up your "Bernard the cuddly dragon-boy" file and go to work on him in the Mesh Form modeler. Let's start there.

Step One

Open the creature's head file and then double-click on your creature's head to open the Mesh Form modeler. Figure 4.108 shows what you should see. Click off to the side to deselect the model. What we're going to do next is to use the Sphere of Attraction tool to make our poor little guy a little more fearsome.

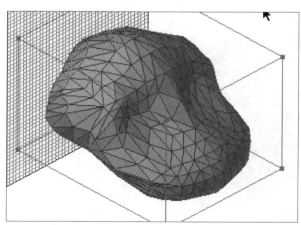

FIGURE *Your poor little creature.*
4.108

Step Two

Click on the **Sphere of Attraction** tool in the toolbar and then choose the **Tool Options** tab in the **Properties** window. Verify that you have **Cubic Spline** as your selected option and that **Radius** is set to **4.00** for the sphere. Now find the middle of your creature's head, and we'll start making him more ferocious by giving him a couple of spikes on his little noggin.

Step Three

You should still be in **Reference** view but if you're not, go there now. Activate the back wall of the drawing plane by option-clicking it in the **Plane Display** tool. See Figure 4.109 for what your window should look like.

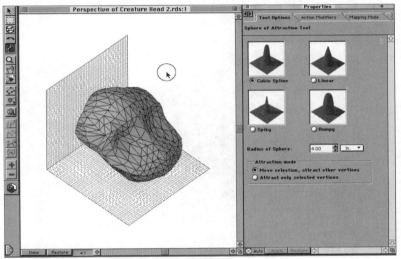

FIGURE *Enable the rear wall of your modeling box.*
4.109

Step Four

Now select one of the points in the middle of your creature's head, and drag up while holding down on the **Shift** key to constrain the movement vertically. Figure 4.110 should be what you wind up with. Now repeat that process on a couple more points to get Figure 4.111.

Now go to a side view to check your spike progress, and move the rear spike back a bit, as in Figure 4.112.

Step Five

Now let's add a more imposing nose. First let's make some changes to our Sphere of Attraction options. You should still have the **Tool Options** open, and

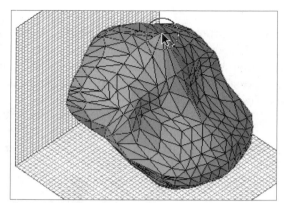

FIGURE
4.110 *The birth of an evil spike.*

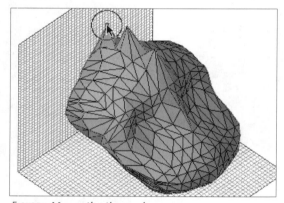

FIGURE
4.111 *More evil spikes are born.*

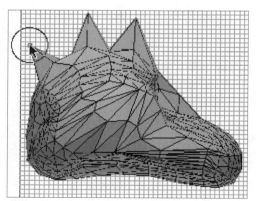

FIGURE
4.112 *Streamlining the spikes.*

I'll assume you do. If not, well, you should know how to get there by now. Choose the **Bumpy** option and put your **Radius of Sphere** up setting to **8.00** inches. Now click on a middle point of your creature's nose and Shift-pull outward to get something that looks like Figure 4.113. Now repeat that process on both sides of the longer nose section, but don't pull these out so far, and you should wind up with something similar to Figure 4.114. Click **Done** to jump into the **Perspective** window and turn on **Best preview**. (See Figure 4.115.)

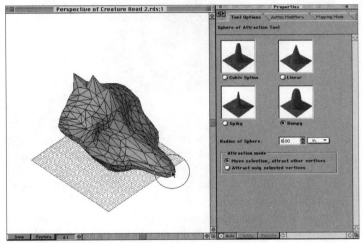

FIGURE *Adding a bigger nose.*
4.113

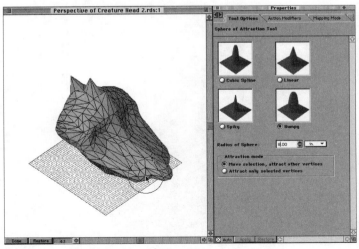

FIGURE *Giving our nose some sides.*
4.114

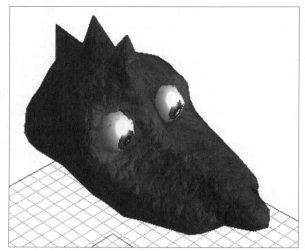

FIGURE **4.115** *Not quite scary yet.*

Step Six

Well, as you can see, we haven't really succeeded in making a scary creature just yet. Let's start by getting rid of those goofy eyes. Select the eyes and delete them. Now let's jump back into the Mesh Form modeler and deepen those eye sockets (we'll add some creepier eyes later). With the **Sphere of Attraction** tool chosen and the default options of **Cubic Spline** and a **Radius** of **4.00**, click on a point similar to Figure 4.116 and Shift-drag backwards to sink in that eye

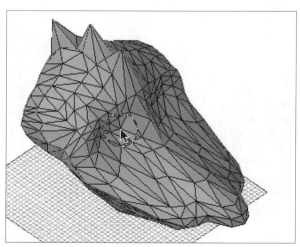

FIGURE **4.116** *Figure 4.116. Use the Sphere of Attraction tool to deepen the eye sockets.*

socket. Do the same thing to the other side as well. Now select the entire model and choose **Subdivide** from the **Selection** menu. Click **Done**.

Step Seven

As you can see, we're getting a bit scarier, but we still have a little way to go. Add a couple of beady eyes, some curvy teeth and a more menacing shader, and we're ready to go. Hopefully our Art Director will like this sketch better. See Figure 4.117 for a slightly more disturbing creature.

— *JOHN W. SLEDD*

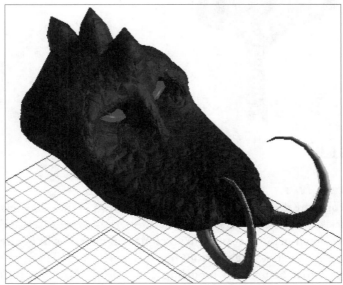

FIGURE *Our dino isn't so friendly anymore.*
4.117

CREATING EASY FOLIAGE

This is a wonderful example of approaching modeling in a not-so-traditional way. My good buddy Kenneth Kepf first started me out on this idea, and it just blossomed (pun intended) into a technique from there.

A couple of tutorials back, we created a tree using Cecilia Ziemer's tree technique. Now we're going to use Ken's technique for leaves to make ourselves some leaves for that poor "nekkid" tree. This won't take long, because the brilliance of this technique is in it's simplicity. We'll cover a couple of other examples of the technique at the end of this tutorial, just so you feel you got your money's worth.

Step One

Let's start with the tree and add a bunch of sphere's to give a cartoony impression of leaves. (See Figure 4.118.) This, by itself, looks pretty good, but if you want individual leaves, you want individual leaves.

FIGURE   *Leaves built with just big spheres.*
4.118

Step Two

Group the spheres and call the group **Leaves Group**. Now select the group and click on the **Deformers** tab in the **Properties** palette. Select **Explode** from the pull-down menu. Set up your **Explode** parameters as in Figure 4.119. Your tree should now look like the front one in Figure 4.120. That's it! You're done! Now wasn't that better than modeling each one of those leaves? You may have to play around with the Explode settings if you want a different look, but this

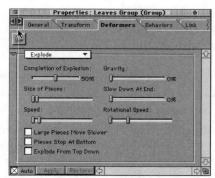

FIGURE   *Using the Explode Deformer to turn*
4.119   *the spheres into clumps of leaves.*

FIGURE **4.120** *Here are the two trees — one with the "exploded" leaves and the original.*

should get you started. Adding a shader with a cellular mix of different shades of green or fall colors can make the results of this technique look astounding.

I have a couple of tips here, though, that you might want to keep in mind. For starters, using the Explode Deformer on that many spheres can slow some machines down quite a bit. If you'd like pretty much the same effect without the overhead, **Boolean** all of your spheres together to create a single object before applying the **Explode Deformer**. Also, if you don't want to be dependent upon the deformer, you can select that group and export it as a .DXF or .3DMF or in Detailer format. This will convert the Deformer settings to actual mesh. Currently, Ray Dream Studio's Mesh Form modeler will not convert another Mesh Form or Primitive object's Deformer properties into stand-alone mesh objects, as it will a Free Form object with a Deformer. This is a bug, however, and has been addressed by the Ray Dream Q&A folks. This bug will most likely be squashed by the time this book goes to print, and then you'll be able to skip the export routine and just do the conversion within RDS.

OK, as I promised, here are some other effects that can be achieved using this technique, and another which is pretty similar. Figure 4.121 shows a Free Form object before and after the Explode technique — great for ferns. Fountain Primitives also make great foliage. Figure 4.122 shows a couple of nested Fountain Primitives. One Fountain has many particles and a green shader for the leaves. The other Fountain has fewer particles and has an orange shader applied. These can be flowers or butterflies or anything your little heart desires. Fountains can be converted to standstill geometry by choosing **Jump In Another Modeler** and then the **Mesh Form** modeler. Try applying an Atomize deformer to the orange fountain to create fruit.

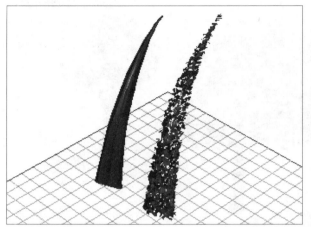

FIGURE **4.121** *The same technique can be applied to free form objects to create other types of foliage such as this fern branch.*

FIGURE **4.122** *The fountain primitive can also be used in this manner to create interesting bushes.*

This technique, and the other Deformer-based modeling techniques that should be dancing through your heads now, should solve many of your modeling woes. We Hope you have fun with them.

— *KENNETH KEPF & JOHN W. SLEDD*

CHAPTER 5

Lighting Tips

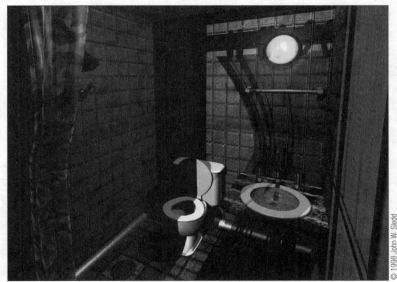

© 1998 John W. Sledd

ACCENTUATE TEXTURES AND BUMP MAPS WITH LOW-ANGLE LIGHTING

Lighting plays a crucial role in achieving and controlling the look of a bump map.

In photography, when you want to accentuate surface texture you tend to lower the light source(s) and "strafe" it across the object — the same method works with Ray Dream Studio.

The idea is to aim the light so that the rays are beaming perpendicular to the object surface rather than at it.

The fact that lights are hidden in **RDS** makes lighting, with this in mind, simple, since you can set various light sources without worrying. Use some lights to accentuate bump, and others to set mood in the scene.

— RICK GRECO

AIMING YOUR LIGHTS

The proper aiming of lights is crucial in a well-lit scene. Take advantage of RDS's light aiming features. Enable your spotlight's **Direct Manipulation** controls by clicking on the icon in the **Light** tab of the **Properties** palette. (See Figure 5.1.) This will show you exactly where your light will fall and give you immediate controls of most of your light parameters.

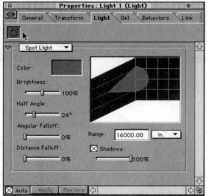

FIGURE **5.1** *Enabling your light's **Direct Manipulation** controls let's you adjust and preview many of your light's parameters in real time.*

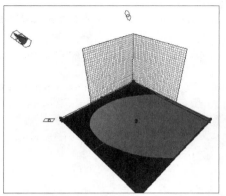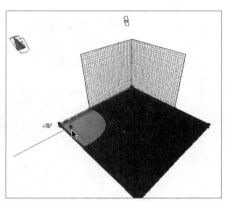

FIGURE
5.2
*The light will follow and center on the hot point when using the **Point At** command.*

Still having trouble aiming your lights? Well then, make use of this nifty feature. As you probably already know, when you select an object and a light (or camera) and choose **Point At** from the **Arrange** menu, the light (or camera) will rotate in whichever direction is necessary such that it points directly at the selected object. What you may not know is that what the light (or camera) is actually pointing at is the object's hot point. So, by moving the hot point of the object, you can determine specific areas for the light to illuminate. (See Figure 5.2.)

If you're still not happy with the amount of control you have, try this little trick. Create a small Sphere, cloak it, and name the little sucker **Light Sight**.

FIGURE
5.3
Setting up the Point At behavior for the Light Sight.

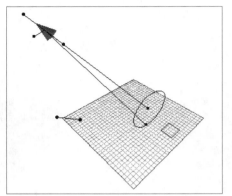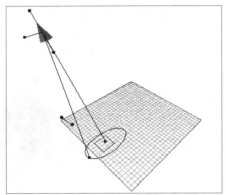

FIGURE **5.4** *The Light Sight tells your light which way to point at all times.*

Now select the light you wish to have total control over, and assign a **Point At** behavior to it. Type **Light Sight** in the text entry field of the **Point At** behavior control panel. (See Figure 5.3.) Now anywhere you move your Light Sight, your light will follow. (See Figure 5.4.) By the way, the same technique works well with cameras. Perhaps I should mention it there too.

— *JOHN W. SLEDD*

NUMBER OF LIGHTS AND RENDERING TIMES

Lights do affect your rendering times. A simple scene with one object and one light, at 320 × 240 pixels, renders in 27 seconds on my machine, but when I add four more lights, the same scene renders in 49 seconds; 22 seconds for four extra lights may not sound like a big deal, but this was a very simple scene rendered at a low resolution. Imagine if you had a scene with one light that took 27 hours to render (not uncommon . . . well, for one light it might be uncommon, but you get the idea). Adding four more lights suddenly shoots your extra rendering time to 22 hours. Almost an extra day.

Keep in mind that I'm not suggesting that you try to use as few lights as possible. Just remember that each light will add to the rendering time. Try not to use any you don't need for your desired effect. Unless, of course, you've got plenty of time to spare (and/or a really fast processor).

— *JOHN W. SLEDD*

A LIGHTING EXERCISE

Spend some time with a ping-pong ball outside and under different lighting conditions. Look closely at how the light changes color according to the source, and also notice how other objects affect the shadows, and how ambient light affects the whole look of the ball. Your goal is to recreate these conditions.

Some 3D programs automatically recreate natural lighting conditions based on your key light source and the objects in the scene, but these are computationally very slow. In Ray Dream Studio, you must position multiple light sources to recreate this look.

— *JOHNATHAN BANTA*

SUN ANGLE AND TIME OF DAY

This tip can easily be studied in the above exercise as well. While you're outside, notice the time of day and how it changes the way your environment is lit. The sun's position moves during the day, causing shadows to be cast in different directions. Keep this in mind when working on a scene that must give the impression of a certain time of day. Suppose you are creating a scene depicting a gunfight at high noon. You render it, and something just doesn't look right. The scene takes place outside, so you're working with only a few light sources — one distant light to represent the sun, and a couple of bulb lights to represent reflected light in some of the darker areas of the town. What could be wrong? Well, you might check the placement of your distant light. You suddenly remember that, when you were having a problem seeing the hero's face because of the shadow his hat was casting, you moved the distant light down a bit so his hat was no longer in the way. That was your mistake. This is supposed to be high noon, yet you set the sun to the 3 o'clock position, and everything in the scene is casting these long, slanted shadows. Move the sun/distant light directly above the scene to get the time of day right, and try adding another light in front of the hero's face or simply cranking up the ambient light to knock down some of the shadows. Bear in mind, though, that ambient light knocks down all of the shadows; there's no way to be selective.

⇨ **Editor's Note:** This is a good place to mention the Wind portion of the Four Elements extension from Rayflect, Inc. 4E: Wind adds Sun and Moon light sources and let's you position them in a sky-sphere fashion. To top that off, the atmosphere reacts with the Sun and Moon very realistically. So if your

FIGURE
5.5
The Wind portion of Rayflect, Inc.'s Four Elements pack makes simulating realistic sun and moon effects a breeze.

scene is supposed to be at high noon and you inadvertantly move the sun down a bit, your atmosphere preview will reflect that change immediately, and it'll be quite obvious that you're not at high noon anymore. All parameters are animatable too, so recording the sun's position throughout an animation is a breeze (heh heh). (See Figure 5.5.)

— JOHNATHAN BANTA

TYPES OF LIGHTS AND WHEN TO USE EACH

You have five basic types of lights in Ray Dream Designer. You have your Spot, Distant, Bulb and Beams lights, which are actual light objects, and then you have your Ambient light, which is an atmospheric effect.

The Spot light casts light in a stream or path like a flashlight. It is used when you want to concentrate light on a certain part of your scene. (See Figure 5.6.)

The Distant light, like the Spot light, casts light in a specific direction but is always beyond your horizon and encompasses the entire scene. For example, if you place a distant light to the left of your scene, it would be impossible to place an object further left than the light. So all of the shadows cast from the Distant light would be in the same direction. Since the rays from a Distant light are parallel, they will not cast soft shadows. Use the Distant light to represent faraway light sources such as the sun. (See Figure 5.7.)

FIGURE
5.6
The Spot light is a focused directional light.

FIGURE
5.7
The Distant light is similar to the Spot light in that it is directional, but it's not concentrated.

FIGURE
5.8
The Bulb light is just like a lightbulb in your house. It provides soft, even, omnidirectional illumination.

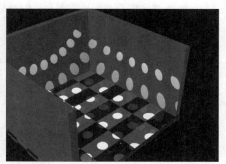

FIGURE
5.9
The Beams light is similar in effect to a disco ball.

The Bulb light is just like the bulb light you have in your ceiling at home. It casts light in all directions from a single source. Use Bulb lights when you want to simulate the typical lightbulb effect or when you want to lighten up a dark room or area evenly in one of your renderings. (See Figure 5.8.)

The Beams light is like using many Spot lights at the same time. It casts a user-defined number of little spots of light. When would you use this? Well, any time you want lots of little lights and you don't want to set up lots of little spotlights — a dance floor perhaps. (See Figure 5.9.)

The Ambient light setting controls overall light in your scene. There is no source for ambient light. It is everywhere, and therefore it casts no shadows. Ambient light is used when you want to soften the effect of shadows and/or to make sure everything in your scene is evenly lit. See Figures 5.10 and 5.11 for examples.

FIGURE **5.10** *Ambient light set at 100%.*

FIGURE **5.11** *Same scene with Ambient light set at 0%.*

USING THE SCENE WIZARD AS A LEARNING TOOL

Confused about how to light a scene that you're doing? Want to know how a pro would light the same scene? Well, you've got the tools necessary to figure this one out right in front of you. Try the Scene Wizard.

Say you're trying to model an office building hallway. Consult the Scene Wizard for a similar scene and study the lighting configuration. (Personally I'd choose the **Indoor Scenes>Indoor Templates>Metallic Entry** option.) Jot down some notes or steal the lights flat out. The Scene Wizard isn't just an instant 3D fix, it's also a valuable learning tool. Each of the Scene Wizard scenes was created with proper photographic techniques in mind. Take advantage of this valuable aid.

— *JOHN W. SLEDD*

VIEWING YOUR SCENE THROUGH THE PERSPECTIVE OF YOUR LIGHTS

Want a good way to see where you shadows will fall? Try viewing your scene through one of your lights.

Open your Camera Properties window by selecting **Camera Properties** under the **Window** menu. Click on the **Position** pull-down menu and, at the bottom of the list, you'll find a list of the lights in your scene.

This is a good way to see exactly where your lights are pointing, and it's a great way of getting different views of your scene that you might otherwise not think of.

— *MARK JENKINS*

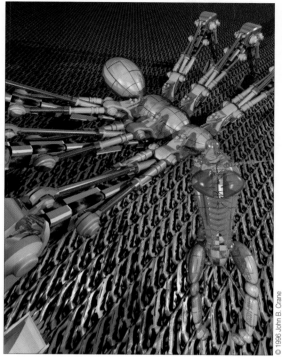

Ant-Acid   John B. Crane

◀ *Ant-Acid* might look mean...and that would be because she *is* mean. Everything about her is mean. See how you can tame her, or a beastie like her, in the **Artist Profiles** chapter.

▶ *Blackjack Progressive Counter* is a glowing example of Ray Dream Studio at work in the world of editorial illustration. Read more about how Rick did it in the **Artist Profiles** chapter.

Blackjack Progressive Counter   Rick Greco

Meta-Hog   Steve McArdle

◀ *Meta-Hog* is an image that touches on all the different areas of *Ray Dream Studio* covered in this book. The well-thought-out use of custom shaders, lighting, camera angle, and composition take a carefully constructed combination of relatively simple objects into a whole new dimension. Get a step-by-step recreation of *Meta-Hog* in the **Artists Profiles** chapter.

▼ Family Room is another great example of just about everything in this book: clever modeling, precise shaders, good composition and realistic lighting top the list.

Family Room   Lisa Abke

◀ *Reflected Mist* is an exercise in detail-obsessed, photorealistic 3D creation. It is a great example of techniques you'll find in the **Shader Recipes and Shader Techniques** chapters as well as **Modeling Techniques** chapter.

Reflected Mist   Lonnie Baily

▶ Human figures aren't as difficult to model as you might think, as *Fox Paw* clearly shows. The **Modeling Techniques** chapter will show you how it's done.

Fox Paw   D. R. Greenlaw

▶ *Fire Canyon* is an excellent example of what can be done with *Ray Dream Studio*'s procedural shaders. It's also a fantastic example of compositional skill. Study the **Shader Recipes, Shader Techniques** and **Thinking in 3D** chapters to learn more about these skills.

Fire Canyon   Lonnie Baily

▼ No, this picture is not intended to make you feel woozy. It's what your image file should look like when you render a RealVR image. The RealVR player wraps this image around a virtual sphere to encompass you in the 3D space. See the **Ray Dream Studio and the Internet** chapter for details on how to create your own RealVR worlds.

Primitive People   Rick Greco

© 1997 Lisa Abke

◀ *Child Playing* shows a great attention to detail (something that is VERY important in the creation of good 3D art) and also demonstrates how lighting can be used to enhance the illusion of depth. You'll find more information in the **Modeling Techniques** and **Lighting Tips** chapters.

Child Playing   Lisa Abke

▶ *Tropical Stream* required some serious scene organizational skills to keep the polygon count from completely suffocating the host machine. Advanced shading and lighting techniques were also used to achieve a great sense of photorealism. The **Thinking in 3D, Modeling Tips, Lighting Techniques, Shader Recipes** and **Shader Techniques** chapters will give you some pointers on how to hone your own skills in these areas.

© 1997 Lonnie Baily

Tropical Stream   Lonnie Baily

▶ *Harry the Handsome Executive*'s not just another pretty face. He always seems to find himself in situations that require a good bit of special effects and modeling techniques to properly recreate. Explosions, Lasers, Plasma Balls and Office Plants are daily fare in Harry's world. See the **Modeling Techniques, Special Effects Tips and Techniques, Lighting Techniques, Shader Recipes** and **Shader Techniques** chapters for more info on these effects.

© 1997 John Sledd

Harry the Handsome Executive   John Sledd

▶ Here's an up-close-and-personal shot of the explosion technique used in *Harry the Handsome Executive.* This effect relies heavily on the Visible Light filters found in Ray Dream Studio 5. You'll find the RDS file for this effect on the CD-ROM in the **Chapter 15** Folder.

© 1996 John Sledd

Explosion   John Sledd

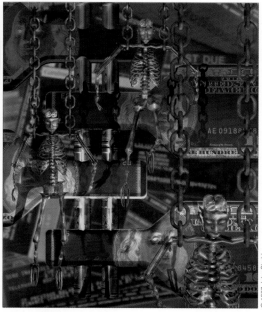

◄ *The Trap* is one of the more brooding examples of the art you can create with Ray Dream Studio. Ray Dream's flexible lighting and texture controls make sure you don't get *chained*-down to any one look.

The Trap   John Sledd

▶ *Flower* shows off Ray Dream Studio's organic modeling capabilites and is also another great example of effective lighting . See the **Modeling Techniques** and **Lighting Techniques** chapters for more information on these topics.

Flower   Sharkawi Che Din

▶ *Runners* utilizes Ray Dream Studio's precision alignment capabilities. Combine this type of structure with RDS's Inverse Kinematics features to make animation a breeze. You'll find more information in the **Modeling Techniques** and **Animation Techniques** chapters.

Runners   Sharkawi Che Din

Fresh Fruit   Lisa Abke

◀ *Fresh Fruit* illustrates how *Ray Dream Studio*'s Free Form modeling tools can be used to create realistic organic shapes, and the **Modeling Techniques** chapter includes several techniques for doing so. This image also does a very good job of using lighting to set the mood of the scene, which is discussed in the **Thinking in 3D** chapter.

CHAPTER

6

Lighting
Techniques

Lighting is often one of the most overlooked components in 3D. Light has the power to turn a mediocre scene into a work of art or a magnificent scene into a stanky pile of still-warm food-court refuse. Most likely it'll be somewhere in-between, but you get the gist.

We hope that, after you've gone through this chapter, you'll be on the way towards that masterpiece and putting more distance between you and that noxious pile of rubbish.

THREE-LIGHT AND FOUR-LIGHT STUDIO SETUPS

Two basic lighting schemes are available that work well in virtually any situation and make it rather difficult really to screw up too badly. They are the three- and four-light setups. These two setups certainly aren't your only choices when lighting a scene, but they will give you a good place to start and an understanding of how light works to augment your scene. Think of lighting as another brush in your 3D artists toolbox. Let's take a look at a couple of our light-brush setups.

The *three-light setup* entails lighting a model using, yep, you guessed it, three lights. The lights are placed in key positions around the model to give you the best detail without washing out everything. Figure 6.1 illustrates the basic three-light setup. In this setup, the three lights are as follows:

The *Key* or *Primary* light provides the most illumination and should be the most powerful light in the scene. This is also the light that should do the shadow casting. It's best to play around with the settings of the light, starting at about 75%. While most programs have a default light value of 100%, you may find that this is too bright and will add too much contrast between the shadows and the illuminated area. It is best to start out lower and add light if needed.

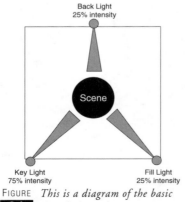

FIGURE   *This is a diagram of the basic*
6.1   *three-light studio setup.*

This light should be located at a 45-degree angle to the front of the model, either to the left or to the right of the camera. The light should be a little bit above head height or over the height of the model. A Spot light with a wide cone would make a good Key light.

The *Fill* light, as its name suggests, fills in the shadowed areas in your model. It's used to soften the contours and make the transition from light to dark areas. You should start out with about 25% on this light and work up if needed. In contrast to the Key light, if the Fill light is too intense, the model could appear washed out.

This light should be located on the opposite side of the Key light at a 45-degree angle to the model. Set this light just a tad lower than the Key light. Both Spot and Bulb lights make good Fill lights. A good render-efficiency trick is to disable the shadow-casting properties of your Fill light, since its shadows are usually overpowered by your key light. Being able to add light without worrying about the additional shadow is one of the benefits of your 3D virtual studio.

The *Back* light is placed behind the model to cast a halo or rim of light around the object. A Back light defines the edges of a model from the background. The Back light, like the Fill light, should start out with an intensity of 25%, which should be increased only if necessary. If the model blends too much into the background, increase the intensity of the Back light. That's what it's there for.

The Back light should be placed directly behind and/or below the model for the best results. Like the Fill light, both Spot and Bulb lights make good **Back** lights.

The *four-light setup* in Figure 6.2 is essentially the same as the three-light setup, with an additional light and a little different placement. With the four-light setup, the Back light can also be placed directly opposite the Key light.

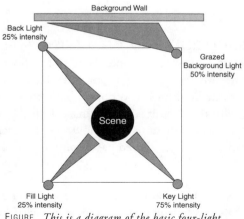

FIGURE
6.2 *This is a diagram of the basic four-light studio setup.*

The fourth light is a *Grazed* background light that is used to illuminate a backdrop screen.

The Grazed light is placed close to the ground plane and is pointed upward at the background screen at a 45-degree angle.

It is best to start the grazed light out at 50% and work up if necessary.

— CRAIG LYN

ILLUSION OF FORM

Now that you have some concept of the lighting schemes, let's tackle one that is similar to both of the above.

Spending hours or even days modeling, shading and arranging a complex scene will become a useless effort if the final composition winds up flat and dull due to improper lighting. Setting the lighting correctly will enable the models to utilize the light more effectively. This is extremely important in creating a sense of weight and form. Regardless of what type of scene or mood you are creating, the ability to set up the proper lighting configuration will help create a more dynamic composition.

The best way to check your scene for this balance is to create a sphere that is about the same size as the whole of the primary objects you are illuminating. By placing this sphere so that it encompasses the objects of your light's attention, you can more clearly observe how your light will strike the objects in the scene. Once you are comfortable with the arrangement of your lights, you can turn off the sphere by making it invisible through the View menu.

The following steps will guide you through the setup of a simple scene of this nature.

Step One

Open the file on the CD-ROM in the CHAPTER 06 folder/directory called **FormB-4.RDS**. This will give you a simple scene to begin with. You can use a scene that you are currently trying to light, but you'll have to make some calculations of your own to make things fit properly. This scene contains a floor, a vase and a spotlight with the default scene settings. Both the floor and the vase have the default red shader on them to show how well this technique can bring separate objects out of even a like-colored background.

Step Two

So we have this floor with this vase on it. Imagine for a moment that instead of having a vase, you have several objects in your scene with lots of curves and such, like this vase. You're under a pretty tight deadline so you can't afford to do a bunch of test renders on a scene this complex. We'll also say, for the sake of simplicity, that you've already grouped all of these objects to make your measurements go more smoothly (aren't you smart).

So now you select your Vase object (or rather, group of vases, as in our own little imaginary world) to get it's measurements. With the vase selected, open up the **Properties** palette (if it's not already open), click on the **Transform** tab and jot down the **Position** and **Size** information. (See Figure 6.3.) You should wind up with **Position** settings of X = –0.17, Y = 16.17 and Z = 7.43. For your **Size** settings you should have X = 10.32, Y = 14.71 and Z = 10.32. You need to pick only the largest dimension here. Since a sphere will have the same dimensions in all fields, you just need to make sure it's going to be big enough. This will give you all the information you need to create and position your light-testing sphere.

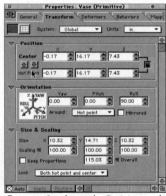

FIGURE **6.3** *Jot down the Position and Size settings for your vase.*

Step Three

Now we're going to create our sphere. Go to the **Insert** menu and select **Sphere**. In the **Properties** palette (**Transform** tab) type in the values that you just jotted down from your vase. In the **Position** box, you should have X = –0.17, Y = 16.17, Z = 7.43, and in the **Size** fields you should have **Size** X, Y, Z = 14.71 (if you have the **Keep Proportions** box checked, you have to enter this number in only one of the fields). This should place your sphere directly over top of your vase. (See Figure 6.4.)

Step Four

Now select your Vase model and make it invisible by choosing **Object Invisible** from the **View** menu. This will make sure your computer wastes no CPU juice on the extra information.

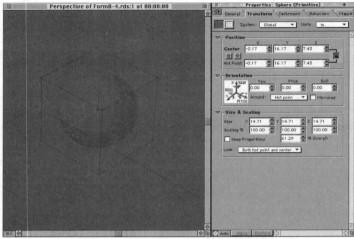

FIGURE **6.4** *Giving the sphere the same Position and Size settings as your vase will position it directly on top of the vase.*

Step Five

Now let's set up the lighting. The most important thing to remember when dealing with lighting is to turn off the **Ambient** light (at least at first — some looks may require you to turn it back on at a later time). Go to the **Render** menu and choose the **Current Scene Settings**. Click on the **Effects** tab and click the little arrow next to **ambient light**. Set the color value to **0%**. (See Figure 6.5.) This should be the first thing you do when you open a new document that you wish to light. It's often a good thing to have on when you're modeling, but when the time comes to light your scene, kill it and then bring it back if necessary. When you're done, close the palette.

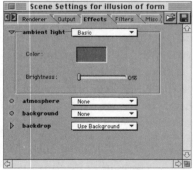

FIGURE **6.5** *Set Ambient light to 0%.*

For this scene we will use four spotlights. I purposely chose spotlights because they will provide a greater control over how the light strikes the objects in the scene. For example, we can isolate the highlights of the specific area of the object without affecting the whole scene. To preserve memory and speed up the rendering process, only the main light will be used to cast shadows. The rest of them will act as fill-in lights. Since we already have a spotlight in the scene, double-click on it to open the **Properties** palette (which should still be open, but ya never know), and take the following steps:

Light 1 — Keylight. In the **Properties** palette, click on the **General** tab and rename the light **Keylight** (might as well call them what they are). (See Figure 6.6.)

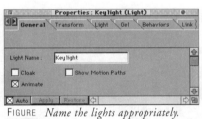

FIGURE *Name the lights appropriately.*
6.6

Now click on the **Transform** tab and enter the following values in the appropriate places: **Position:** X = 63.79, Y = 22.46, Z = 29.84; **Orientation:** Yaw = 95.06, Pitch = −0.13, Roll = 70.24.

When you've done there, click on the **Light** tab and enter the following values: **Color** = white (just make it pretty close to pure white using whatever color system you prefer), **Brightness = 70%, Half Angle = 25%, Angle Falloff = 100%, Shadow = checked at 39%.**

That sets up your first light. Now insert another light by choosing **Insert>Light**, and repeat the above steps but with this information.

Light 2 — Sidelight (don't forget to rename). In the **Transform** tab: **Position:** X = −11.95, Y = 86.89, Z = 13.18; **Orientation: Yaw = 7.43, Pitch = 0, Roll = −89.35.**

In the **Light** tab: **Color = white** (again, just make a white), **Brightness = 63%, Half Angle = 22%, Angle Falloff = 100%, Shadow = unchecked.**

Now insert another light and follow the previous steps but with the next batch of settings.

Light 3 — Fill Light (don't forget to rename). In the **Transform** tab: **Position**: X = –30.78, Y = –41.84, Z = 29.18; **Orientation**: Yaw = –28.41, Pitch = 5.54, Roll = 72.35.

In the **Light** tab: **Color = light yellow, Brightness = 35%, Half Angle = 13%, Angle Falloff = 100%, Shadow = unchecked.**

Insert your fourth light and follow the routine.

Light 4 — Backlight (hope you didn't forget to rename this one). In the **Transform** tab: **Position**: X = –9.34, Y = –12.66, Z = 2.75; **Orientation**: **Yaw = –13.13, Pitch = 0, Roll = 99.0.** In the **Light** tab: **Color = white, Brightness = 100%, Half Angle = 9%, Angle Falloff = 100%, Shadow = unchecked.**

OK. All of the lights are set up. You should have something that looks like Figure 6.7. If not, go back and figure out what went wrong. If so, let's move on.

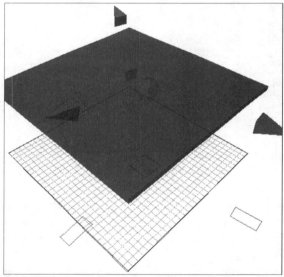

FIGURE *The scene after the lights have been properly set up.*
6.7

Step Six

Let's Insert another camera (select **Insert>Camera**) to shoot this scene. Call the camera **Shooter**, and click **OK**. All other settings should stay as they are. (See Figure 6.8.) The **Properties** palette appears with your new camera selected. Click on the **Transform** tab and enter the following **Position** values: X = 0, Y = 49.79, Z = 30.53; and **Orientation** values: **Yaw = 180, Pitch = 0, Roll = 54.94.**

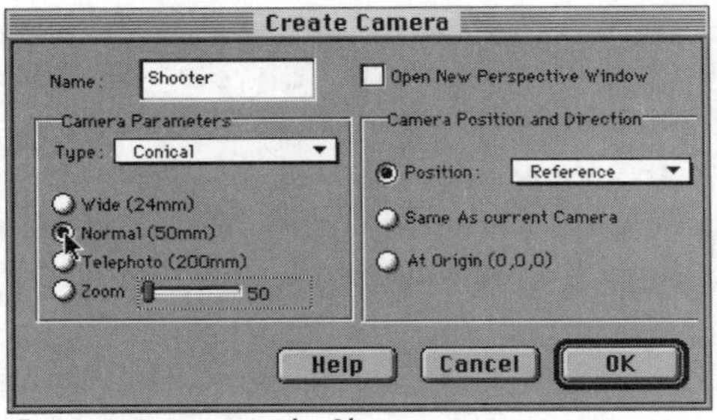

FIGURE **6.8** *Setting up the Shooter camera.*

Step Seven

Now we're ready to test our lighting setup. Open the **Current Scene Settings** palette from the **Render** menu. Click on the **Output** tab and enter the following settings in the **Image Size** box: **Width = 320, Height = 240, Resolution = 72 dpi.** (See Figure 6.9.) Click on the small triangle next to the Camera and choose **Shooter** from the pull-down menu. Close the current setting dialog. Go to **Render>Use Current Settings** to render the scene. You should wind up with something like Figure 6.10.

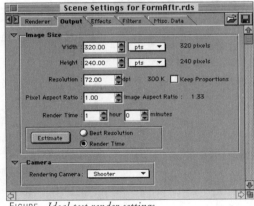

FIGURE **6.9** *Ideal test render settings.*

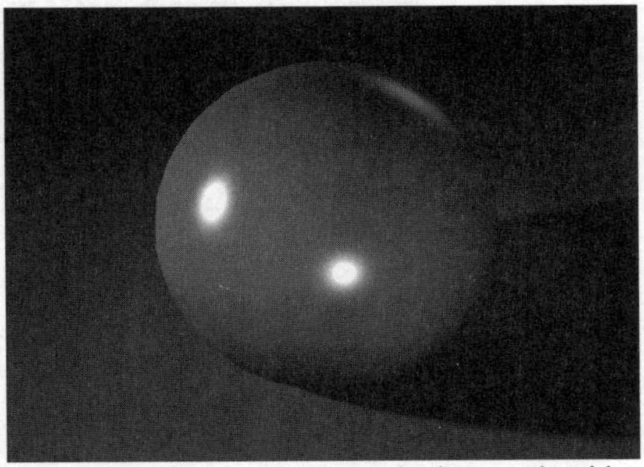

FIGURE **6.10** *Using a sphere as a stand-in for the original models is the most effective and efficient learning process toward understanding how lights affect a 3D surface.*

Analyze the rendered image. Notice how the lights play important roles in building a sense of weight and separate the object from its surroundings. Notice how the differing levels of highlight play upon the surface and actually give the impression that there is more going on around the sphere than there really is. These elements are required to bring the physical characteristics of your models to life.

Step Eight

Play around with your lighting at this point. Once you are satisfied with the result, it's time to render your actual model. Select the sphere and choose **Object Invisible** from the **View** menu. Select the Vase in the **Hierarchy** window and choose **Object Visible** from the **View** menu. Now render away, and hopefully you'll wind up with something close to Figure 6.11.

— SHARKAWI CHE DIN

FIGURE *With the lights set up correctly, the illusion of form becomes*
6.11 *apparent.*

CREATING LENS FLARES USING THE PROFESSIONAL LENS PACK FILTERS

This will give you a quick rundown of how to create an animatable lens flare using the Professional Lens Pack filters that shipped with RDS 5.0. For this example, we will use a Scene Wizard scene.

Step One

Create a new document in Ray Dream Studio by choosing **New** from the **File** menu. If you have **Use Scene Wizard on New** checked in your **Preferences**, you will get the dialog box shown in Figure 6.12, asking you if you want to create an empty scene, use the Scene Wizard, open an existing file, or cancel. Click on **Use Scene Wizard**.

FIGURE
6.12 *If you have Use Scene Wizard on New enabled, this is what you should see.*

If you do not have **Use Scene Wizard on New** checked in your preferences, you will simply get a new empty scene. No problem, just choose **Apply Scene Wizard...** under the **File** menu. You will probably get a warning here that says something about lights and things being replaced but, as long as you haven't done any work here (and you shouldn't have, because I haven't told you to do anything yet), go ahead and click **OK**.

Step Two

Now we have to pick a scene to work on. Well, that Bright Idea logo looks like a fine example of what we're after. (See Figure 6.13.) Double-click on it. You will get the screen shown in Figure 6.14. Double-click on the **Bright Idea** logo again. Now you should be looking at the screen in Figure 6.15. But it doesn't say **Lens** and **Flare** like the one in the picture. Well, make it say that by typing **Lens** in the first field, then hit tab and type **Flare** in the second field. Click on **Done**. Now sit back and watch your machine churn a little bit before it pops Figure 6.16 onto your screen.

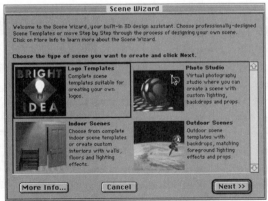

FIGURE *In the Scene Wizard, we're ready to start our lens*
6.13 *flare project.*

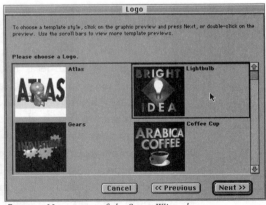

FIGURE *Next screen of the Scene Wizard.*
6.14

Logo Title

Select the sample text in the text field and replace it by typing your own text. Then click on the Done button or press Enter/Return.

Enter text.

Lens

Flare

| Cancel | « Previous | Done |

FIGURE 6.15   *Adding the new text.*

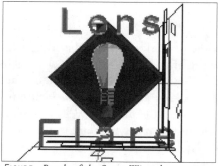

FIGURE 6.16   *Result of the Scene Wizard.*

Step Three

OK, now we're ready to rock. We have to do a quick modification or two to this scene to make it ready for the Lens Flare. The first thing we're going to do is to create a new camera. The camera we're looking through is positioned perfectly for our shot, so we'll leave it there and create a new camera to view the scene through while we make our adjustments. Select **Insert>Camera** under the **Edit** menu. You will get the dialog box shown in Figure 6.17. Set your screen up as shown. We want a new camera positioned at the top of the scene. Now, change your view to Camera 2 by selecting **Camera>Camera 2** under the **View** menu. Now we should be looking down on our logo, as in Figure 6.18. Select the projection of the bulb light that is inside the bulb object (Light 1 is the bulb light. The two Light 2s are the spotlights) using the **Selection** tool as it is shown in Figure 6.18, and choose **Duplicate** under the **Edit** menu. Now

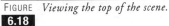

FIGURE *Making a new camera.*
6.17

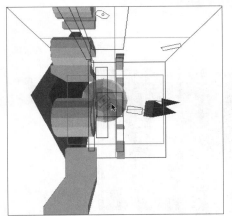

FIGURE *Viewing the top of the scene.*
6.18

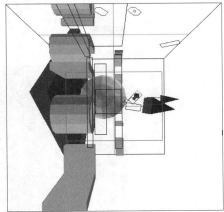

FIGURE *The Lens Flare filter works only on*
6.19 *visible lights, so we have to pull a*
duplicate of the bulb light out where
the filter can see it.

drag the duplicated bulb light in front of the lightbulb model, as shown in Figure 6.19. You should have one bulb light in the lightbulb object and one outside the lightbulb object.

We've done this because the Lens Flare filter works only on lights that are visible in the production frame and are not obscured by any objects — even transparent or semitransparent ones such as this lightbulb model.

Step Four

Now comes the easy part. You might want to save your scene now, just in case something goes awry.

Here's where you will set up the Lens Flare filter. Select **Current Scene Settings** under the **Render** menu, and click on the **Filters** tab. Now click on

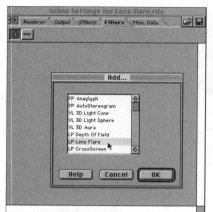

FIGURE *Adding the Lens Flare filter.*
6.20

FIGURE *The Lens Flare dialog box.*
6.21

FIGURE *The rendered Lens Flare effect.*
6.22

the little Plus sign, select the **LP Lens Flare** filter, as shown in Figure 6.20, and click the **Edit** button. Now you should see a Lens Flare dialog box similar to that in Figure 6.21. For this project we're going to leave the default presets intact, but you will want to play around with these at a later time. Feel free to play with them now, if you wish — you can't hurt anything.

Click on the **Preview** button in the upper left-hand corner. This renders a preview of your scene as seen through your camera. If you're happy with the preview, just click **OK**. If you're not happy, remember, I said you could play around if you like.

Your scene is now ready to render. You might as well save again, since you're here. Once you render, you should get a picture that looks very similar to Figure 6.22. Now wasn't that easy? And you didn't even have to think about postprocessing.

— *JOHN W. SLEDD*

GLOWING SIGN TECHNIQUE

This technique was provided by Craig Lyn, author of the *Macintosh 3D Handbook* (also published by Charles River Media). I have rewritten it to be more Ray Dream Studio-specific.

The idea here is to create the effect of backlit letters on a sign using the Glow channel.

I have created the cross sections for the sign using a vector drawing program. (See Figure 6.23.) The reason I have done so is to give me precise control over the

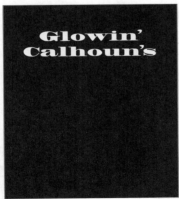

FIGURE **6.23** *First set up the art for the cross sections in a third-party drawing application.*

map size for the Glow channel. Map dimensions are critical, since the Glow channel must line up exactly with the letters on the sign. Notice how this cross section includes both the type and the back wall of the sign. This will allow me to keep the type aligned properly with the sign and its Glow channel, so pay attention. Oh, before I forget, remember that you must convert your type into outlines if you are preparing the art for the cross section in a third-party drawing program. RDS cannot read type imported in this fashion without it first being converted.

Step One

I create a Free Form object for the sign by selecting **Free Form** from the **Insert** menu and name it **Glow sign**. I then import the EPS file of the sign back and text by selecting **File>Import,** and adjust the **extrusion path** to the thickness I want for the actual wall (see Figure 6.24). (I've shaded this particular wall with the Brushed Metal shader from the RDS CD-ROM, but you don't have to be that specific. Just use something that looks, you know, wall-ish.) After the wall is shaded, I click **Done**. This gives me an object that may seem pretty sloppy. A wall with type inside it seems pretty useless, since the type's not even going to show up, right? Read on.

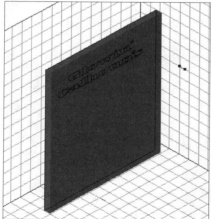

FIGURE *The imported and extruded cross*
6.24 *section.*

Step Two

Here I select the sign object in the perspective window and choose **Duplicate** from the **Edit** menu. This gives me an exact duplicate of the sign object pasted directly over the original. I then double-click on the duplicate in the **Hierarchy** window, which yields the warning dialog in Figure 6.25. I leave the default **Create New Master** selected, since I actually do want to create a new object; and click **OK**.

FIGURE *Jump In warning.*
6.25

When the Free Form modeling window opens, I select the shape that makes up the wall, delete it, and click **Done**. This gives me an object that is just the type without any of the wall. I rename this object **Glow Text** by selecting **Glow sign 1** (which is what RDS automatically named the new master created from the original Glow sign object) in the **Masters** tab and then changing the name in the **Properties** palette's **General** tab.

I then double-click on the original wall object. When the **Modeling** window opens, I choose **Select All** from the **Edit** menu and then **Shift-click** on the box surrounding the type to deselect it. This leaves only the text shapes selected, so a quick jab of the **Delete** key deletes the outlines of text. (I've changed the wall shader here to a basic flat gray material just to make the wall stand out from the text a bit.) I then click **Done** to return to the **Perspective** window.

Now I have an object that is just the back wall, and an object that is just the text. They are still overlapping each other, but I'm planning on fixing that. The important thing to notice here is that they are still aligned as they were when they were one object.

I now send the viewing camera to the **Top** position. This gives me the view I need to move the Glow Text object to a more appropriate position. I click on the

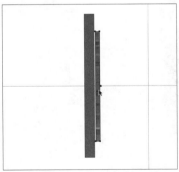

FIGURE *Viewing the two objects from*
6.26 *the top makes alignment easy.*

FIGURE *This is the reference view*
6.27 *of the two sign pieces properly positioned.*

projection of the text object (it will be the smaller one) and drag it so that it's slightly in front of the back wall object. (See Figure 6.26.) Figure 6.27 shows the two objects from the reference view. Notice that the sign is set up properly.

Step Three

Here I create the map that is to be used in the Glow channel to make the text look as if it's back-lit. This is where creating the cross section in the third-party drawing program pays off.

I open the cross section EPS file in a paint program, since I need a bitmapped graphic instead of a vector graphic to place into the Glow channel. The benefit here is that, since the actual sign was created using this same art, all proportions will be correct, and everything will line up perfectly once mapped to the sign back. Once the EPS artwork has been imported into the paint program and rasterized into a bitmap format, I can proceed to Step Four.

Step Four

Now that I have the artwork used to create the cross sections in bitmap format I can apply the halo effect. I do this by applying a five-pixel Gaussian blur to the image. Figure 6.28 shows the art in the paint program with the Gaussian blur applied. I save this file as **Glow Map**.

FIGURE *Halo map with Gaussian blur.*
6.28

Step Five

Here, I go back to the wall object and open it in the Free Form modeler. I prefer to do my shading at the Master level because I find it easier to keep track of my shading if I'm looking at only one object at a time. In addition, if I were to make several duplicates of this file, I could change the shading on all of them by simply changing the shading on the Master object (I know, I mention this all over the place in this book, but I really mean it, dagnabbit).

While the object is open in the Free Form modeler, I click on it using the **Eyedropper** tool. This brings up the **Current Shader Editor**. I go to the **Glow channel** and create a **Subtraction operator**. (See Figure 6.29.) On the left side of the shader tree, I place a color channel with the default color of red. This will be the color of the glow. On the right side of the shader tree, I place a texture map. I then double-click on the right branch of the shader tree and import the Glow Map file. (See Figure 6.30.)

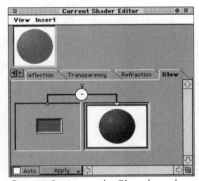

FIGURE *Setting up the Glow channel.*
6.29

FIGURE *Importing the map for the*
6.30 *glow.*

The Subtraction operator allows me to subtract all white areas from the Glow channel while allowing all of the black areas to show through. Since I created the Glow Map as white text on a black background, I must check the **Invert Color** box in the **Shader Editor** to get the desired effect. Otherwise, all of the wall would glow red except for the areas around the letters.

After applying the shader and clicking **Done** to return to the **Perspective** window, I click on the **Masters** tab in the **Hierarchy** window, select the wall object and then click on the **Mapping Mode** tab of the **Properties** palette. I choose **Box/Face Mapping** and click the front face of the cube so that my glow channel is projected onto the object exactly as I have it set up. (See Figure 6.31.)

FIGURE *Select Box/Face Mapping.*
6.31

FIGURE *The rendered wall with glow.*
6.32

Step Six

That about takes care of it. I set up a rendering camera and then render the scene. Figure 6.32 shows the product of this exercise.

This technique can also be used to create lights on buildings for city scenes or for spaceships and space stations to give the impression of many windows. There is no end to the complexity or uses of the maps possible in the Glow channel.

— *JOHN W. SLEDD*

GLOWING LIGHT SOURCES

This is a quick tutorial on how to create subtle yet powerful effects using one of RDS's visible light pack filters. Many of you will beat the Visible Light Cone filter to death all by yourselves (and that's fine by me — it's a killer effect), so I'm going to leave it alone, but you may pass by the Visible Light Sphere filter when your piece could benefit greatly from it. Oh, you might try it once or twice and decide it's not worth the effort. The key, however, is to use it with some finesse, unlike the Light Cone, where bigger and brighter is often better.

The Candle Flame

Creating visible light sources that look like real light sources can be a challenge at times. Take the candle flame in Figure 6.33, for example. As it is, it looks okay, but it could certainly use improvement. The first thing that makes this object challenging is the fact that the flame itself is not the light source of the

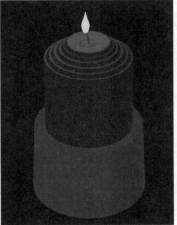

FIGURE **6.33** *A flame without life is like a ... well ... it's just boring.*

scene, but we can fix that by cleverly placing a bulb light in the same place as the flame object and by using the Glow channel on the flame object itself. By doing those two simple things, we've managed to both make the flame look as though it's really made of fire, and make it look as though that fire is responsible for illuminating the scene. So what's missing? Life. The flame has no life. Without animating the flame, you can't give it life through motion, so you have to give it life through spirit. Enter the 3D Light Sphere filter.

Step One

The candle scene is all set up. You've got your flame and you've got your light. (See Figure 6.34.)

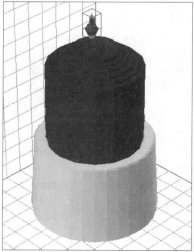

FIGURE
6.34 *Everything you need for a warm and fuzzy candle scene . . . except for the finishing touch.*

All you have to do now is to set up your 3D Light Sphere filter. Let's go ahead and add the filter. Open your Scene Settings palette by choosing **Current Scene Settings** from the **Render** menu. Go to the **Filters** tab and click on the little plus sign. Select the **VL 3D Light Sphere** item and click **OK**. (See Figure 6.35.) Let's just go ahead and accept the default settings and do a test render to see what happens. (See Figure 6.36.)

Step Two

Well, since that didn't really work as planned, I guess the only thing to do is use something other than the default settings (gasp). Don't get me wrong, it's

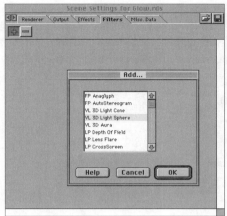

FIGURE *Let's add the 3D Light Sphere filter.*
6.35

FIGURE *I don't know about you, but I*
6.36 *think this looks like <censored>.*

not that bad if you happen to like translucent ping-pong ball glows that wash out your flame and blow out the whole scene, but it could use some . . . what was that word again? . . . ah yes, finesse.

Let us go back into the **Filter** tab of the **Scene Settings** and fix this mess. Click on the **Edit** button in the **Light Sphere** box. (See Figure 6.37.) Looking at the first shot, I'd say we needed to reduce the Range. Wouldn't you agree?

FIGURE **6.37** *Doorway to the Light Sphere settings.*

FIGURE **6.38** *Drag the fog **Intensity** slider back to about 35%.*

Well, you'd be dead wrong if you did. If you reduce the Range, you'll just get a smaller overbearing ping-pong ball glow. How do I know that? Well, it certainly wouldn't be because I actually thought the Range was the problem the first time I did it. Really you want to adjust the **Intensity** of the fog — drag that slider back to about **35%** and click **OK**. (See Figure 6.38.) Now rerender and see what happens. (See Figure 6.39.) Now, if you want to play with the **Range** setting, feel free. The size of your glow is up to you.

— *JOHN W. SLEDD*

(Inspired by Richard Bucci's candle tip from the first edition that I ruthlessly deemed obsolete)

FIGURE *A softer glow is a better glow.*
6.39

PHONY VISIBLE LIGHT BEAMS

In the first edition of this book, Steve McArdle provided us with a technique on creating volumetric lighting effects using geometry and clever shader tricks. Now that actual volumetric lighting is possible using the 3D Light Pack filters that ship with Ray Dream Studio 5, those techniques seemed a bit out of date for this edition. True as that may be, the overall technique still has it's uses. The three most obvious reasons I can think of off-hand are reflections, shape and the power of RDS's shaders.

Since the 3D Light Pack filters are postprocess filters (that is, they are applied after the actual rendering is complete) they will not show up in objects in your scene that have reflective properties, but Steve's technique will.

The 3D Light Pack filters are also limited by their shape for certain effects. You can apply a gel to a light and have that gel be used to calculate the visible beams of light, but if you're looking for a parallel light shaft (that is, one that remains a constant width and does not taper), you're out of luck. With this technique, however, parallel light beams for lasers and transporters are a few more clicks away compared to your standard volumetric lighting filter.

And lastly, when you're after that specific look, it's nice to be able to unleash the power of the RDS Shader editor on your visible light beams.

This technique is more of a lesson in the Zen of RDS than it is a specific project with a specific ending. I'm going to take the essence of Steve's techniques and apply them to a transporter beam. Then we're going to play around with different settings to get your creative juices flowing.

Open the TELEPORT.RDS file in your Chapter 6 directory on the CD-ROM if you want to follow along. Figure 6.40 is what you would get should you render this scene as is. After we're done, however, we'll have a nice, spooky beam coming down to claim our teleportee.

FIGURE   *Teleportee suspended in*
6.40   *midair.*

Step One

This first step is to get acquainted with the scene. I've set most of it up for you, so let me explain what's going on so you'll have some idea why you're doing what you're doing, and when.

What we have here is a figure being suspended in the air by a beam of energy. We want this beam of energy to be visible, and we want to be able to see the figure inside the beam. We'd also like the beam to glow and illuminate the area surrounding it. The obvious solution, the 3D Light Pack filters, simply won't do here for two reasons: The beam must be a uniform size from top to bottom; and this beam is more of a light source than the visible manifestation of light traveling through particle-filled space, so it would need to illuminate not only the teleportee, but the area around the teleportation station as well.

To solve the first problem of the shape of the beam, I modeled geometry to serve as the Transporter Beam. You'll find that object in your **Hierarchy** window. You can't see it now in the **Perspective** window because I've hidden it. We'll get to it later in the tutorial.

To solve the illumination problem, I''ve created two spotlights and assigned a **Point At** behavior to both of them with the **Trans Woman** as the target of their affection. (See Figure 6.41.) The Point At behavior allows me to position the lights in a footloose and fancy-free style because they always remain pointed at their target. I highly recommend the use of that behavior whenever possible.

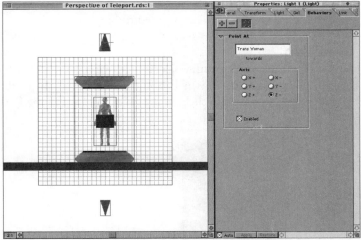

FIGURE   *Using the Point At behavior, positioning the lights is a breeze.*
6.41

A minor problem I ran into was that the lights need to be positioned outside the ceiling and floor of the teleportation station. This meant that the light has to pass through the ceiling and floor of the station to illuminate the teleportee and the ground. There are two ways that this can be accomplished. The first option, and the one I chose, is simply to turn the shadows off for each of the lights. (See Figure 6.42.) Nothing really needs to cast a shadow in this scene because of the position of the beam.

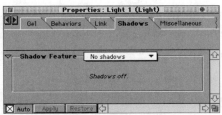

FIGURE   *Turning off the lights' shadows.*
6.42

The second option is to turn off the shadow-casting options on each of the objects that block the light sources. This would be a good option if there were objects just outside the station that really needed to cast shadows. You'd simply turn the shadows off on the objects you don't need shadows from, and leave the feature enabled for the objects that you do want shadows from. If you like, when you've done here, you can go back through the tutorial and try that option instead.

Anyway, on with the show. Now that you understand the crucial points of how the scene was set up, let's proceed to Step Two.

Step Two

Locate the **Transporter Beam** object in your **Hierarchy** and choose **Object Visible** from the **View** menu. This will bring in the beam object that I created. (See Figure 6.43.) Now double-click on the object to open in the **Free Form modeler**.

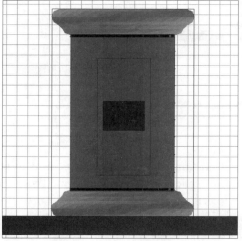

FIGURE   *The Transporter Beam object ready to be*
6.43   *shaded.*

⇨ **Note:** A little history on this beam object: I created it using Cecilia Ziemer's tutorial on the wineglass from Chapter 4. The only difference is that I didn't fill the end cross sections. I didn't want anything interfering with the floor and ceiling of the transport.

Step Three

Now this entire technique from this point on relies on your shader. Let's create a simple initial shader to mimic the effects of a visible light. Your Transporter Beam object should be open in the Free Form modeler at this point. Now click on it with the **Eyedropper** tool to open the **Current Shader editor**. Double-click on the color swatch, and create a light-blue color (I'm a big fan of light-blue lights for some reason, but phosphorescent greens are cool too). Now click on that color swatch and drag it over into the **Glow** tab. This copies the color of the Color channel into the Glow channel. Now **zero** out the **Highlight**, **Shininess**, **Bump**, **Reflection** and **Refraction** channels. Set the **Transparency** value to 75%, apply the shader, and render the file. You should get an image similar to Figure 6.44.

FIGURE 6.44 *The scene already starts shaping up with the use of a simple shader.*

Step Four

Well, that's great, but let's do some more experimenting. Let's go back into the shader of the beam object and jump back into the **Transparency** channel. Instead of the simple **Value** component, let's insert a **Mix** component. In the left branch, insert a **Value** component, and bump it up to 75%. Insert a **Value** component into the right branch, but bump it up only to **25%**. Now select **Insert>Natural Functions>Marble** to insert a **Marble Function** into the **Drop Function here** box at the bottom. Click on the **Direction** pull-down menu and choose the third option. (See Figure 6.45.)

Apply the new shader, and render. You should have something similar to Figure 6.46. Cool, huh. Now jump back into the Shader editor and change the 75% value in the **Transparency** channel to a **100%** value and the **25%** value to a **35%** value, as in Figure 6.47, and rerender. Now you just have bolts of plasma. (See Figure 6.48.)

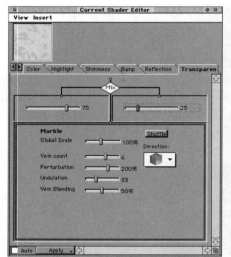

FIGURE **6.45**   *Adding a Marble Function.*

FIGURE **6.46**   *Cool gaseous effects.*

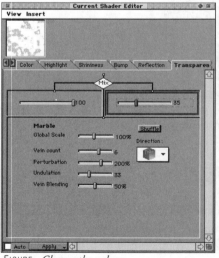

FIGURE **6.47**   *Change the values ...*

FIGURE **6.48**   *... and get plasma.*

With a little Shader editor creativity, you can create complex special effects like those in Figure 6.49 (don't look now, but the recipe for this shader is in Chapter 9).

— *JOHN W. SLEDD AND STEVE MCARDLE.*

© 1998 John W. Sledd

FIGURE **6.49** *Endless possibilities await you with this out-of-date Phony Visible Light technique.*

RADIOSITY FAKE

Ray Dream Studio utilizes *Raytracing*, and therefore can produce reflections of objects; however, it does not currently support *Radiosity*, the ability to reflect light bouncing off other objects in a scene. You can see an example of reflected light by placing a single white light on the ceiling in a room with blue walls. All objects in the room would show a hint of blue, as if being lit up by a faint blue light.

This reflected-light effect causes earth-toned or warm-colored rooms to appear cozy, while rooms with pure white walls may appear antiseptic because all of the reflected light is harsh white. This effect happens outdoors too. While walking in the woods on a sunny day, you may notice a bright green cast of light. This is due to filtering and light reflected by surrounding leaves.

Ambient light can be adjusted in RDS to give overall control over the scattered light in a scene, but reflected light cannot be processed in specific instances such as a white tennis ball sitting next to a red book, or the example below — without using a trick, that is.

Figure 6.50 shows a Ray Dream Studio scene of a ping-pong ball which uses a radiosity workaround. This workaround simulates the effect of specific objects reflecting light — in this case, the table reflecting onto the bottom of

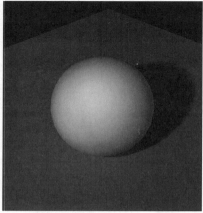

FIGURE   *The fake radiosity effect.*
6.50

the ball and also a little lightness on the table coming from the ball. This effect is hardly noticeable on the pages of the book because it's all about color nuances, so we've included the scene file, as well as a rendered .TIF, on the CD-ROM.

You can observe this effect by looking at the bottom of the ball. Notice that it has a slight green tint that lessens as you follow it up. You can also see a slightly lighter area on the table as the white from the ball strikes its surface.

Step One

The effect of the table's color bleeding onto the ball is accomplished by using a rectangular paint shape applied to the bottom half of the ball Master object. You can create your own file here to play with (it's very simple) or you can open the **RdstyB-4.RDS** file on the CD-ROM. The shader for the ball itself is simply a matte white-ish shader created to simulate the texture of a ping-pong ball. The shader for the radiosity effect has only one channel with information in it, and that is the **Glow** channel. By using unmodified channels for all of the other channels, the underlying shader for the ping-pong ball shows through with only the **Glow** channel being modified by the paint shape's shader.

The reason for using a paint shape is that it provides the most control over where the green bleed starts and stops, because you can resize the shape on the fly and squish or stretch the area affected by the glow.

To apply the paint shape to your ping-pong ball, simply open the ball object, select the **Paint Shape tool**, and draw a square on your ball. It's really best that you don't try to make it right the first time, because it's rather tricky. Just get the shape on the ball. You can then use the **Paint Shape Selection tool** to position and stretch the shape. To get the shape to wrap around the sphere, hold down the **Option** key. This still won't make it easy, and sometimes the shape will snap back. When this happens, simply get a feel for how far you can drag it before it snaps back. Then drag it as far as you can with the **Option** key held down, then drag it a little way without the Option key held down, and repeat these two steps until you have no seam or the smallest seam you can get. A little tip here: if you can get a small seam, you can then click on the Paint Shape and spin it around the sphere so that the seam is in the back and therefore out of view. This trick will save you a good number of headaches.

Step Two

Once you have your Paint Shape drawn, you can begin working on the shader. The first thing you want to do is to go through every channel other than the Glow channel, and hit **Delete**. This will turn all of your other channels into unmodified channels, so that the ball's underlying shader shows through. Then go to work on the Glow channel.

The recipe for this magical radiosity Glow channel is cooked up by inserting a **Mix Operator** into the Glow channel of the Paint Shape's shader. In the left branch, you'll find a color component of black. In the right branch, you'll find a color component of dark green. For the mixer, you'll find a **Gradient Pattern Function** with a **Vertical** Direction and 0% **Turbulence**. (See Figure 6.51.)

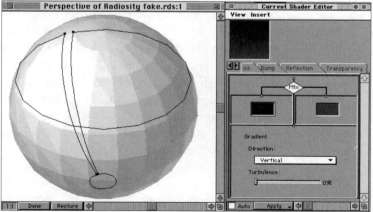

FIGURE **6.51** *The shader settings and Paint Shape placement for the ping-pong ball (notice that the seam for the Paint Shape is hidden by dragging it around to the back of the ball).*

Step Three

For the light cast on the table, a slightly different technique is used — not a paint shape this time, but rather, the original object shader's Glow channel is modified. A mixer is still used, but with a mixer of a Texture Map this time, instead of a procedural. To accurately position the map used as the mixer in the Glow channel, send your camera to the top preset position. From this angle, take a quick screen grab of just the table and ball. (See Figure 6.52.)

FIGURE *A screen capture of a top view of*
6.52 *the table makes a great template.*

Now bring your screen grab into a paint application, if you have one — and you should at least have Painter by now — and create your map based on where the color bleed is to fall.

Make an elliptical selection where the glow is to fall, and fill it with **white**. Now invert the selection and fill it with **100% black**. This should leave you with a pure white ellipse in the middle of a black field. You might want to change your resolution too, since your screen grab is only 72 dpi. You want your map to be as smooth as possible for the final intended use of the image. For the book, we used a resolution of 200 dpi, which is neither the best nor the worst solution but very mid-range.

Now blur the entire map image to soften the edges of the white area and provide a smooth blend. (See Figure 6.53.)

Step Four

Now the map is ready to be applied to the table (which is a flattened cube primitive, by the way). Jump into the table object and open the **Shader editor** by clicking on it with the **Eyedropper** tool (remember, we always shade at the

FIGURE *The grayscale texture map used*
6.53 *for the table's glow.*

Master level). Insert a **Mix Operator** into the Glow channel. Now insert a
Color component with **85% black** into the left channel and a **100% black**
Color component in the right channel. For the Mixer, insert a **Texture Map**
component and open the table glow map that you've just created. The 85%
black of the above branch gives the white area of the map just enough glow to
lighten the table convincingly, while the black of the above right branch is no
glow at all. (See Figure 6.54.) You could have just made your Texture Map
with the proper levels of gray, but using this method, you can experiment in
RDS without having to guess the proper levels in your paint application. It
should also be noted that, whenever using colors of black or white in a Shader

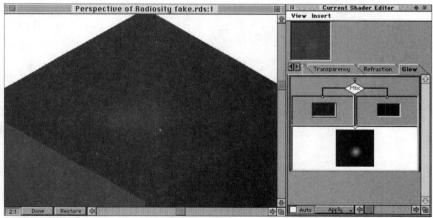

FIGURE *The table's glow requires very low settings to accomplish the desired effect.*
6.54

channel, you can substitute Value components, which often give you a better numerical idea of what you're doing.

We also use the Box/Face Mapping mode to make sure we've projected the shader accurately. (See Figure 6.55.)

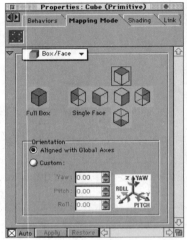

FIGURE **6.55** *Box/Face Mapping was used to project the glow map onto the table.*

When you put it all together, you have a rather convincing radiosity effect.

This type of effect can be used under many circumstances; in our earlier tennis ball/red book example, such a grayscale ramp-map would be mapped onto the tennis ball at the part of the ball's surface that faced the book. A barely perceptible red glow could then be mapped onto the ball, representing the reflected redness of the book it sits next to.

You can also use this technique on the walls of rooms to bleed the colors where walls meet floors and ceilings. You can use it to bleed the color from furniture onto the floors and walls, as well. The Glow channel provides virtually unlimited power when it comes to lighting effects workarounds.

— *RICHARD BUCCI*

USE DIRECT MANIPULATION AND THE POINT AT BEHAVIOR ON YOUR CAMERAS

Ray Dream Studio not only provides you with an excellent way to tell which way a camera is pointing and what the field of view is, but also allows you to edit its parameters using the same visual representations. By simply turning on the Direct Manipulation option in the appropriate camera's Properties palette, you will immediately see the control that awaits you. (See Figure 7.1.) Be sure you're looking at the camera you want to edit though. Turning on the Direct Manipulation option on the camera you're looking through won't do you much good.

In addition to this control, you may find that assigning a Point At behavior to your camera works very well. You can place the name of your main target in the Point At field, or you can use a cloaked object as a virtual "sight" for your camera. To do this, place a sphere or other primitive in your scene, and name it **Camera Sight**. Now cloak the object. Assign a **Point At** behavior to your camera and type **Camera Sight** in the **Point At** field. Now wherever you move the sight, the camera will follow; and since the object is cloaked, it won't show up in your renders.

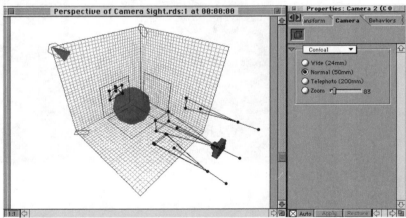

FIGURE *Ray Dream Studio's new Direct Manipulation tools.*
7.1

SAVE POSITIONS AND CREATE ADDITIONAL CAMERAS TOO

Back in the days of Ray Dream Studio 4 (and before), you could save camera positions, but these settings saved only the camera Position and Orientation.

Unless you're the type who likes being irritated, you would most likely create several extra cameras and use them instead of switching preset views — a very good habit.

Well, Ray Dream Studio 5 now has the ability to save a camera's Type and Parameters along with the Position and Orientation in a saved position, so use this often and wisely. When you set up that perfect shot, save it. If you forget and choose another position on your rendering camera, all is not lost, because you can choose the new Last position from the **View>Preset Position** drop-down menu. This should serve as a reminder to save your rendering position immediately. If you forget, change your position and then change it again, you're hosed.

This new position-saving feature does cut down on the need for multiple cameras but doesn't get rid of it entirely. As I mentioned above, you need to be looking through another camera before you can use those groovy Direct Manipulation tools. If you're doing some tricky camera animation, viewing the animated camera through another camera is the only way to go. I personally still find it advantageous to use separate cameras for rendering and for scene navigation. Looking at your whole scene, rendering camera included, helps head off potential errors.

FOCAL LENGTH AND EFFECT

Focal length and effect are photography basics. The higher the numbers in the focal length, the narrower the field of view, and the shallower the depth of field.

A 15mm lens setting is very wide, and will distort objects and make them seem further apart spatially than they really are. For example, consider a camera placed on a road looking down a row of telephone poles: A wide-angle setting will make the poles seem to have a lot of distance between them, and the horizon will seem very far away and less important in the scene, whereas the foreground object will seem bigger and more dominant.

A longer focal length will seem to compress the apparent distance between the poles and the items in the scene — the horizon will seem closer, and there will be less dominance attributed to objects relative to the distance from the camera. See Figures 7.2 and 7.3 for examples of focal length.

Longer focal lengths in photography are usually accompanied by a greater degree of selective focus and, due to the nature of the optics, it is usually difficult to keep more than a certain area in front of the camera in focus. Use

FIGURE *A 24mm depth of field.*
7.2

FIGURE *A 50mm depth of field.*
7.3

RDS 5's Depth of Field filter for this effect — more on that at the end of this chapter.

— *RICK GRECO*

FISHEYE LENS TRICK...ER, I MEAN, "TECHNIQUE"

Many of the optical properties that can be exploited in a real-world 35mm camera can be applied to the virtual camera in RDS. Figure 7.4 shows one of the many effects that can be accomplished with a little ingenuity.

Picture this: you're holding a camera to your eye, poised to take a photograph. You lift a round, reflective ball into place directly in front of the camera lens. Looking through the viewfinder of the camera, the ball fills the frame.

FIGURE   *The fisheye technique employed.*
7.4

On the surface of the ball, you see yourself reflected in the middle of an almost 180-degree view of all that lies behind you. This is the poor man's fisheye lens.

Though the following technique uses, like the above technique, a reflective sphere primitive to achieve a fisheye effect, the concept can be applied using any object with a reflective shader to achieve interesting visual distortions from RDS's virtual camera.

The basic premise is to use a highly reflective object in front of your rendering camera. The camera "sees" the reflection of whatever is in the scene — except itself, of course (ah, one of the beauties of the virtual camera), and renders the scene as a reflection based on the optical distortions created by the shape of the object. Take into account that you can tweak the other shader attributes for varying effects, and you're well on your way to some very creative and unique possibilities for how your virtual camera might see your scene.

To do this nifty Cracker Crack tip, take the following steps:

Step One

Set up your scene normally through a camera with a wide-angle setting of 10mm or less. The lowest you can go with an RDS camera is 6, and in order to get a value of 10, you must first choose the **Zoom** lens and then double-click on the slider and enter a value of **10**. The slider, by itself, skips from 15 to 6.

The wide-angle setting helps you to previsualize and approximate the fisheye's perspective distortion more closely than if a standard setting were used while setting up your scene.

Remember, your fisheye view will bring a great deal of your scene into view; take that into account as you work.

The camera you've just set up will be your render camera, and for this description we'll name the camera **Fisheye**.

Step Two

Create a new camera by dragging the **Camera** icon into the **Perspective** or **Hierarchy** window, and set it to reference your entire scene, including the Fisheye camera. Name this camera **Reference Camera**.

Step Three

While viewing the scene through the reference camera, create a sphere with a diameter about three times the height of the Fisheye camera and position it directly behind the Fisheye camera about four camera lengths from it. This is the sphere you'll point your render camera at to render your scene.

Step Four

Select the sphere and call up the **Current Shader editor** under the **Windows** menu. Place Value sliders in every channel (you can leave the default red in the Color channel if you like — it won't matter with the high reflection value). All values should be **zero**, except **Reflection**, which you set to **100%**. (See Figure 7.5.)

You can place a color or some channel-tree-cocktail in the Highlight channel if you wish, but I would recommend experimenting with the basic technique first before fiddling around with anything too complex.

Apply the shader to the sphere.

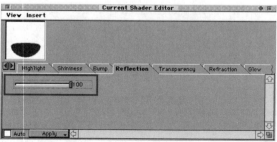

FIGURE
7.5
The Reflection setting is the key to creating a perfect mirror out of the sphere.

Step Five

Select the render cam and the sphere together and point the camera at the sphere using the **Point At** command by selecting **Arrange>Point At**. Look at Figure 7.6 to see how your camera should be positioned in reference to your sphere.

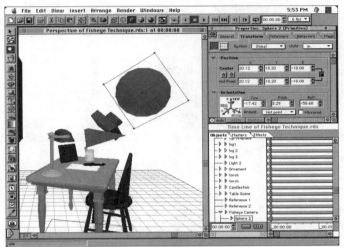

FIGURE   *View of the camera and sphere in relation to the rest of the scene.*

7.6

Step Six

Set the render camera's focal length to **50mm**.

Step Seven

The tricky part comes next. Through some trial and error via test renders, tweak the positions of the camera and the sphere relative to your scene. You can't preview the Fisheye camera's view of the scene in any way other than with test renders, because there is no preview mode that supports reflection. Remember, you are going to render the reflection of the scene on the sphere.

   The general rule of thumb is to create a view through the render camera, activate the production frame, and position the sphere to fill the production frame corner to corner. (See Figure 7.7.)

   Take this moment to select the sphere, open it's **Properties** palette and select the **Rendering** tab. By default, your reflection depth should be 2. You might want to bump this up a bit for the final render. I've bumped this one up

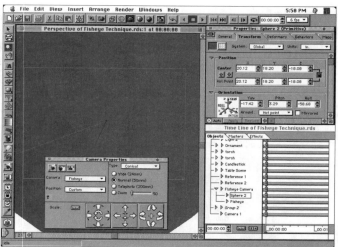

FIGURE **7.7** *View from the rendering camera in Fast Preview mode. Notice how the production frame is totally filled with the sphere.*

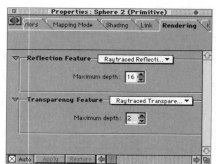

FIGURE **7.8** *Setting the Maximum depth for the Reflection feature on the sphere.*

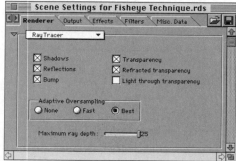

FIGURE **7.9** *Be sure Reflection is enabled, because this technique relies on it.*

to about 16, which may be overkill, but I wanted to make sure we get as much information as possible. (See Figure 7.8.) Keep in mind that the higher the depth setting, the longer the render. Start out with the default and work your way up if you aren't satisfied with your last couple of test renders before the final one.

When you set up your render settings, use the **Ray Tracer** and be sure to enable **Reflection** in the **Render Settings** dialog box (you could use the Adaptive renderer, but since this scene is all reflection, it really doesn't matter). Keep in mind that since you are rendering a reflection, the scene will take much longer to render than if it were rendered through a normal camera setup. (See Figure 7.9.)

— *RICK GRECO*

CREATING A DEPTH-OF-FIELD EFFECT WITH THE PROFESSIONAL LENS PACK FILTER

You can now create realistic depth of field without ever leaving Ray Dream Studio by using the Depth-of-Field portion of the Professional Lens Pack plug-in that ships with Ray Dream Studio 5. To illustrate the effect, we'll use a scene provided by Rayflect, Inc., creators of the Pro Lens pack. (See Figure 7.10.)

FIGURE *The scene is ready to be rendered.*
7.10

Step One

Open the scene that you wish to add the Depth-of-Field effect to. Open the **Scene Settings** window by selecting **Render>Current Scene Settings**, and click on the **Filters** tab.

Step Two

Click on the Plus sign button, choose **LP Depth of Field**, and click OK. (See Figure 7.11.) Click on the **Edit** button, and when the menu pops up, as in Figure 7.12, click on the **Preview** button. This will do a mini-render of your scene.

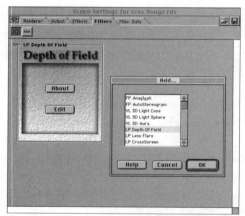

FIGURE 7.11 *Adding the Depth-of-Field plug-in to the Scene Settings Filters tab.*

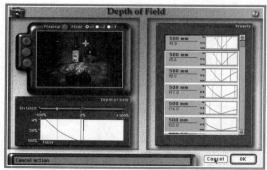

FIGURE 7.12 *The preview makes it easy to specify the proper settings.*

© 1998 Fred Beltran

FIGURE *The scene rendered with the Depth-*
7.13 *of-Field plug-in*

Step Three

After your preview has rendered, click on the **Red** plus sign and then click on the object in your preview that you wish to remain in focus. Then click on the **Green** plus sign and click on the foreground object you wish to be out of focus. Finally, click on the **Blue** plus sign and then click on the background object you wish to be out of focus. Then click **OK** and render your scene. Figure 7.12 shows the scene rendered in all its splendor.

— *RAYFLECT, INC.*

Shader Tips

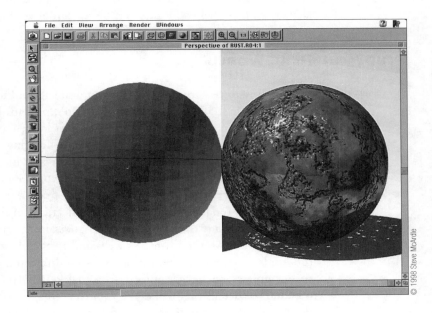

Shading is probably the most important part of the 3D process when it comes to giving a sense of realism to a scene. No matter how detailed and realistic your models, no matter how artistic your lighting and your composition, if your shaders aren't good, it will all look as if it came straight out of a computer.

In light of this revelation, you'll be pleased to know that Ray Dream Studio has some of the most powerful shader capabilities of any 3D software package. All of the images in this book are testimony to just what can be done using Ray Dream Studio's shaders and you've probably seen several other examples as well. The tips in this chapter, along with the recipes and techniques in the following chapter, will get you up to speed on creating and applying shaders and will help you improve the realism of your images.

STUDY THE REAL WORLD

Hemingway once wrote: "How can you write about life if you haven't lived it?" If he had been a 3D artist instead of a writer, perhaps his question would have been: "How can you model life if you haven't looked at it?" Good artists spend time studying the world around them and noticing the details that end up making the difference between approximation and duplication.

As a simple example, consider an old copper kettle. If you examine it closely, you'll see that it has multiple layers of color, gloss, shininess and reflective qualities. You'll also notice that the reflections in the kettle are neither perfect nor consistent; there are minor variances in the surface of the kettle (perhaps a few not-so-minor ones as well) and in the gloss of the finish. These are the kinds of detail that you probably wouldn't think of putting into a kettle shader unless you first examined an actual kettle. For this reason, they're also the kinds of details that will make your final image look like an old copper kettle instead of a computer-generated kettle. Take the time to do your research, and you'll impress everyone — including yourself — with the results.

— *TONY JONES*

ADD COMPLEXITY

In light of the previous tip, it should come as no surprise that the key to realistic shaders is to build complexity into them. Ray Dream Studio makes this easy to do using the Shader editor's various operators and functions to create shaders that are made up of several different levels of detail. In particular, the **Add** and

Mix operators should become an integral part of your shader vocabulary, as should the **Natural** and **Pattern** functions. You'll be amazed at how versatile these shader components can be, especially when used to create and enhance details. The next chapter includes several excellent examples for you to study.

Make sure you also take advantage of as many Shader channels as possible when building your shaders. At the very least, each shader should include something in the Color, Highlight, Shininess and Bump channels, even if it's just something subtle. It may not seem as if it makes a big difference, but even a small degree of added complexity will have a big effect on the resulting images.

— *CHRISTIAN NAKATA, STEVE MCARDLE, CECILIA ZIEMER & TONY JONES*

LEARN BY EXAMPLE

One of the best ways to learn is to take something apart to see how it was put together. This is as true of Ray Dream Studio's shaders as it is with anything else; any of the shaders that come with Ray Dream Studio are a learning experience waiting to happen. (See Figure 8.1.) Make sure you spend some time looking at the ones you find interesting to see what techniques and settings were used to create different effects. (You'll find several more advanced shaders in the next chapter.)

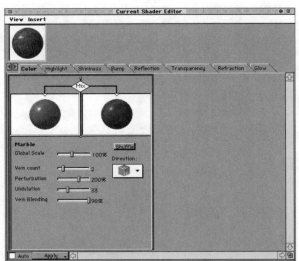

FIGURE **8.1** *The sample shaders included with Ray Dream Studio make great learning tools if you spend some time studying how they were put together.*

As a bonus, you'll find that many of the shaders that come with the program, especially those that are included on the Ray Dream Studio CD-ROM, include Texture Maps that can be saved to disk and then used in your own shaders.

— JOHNATHAN BANTA

USE FLAT PREVIEW

When using the Shader editor, you can preview your shader in one of two modes. The default mode is Sphere Preview, which gives you a rough idea of how your shader will look when applied to an actual object, and is the best way to preview the effects of the Highlight, Shininess, Bump, Reflection and Refraction channels. When you're working on the Color, Transparency and Glow channels, however, you may prefer to switch to Flat Preview mode (select **Flat Preview** from the **Shader editor**'s **View** menu). Flat Preview mode shows more detail than Sphere Preview and makes it easier to see how different function settings will affect the shader. It also helps you see exactly how different subshaders are being combined when using one of the shader operators. (See Figure 8.2.)

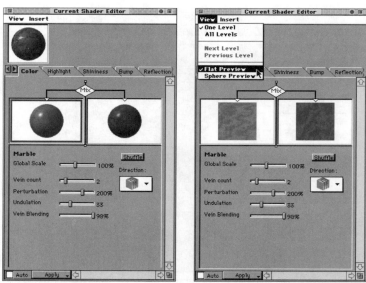

FIGURE **8.2** *Selecting **Flat Preview** from the **Shader editor**'s **View** menu will often give you a better idea of what your shader looks like and what different operators are doing.*

When using Flat Preview mode, keep in mind that switching preview modes will affect only the current shader level. If you're using subshaders, you must jump into the subshaders and switch on their preview modes as well. The exception to this is if you're using the View>All Levels option. When viewing all levels, you can change the Preview mode and then switch back to View>One Level and all previews will be in whatever mode you chose.

— *Craig Patchett*

TEST EVERYTHING IN THE COLOR CHANNEL

If you're using functions or operators in any of the non-Color channels, it can be difficult to see exactly what effect they're having on the shader. This is especially true in the Transparency and Refraction channels, where the effects can be subtle, and where it can also take a long time to create a test render. One solution is to create a new shader for each channel and build the non-Color channels of your final shader in the Color channels of the new shaders. This not only lets you see the effect of the settings for each channel in the Shader editor's Flat Preview mode (as mentioned in the previous tip), it also lets you apply the test shader to your objects and create quick test renders. (See Figure 8.3 for an example.)

When you're satisfied with the results, you can copy the Color channel from your test shader into the appropriate channel on your final shader using Ray Dream Studio's drag-and-drop capabilities. You'll find that this procedure will save you a lot of time and guesswork when working with more advanced shaders.

— *Craig Patchett*

FIGURE *By first building the Transparency channel for the shader shown on the left in the Color*
8.3 *channel, it was easy to generate quick test renders, as shown on the right.*

CONTROL THE INTENSITY OF YOUR CHANNELS

If you're using complex shader functions or operators in any of the non-Color channels, you can use the Multiply operator as a "volume" control to adjust the intensity of the function without having to change the function itself. The Multiply operator simply multiplies its two subshaders together. If you use a Value slider as one of the subshaders and your Shader function as the other (see Figure 8.4) you can adjust the intensity of your Shader function simply by changing the Value slider setting. A setting of 0 will turn your function off completely, a setting of 50 will turn it on halfway, and a setting of 100 will turn it on full strength.

— STEVE MCARDLE

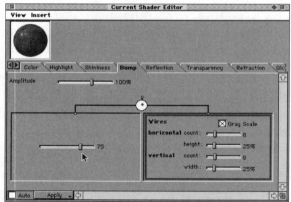

FIGURE **8.4** *A Value slider on one side of a Multiply operator can be used as a "volume" control.*

USE THE BROWSER TO COPY CHANNELS

Ray Dream Studio's drag-and-drop capabilities make it easy to copy subshaders within a channel or from one channel to another — just drag the shader onto the appropriate channel tab. But what if you want to copy, say, the Color channel into a subshader in the Bump channel, as was done for the example in Figure 8.4?

Ray Dream Studio makes this relatively painless, because each file in the Browser has its own editor. In other words, you can have two or more Shader editors open at the same time, which means you can copy any nested component from a Shader Document in the Browser to any nested component of your current Shader editor (or other Browser Document) and vice versa.

You can also store specific shader channels, no matter how many layers deep, as separate Shader Documents for later use. To do this, simply delete the components in the channels you don't wish to keep, thus leaving an "unmodified channel" in it's place, and then drag the resulting shader into the Browser, if it's not already there. It helps if you create specific folders for such things so you won't mistakenly edit any shaders you want to keep intact and so you'll know where to find your custom shaders and semi-shaders.

When you drag a shader with information in only one or a few channels from the Shader Browser onto an object or another shader, only the contents of the channels containing information in that shader will be applied to the destination object. This means you can change just an object or shader's bump, color, glow or any combination of the above and more without affecting the rest of the shader.

Copying and swapping subshaders in this manner instead of just recreating them in the new channel is a real time-saver when you're working with complex nested shader components, especially when certain aspects of the nested components need to match up for alignment purposes, or when the nested components and mixes are complex or just difficult to navigate to.

Something that has proven to be very useful is the creation and maintenance of a "Scratch Pad" shader folder. This folder serves as the container for shaders you create from bits and pieces of other shaders and that you want to store somewhere temporarily. By maintaining a folder of this nature, you always have somewhere to place your scratch components without fear of overwriting other favorite shaders.

— *RICHARD BUCCI & JOHN W. SLEDD*

REFLECT SOMETHING

When creating reflective surfaces, especially highly reflective surfaces such as chrome and glass, make sure you give your surfaces something to reflect. While this may seem obvious, reflective objects often extend the camera range to the side of and behind the camera, in which case you need to extend your modeling area beyond what appears within the production frame. You can see the difference this makes by looking at the example images shown in Figures 8.5 and 8.6. Figure 8.5 is limited to objects that appear on-camera. Figure 8.6 includes additional off-camera objects to create more realistic reflections.

You can also enhance reflections using the Reflected Background option in the Effects tab of your Scene Settings palette, but the way this feature works makes it difficult to use to create realistic reflections for anything other than simple background-type images (for example, clouds, color gradients and so

FIGURE
8.5 *Reflective surfaces don't look their best unless they have something to reflect.*

FIGURE
8.6 *You may need to add additional off-camera objects to your scene in order to create realistic reflections.*

on). Keep in mind, however, that RealVR renders do a great job in the Reflected Background option. If you have to model a complete room today, do a RealVR rendering of it so you'll have a quick-something to reflect in the simple scene you have to do tomorrow.

If your reflective object is flat or reflective in only a limited area, you might also try creating a large flat or curved surface, applying an image map to it, and positioning it just out of camera range so it is reflected in the object. Where possible, however, your best bet is to add additional models to your scene. Even simple ones, appropriately chosen, will add to the believability of the scene.

— *DEREK CARLIN, JOHNATHAN BANTA & JOHN W. SLEDD*

USE COLOR IN THE REFLECTION CHANNEL

Unless a surface is perfectly reflective, its color will be evident in its reflections. As a result, you'll find that a shader will give you richer, more realistic reflections if you copy its color into the Reflection channel. You can use the Multiply operator to control the strength of the reflection (as explained earlier in this chapter) if you're using a light color and low reflectivity, or the Add operator if you're using a dark color and high reflectivity.

— *RANDY HOLLINGSWORTH*

CHANGE THE DEFAULT APPLY MODE

Two modes are used to apply a shader to an object. The Apply Non-Empty Channels mode applies only those shader channels that contain settings, leaving the other channels with the settings of the object's previous shader. This is useful when you want to modify the Bump channel, for example, without affecting the other channels. The Apply All Channels mode completely replaces the object's previous shader with the one you're applying. (See Figure 8.7.)

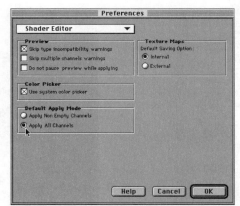

FIGURE *You can change the Default Apply mode*
8.7 *for both the Shader Editor and the*
Shader Browser.

If you hold down the **Apply** button in the **Shader Editor** or **Shader Document** window, you can select one of the two modes from the menu that appears. If you just click the **Apply** button, however, or apply the shader by dragging the shader preview from the **Shader editor**, **Shader Document** or **Browser** window to an object in the **Perspective**, **Hierarchy** or **Modeling** window, then the shader will be applied using the default mode, which is initially set to **Apply Non-Empty Channels**.

Depending on how you work with shaders, you may find it useful to change the default mode to **Apply All Channels**. You can do this by changing the **Default Apply mode** setting in the **Shader editor** sections of the **Preferences** dialog box. (See Figure 8.7.)

— *STEPHANIE ARVIZU*

USE IMAGE MAPS AS MASKS

If you set up a Mix operator with a grayscale or black-and-white Texture Map as the mix function, the Texture Map will act as a mask for the two mix functions. In Figure 8.8, for example, the initials RDH are masked out of a dark marble subshader and overlaid on top of a light marble subshader, complete with antialiased edges. (The original texture map file was antialiased.)

FIGURE **8.8** *Texture Maps can be used as masks.*

While the same effect could be accomplished in an image-editing program and brought into Ray Dream Studio as a simple Texture Map, doing it this way has several advantages. First, a grayscale Texture Map takes a lot less memory than a full-color one. Second, you can mix procedural shaders rather than limit yourself to a single bitmapped Texture Map. (Chapter 2 pointed out the advantages of this.) Third, the same mask can be used in multiple channels to create complex effects. Finally, since a Texture Map can be a movie, this technique opens up a whole range of possibilities when used in your animations.

— *RICK GRECO*

ADJUST SLIDER SETTINGS FROM THE KEYBOARD

This is a simple tip that will make the process of setting up your shaders a lot easier: Any of Ray Dream Studio's Slider controls can be controlled from your keyboard for greater precision and ease of use. Just click on a slider to activate it, then use the cursor control keys and/or the number keys to adjust it.

Pressing the **Right** or **Up** arrow [or the **plus** (+) key] will increase the slider value by one. Pressing the **Down** or **Left** arrow key [or the **hyphen** (-) key] will decrease the slider value by one. Pressing the **Home** key will set it to zero, while pressing the **End** key will set it to its highest value. The number keys will move the slider a certain percentage along its range, with 1 being 10% of the highest value, 2 being 20% and 0 being 100% — the same as pressing **End**.

— *STEPHANIE ARVIZU*

TRY DIFFERENT MAPPING MODES

If a shader doesn't look right after you've applied it to an object, try using a different Mapping Mode. Mapping Modes are accessed by selecting an object, then clicking on the **Mapping Mode** tab in the **Properties** palette (select **Properties** from the **Windows** menu or type **Command/Ctrl-T**) The Mapping Mode determines how shaders and 3D Paint tools are applied to an object. (See Figure 8.9.) Changing modes can make a big difference in how a shader looks on an object. Read the corresponding section in the *Ray Dream Studio User Guide* to brush up on the basics, then experiment with several different objects and shaders to see how the different modes work. You may find that this single tip alone can solve a lot of your shader problems.

— *ROBERT LOMINSKI*

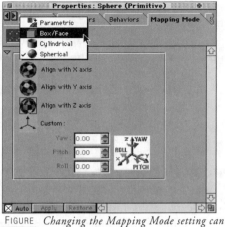

FIGURE
8.9
Changing the Mapping Mode setting can make a big difference in how a shader appears on an object.

ALWAYS SHADE AT THE MASTER LEVEL

OK, so perhaps I've said this 400 times in the book already, but I really mean it. Applying your shaders at the Master level will save you lots of heartache in the future. No, you don't always have to apply your shaders at the Master level, but it's a great habit to get into; and the day you don't, you'll most likely wish you had.

— JOHN W. SLEDD

THE WHITE IS INVISIBLE OPTION VERSUS A MASK

A lot of people have asked me when to use the White Is Invisible option rather than a mask. For a start, let me just say that it's typically not an either/or situation but most often a matter of using both — that is, if you want to get the most out of the option. The only time I can think of in which the White Is Invisible option should be used and a mask shouldn't is when you have a odd-shaped, non-antialiased logo or texture that you want to apply to an object, but you want the object's primary shader to show through around the edges of your paint-shaped logo.

Since a paint shape shader's Transparency channel carries through to the underlying shader if there is any component in it whatsoever — in other words, if you simply place a mask in the Transparency channel of a paint shape, you'll just cut a hole in your underlying object — you must use a White Is Invisible option in your color channel so that the area around your logo will be ignored. You would then delete any component in your Transparency channel to leave the channel as an "unmodified channel," which means there's nothing in it to use, so that your underlying shader's transparency settings show through.

The key comparison here is that White Is Invisible completely ignores solid-white pixels, whereas a grayscale mask offers a range of levels where black is 0 and white is 100. So even where you have white in a mask, it's as though you were assigning a value of 0 to that area of the image. On the other hand, having areas of pure white in a texture map that has the White Is Invisible option checked is like saying everything that is 100% white will be treated as an "unmodified channel," which means that everything that is 100% white will be ignored and anything in the shader under it will be visible through these areas of 100% white.

Another tidbit that should help you differentiate between the two is knowing that masks are usually used to mix two components of a Shader channel, whereas the White Is Invisible option works within a single Texture Map component.

Keep in mind that White Is Invisible ignores only pure, 100%-white pixels. Pixels which are 99.9% white or darker will show up. This means that images with antialiased edges will have a halo around them when applied with the White Is Invisible option checked. What do you do when this happens and you have no way of getting a non-antialiased version of your logo? You use a mask along with the White Is Invisible option. Turn to the next chapter to find out how. I've included a tutorial with several variations of the White Is Invisible option in use.

— John W. Sledd

Shader Recipes

Those of you who have experience with other 3D applications know how incredible RDS's Shader editor is in comparison. Those of you whose 3D experience has been mostly with RDS most likely take the Shader editor for granted — I know I did until I gained experience with other 3D apps.

As soon as you grasp the basic concepts behind building a shader in Ray Dream Studio, it suddenly becomes clear that there isn't much you can't do with shaders. From realistic imitations of real-life surfaces to wild creations that previously existed only in your imagination, Ray Dream Studio's shaders are capable of almost anything. The trick is in understanding how to combine all the different features shaders offer in a way that gives you the results you're looking for.

This chapter and the next one will show you a variety of different ways to get the most out of shaders, from step-by-step breakdowns of specific shader effects to general techniques that can be applied to a variety of shader types. By the time you've finished reading through these two chapters and experimenting with the information they offer, you'll have already built the foundation for your own shader library.

This chapter serves up a variety of shader recipes that explore different shader features and capabilities. Follow step by step to expand your shader library or use the recipes as a learning tool that will help you learn how to build complex shaders of your own design.

RECIPES

When it comes down to creating a specific shader, the first thing you need to do is make sure you understand all the capabilities that Ray Dream Studio's Shader editor has to offer. Brush up on each shader component and the ways in which they can be combined, along with the effect of each Shader channel, by rereading the "Shading Objects" and "Creating Shaders" chapters of the *Ray Dream Studio 5 User Guide*. The recipes presented in this chapter assume that you have at least a basic understanding of shader components and channels; the first recipe will walk you through the creation process to help you get up to speed.

While you do have the option of just taking the recipes in this chapter and using them to create specific shaders for your shader library, I would encourage you also to study the way they are put together and the way each uses the different shader components and channels. Each shader in this chapter has been included not only for the effect it creates (although each shader is useful in itself) but also for the way in which it uses different techniques to achieve that effect. By gaining an understanding of how these shaders work, you will start to develop the skills necessary to develop your own shaders, which is what this chapter is all about.

FIRST THINGS FIRST

Since the first edition of this book, I've received many requests for a tour of the Shader editor and its various components, so here it is. After we've finished, you should have more than a decent understanding of what you're doing during the rest of the recipes and tutorials in this chapter. By "understanding," I mean that you'll know why you're putting a certain function here or why this operator goes there. So, shader kiddies, put on your thinking caps, 'cause here we go.

Step One

Launch RDS and create a new file. Once the file is open, insert a sphere primitive into your scene in any way you please. Select the sphere if it's not already selected, and choose **Current Shader Editor** from the **Windows** menu. The **Shader editor** should pop up, looking similar to Figure 9.1.

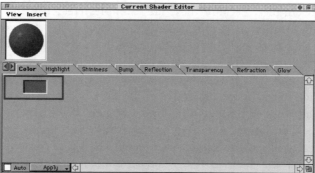

FIGURE **9.1** *The Current Shader editor with the default shader that RDS always assigns to new objects.*

Step Two

Click on the **Insert** menu at the top of the Shader editor and notice that Color has a checkmark by it. Take a moment to go through your options. Ignore the Composite and Global Mix stuff at the very top — we'll cover that later. Just take a look at your other options. Figure 9.2 shows what you should be look-

FIGURE   *This is a list of the components*
9.2   *available for a channel in your Ray*
          Dream Studio Shader editor.

ing at. If you haven't purchased Rayflect, Inc.'s Four Elements package, you won't see the Four Elements Shaders option. Likewise, you may not have the COM examples, because these are examples created using the Ray Dream's Software Developers Kit for those who wish to create their own shaders. As an artist, feel free to experiment with these but be aware that they are for example purposes only and are unsupported by MetaCreations.

You may even have other components installed that do not appear here (these were all that were available at the time of this writing) but that's OK — they'll all work in basically the same way. Let's take a few moments to go over the ones that shipped with Ray Dream Studio and so are supported.

First in line is the Value component. The Value component places a slider in your current channel. The Value component simply adds to your channel a controllable spectrum of black to white. Go ahead and select the **Value component** and watch what happens.

You should now have a Value operator in your Color channel. The slider should be at 0, and your Shader preview should have turned into a solid black sphere with a tiny white highlight. This is because you have essentially changed the color of this shader to black because a value of 0 equals black. Now click on the slider and move it to **50** (you can also double-click the slider and manually enter 50). Now your Shader editor should look like Figure 9.3. Your Sphere preview should be a medium gray color, because a value of 50 equals a 50% gray.

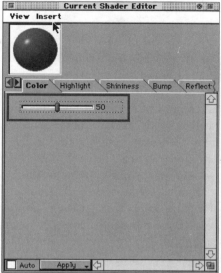

Figure A value of 50 is the same as a 50%
9.3   gray color.

Those of you out there who use image editing apps with alpha channel capabilities should hear a teeny bell in the back of your head going ding ding ding.

Now go ahead and slide the Value slider up to **100**. This will turn your shader Color channel to a solid white, because a value of 100 equals pure white. This is the basis on which all shader operations in RDS work. Every component is based on a color or mixture of colors, and most of these, such as the Functions, are limited to gray values just like this one. It is important to understand that you could just as easily drop a Color component in here and make it white for exactly the same results. The reason you would want to use a Value slider is simply because it's less information to deal with than a color if a spectrum of black to white is all you need, which is often the case in the other channels. Of course, this completely depends on how your own brain works. If you understand colors better, then by all means, do what works the best for you.

This is a very basic usage of the Value component. In the Color channel, most people would simply drop a color and make it white because that's what would make most sense to them (certainly makes the most sense to me), but the Value component has many other uses for mixing and controlling the appearance of other components in all of the channels. For example, a Value of 50 in the Transparency channel would make the object 50% transparent. Likewise, a color of 50% gray would also make the object 50% transparent but it's often easier to just drop the Value component in there and go with the numbers. Stay tuned for more on this.

Now let's go ahead and move on to the Color component. Please don't confuse this with the Color channel. Any component can be inserted into any channel. The Color channel is simply the channel that controls your object's color, whereas a Color component is what you use when you want to insert a flat color into any of your channels. Go ahead and insert a Color component into the Color channel. This will replace your Value component with the default red color. Double-click on the **color swatch** and play around with the color picker. This Color component works exactly like the Value component except that it offers a hue value in addition to the gray values found in the Value component. You can use the Color component in any of the Shader channels (and branches thereof), but in many instances, only the gray value or luminosity value will be used. In other words, the channel (or branch of the channel) will use only the gray equivalent of the color. The Bump channel is a good example to use here. The Bump channel doesn't care about hues or colors. All it cares about are white, black and the 254 levels of gray that fall in between. It reads 0 (or black) as low and 100 (or white) as high, and everything else simply falls in the middle. Don't let the fact that we're talking about 0 to 100 in the Value component but 256 levels of gray confuse you. Think of the 0-to-100 range as the percentage representation of 256 levels of gray. (See Figure 9.4.)

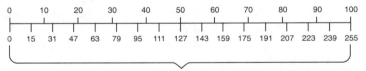

Notice that 0 is an actual level (black) and 255 is the top level (white),
so "Level 0" + 255 = 256 levels.

FIGURE   *This is how the 0-to-100 range stacks up to 256 levels of gray.*
9.4

Different color pickers refer to a color's value and hue differently, but basically the value or lightness of a color is the same as a gray value. To understand how this works, just think about how a black-and-white television displays colors. It doesn't; it displays the gray values of the colors. Or better yet, think about the grayscale images in this book. Most started out as color images, but once the color was removed, only the gray values remained.

The Color component can create interesting effects when placed in channels other than the Color channel. For example, a Color component placed in the Highlight channel will give the highlight the value of the gray value of the color and will also tint that highlight with the hue of the color. If you use the example of the Transparency channel above but with a Color component, the object would have a transparency equal to the color's gray value but would also be tinted with the hue of the color.

Now let's move on to the Texture Map component. This component allows you to place bitmaps into your Shader channels for use as base shaders, mixers or whatever you see fit. You can use color textures such as photographs and custom-painted textures, or grayscale and black-and-white textures. Placing a color or grayscale map into a Shader channel is like assigning a different Value or Color component for each pixel in the map. Feel free to import a Texture Map such as the RDH.JPG or RDHCOLOR.JPG files included on the CD-ROM in the folder for Chapter 9.

The Movie component is just like the Texture Map component except that you import . . . yep, you guessed it . . . movies. So not only do you get the range of values and hues available with the Texture Map component, you also get the ability to change those based on the different frames on your movie source file.

The next item in line is the Operators menu item. The operators give you tons of power because they are how you mix your various other components when a simple, one-component channel isn't enough. We're going to skip the lengthy explanation on operators right now because you really need to know what the other components do first. In Chapter 2 we talked quite a bit about pattern and natural functions, which are our next menu items. Feel free to drop one into your open Color channel. Pick something other than the formulas, though — why don't you make it easy on both of us and start by inserting a Checkers Pattern function. Notice now that your Sphere preview is covered in black-and-white checkers, as in Figure 9.5. This goes back to what I mentioned

FIGURE **9.5** *The Checkers function creates alternating values of 0 and 100.*

earlier about how the Value component was really the basis for all of the other components. What the Checkers function does is to set up a grid of squares with alternate values of 0 and 100. In the Color channel this equates to alternating colors of black and white. To get a better idea of what's going on here, go to the **Shader editor's View** menu and choose **Flat Preview**. This, as mentioned in Chapter 8, gives us a great representation of what's going on with our function before it gets wrapped around our 3D object. (See Figure 9.6.)

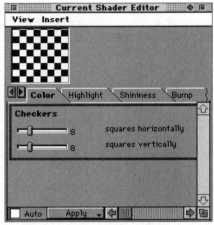

FIGURE **9.6** *Viewing the function in Flat Preview mode can give you a better idea of what you're doing.*

If you count your checkers and compare that to the settings, you'll see that you have eight squares running horizontally and eight squares running vertically. Change those values to two squares horizontally and six squares vertically, and watch how your preview updates. So what you're seeing in the preview window is exactly what would be mapped to your 3D object. Switch back to **Sphere preview** to see what I mean.

Notice how the Checkers function gives you values only of 0 and 100 (or white and black). The same is not true for all the functions. Insert a **Wire pattern function** to see what I mean. When you get the Wire function inserted, change the parameters to two horizontal wires and two vertical wires. Leave everything else the same, and you should wind up with a window-looking preview like the one in Figure 9.7. The Wires function does give you a mix of 0 and 100 at first, but by checking the Gray Scale checkbox, the Wires will then blend from black to white using gray values. Go ahead and click on that **Gray Scale** box, if you haven't already, and notice how your preview changes to blend the colors between the white and the black to make them much softer.

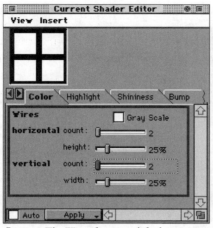

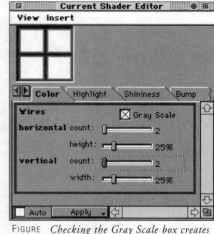

FIGURE **9.7** *The Wires function defaults to strict 0 and 100 values.*

FIGURE **9.8** *Checking the Gray Scale box creates a soft blend between the values.*

(See Figure 9.8.) Take note that when you use Wires in the Bump channel, you'll get a much more pleasing bump by checking that box.

Now go ahead and play around with the other functions. Insert a few Pattern and Natural functions to get an idea of what each looks like. Play around with the settings and bounce back between Flat and Sphere previews to see what the functions look like both ways. Basically what you should figure out here is that the Pattern and Natural functions are, for all practical purposes, creating a texture map that is placed on your model. The only difference is that the functions are calculated at rendering time, whereas a texture map is already there. Like a texture map, functions assign several different values across the surface of your model.

When you've finished playing here, move on to Step Three, and we'll toss some operators in there to see where the use of functions really shines.

Step Three

By now you should have a good idea of what the different components do, and especially what the functions do. You should be aware that the functions by themselves create only grayscale images. You might even be wondering what good that is. Well, here's where you find out. Now, while the component of your Color channel is selected, I'd like you to insert a **Mix Operator** into the Color channel. You should get what looks like Figure 9.9. This is called a *Shader Tree.*

Notice how the different boxes (or branches) have different comments in them, such as "Drop first shader here" or "Drop second shader here" and "Drop function here." You can ignore these comments. If you try to drop an

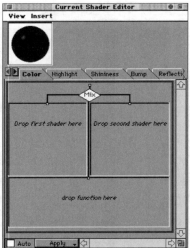

FIGURE
9.9 *A Mix operator in the color channel creates what is known as a Shader Tree.*

actual shader where it says to drop a shader, you'll get only part of that shader, so let's just look at these boxes as all the same for now. As you get more acquainted with how RDS works, you'll be able to make more sense of those.

Each of these boxes is just like the root level of the channel in which you were dropping components in the first part of this tutorial. The only real difference is that the Drop Function Here box can use only grayscale information. Are things starting to click yet? I hope so. I want you to take a moment to notice how these different boxes are selected. The first thing you should notice is that the entire Mix component (all three boxes and the little Mix diamond) has a gray box around it. Now I'd like to you click on the first box that says **Drop First Shader Here**, and notice that the entire Mix component deselects and that only the Drop First Shader Here box is selected. Just jump around from box to box and select them. I don't want you to put anything in any of them yet, just notice how they are selected. Whatever you have selected in your channel when you insert a component will be replaced by that component. So if you have all three boxes selected (do that by clicking anywhere outside the other three boxes), and you insert another component, you'll wipe out the entire Mix operator. However, if you have only one of the three boxes selected and you insert a component, only that box will be replaced by the inserted component. The exception to this rule comes when you insert another operator, such as Add or Multiply. When you do this with the entire Mix operator selected, you replace only the operator. The information in the two branches remains the same, but the Drop Function Here Box will disappear because it's not needed for the other operators. With that out of the way, lets make a tree, shall we? A Shader Tree, that is.

The first thing I want you to do is select the **Drop Function Here** box and the **Insert a Checkers function** from the Pattern Function menu item. This places the Checker function into the role of Mixer for the two branches. What you'll wind up with when you insert this function is exactly what you had when you inserted a Checkers function all by itself: A black-and-white checkered sphere. The reason for this is that, since you don't have anything in the two channels, you're not really mixing anything, so you just get the Checkers function all by itself. Now I'd like you to select the **Drop First Shader Here** box and insert a **Color component**. Now you should see that your black checkers have changed to red checkers. This must mean that values of 0 in the mixer are 100% of the left branch and values of 100 are 100% of the right branch. Now click on the color swatch you've just inserted and drag it over to the **Drop Second Shader Here** box. This will create a duplicate of the red color swatch in the LEFT branch of your Shader Tree, and your sphere will once again turn solid red. Since this is a waste of a good Shader Tree, double-click on the left color swatch and make it a nice dark-blue color. You should wind up with something similar to Figure 9.10. Change your view to **Flat preview**.

Now let's play around with some different components in the bottom box. You aren't really limited to functions here; whatever you put in here, whether it be a texture map, movie, Pattern function or value, will simply be the mixing

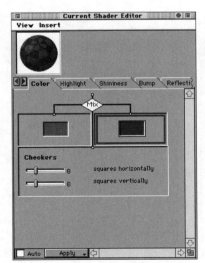

FIGURE *A simple Shader Tree in the*
9.10 *Color channel.*

function of the Mix operator. It will be what controls how the two sides of your tree interact with each other. Currently the Checkers function is defining which color should be where, but now we're going to make a different color out of our existing colors. First let's select the current **Checkers function** at the bottom of the tree and insert a **Value component**. What you'll wind up with here is a flat swatch of red in your Shader preview window. You can think of this Value component as the balance control on your stereo. If it's all the way to the left, you get 100% red, but move the Value slider to 50, and you'll get a nice shade of purple. This is because you're telling the tree to give you 50% of the left branch and 50% of the right branch. Likewise, if you slide the slider all the way over to the 100 mark, you'll get 100% of the blue in the right channel. Pretty simple concept, eh? Just to drive this point home, insert a **Gradient Pattern function** into the box where your Value component is. You'll now see how your colors blend from red to blue. Feel free to play around with inserting a few more patterns and such into that bottom box. Also feel free to tweak around with their parameters to see what you wind up with. You should now have a pretty good grasp of the concepts behind the basic Shader Tree structure and what those mixers mean.

Step Four

Now let's go back and reinsert that **Gradient function** as the mixer. This time, however, we're going to mix things up a bit (pun intended, of course). You should now have a Shader editor that looks like Figure 9.11.

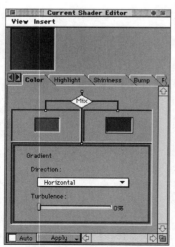

FIGURE
9.11 *A simple Shader Tree with a Gradient mixer.*

Now we're going to make this shader tree a little more complex. Start by selecting the box with the red color component in it. Now I'd like you to insert an **Add operator**. This will give you a blend of gray to blue instead of the red to blue we had previously. (See Figure 9.12.) It's gray because we haven't done anything to it yet. Double-click on the left branch (the one with the big gray swatch in it), and you'll get Figure 9.13.

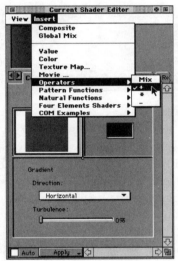

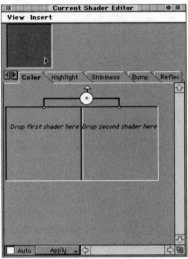

FIGURE *Inserting an Add operator*
9.12 *into the left branch.*

FIGURE *Jumping into the subshader.*
9.13

What we've done here is to jump into the subshader of the current branch of the Shader Tree. To give you a better idea of what's going on, click on the little black **arrow** that is now in your Shader preview window and select the **preview** of the gray-to-blue blend. Now go to your Shader editor's View menu and select **All Levels**. This expands each of the nested shaders so that you can see all your components at the same time. This is very handy and makes shader creation much easier, but it's practical only if you have a big monitor. Those of you with smaller monitors may find it easier just to jump in and out of your subshaders as needed. Remember, though, that the key to keeping track of where you are is that little black arrow that will pop up in your Shader preview when you're in a nested shader.

We now have a relatively complex Shader Tree. It doesn't look that complex because we haven't made much of the Add operator in the left branch. To do so, let's add a Color component in the left branch of the subshader and a Spots function (it's in the Natural Functions menu) in the right branch. Double-click on the **Color component** and make it a very light blue. Now

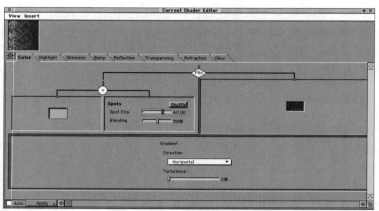

FIGURE   *A moderately complex Shader channel.*
9.14

adjust the **Spots function** so that the spot size is **60** and the blending is **53%**. Figure 9.14 shows what the shader should look like and just exactly how quickly the All Levels feature can eat up your screen real estate. Compare it to Figure 9.15, which is what you get with the View>One Level option. It's much more compact and even gives you a good preview of your other branch but at the expense of having to jump in and out of your subshaders.

The Add operator added the gray values of the Spot function to the light-blue color. As you can see, this creates a dappled look in the subshader for the

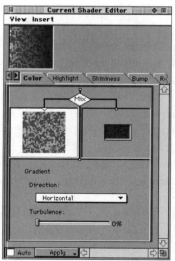

FIGURE   *The much more compact*
9.15 *View One Level option.*

left side of the main Shader Tree, which then blends into the solid blue color on the right side of the main tree.

Step Five

That about concludes this basic shader creation tour. We stayed within the Color channel because, as we mentioned in Chapter 8, that's the easiest way to preview your settings. Now I'd like to encourage you to experiment a bit. Add different components as your mixer. See how many nested shaders you can create without going batty waiting for the redraws or getting lost in the endless maze of nested subshaders. The possibilities really are limitless. And when you've finished there, remember that you have seven more channels to play with. Different combinations in the different channels can build just about anything your twisted mind can cook up. Not everything has to be this complex, and some other effects may require even more complexity, as you will soon see. The key is to understand how the Shader editor works. It's really a very basic yet extremely powerful tool. Continue on with the other recipes in this chapter and hopefully you'll get the hang of what's going on very quickly.

— *JOHN W. SLEDD*

BEACHBALL

This beachball shader is an excellent example of how to use Shader Trees to accomplish things that couldn't be done using a single-level shader. By nesting multiple Checkers functions to create, in effect, checkers of checkers, this shader extends the usual two-color limit of the Checkers function to eight. (Each stripe in Figure 9.16 is a different color.) This principle of nesting can be applied to other functions as well and is the key to building complexity and detail into your shaders. You'll see other examples of it throughout this section.

© 1998 Steve McArdle

FIGURE **9.16** *By nesting the Checkers function, you can extend the number of colors that it can mix.*

You should at least be familiar with creating nested shaders (especially if you lived through that tour) but we'll walk you through this one step by step anyway. Subsequent recipes in this chapter, however, will show and describe the various shader levels and leave it up to you to recreate them.

With the exception of default settings (Value slider set to 50) in the Highlight and Shininess channels, this shader is built entirely in the Color channel. A complete view of the Shader Tree for the Color channel is shown in Figure 9.17. We'll build it from scratch, starting from the top and working our way down the branches.

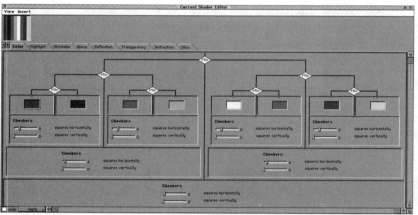

FIGURE 9.17 *This Shader Tree for the beachball shader is relatively straightforward. What makes it work is the settings for each Checkers function.*

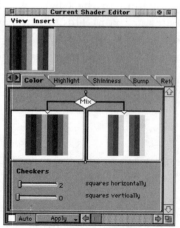

FIGURE 9.18 *The top level of the final beachball Shader Tree.*

Figure 9.18 shows the top level of the shader, which mixes together two four-color subshaders using the Checkers function to create the eight-color shader.

Step One

Create a new document, insert a sphere to be your beachball and open up the **Current Shader editor**. Choose **Flat Preview** right away because it will really help you get the hang of this shader. Now click on the **Color** tab and insert a **Mix operator**. Click on the **Drop Function Here** box at the bottom of the mix to highlight it and insert a **Checkers Pattern function**. Set the sliders to **2** squares horizontally and **0** squares vertically. Your shader editor should look like Figure 9.19.

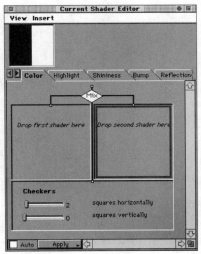

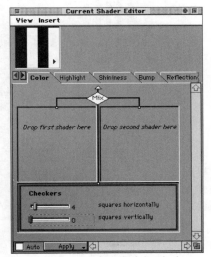

FIGURE **9.19** *Here's where we start.*

FIGURE **9.20** *The second level of the Shader Tree.*

Step Two

Select the **Drop First Shader Here** box at the top left of the mix to highlight it, and insert another **Mix operator** (yes, just as you did in Step One). Double-click on the **square** to jump into the subshader.

Now select the **Drop Function Here** box, just as in Step One, and insert another **Checkers function**; only this time, set your Checkers parameters to **4** squares horizontally and **0** squares vertically. Your Shader editor should look like Figure 9.20.

Step Three

Select the **Drop First Shader Here** box in your current level and insert yet another **Mix operator**. Double-click on it to jump into the third level of your

Shader Tree. Select the **Drop Function Here** box at the bottom and insert another **Checkers function**. Give this one the settings of **8** squares horizontally and **0** squares vertically. Your Shader editor should look like Figure 9.21.

Now it's time to add some color. Select the **Drop First Shader Here** box and insert a **Color component**. Double-click on the **color swatch** and make it the first of your eight colors for your beachball; click **OK**. Now drag that Color component into the **Drop Second Shader Here** box. Double-click on it and make it the second of your eight colors. Your Shader editor should look something like Figure 9.22.

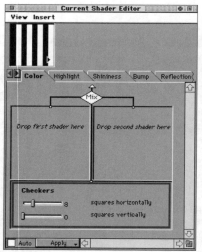

FIGURE *Here's where we start.*
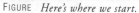
9.21

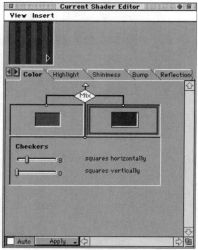

FIGURE *We're finally adding some color.*
9.22

Step Four

The rest of the shader is easy, but pay attention to what happens as we jump from the third to the second to the third levels in our Shader Tree. Click on the little black **arrow** in the **Shader Editor** preview and select the second level, as shown in Figure 9.23.

Now you should be looking at the second level of your tree. Notice how you have a preview in the left branch and Drop Second Shader Here in the right branch still. Also take notice of your Shader preview in the top left corner. Notice how you're alternating the two stripes of color you've just created with one stripe of white. (See Figure 9.24.) This is because the two colors you've just created appear only where your Checkers function is black in the current level. We're now going to add two more colors to where the white stripes are by selecting the **left branch** and dragging it to the **right branch** where it says **Drop Second Shader Here**. This makes a duplicate of that nested

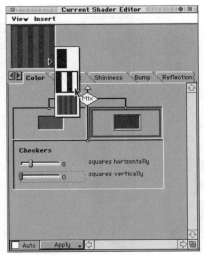

FIGURE
9.23
Selecting the second level.

shader in the right branch. Now double-click on the **right branch** that you've just copied and, when it opens, change your colors to the third and fourth colors that you want in your beach ball. When you've finished, jump back down to the second level, as shown in Figure 9.25, and you'll see how you have two repeating patterns of your four colors.

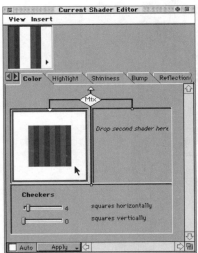

FIGURE
9.24
The two colors you've just created now alternate with stripes of white.

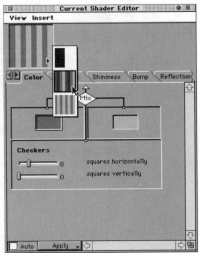

FIGURE
9.25
After you've changed the duplicated colors, jump back to the second level of your Shader Tree.

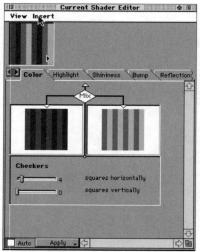

FIGURE
9.26
The second level completed.

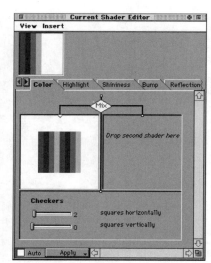

FIGURE
9.27
Back to the first level with the first four colors done.

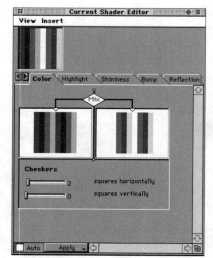

FIGURE
9.28
What your final first level should look like after changing your last four colors.

Step Five

Figure 9.26 is what the second level of this particular branch should look like. Now click on that little black **arrow** again and jump back down to the first level of your shader tree. Figure 9.27 shows what you should see. Notice that you now have your four colored stripes followed by one large stripe of white. This large stripe of white is just begging to be filled with four more colors. Add these four colors by clicking on the **left branch** and dragging it into the **Drop Second Shader Here** box in the right branch. This copies the multiple nested shaders for the left branch into the right branch. Now all you have to do is to go into each of these nested shaders and change their colors, just as you did in Step Four, to get your fifth, sixth, seventh and eighth colors, until you wind up with Figure 9.28.

— *STEVE McARDLE AND JOHN W. SLEDD*

CERAMIC TILES

As we mentioned in Chapter 2, you can easily create complex tile effects using a single shader on a flat surface, as shown in Figure 9.29. This shader is an excellent example of how to combine different functions (Checkers and Wires, in this case) and use multiple channels to build a complex effect. It's also a good example of how you can use shaders to simplify the modeling process; the tiles could also have been created by modeling individual tiles and duplicating them. You'll see several examples throughout this chapter of how the Bump channel and the Transparency channel can be used as modeling tools.

FIGURE
9.29 *Checkers and Wires combined in multiple channels can be effective.*

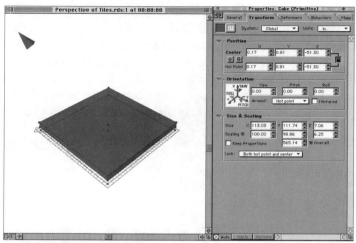

FIGURE
9.30 *Setting up the ceramic scene.*

Step One

Let's start this round by creating a new file, inserting a cube and sizing it as in Figure 9.30 so you'll have something to drop the shader onto. Now click on the object with the **Eyedropper tool** to open the **Current Shader editor**.

The best place to start in creating the ceramic tile shader is to build the Shader Tree for the Color channel. (See Figure 9.31.) This tree mixes a Checker subshader with a grout color using the Wires function. The different levels of the Shader Tree are shown in more detail in Figures 9.32 and 9.33.

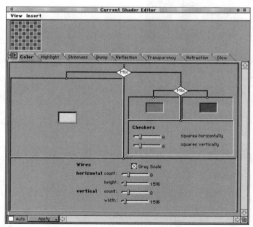

FIGURE
9.31 *The Shader Tree for the tile Color channel mixes Checkers and Wires.*

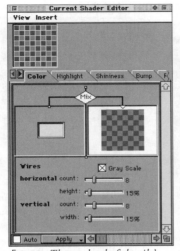

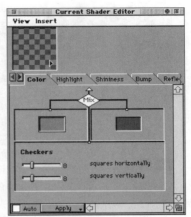

FIGURE **9.32** *The top level of the tile's Color channel tree.*

FIGURE **9.33** *The right subshader from Figure 9.32.*

You can use whatever colors you like for the grout and the checkers pattern. We won't grade you on color theory right now, but if you'd like to match the example, I used a gray and a brown for the checkers and a lighter gray for the grout.

Step Two

Leave the Highlight and Shininess channels at their default values (**Value** slider set to **50**). The Bump channel is used to raise the tiles above the grout using the Wires function. The Shader Tree for the Bump channel is shown in Figure 9.34 and in detail in Figures 9.35 and 9.36.

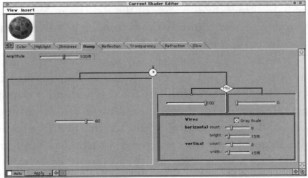

FIGURE **9.34** *The Shader Tree for the tile Bump channel uses Wires to raise the tiles above the grout.*

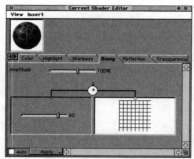

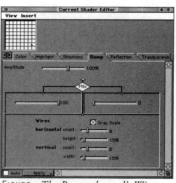

FIGURE **9.35** The top level of the tile's Bump channel uses a Multiply operator to control the tile height.

FIGURE **9.36** The Bump channel's Wires subshader uses the Gray Scale option to curve the tiles' edges.

Notice two things about this channel. First, a Multiply operator is used to control the height of the tiles. (See Figure 9.35 above.) Increasing the Value slider on the left of the operator will raise the height of the tiles; decreasing it will lower the height. Second, in the Wires subshader (see Figure 9.36 above), the Gray Scale option is turned on to curve the edges of the tiles. Turning the Gray Scale option off will give you tiles with perpendicular edges. Try it and see. You might also want to play around with the new Amplitude slider. This will give you a deeper and shallower bump, depending on the setting. In fact, you most likely won't even need the Multiply operator here if you're using RDS 5; I've left it in for those out there still using RDS 4.

Step Three

The final step in creating the ceramic tiles shader is to create the Reflection channel. The challenge here is to make the tiles reflective while keeping the grout nonreflective. The Shader Tree to accomplish this is shown in Figure 9.37.

Figure 9.38 shows the top level of the Reflection Shader Tree. This level is another example of how Multiply can be used as a "volume control" for a complex shader. Increasing or decreasing the slider will increase or decrease the amount of reflection. This makes it easy to test different amounts of reflection without having to change all the color values in your subshader.

Figure 9.39 shows the subshader for the Reflection channel. It's the same as the Color channel except that it uses black (a Value of 0) for the grout color. This results in the grout having no reflection. The tiles' color is used in the right subshader to prevent the rendered color from washing out. (Try replacing the subshader with a Value slider set to 100 and see what happens.)

— *STEVE MCARDLE*

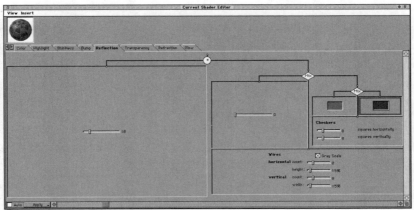

FIGURE 9.37 *The Shader Tree for the tile Reflection channel mixes Checkers and Wires to create reflective tiles and nonreflective grout.*

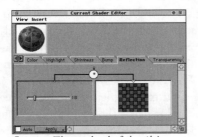

FIGURE 9.38 *The top level of the tile's Reflection channel also uses a Multiply operator.*

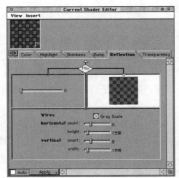

FIGURE 9.39 *The Reflection channel sub-shader is the same as the Color channel, except for black grout.*

RIPPLED WATER

Realistic water is perhaps one of the most sought-after 3D effects and also one of the most elusive — unless, of course, you have Rayflect, Inc.'s Four Elements pack or the following tutorial. One solution is to use texture maps in the Bump channel to create a rippled effect, but this approach brings with it all the shortcomings of texture maps that were discussed in Chapter 2. A better approach is to use Ray Dream Studio's built-in functions to create a procedural shader, which is easier to do than you might think. Figure 9.40 shows the results, while Figure 9.41 shows the Bump channel that makes it work.

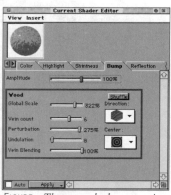

FIGURE **9.40** *A realistic water effect such as this can be creating using a surprisingly simple procedural shader.*

FIGURE **9.41** *The water shader creates its effect almost entirely from this basic Bump channel mix.*

There really isn't much to this shader. The Wood function creates the rippled effect (create another shader with this Wood function in the Color channel to see what it looks like) while the Amplitude slider controls how strong the ripples are. You can experiment with the Wood function settings to get different effects. A Perturbation setting of 300 and an Undulation setting of 5, for example, will give you choppy water. The Cellular function can also be used in place of or in addition to the Wood for great water effects.

Several other channels are used to complete the effect. The Color channel should contain a blue or aqua color, the Highlight channel should contain a Value of 40, the Shininess channel should contain a Value of 70, and the Reflection channel should contain a Value of 50. If you want your water to be transparent, try adding a Value of 6 to 9 in the Refraction channel and a Value of 30 or higher in the Transparency channel, depending on how murky you want the water to appear.

— *STEVE MCARDLE*

CORK

As mentioned earlier, Ray Dream Studio's shader trees are especially good at adding detail to shaders, which is essential for developing realistic shaders. (Reality is almost never simple.) This Cork shader is an excellent introduction to this technique and uses several shader levels to create a very realistic effect, as shown in Figure 9.42.

FIGURE
9.42   *Nested shaders are the key to the subtle details that give this Cork shader a realistic look.*

Step One

Most of the detail for this shader is in the Color channel, with a little help from the Bump channel. The Shader Tree for the Color channel is shown in Figure 9.43. Although it's not overly complicated, the way the different levels are built and combined give it a complex look.

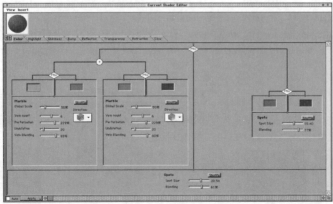

FIGURE
9.43   *While the Shader Tree for the Cork shader's Color channel isn't overly complicated, it adds enough extra detail through nesting to give the shader a complex look.*

The top level of the Color channel is a Mix that combines two subshaders using the Spots function to create the cork effect. (See Figure 9.44.) You can adjust the **Spot Size** slider to change the scale of the effect and also use the **Shuffle** button to try slightly different variations on the way the spots appear.

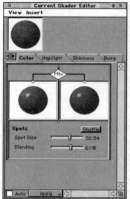

FIGURE **9.44** *The top level for the Color channel is a Spots mix.*

Step Two

In this step you'll build the left subshader for the top level, which combines two wood-like subshaders using the Add (+) operator. (See Figure 9.45.) The Add operator combines the two subshaders by adding their values. This has the effect of blending the two and is a great way to add a little extra complexity to a shader or subshader. Figures 9.46 and 9.47 show the subshaders that are used in this mix. Figure 9.46 uses the Marble function to create a burled wood effect, while Figure 9.47 uses the Marble function with two similar colors to create a subtle flecked effect. When these two subshaders are combined, the

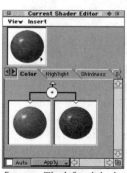

FIGURE **9.45** *The left subshader for Figure 9.44.*

FIGURE **9.46** *The left subshader for Figure 9.45 is a simple burled wood effect.*

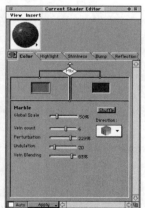

FIGURE **9.47** *The right subshader for Figure 9.45 is a subtle flecked effect.*

result is a more realistic wood effect than the subshader in Figure 9.46 alone could offer.

In both of these subshaders, and in any shader that uses the Marble or Wood functions, the Global Scale slider can be used to adjust the scale of the shader relative to the object you are applying it to.

Step Three

The last step in building the Color channel component is to create the right subshader for the top level. (See Figure 9.48.) This subshader is a simple Mix using the Spots function to combine two contrasting colors into a flecked pattern that will add a composite look to the cork when mixed with the wood subshader we've just built. Once again, you can change the scale of this subshader by adjusting the **Spot Size slider**. You can also give the spots a softer or harder look by adjusting the **Blending slider**.

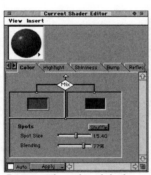

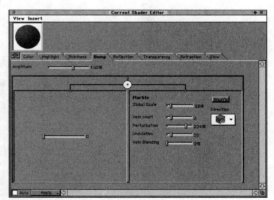

FIGURE **9.48** *The right subshader for Figure 9.44 adds a composite look.*

FIGURE **9.49** *The Bump channel for the cork shader uses the Marble function with minimal Vein Blending to create a perforated effect.*

Step Four

The Bump channel completes the primary cork effect by using the Marble function to add a perforated look to the cork surface. (See Figure 9.49.) This is accomplished by using a high Perturbation setting and a low Vein Blending setting. Notice also how the Add operator is used with a Value slider to control the depth of the effect. Try changing each of these settings to see how the shader is affected.

Complete the shader by adding a **Value** of **18** to the **Highlight channel** and a **Value** of **8** to the **Shininess channel**.

— *STEVE MCARDLE*

WOOD

If you've been following along with the rest of this section, it shouldn't come as a surprise to learn that the secret to creating a realistic wood shader is to build detail using nested subshaders. Both the Wood and Marble functions can be used to create wood shaders, but neither will be very effective unless you nest them to build complex details into the shader. (A close look at any wood surface will show that there is more involved than simply swirling two colors together.) You can do this by building details into the grain using the Mix operator or simply by building a layered effect using the Add operator. The shader in Figure 9.50 uses the layered approach. You can find an example of the other approach in the Marble shader presented later in this section.

© 1998 Steve McArdle

FIGURE **9.50**   *The secret to realistic Wood shaders is to build detail using nested subshaders.*

Step One

Let's create a new file, as in the past, and insert some object to apply the shader to. With the object selected, open the **Current Shader** editor. This wood shader is built entirely in the **Color** channel, although you could vary it by adding a **Bump** channel and other qualities. The example in Figure 9.50 above adds a **Value** of **90** in the **Highlight** channel, a **Value** of **50** in the **Shininess** channel, and a **Value** of **18** in the **Reflection** channel to add a polished effect, so if you want to create that exact wood, go ahead and enter those values now. Figure 9.51 shows the completed Shader Tree for the Color channel. As you can see, it builds a layered effect by combining four Wood functions using the Add operator.

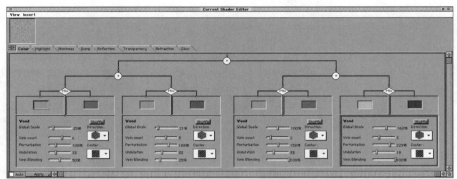

FIGURE
9.51
The Shader Tree for the Wood shader's Color channel is a good example of how to build levels of detail using the Add operator.

With your **Current Shader** editor open, insert an **Add** operator into the Color channel. Select the **Drop First Shader Here** box and insert another **Add** operator. Your Shader editor should look like Figure 9.52. Now double-click on the left branch, and you'll jump to level 2. Select the left branch and insert a **Mix** operator, as in Figure 9.53. Jump into that newly created branch, and you'll see an empty Mix operator tree. Start this tree by inserting a color component in the **Drop First Shader Here** box. Make that color a light blonde wood color and click **OK**. Now drag that color swatch into the **Drop Second Shader Here** box and change the color to a darker version of the first. When you've done that, click on the **Drop Function Here** box, insert a **Wood Natural** function,

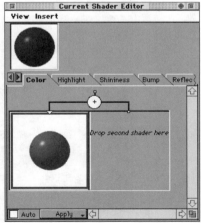

FIGURE
9.52
The top level of the Color channel being built.

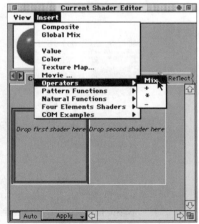

FIGURE
9.53
Adding the left subshader for Figure 9.52.

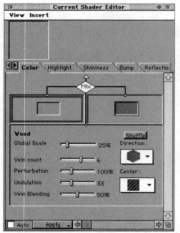

FIGURE **9.54** *Creating the first Wood subshader.*

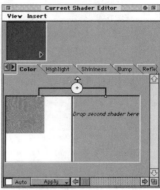

FIGURE **9.55** *Getting ready to create the right subshader.*

and give it the parameters shown in Figure 9.54. Now jump up a level and see what you have. Your Shader editor should look like Figure 9.55.

Step Two

The next step is to create the right subshader for Figure 9.55. Since this subshader also uses the Wood function, the best course of action would be just to copy the left branch into the right, as we've done so many times so far. (See

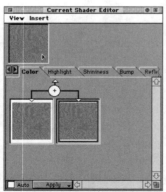

FIGURE **9.56** *The left subshader is copied into the right.*

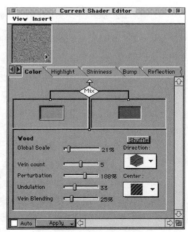

FIGURE **9.57** *Here's what your right subshader should look like.*

Figure 9.56.) The right subshader uses settings similar to those of the subshader we've just created, so the two will complement each other nicely when
mixed. Double-click on the right branch and enter the wood settings shown in
Figure 9.57. Change the two colors to just two more complimentary wood-ish
colors — no numbers please, just eyeball it. Think of this as though you're
painting and mixing your colors on the fly.

Step Three

Now jump up out of that level, and you'll see that you have your first two
Wood subshaders built. From here, jump up to level 1; let's build the right subshader for the top level of the Color channel. Since you already have an entire
side built, this will be a cinch. Start by dragging the left subshader over to the
right to copy it. (See Figure 9.58.)

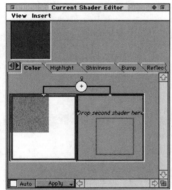

FIGURE *Dragging the left branch to*
9.58 *make the right.*

Jump into the right subshader by double-clicking, and then jump into that
subshader's left subshader. The Wood function is used again for this subshader,
this time to generate a soft, swirling effect by increasing the Vein Blending setting and decreasing the Vein Count. Set your Wood parameters up to match
Figure 9.59. This effect will be used to reduce the uniformity of the mix we
created in the previous steps, and to soften it somewhat as well. You'll also
want to repeat the steps of changing the colors. Don't go too wacky with them;
just use slightly different shades or hues.

Now jump up a level and then jump into the right subshader. Again,
change your colors slightly and give your Wood Mix the settings shown in
Figure 9.60. Now jump up a level, and you should see your two new Wood

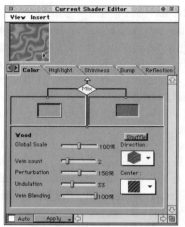

FIGURE
9.59 *The left subshader of the right branch.*

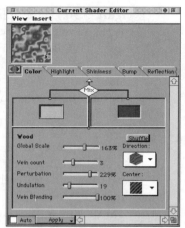

FIGURE
9.60 *The right subshader of the right branch.*

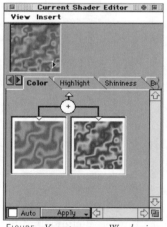

FIGURE *Your two new Wood mixes.*
9.61

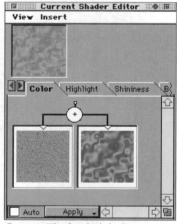

FIGURE *The finished shader.*
9.62

mixes, which create a more turbulent, more contrasty, swirling effect to mix with the subshader on the other side. (See Figure 9.61.)

Step Four

Jump up to the top level of your shader by clicking on the black arrow for the final time. Figure 9.62 shows the final shader.

— *STEVE MCARDLE*

CLOUDS

Creating a Clouds shader is an excellent example of how you can use Ray Dream Studio's shader functions to create effects that go beyond what you might think the functions are capable of. (See Figure 9.63.) This particular shader, for example, is built using layered Marble functions, and takes advantage of the effect you get when turning up the Marble function's Perturbation and Vein Blending settings together. As mentioned in Chapter 2, both the Marble function and the Wood function are well worth exploring in this way, especially when used in a combination of different channels.

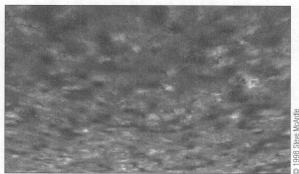

© 1998 Steve McArdle

FIGURE *The Marble function is just as versatile as the Wood*
9.63 *function, as you can see from this Cloud shader.*

Step One

This particular shader is created entirely in the Color channel, although you could get fancy and add a Transparency channel if you wanted to. Its Shader Tree is shown in Figure 9.64. (Parts of the Shader Tree have been compressed slightly in Photoshop so that it will fit on the page.) Notice how the Marble function is used to create several basic cloudy effects that are then combined using the Spots function to create a more complex effect. The Spots function is used along with a low Blending setting to create a wispy transition between the different Marble functions.

The first step in building this shader is to create the top-level Mix. This level combines two different cloudy subshaders using the Spots function to create a layered mix of the two, as mentioned in the previous paragraph. Figure 9.65 shows the settings used for the Spots function. You can also go ahead and create the left subshader for the Mix, which is just another Mix of two cloudy subshaders using the same Spots function and settings as the top level. (See Figure 9.66.)

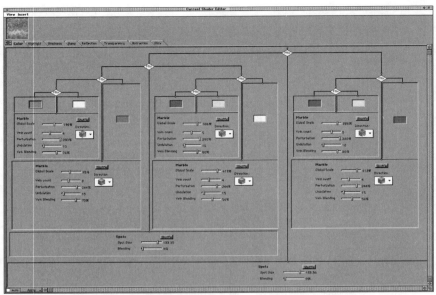

FIGURE
9.64 *This relatively complex Shader Tree for the Cloud shader's Color channel is still focused primarily on building detail. (It's been modified slightly to fit the page.)*

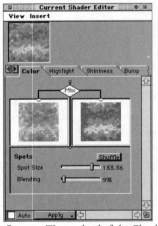

FIGURE
9.65 *The top level of the Cloud shader Color channel.*

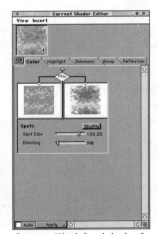

FIGURE
9.66 *The left subshader for Figure 9.65.*

Step Two

The next step is to create the left subshader for Figure 9.66 above. (See Figure 9.67.) This subshader creates a mix of a simple Cloud subshader with a plain blue color, using the Marble function to create a more complex cloud effect than the subshader alone provides. The Cloud subshader for this level is shown in Figure 9.68; it's a basic Marble Mix of two colors: a light blue and a white. Notice how the Marble functions in both the original subshader and its Cloud subshader both use high Perturbation and Vein Blending settings to achieve their effects. Also notice how the two Marble functions use different Direction settings. These Direction settings are consistent across each shader level, which helps build up the multilayered effect that is so evident in Figure 9.68.

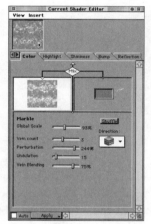

FIGURE **9.67** *The left subshader for Figure 9.66 starts to build the cloud detail.*

FIGURE **9.68** *The left subshader for Figure 9.67 is a basic Marble Mix of two colors.*

Step Three

The third step is to create the right subshader for Figure 9.66 above. (See Figure 9.69.) This subshader is similar to the left subshader that you created in the previous step in that it mixes a Cloud subshader with a solid blue color using the Marble function. This time, however, the effect is bolder and has more contrast, which mixes nicely with the wispy effect of the left subshader.

Figure 9.70 shows the Cloud subshader for Figure 9.69 above. Notice that its settings are very similar to those for the subshader in Figure 9.68 above. The only significant differences are in the Global Scale and Vein Count settings and in the colors, which are now different shades of dark and light blue. This helps to maintain a relationship between all the subshaders as they are mixed, and prevents the result from becoming a muddled mess. A similar relationship exists between the settings for the subshaders in Figures 9.67 and 9.69 above, and these relationships extend to the subshaders in the next step as well. As you build complex nested shaders, make sure you build these types of relationships into them, so that you'll end up with more cohesive results.

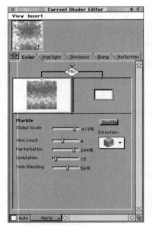

FIGURE
9.69 *The right subshader for Figure 9.66 adds a bolder cloud effect.*

FIGURE
9.70 *The left subshader for Figure 9.69 is another basic Marble Mix.*

Step Four

The final step is to create the top level's right subshader, which is the same as the one in Figure 9.69 above. (See Figure 9.71) The only difference is that it uses a dark blue color on the right side of the Mix instead of white. This has the effect of adding a little blue sky back into the final cloud Mix, as you can see by looking again at the top-level Mix in Figure 9.65 above.

— *STEVE McARDLE*

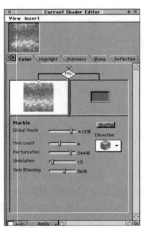

FIGURE
9.71 *The right subshader for the top level of the clouds.*

ROCK

Two tricks are used to create realistic-looking rocks. The first is to create a realistic model, which was covered in Chapter 4. The second is to create a realistic shader, and this is a task for which Ray Dream Studio's Shader functions are a perfect match. (See Figure 9.72.)

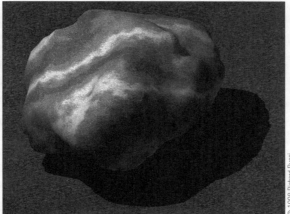

© 1998 Richard Bucci

FIGURE **9.72** *A simple Marble function gives this rock its patterns, while the Spots functions provide the details.*

The Marble and Spots functions are the keys to creating an effective Rock shader, and once again nested subshaders add significantly to the degree of realism. (See the Color channel Shader Tree in Figure 9.73.) When creating any type of Rock shader, you'll do well if you have an actual rock in front of you for inspiration; pay particular attention to the different levels of detail that make up its texture.

Step One

Figure 9.74 shows the top level of the Rock shader's Color channel. As you can see, it is a simple Marble Mix of two subshaders. The first step in building this shader is to create the **Mix** and set up the **Marble** function as shown in Figure 9.74. Once you've created the subshaders, you may want to come back to this level and play around with different settings for the Marble function. In particular, the Global Scale, Shuffle, and Direction settings will play a big role in how the shader appears on a particular object. Experiment with different settings, apply them to your object, and use small test renders to get a quick sense of which settings look the best.

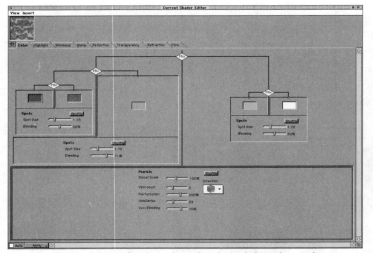

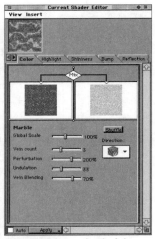

FIGURE **9.73** *The Shader Tree for the rock's Color channel shows how judicious use of the Spots function can add complexity to a simple Marble function.*

FIGURE **9.74** *The top level of the rock's Color channel creates the rock's veins.*

Step Two

The next step is to create the left subshader for the Marble Mix. As shown in Figure 9.75, this subshader creates a Spots Mix from a dark-colored subshader and a light, solid color using a high Blending setting to create a speckled effect. The dark subshader is also a Spots Mix, using two slightly different shades of the same earthy color and a small Spot Size setting to create a subtle random effect. (See Figure 9.76.) This adds one more level of detail to the shader and contributes to its realism. (Try using a solid color instead and notice the difference.)

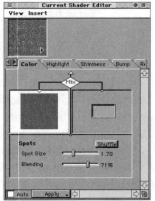

FIGURE **9.75** *The left subshader for Figure 9.74.*

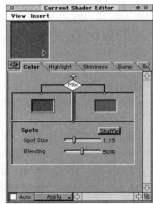

FIGURE **9.76** *The left subshader for Figure 9.75.*

Step Three

The third step is to create the right subshader for Figure 9.75 above, which, like the one you've just created, is a simple Spots Mix using two slightly different shades of the same pink-tan color to add a random effect. (See Figure 9.77.) For a variation on this subshader, try mixing the two colors using a **Marble** function with a low **Global Scale** setting to create a subtle "veins within a vein" effect.

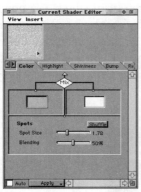

FIGURE **9.77** *The right subshader for Figure 9.74 above.*

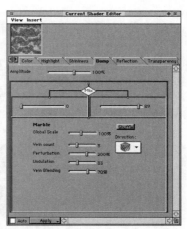

FIGURE **9.78** *The Bump channel for the Rock shader uses the same Marble function as the Color channel.*

Step Four

The final step is to create the Bump channel, which is shown in Figure 9.78. To make sure the veins in the Bump channel match those in the Color channel, copy the **Marble Mix** from the **Color** channel by dragging it onto the **Bump** tab. For this example I changed the Mix shaders to Value sliders for a smoother effect, but you could leave them alone for a rougher look. Try it both ways and see which one you prefer. You can also change the contrast in the Spots subshaders to increase the roughness even more.

Although this particular Rock shader doesn't have any Highlight or Shininess settings, you could also copy the **Color** channel into the **Highlight** and **Shininess** channels for a more complex effect. If you do, make sure you change the colors in the subshaders to darker values; most rocks aren't very shiny unless they're wet or polished. If you're feeling adventurous, try copying the **Color** channel to the **Transparency** channel to add some quartz veins to your rock.

— *RICHARD BUCCI*

BRICKS

By now the word "bricks" should automatically trigger the word "Wires" in your mind when it comes to creating a shader. However, the Wires function by itself is capable of creating only a grid pattern, which can quickly become monotonous. Bricks tend, for example, to be laid in some sort of alternating or offset manner that goes beyond a simple uniform grid. Fortunately, there is a way to achieve a similar effect in Ray Dream Studio without having to resort to using a Texture Map in the Bump channel.

The secret to this technique, the results of which are shown in Figure 9.79, is a carefully orchestrated Mix that combines the Wires and Checkers functions. Although it takes a little experimentation to get the hang of it, you'll find that the basic concept behind it is one you can use in a number of ways to get a variety of Shader effects.

© 1998 Cecilia Ziemer

FIGURE **9.79** *A carefully planned Mix of Checkers and Wires can result in some interesting brick patterns.*

The only real step involved in creating this shader is to create the Bump channel, shown in Figure 9.80 (you can put anything you want in the other channels). It may be a little hard to visualize exactly how the Wires and Checkers functions are interacting with each other here, so I copied the **Bump** channel into the **Color** channel of a new shader, reduced the number of wires and checkers proportionally, and set up the **Wires** and **Checkers** as subshaders so you could see what's going on. Figure 9.81 shows the result.

By using different combinations of vertical and horizontal settings in both the Wires and Checkers functions, you can create a variety of patterns. Make sure you preview these patterns in Sphere Preview mode as well as Flat Preview

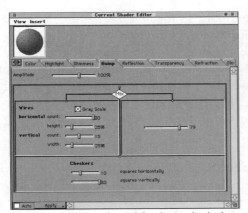

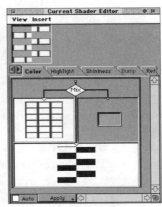

FIGURE
9.80
The Bump channel for the Bricks shader uses an interesting Mix of Wires and Checkers to achieve its effect.

FIGURE
9.81
A visual depiction of what the Bump channel is doing.

mode, however, because Flat Preview mode doesn't always give a completely accurate preview when using this technique.

— *CECILIA ZIEMER*

LASER BEAMS

You've already seen how handy functions can be in the Bump and Color channels, but you might be surprised to see how useful they can be in the Transparency and Glow channels. By taking advantage of the Gradient Pattern function, you can easily create a convincing pulsed laser effect, as shown in

FIGURE
9.82
A little creative use of the Gradient function in the Transparency and Glow channels goes a long way toward creating special effects.

Figure 9.82. Each laser pulse in the image is nothing more than a basic cylinderlike object with this shader applied to it.

You should be able to come up with a number of different applications for this Shader. It was also used for the visible light beams in Chapter 6, "Lighting Techniques," and it will be used again in the next technique, but we'll do this one first because it's a little less complicated. It should inspire you to do some more experimentation on your own.

Step One

This is another simple shader to create, as you can see from Figures 9.83 and 9.84. Apart from a solid color in the Color channel (the color of your laser), these two basic Mixes are all it takes to create the pulsed laser effect. Actually, they're really the same Mix, with the exception that the Transparency channel mixes a 0 Value (black) with a 100 Value (white), whereas the Glow channel mixes the color from the Color channel with a 0 Value (black). This will create a Shader that goes from opaque to completely transparent while fading from a colored glow to no glow at all. When applied to a cylinder, this will create a bright glow at one end of the cylinder, fading away to nothing at the other end.

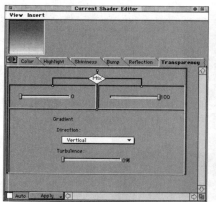

FIGURE **9.83** *The Transparency channel uses a Gradient function to create a blend from 0% to 100% transparent.*

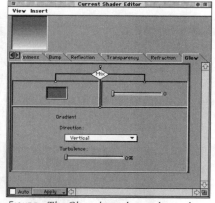

FIGURE **9.84** *The Glow channel uses almost the same Mix as the Transparency channel.*

Step Two

The second and final step in creating this shader is to make sure the fade goes from the front to the back of your cylinders rather than from one side to the other. To do this, click on the **Mapping Mode tab** of the **Properties palette** dialog box and set the **Mapping mode** and **Direction** as shown in Figure 9.85.

The settings for the Mapping Mode are completely dependent on the orientation of the object at the time of creation and the orientation of your gradient.

Another nifty feature to remember here is the Aura filter that shipped with RDS 5. Since you're using the Glow channel, you can also enable the Aura filter for an interesting plasma effect. (See Figure 9.86.)

— *STEVE MCARDLE AND JOHN W. SLEDD*

FIGURE 9.85 *The Mapping mode and Direction for this Shader are critical for getting the desired effect.*

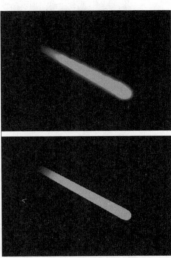

FIGURE 9.86 *The Laser bolt with and without the Aura filter applied.*

TELEPORTER

As you may remember from Chapter 6 and that cool Teleportation Station tutorial, I did promise to divulge the recipe for the shader, so here it is. (See Figure 9.87.) The technique is based on the same concept as the Laser shader technique above but is just a tad bit more complicated. Unlike the Laser shader, this one is built in the Transparency channel. The only thing in the Glow channel is the color of the glow. You don't really need anything else in the Glow channel — because 100% transparency counts for glows too — unless you plan to use the Aura filter. The Aura filter isn't affected by the Transparency channel, only by the Glow channel, so unless you want the invisible portions of your energy beam to have an aura, you need to mask out the areas that you don't want to glow. In the case of the teleportation beam, I didn't want to use the Aura filter so I saved myself some time in the creation of the Shader.

FIGURE *The Teleportation Station.*
9.87

Step One

I'm not going to show you the All Levels version of this one because it's about eight miles long, so let's just start by inserting the color that you want for your teleportation beam in the **Color** channel. This isn't absolutely necessary because all of the color comes from the Glow channel, but do it anyway, just to practice the technique. You can always experiment with adding different colors in the **Color** and **Glow** channels for mysterious effects. When you get the color you want, drag the color swatch over to the **Glow** tab to copy it into the **Glow** channel. Now make sure the values for **Highlight** and **Shininess** are set to **0**. We don't want our energy beam to have a real surface quality.

Step Two

Now we'll get to work on the Transparency channel. Figure 9.88 shows the top level of the Transparency channel — looks simple enough from here. Don't worry though, it gets good and sticky when you crack it open. Nothing you haven't seen before though, just a little more of it.

As you can see, you'll want to insert a **Mix operator** in this top level. Insert a **Value** into the right branch and a **Gradient** function into the **Drop Function Here** box. Set both up as shown.

Now let's insert another **Mix operator** into the **Drop First Shader Here** box (the left branch). Figure 9.89 shows you what you'll be doing here. As with the last one, insert a **Gradient** function into the **Drop Function Here** box, and then let's get to work on the left side of the mix.

Insert a **Multiply operator** into the left branch, and jump inside. In the left branch I'd like you to insert a **Wires** function and on the right, pop in

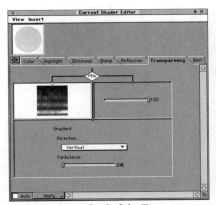

FIGURE
9.88 *The top level of the Transparency channel is a simple-enough concept.*

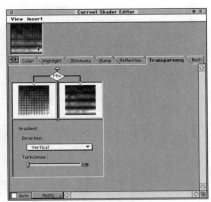

FIGURE
9.89 *This is what you're working toward in the left branch of the Transparency channel.*

another one of those **Gradient** functions I seem to like so much. Set the parameters as shown in 9.90. Notice that I added a little turbulence to the Gradient in this one. By looking at the preview you can see what's going on. Basically we're creating a blend of the Wires and the Gradient, and by adding some Turbulence, we're getting a good smoky effect. Once you have done that, jump back up a level, and we'll go on to Step Three.

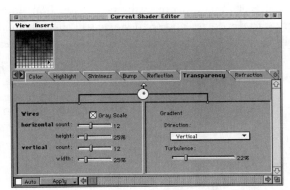

FIGURE *The functions start getting more interesting.*
9.90

Step Three

Now let's tackle the right subshader. Figure 9.91 shows you what we're aiming for here — another smoky-looking Gradient and another Wires function — so go ahead and copy the left branch into the right branch. The only difference is that we're changing some of the parameters. I'm giving the Gradient a little more

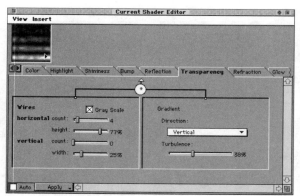

FIGURE *Finishing the right side of the teleportation Shader Tree.*
9.91

Turbulence to offset it from the last smoky Turbulence, and I'm also changing the Wires parameters to create a pulse-beam kind of effect as opposed to a grid effect.

Jump back up a couple of levels when you've finished. All you have to do now is to map the white shader to a cylinder and set the **Mapping mode** so that it maps properly. For the sample at the beginning of the tutorial, I used a Free Form object made from an extruded circle, so I set the Mapping mode as in Figure 9.92. All of these Mapping modes are based on the objects' orientation in the modeling window, so use that as your guide. If you're not just dying to play with your own Shader function combos by now, I just don't know what's wrong with you. Best go to the doctor and see if you're still alive. Just in case you're simply not so easily excitable, we have more for you to do, so keep reading.

— JOHN W. SLEDD

FIGURE *Setting the Mapping mode properly*
9.92 *is critical.*

RUST

This shader is the most complex in this section in terms of the number of channels it uses and the visual effect it creates, but it is still relatively simple once you have an understanding of how Ray Dream Studio's Shader channels and functions work. It's an excellent example of how the different channels can be set up so they build on each other to create a complex effect. Try rendering the shader in Figure 9.93 after each step to see how each channel adds to the overall look of the shader.

FIGURE **9.93** *The Marble function was used in several channels of one Shader to create this complex rust effect.*

Step One

The first step is to build the Color channel, as shown in Figure 9.94. Figure 9.95 shows the top level of this channel, which mixes a solid gray with a rusty red subshader using the Marble function. The subshader is shown in Figure 9.96; it mixes two different shades of dark reddish rusty brown using the Marble function.

Notice how the settings for the Marble function in the subshader are almost identical to those for the Marble function in the top level. The only significant difference is in the Undulation setting. This allows for a more harmonious mix between the gray and the subshader in the top level.

Step Two

The next step is to add the Highlight and Shininess channels. The Shininess channel is easy; it has a Value of 54. The Highlight channel is another Marble function, as shown in Figure 9.97. Notice that it uses different settings from the ones in the Color channel, which adds another subtle level of complexity to the shader. (Try copying the **Color** channel to the **Highlight** channel instead, and notice the difference.)

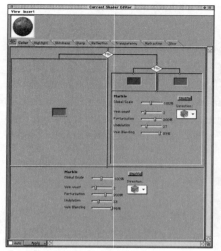

FIGURE **9.94** *The Shader Tree for the rust Color channel isn't very complicated.*

FIGURE **9.95** *The top level of the Color channel mixes gray with a rust subshader.*

FIGURE **9.96** *The right subshader for Figure 9.69 creates a rust-colored Mix.*

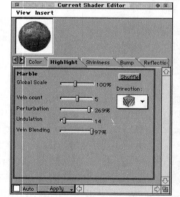

FIGURE **9.97** *The Highlight channel uses its own Marble pattern settings.*

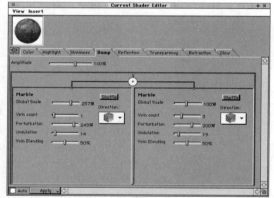

FIGURE **9.98** *The Bump channel mixes two contrasting Marble functions using the Add operator to create a layered effect.*

Step Three

The third step is to create the Bump channel, which is shown in Figure 9.98. This channel layers two Marble functions together using the Add operator to create a more complex effect than one function alone would give. Notice that the two functions have different Global Scale and Direction settings, which adds to the complexity of the layered effect. (Try using similar settings instead to see what effect this has on the shader.)

Bear in mind also that using the Marble function (or any other function for that matter) by itself is the same as using it in a mix with black and white as the subshaders. This will maximize the effect it has in any of the non-Color channels, so you may want to add a **Multiply** operator with a **Value** slider to allow you to control the intensity of the effect, or if you're using RDS 5, you can use the **Amplitude** slider for the same effect.

Step Four

The fourth step is to create the Reflection channel, which is shown in Figure 9.99. This channel is a copy of the Color channel with the right subshader replaced by a solid black Color. This has the effect of making the rusted areas nonreflective. Make sure you create it by dragging the **Color** channel **Mix** onto the **Reflection tab** to ensure that the settings are identical. You can then select the subshader and choose **Color** from the **Component** menu — or, just to make sure we beat that dead horse a little more, you can use a **Value** of **0**.

Step Five

The final step in building the Rust shader is to create the Transparency channel, which is shown in Figure 9.100. This channel adds a finishing touch to the shader by creating sections on objects that the shader is applied to that look as though they've been rusted through. The high Perturbation setting and low Vein Blending setting are the key to this channel, although you could use lower Perturbation settings if you wanted larger holes.

— STEVE MCARDLE

FIGURE **9.99** *The Reflection channel uses the Color channel's Marble settings.*

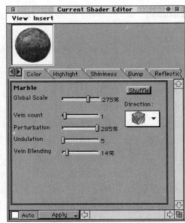

FIGURE **9.100** *The Transparency channel creates "rusted-through" patches.*

MARBLE

In Chapter 2 we talked briefly about building an effective marble shader and how the key was to nest Marble functions to build up a layered effect, which should be second nature to you at this point in the book. You've seen throughout this section how effective the Marble function can be, so it should come as no surprise that it is particularly adept at creating realistic Marble shaders. (See Figure 9.101 for an example.) If you're willing to take the time to experiment with your layers and base your shaders on real-world examples, you'll be able quickly to build up a very realistic Marble shader library without ever having to resort to Texture Maps.

FIGURE
9.101 *It should come as no surprise by now that the key to an effective Marble shader is to nest Marble functions.*

Step One

Unless you're trying to create a roughened marble effect, Marble shaders are built almost exclusively in the Color channel. (You'll probably want to add some Value components in the Highlight, Shininess and Reflection channels as well, to create a polished look.) Figure 9.102 shows the Color channel Shader Tree for the Marble shader used in Figure 9.101.

The first step in building the Color channel is to create the top-level Mix, which combines two subshaders using the Marble function. (See Figure 9.103.) Both subshaders are built with Marble functions themselves and create a layered effect when combined. The left subshader adds to the level of complexity by combining two more subshaders using the Add operator, as shown in Figure 9.104. Go ahead and set up this subshader as well.

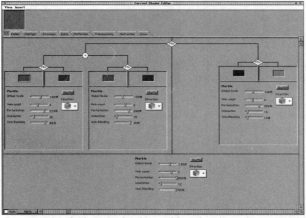

FIGURE **9.102** *The Shader Tree for the marble Color channel uses nested Marble functions to create a layered effect that gives the shader its realism.*

FIGURE **9.103** *The top level of the Color channel mixes two Marble subshaders.*

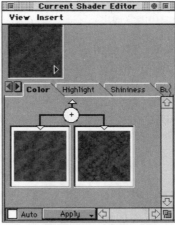

FIGURE **9.104** *The left subshader for Figure 9.103.*

Step Two

The next step is to create the subshaders for Figure 9.104, both of which are Marble Mixes that combine two solid colors. The left subshader is shown in Figure 9.105 below; it mixes two shades of green. The right subshader is shown in Figure 9.106; it mixes two slightly different shades of green.

Notice that the two Marble functions used to create these subshaders have very little in common with each other and even have opposite Direction

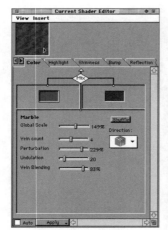

FIGURE **9.105** *The left subshader for Figure 9.104.*

FIGURE **9.106** *The right subshader for Figure 9.104.*

settings. This creates a more complex Mix than two functions with similar settings would.

Step Three

The final step is to create the right subshader for the top level. This subshader adds a thin, sharp, light-green vein to the shader; it is shown in Figure 9.107. Notice that it uses a low Vein Blending setting to achieve the sharp, contrasty effect. It also uses different settings and a different Direction from the two sub-shaders in the previous step, to add even more complexity to the shader.

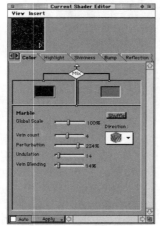

FIGURE **9.107** *The right subshader for Figure 9.103.*

The version of this shader used for Figure 9.101 includes a Value of 80 in the Highlight channel, a Value of 80 in the Shininess channel, and a Value of 30 in the Reflection channel.

— *STEVE MCARDLE*

GLOBAL MIX SHADERS

I couldn't let this whole section go without saying something about Global Mix shaders. You probably won't use them a lot, but when you need one, you'll be very glad the option is there. Global Mix shaders are a way to mix entire shaders in much the same way that you have been mixing colors, functions and subshaders. With a Global Mix shader, you can mix two completely different shaders with completely different Color, Highlight, Shininess, Bump and other channels using exactly the same methods you've been using to mix components within individual Shader channels. In this example, I used the Cork and Tiles shaders we created earlier this chapter. We'll call our new shader Corky Tiles. The shader used in Figure 9.108 would have been a nightmare to create in one shader because it would have required subshader on top of subshader on top of subshader, and they would have all had to match up in every channel. Imagine matching the Bumps up with the Color in all of the nested shaders you've created in these two shaders.

So how do you create such a shader? It's simple.

FIGURE **9.108** *The Global Mix shader makes the creation of extremely complex shaders much easier.*

Step One
Create a new shader, which will be your Global Mix shader.

Step Two
Choose **Global Mix** from the **Insert** menu.

Step Three
Drag your first prebuilt shader into the left branch and drag your second prebuilt shader into the right branch. You don't have to use Cork and Tiles here if you simply want to create your own shader, but they are available on the CD-ROM, if you want to use them.

Step Four
Insert the function of your dreams into the **Drop Function Here** box and adjust to taste. That's all there is to it. (See Figure 9.109.) The Global Mix works on the same premise as any of the other functions and operators.

— John W. Sledd

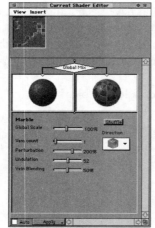

FIGURE
9.109
This Global Mix shader created the effect of sand spilled on a tile floor.

GLASS

A Glass shader may seem fairly straightforward, but if you try to create one you'll quickly find that it can be extremely frustrating and time-consuming to get the settings just right, especially considering how long it takes to do each test render. I thought I'd finish this section by saving you a little time and effort and giving you a good place to start.

Figure 9.110 shows a basic Glass shader applied to a flask object. There is also a liquid partially filling the flask. All the channel settings for this shader are simple ones. It has a touch of a dark aqua color — though this will vary depending on the type of glass you're trying to create — a maximum Shininess setting (Value of 100), a maximum Highlight setting (Value of 100), a fairly high Reflection setting (Value of 73), a low Refraction setting (Value of 13), and a high Transparency setting (Value of 90 for this example, although this too will vary depending on the type of glass).

© 1998 Steve McArdle

FIGURE **9.110** *As simple as a Glass shader may seem to be, the right settings make a huge difference in appearance.*

While these settings will give you a good, basic Glass shader, bear in mind that what makes glass look like glass are its reflections, highlights and, to a lesser degree, refraction. Make sure, therefore, that you set up your lighting carefully and include other objects or a reflected background to complete the effect. You might also want to study professional photos of glass objects to see how the photographer placed the lighting and what is reflected in the glass. (Hint: large, glowing, flat surfaces can come in handy.) With curved objects, you'll also find that you get better reflections if you increase the object's Surface Fidelity. (Select **Surface Fidelity** from the **Geometry** menu in the **Modeling** window.)

—STEVE MCARDLE

CHAPTER 10

Shader Techniques

© 1998 Richard Bucci

Now that you've mastered the process of putting together a shader and taking advantage of the different shader operators and functions Ray Dream Studio offers, it's time to take a look at a few techniques that will allow you to enhance your shader abilities even further. The techniques presented in this chapter cover several different areas, but all are extremely useful and will quickly become an essential part of your shading toolbox.

CREATING TEXTURE MAPS FOR RELATIVELY FLAT OBJECTS

Chapter 2 mentioned how important it is to make sure any Texture Maps you use in a shader are large enough that they won't pixellate in the final rendered image. It's also important to make sure that Texture Maps are the right shape, because otherwise Ray Dream Studio will stretch them to fit the object you're applying them to, and they will look distorted. Finally, in many cases you want to make sure that the Texture Map is properly aligned on the object. While this may not be important if your Texture Map is a simple texture, it's very important if the Texture Map is designed to add specific details to the object, as is the case in Figure 10.1.

Fortunately, all three of these Texture Map issues can be taken care of at the same time using the technique presented here. It's very straightforward and will make a great difference in most situations where you need to use a Texture Map on a relatively flat object.

© 1998 Craig Lyn

FIGURE **10.1** *The key to using Texture Maps is to make sure you create them at least as large as they will appear in the final rendered image.*

Step One

The first step is to position an Isometric camera directly above the surface of the object you want to create the Texture Map for, and point the camera so its line of sight is as close to perpendicular to the surface as possible — this will prevent distortion. You'll find this a lot easier to do if the object is parallel to one of the

Working Planes in the Perspective Window. If your object is already rotated into its final position in the scene, and you don't want to change it, you can copy it into a new scene and use the copy for this step and the following one.

Step Two

Next, think about how large the model will appear on the screen in your final render. Zoom in on the model until you feel it is scaled appropriately. Then zoom in a little bit more to give yourself a safety margin. Now render the scene at a size and resolution that's just high enough to show you any details that will be important for positioning the Texture Map. (Figure 10.2 shows the resulting render for our example spaceship.) The only thing you'll be using this render for is to determine the shape and size of the object and any relevant details, so you may also want to turn off some of the Render settings to speed up the render.

FIGURE
10.2   *Create a render of your object using an Isometric camera that is above and perpendicular to your object.*

Step Three

Open the rendering of your object in an image-editing program and crop it to the outer edges of your object. Figure 10.3 shows how the render in Figure 10.2 above was cropped to the the outer edges of the wing of the spaceship — the first thing we'll create a Texture Map for.

FIGURE
10.3   *Crop the render so that the object you'll be creating the Texture Map for completely fills the frame.*

Step Four

Using the rendered object as a guide, start to create your Texture Map on top of the cropped image (as shown in Figure 10.4), making sure the Texture Map overlaps the rendered object slightly to allow for a margin of error. If you're using an image-editing program that supports layers, create your Texture Map in a separate layer. This will allow you to leave the original render intact in case you make a mistake and need to erase part of the Texture Map. It also allows you to make the Texture Map layer partially transparent during the creating process so that you can see how the Texture Map lines up with specific details on the rendered object.

FIGURE *Once you've cropped your image, you can start*
10.4 *creating your Texture Map over it.*

When you've finished creating the Texture Map, remove any remaining parts of the original render (or delete/hide the render layer) and save the Texture Map in a file format that Ray Dream Studio can import, such as Photoshop 2.5, PICT, RIFF or PCX. Figure 10.5 shows the finished Texture Map for our example.

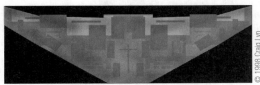

FIGURE *Once your Texture Map is complete, remove any*
10.5 *remaining parts of the original render and save*
it to a file.

Step Five

The next step is to create a shader with your new Texture Map in the Color channel. Open the shader for the object you want to map this thing onto, and insert a **Texture Map** component into the **Color** channel. Select your Texture Map **file** from the file dialog box that appears and make sure the **Better (but slower) sampling** option is selected, as shown in Figure 10.6. Your shader is now ready to be applied to your object, although you can embellish it first, if you like, by editing the other channels.

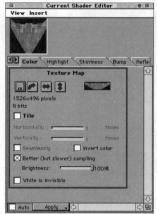

FIGURE *Create a new shader and*
10.6 *import your Texture Map.*

Step Six

The final step is to apply your new shader to your object. The best way to do this is to apply the shader to the object as normal and use the **Box Mapping mode.** Since Ray Dream Studio uses your object's bounding box as its guidelines for this type of mapping, the black areas around the wing will essentially be projected into nothingness. This is another reason for using this technique for the creation of your maps. Depending on the orientation of your model in the modeling box, you might want to use a different projection setting, but for this particular object, Figure 10.7 was perfect. When you've finished, switch to **Better Preview mode** to see how the Texture Map looks. (See Figure 10.8.)

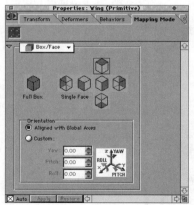

FIGURE *Using the Box Mapping mode*
10.7 *projects the map onto the wing exactly as we want it.*

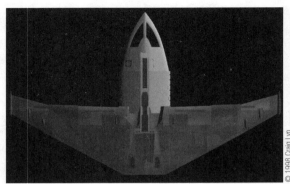

FIGURE *The wing is perfectly mapped.*
10.8

⇨ **Note:** You can use this technique to create Texture Maps for simple cylindrical objects as well. The only difference is that you'll need to compensate for the curvature of your object in Step Three. Crop your rendering to the top, bottom, and sides of your object. Multiply the width of the cropped image by π (3.1416) and widen the image to the result (the object's circumference). Fill this entire image with your Texture Map and apply the resulting shader to your object in Step Six using the **Cylindrical Mapping mode** instead of Box Mapping.

CREATING TEXTURE MAPS FOR IRREGULAR OBJECTS

Irregular shapes such as the one shown in Figure 10.9 present a unique challenge when you need to apply a Texture Map, but as Figure 10.10 shows, it's a

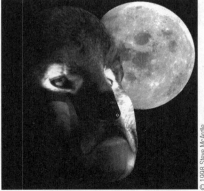

FIGURE *The irregular object from Figure*
10.9 *10.10 as it was originally created.*

© 1998 Steve McArdle

FIGURE **10.10** *Creating or modifying a detailed Texture Map to fit an irregular object is surprisingly easy.*

challenge that can be overcome. This technique will show you how to position and adjust any Texture Map properly to fit perfectly on any object.

Step One

The first step in creating a Texture Map for an irregular object is to decide how you want to apply the Texture Map to your object. Ray Dream Studio offers several Mapping modes, each of which will have a different effect on the final image. (They're set in the Properties palette under the Mapping Mode tab.) The one you choose will depend on how your object was created and how it will be viewed. Typically you'll want to try the default Parametric Mapping mode first, if your object was created in Ray Dream Studio, that is; sometimes the Box, Cylindrical, or Spherical Mapping modes will offer better results (if your object was imported from another program, these will be your only choices.) If you will be showing only one side of the object in your renders, as is the case in our example, you may want to try the Box Mapping mode (as shown in Figure 10.11) because it's probably the easiest and most straightforward method. Always start with your best guess because you can always change it if you don't like what you see.

⇨ **Note:** If you are going to be animating the vertices or the shape of your object, Parametric Mapping is the best option because it will keep your map aligned with the surface of your object in the best possible way. Using the other Mapping modes may cause distortion because your map scoots around on the surface of your model as it moves.

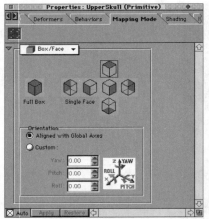

FIGURE   *The first step in creating a Texture*
10.11   *Map for an irregular object is to*
choose the appropriate Mapping mode.

If you're not already familiar with the different Mapping modes and their options, this technique is the perfect opportunity to experiment and learn more about them. At the end of the next step, change to each of the different modes and see what effect it has on the shader. You may want to create and save test renders of each for later reference.

Step Two

The next step is to create a numbered grid, which will be used to determine where the features on your Texture Map will be positioned on the object. Although it doesn't really matter what the size and proportions of the grid are, you'll want to make sure it's roughly proportional to the size of your Texture Map if you are adapting an existing Texture Map. If you're building a Texture Map from scratch, then use the proportions of your object as a rough guide. Either way, the number of squares in the grid should be proportional to the amount of detail in your Texture Map — the more details, the more squares. Finally, the pixel resolution of the grid isn't really important either; the example grid shown in Figure 10.12 is a 72-dpi screen shot from a page layout program.

Step Three

Once you've created your grid, the next step is to apply it to your object. To do this, create a new shader, select the **Color** channel, select **Texture Map** from the **Shader editor**'s Insert menu. Then select your grid file in the file dialog box that appears. Make sure your object is selected and click on the **Apply** button in the **Shader editor** to apply the grid. Create a test render of your object and print it (or you can simply keep the render open while you're editing your

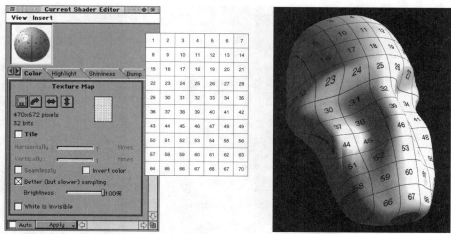

FIGURE 10.12 *By creating a numbered grid and applying it to your object, you can create a reference image that will let you see how a shader will be mapped to your object.*

map — if you have the RAM, that is). You'll use it as a reference guide to build or manipulate your Texture Map.

This is the time to determine whether you've chosen the appropriate Mapping mode for your object. If the grid is not being applied to your object the way you want (especially if it looks too distorted), try some of the other Mapping modes to see if one works better. If you'll be animating your object or rendering it from different views, look at it from several angles as well to make sure that the grid is behaving the way you expect over the entire object.

Step Four

Now that you have your rendered, gridded object as a reference guide, you will create a second reference guide by opening up your Texture Map in an image-editing program — ideally, one that supports layers — and overlaying your grid onto it (make the grid mostly transparent) so you can see how the Texture Map aligns with the grid. (See Figure 10.13.) If necessary, resize your grid so that it is the same size as your Texture Map.

By comparing this second image to the test render from the previous step, you can see exactly what changes need to be made to your Texture Map so that everything lines up properly on your object. Alternatively, if you're building your Texture Map from scratch, you can build your Texture Map over the blank grid, using the test render as a guide to determine where to place your details.

For example, if you compare the image in Figure 10.13 to the test render in Figure 10.12 above, you can see that the eyes are too high and a little too far apart, and the mouth stretches up too far at the corners. (Figure 10.14 shows the unmodified Texture Map from Figure 10.13 applied to our object.)

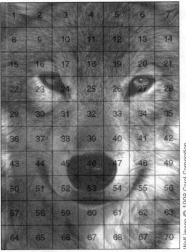

FIGURE **10.13** *Overlay the grid on your Texture Map to use as a guide.*

FIGURE **10.14** *The Texture Map in Figure 10.13 would look like this on our object.*

Step Five

The final step is to manipulate or create your Texture Map so that all the details line up properly with the grid, then apply it to your object using the same method you used to apply the grid in Step One. (See Figures 10.15 and 10.16.)

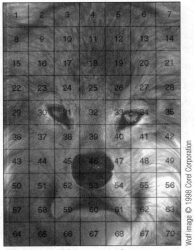

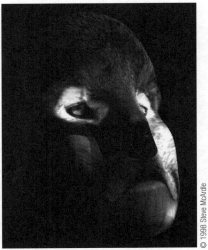

FIGURE **10.15** *Build or manipulate your map to align to the grid.*

FIGURE **10.16** *Your first test render with your Texture Map should be perfect.*

If you're working with an existing Texture Map such as the one in our example, you'll find that the easiest way to manipulate it is with Kai's Power Goo from MetaCreations, which lets you turn your Texture Map into a piece of virtual putty and slide features around at will. Whichever technique you use, however, you should find that you have a perfect match the first time around, thereby saving yourself the hours of adjustments and rerenders that a trial-and-error approach would require.

— *Bård Edlund, Steve McArdle*

WORKING WITH DETAILER

For those of you out there with MetaCreation's Detailer, the above process can be streamlined a little bit, especially if you're creating your Texture Maps from scratch. This is a little demonstration on getting a smooth path between Detailer and RDS. Figure 10.17 shows a nice snake head whose textures are 100% Detailer. In case you haven't noticed yet, the model is the same one that was used for the wolfman in the tutorial above. It just goes to show that it's all a matter of how you look at things.

FIGURE *A snake, by any other name . . .*
10.17

Step One

The first thing you want to do is to export your model from RDS to be used in Detailer. Your export settings can mean the difference between a smoothly running project and one that leaves you brimming with an overwhelming feeling of disgust. I know about both first-hand, so I hope I can save you a little trouble by walking you through a simple setup.

In order to export a Detailer file from RDS, you must first select the object you want to export. Although Detailer does allow you to import a whole model built from many objects, I certainly don't recommend it. Detailer allows up to five separate maps per object. Those five maps, coupled with Detailer's hefty screen real-estate requirements, are plenty for you to deal with without having to navigate through the maps for several more objects. So with that out of the way, select the object you wish to export and choose **Export** from the **File** menu. When the Export dialog box pops up, change the file type to **Detailer** via the pull-down menu at the bottom. (See Figure 10.18.)

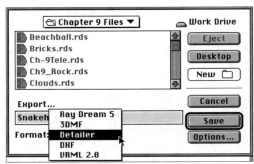

FIGURE *Setting up your Export dialog box.*
10.18

Now before you start exporting things, there are a few more changes you need to make. Click on the **Options** button and I'll tell you about them. Figure 10.19 shows you the default Detailer export options. You have three main boxes: Export, Surface Fidelity and Image Files. In the Export box you'll most likely only be concerned with the Geometry Only radio button, because you'll be shading the thing in Detailer.

⇨ **Note:** This ability to export shading does come in handy for certain things, such as exporting RDS's procedurals for use in Detailer or if you just need a texture for a Painter file you're working on. This option creates bitmaps from your procedurals and can be very useful.

Since we're not going to be exporting any shader info right now, all you need to be concerned with is the Geometry Only radio buttons and the Surface Fidelity. To start, click on the **As a Single Object** radio button under the **Geometry Only** radio button. This exports your object as a single-mesh object, so you have to deal with only one set of maps.

As for the Surface Fidelity, the golden rule is the lower the better. Now, this doesn't mean to crank it down to nothing; it means the lowest you can get away with without sacrificing quality. A setting somewhere in the middle is usually plenty for those times when you don't feel like experimenting, but if you do have the time to test the waters, just go with the default setting. If it looks OK when you import it into Detailer, then all's cool that ends cool and you've saved yourself some RAM and processor time. If it looks blocky and like a pile o' bricks, then you'll want to nudge up the Surface Fidelity and try it again. Just keep going until it looks good. When you have your options set up as shown in Figure 10.20, click **OK** and then click **Save**, and we're on to Step Two.

⇨ **Note:** If you'll be importing only the shading information that you create in Detailer, a low Surface Fidelity setting doesn't matter.

FIGURE **10.19** *The default Detailer export options.*

FIGURE **10.20** *The preferred Detailer export options.*

Step Two

Now you're ready to open up Detailer and get to work on this slimy critter. When you get Detailer open, go into the **Edit>Preferences>Model** window and make sure the **Ray Dream Compatible** box is checked. (See Figure 10.21.) The reason for this is that Detailer allows you to use different Mapping options for the different maps For example, your Texture map can have Implicit mapping and your Bump can have Spherical mapping while your Highlight has Cubical mapping. Ray Dream Studio doesn't let you have different Mapping Modes per Shader channel, so clicking this option makes sure that Detailer maintains the same Mapping options for all of the maps.

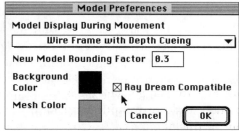

FIGURE **10.21** *Checking the Ray Dream Compatible box makes sure that all of your Detailer Mapping modes stay the same as they were in Detailer.*

Now we want to open our newly exported Detailer file. Because we exported as a native Detailer file, all you have to do is to choose **Open** from the **File** menu, make sure the **Model** radio button is selected, and then navigate to the appropriate file. Once the model is in, you're ready to go. You now need to orient the model so that you have a front-on view because you're going to be using a Projection Mapping type. Do that by selecting the **Virtual Trackball** tool and then dragging around inside the **3D View** window, or by using the **Virtual Trackball** controls. (See Figure 10.22.)

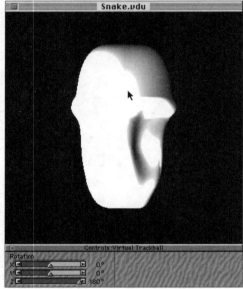

FIGURE   *We want to see our model head-on.*
10.22

Step Three

Let's create a map. I usually create my Texture Map first because I use it to create my Bump map. To create a map from scratch, choose **Map>Load>Texture**; set up your file as shown in Figure 10.23 if you're using the same model as I have. One definitely confusing thing about Detailer is its use of the terms *Rows* and *Columns*. This is confusing because typically you see dimensions referred to as *Height* and *Width*. *Rows* and *Columns* refer to the same thing — but it's backwards. *Rows* are rows of pixels *horizontally* or widthwise, and *Columns* are columns of pixels *vertically* or heightwise. So they are simply Width and Height in pixels.

Once you get past that little hurdle, you get to the dialog box shown in Figure 10.24. This is the Set Mapping Options dialog box for your newly created

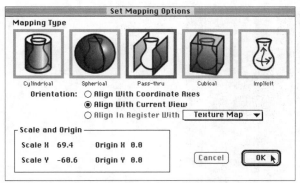

FIGURE *Creating the Texture Map to the proper*
10.23 *proportions.*

FIGURE *Setting Detailer's equivalent of Mapping Mode.*
10.24

Texture Map. Select **Pass-thru**— which is essentially the same as RDS's Box Mapping mode set on one face — and click on the **Align with Current View** radio button. This is why we oriented the model in a forward view in Step Two.

Step Four

Now we're ready to create a scaly Texture Map. I choose the **SURFACE0422** pattern from the Detailer Patterns library, scale it to **35%** and fill the Texture Map using the **Paint Bucket Fill** tool. This gives me a great scaly texture to start with. (See Figure 10.25.) Turning on the **Display Mesh** option gives me a great mesh representation of my model to work from. (See Figure 10.26.)

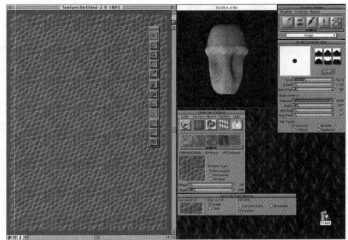

FIGURE **10.25** *A fill of one of Detailer's patterns makes great scales.*

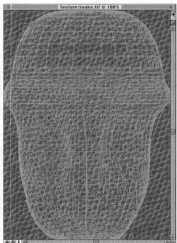

FIGURE **10.26** *Turning on the **Display Mesh** option provides an outline that can be used as a template.*

Step Five

A few color alterations here, filling some selections with lower-scaled patterns there, some distortion over yonder, and I wind up with the map in Figure 10.27. I plan to use this map for my Bump map, so I go to **Map>Load>Bump**

Apply Bump Map

Map Source

Current Map: SnakeBmp.tif
○ Remove current map
◉ Copy image: Snake.tif ▼
○ Open image...

Make new image using...
○ Blank
○ Pattern
○ Texture
Image size

Cancel   OK

FIGURE **10.27** *The finished Texture Map.*

FIGURE **10.28** *Detailer makes it easy to create a new map copied from existing maps.*

and click on the **Copy Image** radio button. SNAKE.TIF — that's what I named the texture file — is automatically highlighted because I don't have any other maps open. (See Figure 10.28.) Then I click **OK**. This gives me a perfect copy of my Texture file in the Bump map file. Since the Bump map used only gray values, and since it's much easier to see the gray values when the file is actually gray, I turn the Bump map into a grayscale file by choosing **Effects>Tonal Control>Adjust Colors** and cranking the **Saturation** slider down to **–139**. I then toy around with the **Brightness/Contrast** settings until I get a nice, contrasty image. A little bit of paint here and there to mix things up, and I wind up with the Bump map in Figure 10.29. I also drop the **Specular** settings and increase the **Bump map Adjustment** as in Figure 10.30. Figure 10.31 shows the final snake head in Detailer's 3D View window.

Step Six

Now we're ready to head back into RDS for rendering and animation. One thing I want to point out here is that Detailer and RDS provide a great way just to swap Texture Maps without replacing the actual geometry — at least theoretically so. This is a great thing because spline-based objects, like those from RDS's Free Form modeler, are much smaller than polygon-based objects like those Detailer uses. The problem (and why I said "theoretically") is that I've never used that option. I don't know why. I just clicked with this way of

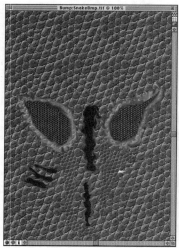

FIGURE
10.29
The finished Bump map.

FIGURE
10.30
Dropping the Specular settings and increasing the Bump map Adjustment.

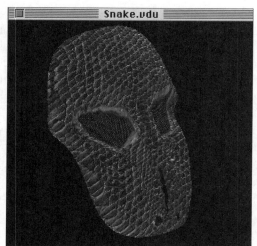

FIGURE
10.31
The final snake head in the 3D View window.

doing things and have stuck with it, so I encourage you to use what you learn in this technique and then mess around until you figure out how to take advantage of that option. I'll get around to it some day, I'm sure. This is why it's so important to do lots of experimentation. Those who are considered pros often get stuck in their ways. You know the old adage about teaching old dogs new tricks. The same thing applies here, except that I think it's easier to teach an old dog than an old 3Der.

Anyway, the dirty old way I usually do it is either to open up the file that I exported the model from or to create a completely new file. In this instance, I created a completely new file. I wanted to keep the old head in its own file for archival purposes.

To do this, I choose **Import** from the **File** menu and select my **SNAKE.VDU** file. Here's where you get that little snippet about importing the shading only. This, of course, would require that you are importing the Detailer information back into the same file that you exported the model from. All of the necessary directions are shown in Figure 10.32.

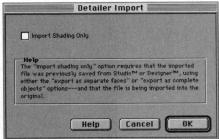

FIGURE   *The RDS Detailer Import dialog box.*
10.32

Because we're going into a new file with no geometry to speak of, I'll leave that box unchecked and click **OK**. This will import the geometry and shading ready to be repositioned, animated, and added to more objects to form a complete model — or whatever you can dream up.

I've just about finished yammering about this Detailer stuff but I want to point out one more thing before I leave it alone. If you select an object in RDS that has been mapped in Detailer, you may notice that you have trouble changing the shading attributes. The reason is that Detailer maps in RDS are not applied directly to the surface of your objects themselves but instead are applied via a paint shape. If you select your Detailer-shaded model and then check out its Shading tab in the Properties palette, you'll see that there is no primer but that there is a Shader Element present; expanding the little arrow beside Element will give you the information for your Detailer-bred paint shape. (See Figure 10.33.) The Detailer/RDS combination is a wonderful addition to any 3D arsenal.

— *JOHN W. SLEDD*

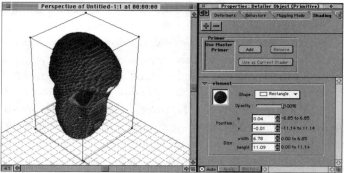

FIGURE **10.33** *Detailer maps are applied to your objects via a paint shape.*

CREATING CUTOUT FIGURES

There are no rules that say everything in your scene has to be a 3D model, especially if you're rendering your scene from only one angle. Adding complex finishing touches such as plants, animals, or even humans can be simple if you take a 2D approach. Figure 10.34 for example, includes several human figures that would have been extremely time-consuming to model and extremely challenging to add in postproduction, due to the complex reflections and shadows in the scene. Instead, they were added as the 3D-graphics equivalent of cardboard cutouts, using the technique shown on the following pages.

© 1998 John Stephens

FIGURE **10.34** *The human figures in this scene are the 3D equivalent of cardboard cutouts, but still add tremendously to the scene.*

This is another technique that requires the use of an image-editing program, and although Photoshop is used in this example, any image-editing program will do. You may also need to use an illustration program such as Illustrator.

Step One

The first step is to crop the image you'll be using so that the edges of the cutout object touch all four sides of the frame. In Photoshop, the easiest way to do this is to use the Selection tool to select the object, copy the selection, create a new document using the default settings (which will be the correct size for the selection you copied), paste the selection, and save the document (keep the selection active). This file will be used for the Color channel of your object shader. (See Figure 10.35A.)

If you want your object to have soft edges, you should also create a mask by filling your selection with black and saving the result in a separate file. This file will be used for the Transparency channel of your object shader. (See Figure 10.35B.)

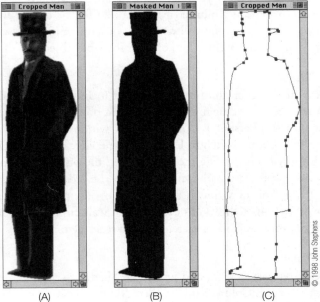

(A)   (B)   (C)

FIGURE *Use an image-editing program to crop your original image,*
10.35 *create a mask (optional), and create an outline path.*

Step Two

The next step is to create the outline path that will define the shape of your object. There are several ways to do this. If you're using Photoshop, the easiest way is to convert your selection into a path using the **Make Path** command in the **Paths palette** menu to create a path based on your selection (see Figure 10.35C), then choose **Export** from the **File** menu and select **Paths to Adobe Illustrator** from the submenu that appears. This will ensure that your path matches the cropped image from Step One as closely as possible.

If you're not using Photoshop, you may need to import your cropped image into an illustration program and create a path manually based on the image. If this isn't an option, make sure you create a Transparency mask in the previous step, skip the next step, and apply your shader in Step Four to a flat, rectangular object with the same proportions as your cropped image. If your cropped image were twice as high as it was wide, for example, you would create a rectangle object that is twice as high as it is wide.

⇨ **Editor's Note:** If you take this flat object route, be sure either to zero out your **Highlight** and **Shininess** channels or to use the same mask that you used for your Transparency channel as a mixer in these two channels. The reason is that even 100% transparent objects can have highlights on them which will give away your secret in a glance. It should also be noted that, if you are using any volumetric effects like fog or clouds in your scene, the flat-mapped technique will not work because volumetric effects have a tendency to give away the edges of your invisible objects.

Step Three

The next step is to create the cutout object in Ray Dream Studio. Create a new **Free Form** object by dragging the **Free Form** object **Creation tool** icon from the toolbar into the **Perspective** or **Hierarchy** window. The **Free Form Modeling** window will appear. Switch to **Drawing Plane** view by typing **Command/Ctrl-5**. Select **Import** from the **File** menu and open the outline path file you created in the previous step. The path will appear on the cross-section plane, as shown in Figure 10.36. You may find it necessary — or just useful — to adjust the size of your cross-section at this point by selecting **Scale** from the **Geometry** menu and entering appropriate horizontal and vertical scale factors.

Step Four

The next step is to create and apply the Shader to your object. Create a new Shader, select the **Color** channel, select **Texture Map** from the **Shader editor's Insert** menu, and select your cropped image file in the file dialog box to insert your image file as a Texture Map. (See Figure 10.37.) If you created a mask file, select the **Transparency** channel and repeat the last few steps to insert your mask file into the **Transparency** channel. Depending on your scene's lighting, you may also find it useful to copy the **Color** channel into the **Glow** channel and use a **Multiply** operator to control its strength. Click on the **Apply** button in the **Shader editor** to apply your Shader. It should fit your cross-section shape perfectly (See Figure 10.38.)

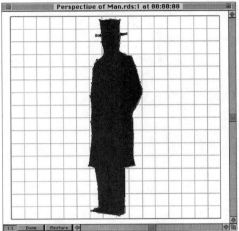

FIGURE **10.36** *Import your outline path into the default cross-section to create your object.*

FIGURE **10.37** *The cropped image file is used as a Color Texture Map.*

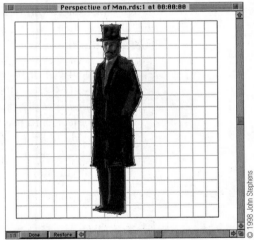

FIGURE **10.38** *Once applied, your Shader should fit the cross-section shape perfectly.*

© 1998 John Stephens

Step Five

The last step is to flatten your object. Switch back to **Reference** view by typing **Command/Ctrl-0**. Click on the **Sweep Path** plane to activate it and shorten the **Sweep Path** by dragging its right endpoint toward the left endpoint while holding down the **Shift** key — this will keep the **Sweep Path** perpendicular to the cross-section. The shorter you make the **Sweep Path**, the

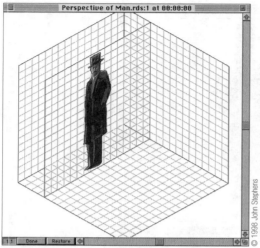

Perspective of Man.rds:1 at 00:00:00

© 1998 John Stephens

FIGURE *The last step is to shorten the Sweep Path to*
10.39 *flatten your object.*

flatter your object will be. (See Figure 10.39.) When you've finished, click on the **Done** button to return to your scene, and then scale and position the object within the scene.

⇨ **Note:** Because your object is flat, it's important that you position it carefully within your scene to make it appear as realistic as possible. For best results it should be directly facing the camera (you can assign a Point At behavior to your objects and use the camera as the target for this) and you should try to avoid side-lighting. You'll need to be careful with reflections as well; if an object reflects the side of your cutout, you'll give away your secrets and destroy the illusion!

— JOHN STEPHENS

APPLYING ONE SHADER ACROSS MULTIPLE OBJECTS

There are times when the easiest way — or the only way — to model a single object is to create multiple objects and group them. The only problem with this technique is that when it is time to apply a complex Shader, the Shader will be applied differently to each object in the group, destroying the illusion of the group being a single object. Fortunately you can get around this by taking advantage of Ray Dream Studio's Detailer export function — even if you don't have Detailer. While this solution can get a little unwieldy if you're working

© 1998 Steve McArdle

FIGURE **10.40** *This technique makes it easy to apply a single Shader continuously across a group of objects (five in this case).*

with several different groups, it works like a charm when used in moderation, as you can see in Figure 10.40.

Compare this image to the preview of the original grouped object in Figure 10.41. You'll see just how much of a difference this technique can make.

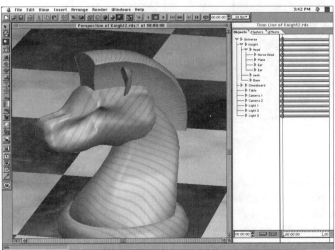

FIGURE **10.41** *This preview of the knight in its multiobject form shows how each object appears separate from the others because of a lack of continuity in the Shader.*

Step One

One important aspect of using Detailer objects that you create from within Ray Dream Studio is that they will be imported with the same position, orientation and size as the original object or group. Since it's faster to manipulate and preview Ray Dream Studio objects than it is Detailer objects, you may want to position your grouped object where you want it to appear in the final image. When you've finished, select the group of objects that you want to consolidate and export them by choosing **Export** from the **File** menu and using the Detailer file format as described in the the "Working with Detailer" tour a couple of tutorials back. In case you don't feel like going back, Figure 10.42 shows a sample of what your Detailer Options might look like. You definitely want to export **Geometry Only** with **As a Single Object** selected. After all, that's what this whole tutorial is all about. Like the "Working with Detailer" example, your Surface Fidelity settings are completely flexible. You simply want the smoothest file for the least cost in polygons. In this sample, though, they've been increased a tad from the default settings, just to make sure we get a smooth knight. Don't worry if your Detailer export takes a while. Your machine is most likely not locked up, as you might think. It's merely calculating a lot of polygons for the conversion. This is one reason to keep the Surface Fidelity as low as possible.

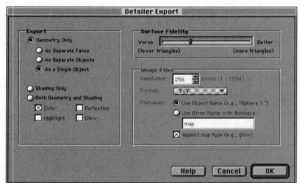

FIGURE **10.42** *When exporting the Detailer object, set the Import options as shown above.*

Step Two

The next step is to import your Detailer object into your original scene. To do this, choose **Import** from the **File** menu. Select your Detailer object file and click on **OK**. An Options dialog box will appear. (See Figure 10.43.) Ignore the Import Shading Only box and just click **OK**.

Notice that your new knight appears in exactly the same space as the original knight. (See Figure 10.44.) You could have deleted the original before the import,

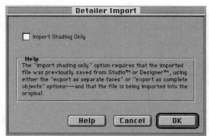

FIGURE **10.43** *When importing the Detailer object, ignore the Import Shading Only box and just click OK.*

but I wanted to keep it around in case I wasn't happy with the Surface Fidelity quality. I also wanted to steal the Shader from it first. At this point, you can delete the original, cloak it, make it invisible or whatever you like — but be sure to steal that Shader first and apply it to the Detailer object. Figure 10.45 shows the imported and shaded Detailer knight with the mapping as it should be.

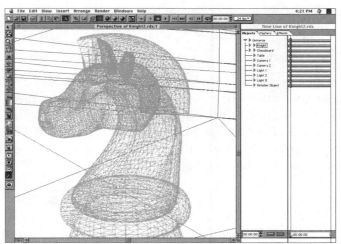

FIGURE **10.44** *When you import the Detailer object, it will appear with the exact position, orientation and size of the original grouped object.*

⇨ **Note:** Many of you might be wondering why you couldn't just use the Boolean operations to do the same thing. The answer is: well, you could. The thing is that you'd have to do it two objects at a time. With this option, you have only a couple of steps. If you're creating a single object out of only two or three objects, Booleans might be a better solution and they'd also be a tad more efficient because they get rid of unneeded geometry, unlike the

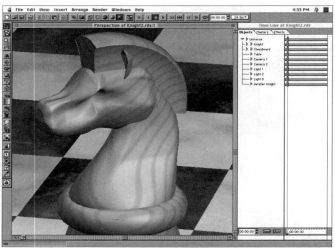

FIGURE *Shader mapping as it should be.*
10.45

Detailer trick. Notice, in Figure 10.44, how the area of the mane that is embedded in the head is still there. With a Boolean operation, this geometry would be clipped away. It's a tradeoff really, and with a file made up of this many objects, the Detailer trick is the quickest solution.

Those of you who had the first edition of this book might be wondering why we changed this tip to use a Detailer export instead of a DXF. The answer to this one is simple: the Detailer file format wasn't available at the time of the first edition. The Detailer file format also supports the Parametric Mapping mode, whereas DXF is very limited in the area of mapping. The Detailer file format is much better suited to the Detailer format.

— *STEVE MCARDLE AND JOHN W. SLEDD*

MODELING WITH THE TRANSPARENCY CHANNEL

This technique could just as easily have been included in Chapter 4 as a modeling technique, but it's completely dependent on Shaders, so it has been included here instead.

When you set out to design and build your models, one of the first things you should do is take the Transparency channel into consideration. Anything that includes holes or openings that would be difficult or impossible to model using other methods can probably be done using the Transparency channel. You can even use it in more complex ways to model multiple flat objects from a single, simple object. But a good place to start is with the basics, an example of which can be seen in Figure 10.46. This model would be virtually impossible to create using any other method, but as you'll see in the next few pages, it is nothing more than a simple sphere and an equally simple Texture Map in the Transparency channel.

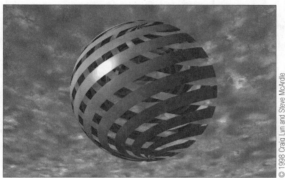

FIGURE **10.46** *The Transparency channel can be used to create modeling effects that would otherwise be impossible.*

Step One

Once you've created your basic object, the first step is to set up your Shader and, in particular, the Transparency channel. (See Figure 10.47.) Although most of the time you'll probably want to use a custom Texture Map, anything will have *some* kind of effect, so feel free to experiment with various Shader components, especially the Shader functions. When you've finished, apply the Shader to your object.

FIGURE **10.47** *Set up a Shader with a Texture Map or procedural Shader function in the Transparency channel.*

Step Two

The only other step in this technique is to render your object (although you may also want to experiment with different Mapping modes, as discussed in the previous technique). When doing so, just make sure you select the **Adaptive or Ray Tracer** renderers and turn on the **Transparency** and **Lighting Through Transparent Objects** settings in the **Current Scene Settings** palette's **Render** tab, as shown in Figure 10.48. Whether you have **Refracted Transparency** checked or not is up to you. If you didn't use any refraction in your Shader, then you don't need it enabled.

FIGURE **10.48** *When using the Transparency channel, make sure your Renderer settings are set appropriately.*

⮕ **Note:** If you need more precision in the placement of the transparent area or if you want to use transparency in only a limited area, create a Shader that is empty in all channels except the Transparency channel, and then use a 3D Paint Shape Creation tool to apply it to your object. You can also use the 3D Paintbrush tool to create the transparent area manually if you prefer.

The 3D Paint tools are especially useful if you want to create simple windows in your objects or to create cutaway views to show what's happening inside an object. Experiment with both methods to see what each can do.

— CRAIG LYN

THE "WHITE IS INVISIBLE" OPTION DEMYSTIFIED

I promised this in Chapter 8 and here it is. People are always asking me what good the White Is Invisible option is at the bottom of the Shader editor's Texture Map and Movie components. (See Figure 10.49.) Well, I'll show you. White Is Invisible is a very specialized tool and is a little misleading. Most, including myself, assume at first that White Is Invisible has something to do

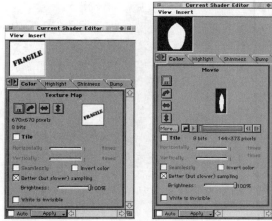

FIGURE **10.49** *The White Is Invisible checkbox is found at the bottom of the Texture Map and Movie component windows.*

with transparency. So we try, in vain, to punch holes though things or create odd transparency masks using this White Is Invisible checkbox.

Basically, White Is Invisible might be better served by the names "White is ignored," "White is a vacuum" or "White is unmodified." White isn't so much invisible when this box is checked as it's simply treated as not being there at all. So it's not invisible, it's just not there. The Shader editor simply ignores all areas of the map that are 100% white. It essentially turns the areas of 100% white into an unmodified channel but leaves the areas that aren't 100% white untouched. Now this seems logical at first, but the first problem you run into is that White Is Invisible doesn't work like everything else in the Shader editor. What I mean by this is that everything I've ranted and raved over about Shader editor and its components would lead one to believe that a pixel that is shaded 99% white would be ignored just a little less than 100% white. This is not the case with White Is Invisible. Anything less than 100% white is seen perfectly clearly by the Shader editor. No ignoring takes place at all. So this adds just another layer of mist over the true sense of White Is Invisible.

In order to help you better understand White Is Invisible, I've put together a project where it is extremely handy. The first part of this project is the cardboard box shown in Figure 10.50. In this example, I had a box whose main cardboard texture was made with a nested procedural texture. The problem was that I wanted to add the words "Fragile" to the side of the box. I also wanted the type to look spattered and a little translucent as though it had been spray-painted onto the box. This would be easy enough to do in an image-editing application, but you'd have to export your procedural textures as a map and then use that map to mix with the type in your paint program. You'd also

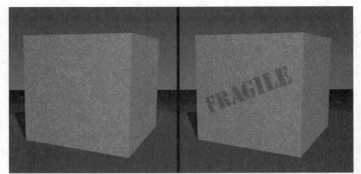

FIGURE **10.50** *The White Is Invisible option makes adding the type to this box a breeze.*

have to make sure you had your colors right, and your file size would increase due to the added overhead of the additional Texture Map. Using this technique lets you retain complete control from within RDS. Suppose you wanted to change the colors of any aspect of the box: the type color, any component of the cardboard texture or anything else. If you used a Texture Map, you'd have to go back and change the actual Texture Map, but by using this technique, you can change anything you desire right in RDS.

Let's go through the creation of this Fragile shader. We'll even cover the what-ifs to show you why it was done this way.

Step One

I have my box. I built the Shader out of nested Mix operators and Spots functions but now the time has come for me to add the "Fragile" text to the side of the box. The first thing I do is to create a Texture Map file to use as my text mask in Adobe Photoshop. (See Figure 10.51.) To get the soft-edges effect, I run a 3-pixel Gaussian Blur to the text to get Figure 10.52. This is the file I plan to use for my Mixer. I could have simply made the text red but, as I mentioned above, I wanted to be able to adjust the color from within RDS, so I've left it as a grayscale file and plan to use it along with an operator.

FIGURE **10.51** *The text was created in Photoshop.*

FIGURE **10.52** *A Blur was added to give me my soft edges.*

Step Two

I open the RDS box file to add my text to the box. Because I want the text to appear on only one side of the box, I use the **3D Paint Shape** tool and draw a shape on the appropriate side of the box which is only slightly smaller than that particular face of the box. (See Figure 10.53.) I double-click on the paint shape with the **Paint Shape Selection** tool to open the **Current Shader editor** for the paint shape. If you don't use the **Paint Shape Selection** tool, you run the risk of selecting and changing the box's Shader. When the Shader editor pops up, the first thing I do is to go through all of the channels except the Color channel and hit **Delete**. This turns all of the other channels into Unmodified channels, which simply means that in the paint shape these channels will be ignored and the box's primer will show through. (See Figure 10.54.)

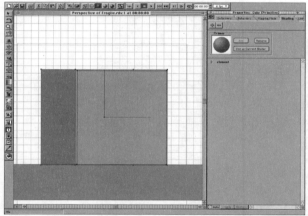

FIGURE *Drawing the paint shape on the box.*
10.53

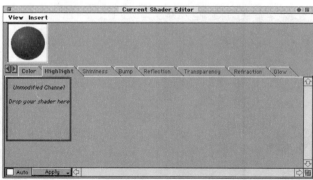

FIGURE *Creating Unmodified channels.*
10.54

Step Three

Now comes the Color channel. For this channel my goal is to make the black areas of the "Fragile" map I've just created red, and I want the other areas to show through to the box's texture. I accomplish this by inserting a **Subtract** operator in the channel. On the left branch of the channel, I insert a **Color** component and leave it at the default **red**. For the right branch, I insert a **Texture Map** component and load in my "Fragile" map. (See Figure 10.55.) I use the Subtract operator because I want to subtract all areas of the mask that are white from my red Color component. Notice that I haven't checked the White Is Invisible box yet. I apply this map, figuring I've finished. Figure 10.56 is the result. As you can see, it hasn't worked out exactly right.

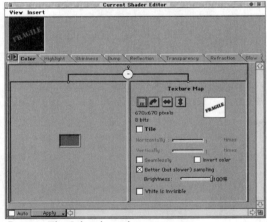

FIGURE *The Color channel setup.*
10.55

FIGURE *This isn't exactly right.*
10.56

The reason this didn't work is because I simply subtracted everything from the Color operator but because the Shader has to put something there, it put a level of 0 just as it was supposed to. Since 0 equals black, this is what I wound up with. I figured: hmmm, clearly, if I don't want the black areas to show through, I need to copy that "Fragile" mask into my Transparency channel. So that's what I did. The Shader preview looked like exactly what I wanted. (See Figure 10.57.) I rerendered, and Figure 10.58 shows what happened. Whereas this might be cool, floating text in front of an empty box was not what I wanted. The reason this didn't work was because when I inserted the map into the Transparency channel, the channel was no longer an Unmodified channel. At this point I thought about the White Is Invisible option, but knew that if I enabled it here, I'd simply get a semitransparent area around each letter, because transparency is transparency when in the Transparency channel. The Transparency channel was not what I

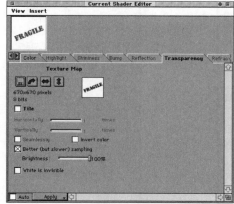

FIGURE
10.57   *Copying the text mask into the Transparency channel looks like a good idea . . .*

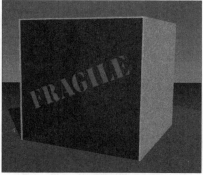

FIGURE
10.58   *. . . apparently it isn't.*

wanted to use here, so I deleted the Texture Map to make the Transparency channel and Unmodified channel once again.

Step Four

After deleting the map from the **Transparency** channel, I headed back into the **Color** channel because I knew exactly what I had to do — check the **White Is Invisible** box for my Texture Map. (See Figure 10.59.) That would certainly give me what I needed. Figure 10.60 showed me otherwise. This was another nifty effect that I jotted down in my List o' nifty effects, but it still wasn't what I wanted. Apparently the problem here was the blur around the outsides of the letters. So I was stuck. How do I get fuzzy edges while using White Is Invisible? And then it hit me — dithering!

FIGURE *Checking the **White Is Invisible** box.*
10.59

FIGURE *So I wasn't as smart as I thought —*
10.60 *cool effect, though.*

Step Five

With my newfound boost of creativity, I headed back into Photoshop, where I opened my blurred text mask. Once the file was opened, I changed its mode to **Bitmap**. Since Photoshop needs some clue as to what to do with the gray values in an image you're turning into a bitmapped image composed of only black-and-white pixels, it presents you with the dialog box in Figure 10.61. I chose the **Diffusion Dither** option because it takes your gray values and creates diffused black dots in an attempt to simulate the gray values. For example, an area composed of 50% gray pixels would be represented by an area containing equal numbers of white and black pixels when diffused. Figure 10.62 shows the same image before and after dithering.

I chose to double the resolution because I wanted very small dots for my screen. Quadrupling them would have actually created a closer match to the grayscale version, but I like the choppiness of the 300-dpi bitmap version. It adds more of a spattered effect. A cool thing about this bitmap technique is that the bitmap files are much smaller than their gray siblings.

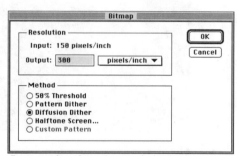

FIGURE *Photoshop's Bitmap dialog box.*
10.61

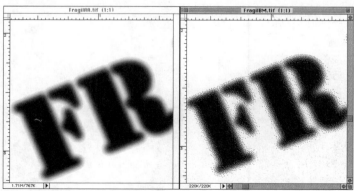

FIGURE *The text mask before and after dithering.*
10.62

With that done, I headed back into RDS where I replaced my grayscale version of the text in the Color channel with the dithered bitmap version (See Figure 10.63.) The rerender shown in Figure 10.64 was almost perfect. The "Fragile" part was just a little opaque for my tastes. I wanted a bit of the underlying box texture to show through. I accomplished this by going into the **Properties palette** and clicking on the **Shading** tab. I expanded the little blue arrow beside the element and changed the **Opacity** to **50%**. (See Figure 10.65.) Rerendering the image this time gave me Figure 10.66, which is what I'd set out to do. All this would have been so much easier had I just used White Is Invisible properly from the start — but then we wouldn't have learned what all those other options do.

FIGURE **10.63** *The Shader editor with the bitmap version of the text.*

FIGURE **10.64** *This render is almost perfect.*

FIGURE **10.65** *Adjusting the opacity of the paint shape.*

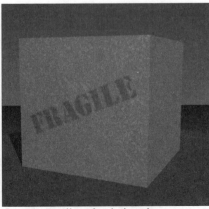

FIGURE **10.66** *Finally, a finished render.*

Step Six

I enjoyed doing that one so much that I decided I needed to add some hazardous-looking symbols to the box as well. I had two symbols. One was a non-antialiased symbol, which means that there were no smooth blends between colors; and the other was antialiased which means that its edges were smooth because the colors blended between each other. Figure 10.67 shows both symbols up close and in full view.

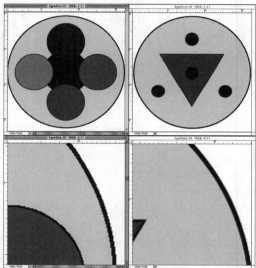

FIGURE *Both of the symbols I had to work with.*
10.67

The non-antialiased version would be a breeze based on what I'd just found out about the White Is Invisible option. Since the file had hard edges around the outside of the circle, I knew that I wouldn't have a problem with silhouetting as I had with the type. I drew a paint shape on the top of the box, just as I did on the side of the box in Step Two, and prepared my new Shader in the same way — but this time I didn't need any trick operators or anything of that nature. I simply inserted a **Texture Map** component and imported the non-antialiased symbol. I checked the **White Is Invisible** box and applied it. (See Figure 10.68.)

The rendering in Figure 10.69 shows that this was perfect. The reason it worked was simply because since the edges were not antialiased, there were no levels of white in the symbol except for the outside areas, which we didn't want to show. The great thing about these techniques is that RDS will do all of the antialiasing for you. It'll automatically create antialiased versions of your artwork when it renders the file with antialiasing turned on. Of course it helps to

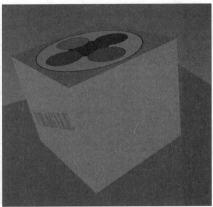

FIGURE
10.68 *The Shader with the first symbol.*

FIGURE
10.69 *This image was perfect from the start.*

have pretty high-resolution artwork when it's not antialiased, but that's often easy to do or find.

The next symbol proved to need a little more work. Since the art had been antialiased, however, there was a smooth blend between the black border of the symbol and the white area surrounding it. Simply importing and applying this symbol, as with the first one, with the **White Is Invisible** box checked yielded the render in Figure 10.70.

I fixed this by creating a non-antialiased mask for the symbol to use in the same way as I did with the text. I opened the symbol in Adobe Illustrator and drew a circle around the symbol that was only slightly smaller than the outside

FIGURE
10.70 *Antialiased edges create a slight halo when used with the White Is Invisible option.*

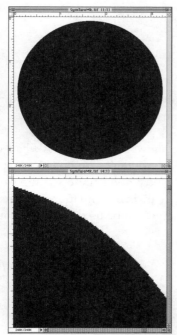

Rasterize Adobe Illustrator Format

Image Size: 248K

Width:	3.354	inches ▼
Height:	3.354	inches ▼
Resolution:	150	pixels/inch ▼
Mode:	Grayscale ▼

OK
Cancel

☐ Anti-aliased   ☒ Constrain Proportions

FIGURE *The Illustrator Rasterize dialog box.*
10.71

FIGURE *The mask for the second symbol.*
10.72

edge of the circle just enough to make sure I clipped off the feathered edges. I then deleted the symbol from the Illustrator file and saved it. I opened this file in Photoshop and unchecked the **Antialiased** checkbox so that I wouldn't repeat the same mistake. (See Figure 10.71.) This left me with the file shown in Figure 10.72, which I saved for use as a mask for my second symbol.

The next step was to create a Subtract operator for the Color channel as I did with the text file, but in this Shader I used the original logo as the left branch (instead of the Color component) and the mask in the right. Figure

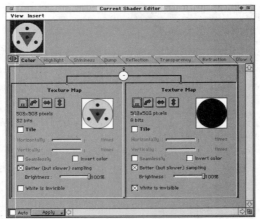

FIGURE   *The Shader for the second symbol.*
10.73

10.73 shows what the Color channel looked like at this point. Notice that I used the White Is Invisible option only on the mask branch. That's the only one that it's important for.

Rendering the file this time showed that the mask had clipped off the outer edges of the second symbol, leaving me with no halo. (See Figure 10.74.)

By now you should have a pretty good understanding of the White Is Invisible option and how to use it in many situations. You're not limited to using it in the Color channel either; it can be used anywhere you need part of a Texture Map to be ignored.

— *JOHN W. SLEDD*

FIGURE   *All the pieces come together for the final*
10.74   *White Is Invisible project render.*

WET ON THE BOTTOM, DRY ON THE TOP

This last tutorial is basically exactly the same tutorial as the Radiosity fake tutorial from Chapter 6. The reason they are so similar is because they are two aspects of the one technique sent in by Richard Bucci. Since that technique is so similar, I'm going to make this one very short. Hey, it's the least I can do for making you fight through that last monster. If you have problems with gaps in this version, please refer back to the tutorial in Chapter 6 to bring you up to speed. They really are the same techniques. That one was placed in that chapter because it's a lighting technique. This one is included here because it's a technique to make your objects' surfaces appear more realistic. Figure 10.75 shows the effect we're after. Notice how the beachball is wet and reflective at the bottom yet dry and nonreflective on top. Compare that to the image in Figure 10.76 and you'll see the difference. Notice how much more realistic the first image is and how you can almost feel the differences between the two balls. The good news is that this technique is a simple one requiring only two short steps, so I'm not even going to bother calling them steps. Just keep reading to figure out how to do this.

FIGURE **10.75** *A beachball afloat in a cove.*

FIGURE **10.76** *A beachball afloat in a cove, yet somehow it remains dry.*

The basic idea behind this tutorial is to use paint shapes and Shader functions to mix up the surfaces of your objects. The beachball Shader is simple enough as it is, but the reflection that blends from the bottom to the top requires a little more thought.

Like the tutorial in Chapter 6, this one relies on a Gradient function. This Gradient function could be used as a mixer in the Reflection channel to blend the reflective qualities from the bottom of the ball to the top. The problem is that you can't control how the Gradient blends. For example, you might want the blend to be short from wet to dry. If you simply place the Gradient function as a mixer in the Reflection channel, you're stuck with the blend you get. However, if you use it in a paint shape, you can control the blend simply by adjusting the size of the paint shape. You want the blend to go from the bottom of the ball to the middle? Simply size the paint shape to go from the bottom to the middle. You want it to go up only about a third? Just resize the paint shape. It's as simple as that.

So the basic step is to create your main Shader as though it were the surface of your object. You then place your paint shape on the object and use that as the surface condition of your object. For this one, the paint shape is the surface condition wet. So the Shader for the paint shape is merely a Mix operator in the Reflection channel which uses two Value components as the right and left branches and a Gradient function as the mixer. Figure 10.77 shows the Reflection channel tree for the paint shape. That's it. That's all you need to know. Figure 10.78 shows the final scene of the lost beachball.

— *RICHARD BUCCI*

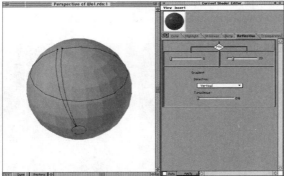

FIGURE **10.77** *The Gradient Function in the Reflection channel creates the illusion of variable moisture on the bottom of the ball.*

FIGURE **10.78** *The final lost beachball is wet where it should be wet and dry where it should be dry.*

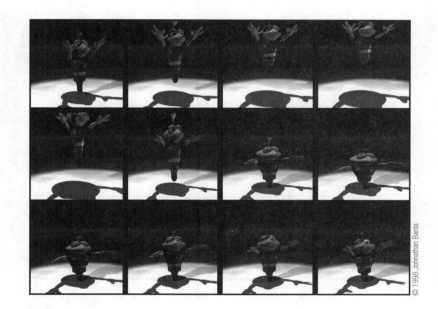

ANIMATED AMBIENT LIGHT

Remember that virtually everything in Ray Dream Studio is animatable —
even the Ambient light. Animating ambient light in conjunction with your
other lighting is a great way to create your fade-ins and fade-outs right in Ray
Dream Studio.

For this example, we have animated a fade-out. We did a one-second animation at 12 frames per second, where the ambient light starts out at 100%
and fades to 0%, thereby closing the scene in total darkness.

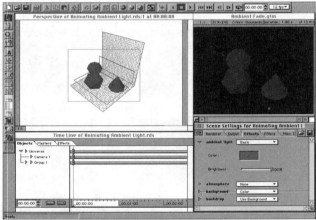

FIGURE   *The beginning of the Ambient light animation.*

11.1

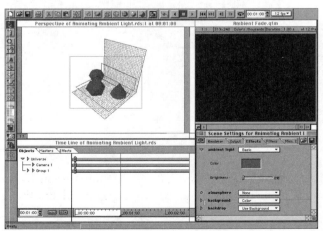

FIGURE   *The end of the Ambient light animation.*

11.2

Figure 11.1 shows the animation at frame 0:00. In this frame, the Ambient light has been set to 100% (the default ambient light setting for RDS 5 is 60%).

Moving to frame 1:00 we set the ambient light at 0% by selecting **Render>Current Scene Settings>Effects Tab>Ambient light,** which creates a key event. (See Figure 11.2.)

FIGURE *Animating the Ambient light creates an interesting fade-out.*
11.3

Figure 11.3 shows the gradual fade-out at work.

— *AARON PUTNAM*

ANIMATED FOG

Atmosphere effects can be animated too. You can have Distant Fog roll in to encompass a scene with a lighthouse or, as in the scene in Figure 11.4, a Cloudy Fog can rise up from the ground and engulf an entire city.

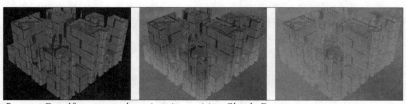

FIGURE *Engulf your scene by animating a rising Cloudy Fog.*
11.4

⇨ **Editor's Note:** These effects can be expanded upon by animating the new Fog Volumetric Primitive or by using Rayflect, Inc.'s Four Elements Extension.

— *AARON PUTNAM*

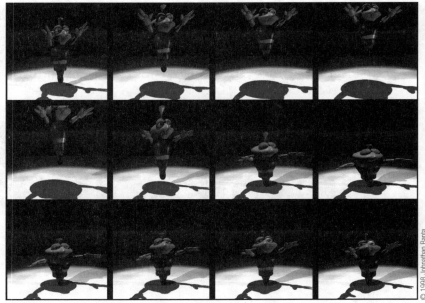

© 1998 Johnathan Banta

FIGURE *Animating the Stretch deformer can breathe new life into your character*
11.5 *animations.*

ANIMATING DEFORMERS

Use deformers to give your animations a lifelike elasticity. Without deformers, the character in Figure 11.5 would seem rigid and dry. Clever use of the Stretch deformer "springs" this animation to life. Notice how the body stretches during takeoff and then squashes upon landing.

— *JOHNATHAN BANTA*

ANIMATING MASTER OBJECTS AND GROUPS FOR MASS EFFECT

Be sure not to overlook the power of animating Master objects. Just as you can change the shading on a group of objects that are based on the same Master object simply by changing the shading on that Master, you can also animate a group of objects that are based on the same Master object by animating only the Master object.

In Figure 11.6, we have a school of goldfish made up of instances of the same Master object. We can animate the swimming motion of this entire school at the same time by modifying the master fish. In figure 11.7, we have a view of the master fish object in the modeling window at frame 0:00. In figure 11.8, we have the same master fish object at frame 2:00 with the tail swishing

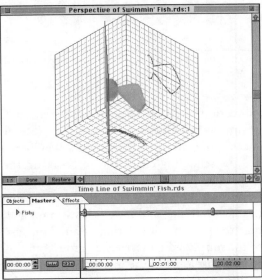

FIGURE *The unanimated school of fish.*
11.6

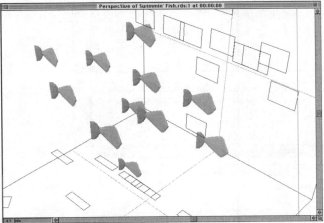

FIGURE *The master fish at the beginning of its tail-*
11.7 *flicking motion.*

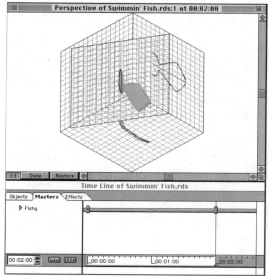

FIGURE
11.8
The master fish at the end of its tail-flicking motion.

FIGURE
11.9
The motion of the instances of the master fish is dictated by the motion created at the Master level.

in the opposite direction. Add an Oscillate tweener, and the entire school swims in unison from the modification of one object. (See Figure 11.9.) For an added effect, you can group all the fish and add a Wave deformer to the group to further enhance the schooling effect and to break up the fact that they all flick their tails at the same time.

Now if you create a Master group from that group, you can duplicate that group as many times as you like, and have fish swimming all over the place. If you want to change the position or coloring or anything else of any of the fish in all of the groups, simply edit the Master group, and all instances of the group will be updated, just as all of the instances of the fish master object were updated — pretty nifty, eh?

— JOHN W. SLEDD

ANIMATE THE TRANSPARENCY CHANNEL FOR SPECIAL EFFECTS

Animating the Transparency channel can create some clever special effects. For instance, you can animate a ghostly apparition fading into your scene and then slowly fading back into nothingness. (See Figure 11.10.) Or you can place movie maps (quicktime or avi format) into the Transparency channel to make objects appear and disappear in a puff of smoke.

FIGURE   *The figure starts out with a transparency setting of 44%, which dwindles to*
11.10   *0%, creating a complete fade-out of the object.*

BANKING ON CURVES

Many of you will animate some sort of flying thing at one time or another, whether it is an airplane, a spaceship or a mechanical owl. When animating flying things, pay very close attention to banking. When you see a jet fighter take a sharp turn, it doesn't turn on the Z axis (Yaw) and go in the other direction, as your car would. It must bank — change angles in both Pitch and Roll — to make all of the forces of physics happy so that they will oblige in the request for a direction change.

Since the 3D world really doesn't care that much about physics in general — there are exceptions, as you should know if've you read your *Ray Dream Studio User Guide*— you, the animator, must add these effects to maintain the believability of your animations.

— *JOHN W. SLEDD*

USING MOVIES AS GELS TO CREATE REALISTIC SHADOWS

Use movies as gels for your lights to add more realism. An animation of an outdoor scene will have more impact if the shadows cast from the leaves in a tree move as if there is a slight wind blowing. This can be accomplished by slipping a movie of moving leaves, either real or electronic, into the gel channel of your light source.

AVOID VIBRANT COLORS IF OUTPUTTING TO VIDEO

If your animation is to be broadcast or played on your TV, there are some color issues you need to be aware of. Just as the RGB color palette used by television screens and your monitor has a larger range than the CMYK palette used for color printing, your multiscan computer monitor's color range is much broader than your TV NTSC monitor's color range. If you have postproduction software, you can go ahead and render with the full 24-bit color palette and then convert your animation to an NTSC-safe palette before committing it to tape, but be prepared to lose some colors. If you don't have video postproduction software, the warning to beware of vibrant colors is something you will need to pay attention to while creating your animation.

Red is a very good example of a color to watch out for. Some shades of red tend to bleed on a TV screen and generally behave poorly, so use them sparingly.

Russ Andersson of Autonomous Effects has created an extension that will help you out tremendously with this type of problem and will give you lots of creative options as well. It's called TV Tweaker, and it'll do just about any postprocessing effect you can think of, right in RDS, including choosing the best NTSC-safe color options.

USING THE OSCILLATE TWEENER TO PROVIDE AN ENDLESS LOOP

Suppose you want to do an animation against an animated background that you found on a CD-ROM. (See Figure 11.11.) The problem is that the anima-

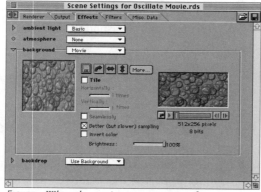

FIGURE
11.11
When the movie you want to use for a background or a gel is shorter than your animation, use the Oscillate tweener to loop the movie as many times as you need.

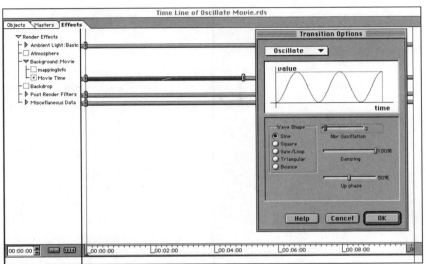

FIGURE
11.12 *Just type in the number of times you need the movie to repeat, and render your animation.*

tion from the CD-ROM is five seconds long, and you want it to repeat throughout your 10-second animation sequence.

Currently, Ray Dream Studio does not provide an obvious way to loop a movie. What it does have is perhaps not so obvious but nonetheless effective.

Set up your movie to play throughout the animation, and then use the Oscillate tweener (see Figure 11.12) to specify the number of times you'd like it to play. It works wonders — trust me.

12 Animation Techniques

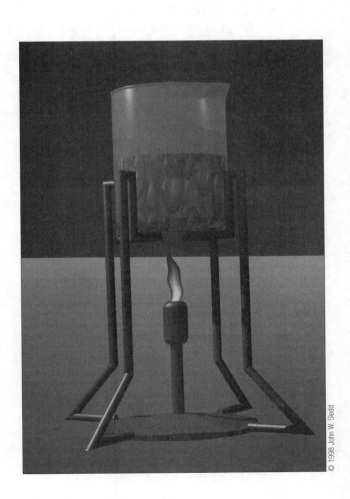

ANIMATING BUMP MAPS

Animating the Bump channel can be used to create a wide variety of effects from rippling water to spontaneously emerging text. RDS provides many ways to animate the Bump channel. You can place a movie in the Bump channel, or you can animate procedurals such as the Marble or Wood procedurals to get a veiny effect. You can also animate mixes of the Shader Tree or simply animate a slider, as we are going to do in this tutorial. Our goal here is to animate text rising up out of the texture of a wall.

Step One

Create a new scene by choosing **New** under the **File** menu.

Step Two

Create a cube by choosing **Cube** from the **Insert** menu. We're going to map the Bump onto the front face of the cube, so select the cube and open the **Properties palette**. Click on the **Mapping Mode** tab, choose the **Box/Face** Mapping mode and select the **Front Face.** (See Figure 12.1.) Now click on the cube with the **Eyedropper** tool to bring up the **Shader editor**. Change the color in the Color channel to a medium shade of gray.

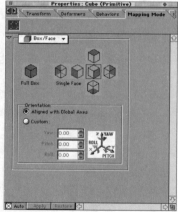

FIGURE **12.1**   *Use the Box/Face or Projection Mapping mode for the best placement of your Bump.*

Step Three

Here's where we apply the Bump map. I created the Bump Texture Map ahead of time in an image-editing application. (See Figure 12.2.) Click on the **Bump**

FIGURE **12.2** *Give your Bump maps a little Gaussian blur to extend the Bump range.*

FIGURE **12.3** *The Bump channel's Texture Map.*

tab in the **Shader editor** and insert a **Texture Map** component. Navigate to the file you wish to use for the Texture Map and click **Open**. Your **Shader editor** should look somewhat like Figure 12.3.

Since we want the Bump to fade in over time, drag the **Amplitude** slider down to **0%** and apply the **Shader**. (See Figure 12.4.)

FIGURE **12.4** *Zero out the Amplitude slider.*

Step Four

If you rendered this frame of the animation, you would not see your Bump. That's because we dropped the Amplitude or level of your Bump map down to zero. It's there, but we're putting a cap on it with that Amplitude slider.

To fade your Bump in from the zero level, where it is now, to a 100% Bump, drag the **Current Time Bar** to the time in the animation where you want the Bump to be at 100% and bring up the **Shader editor** again. Click on the **Bump** tab and drag the **Amplitude** slider to **100%** (or more, if you're feeling feisty). This will bring the Bump to it's full glory. (See Figure 12.5.) Click **Apply** in the **Shader editor** and return the **Current Time Bar** to **0:00**.

Now move your camera to the front of the cube by choosing **Preset Position>Front** from the **View** menu. Position the cube in the center of your Production Frame. Render your animation and watch the Bump fade in, as in Figure 12.6.

— CRAIG LYN

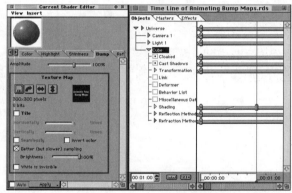

FIGURE *Setting the Bump level to the desired height.*
12.5

FIGURE *The Bump gradually fades into the object.*
12.6

ANIMATED FLASH OF LIGHT

In this example we're going to create an animated Glow map. The effect that we're trying to achieve in the final rendering is a flash of light or glint crossing the surface of the model, which is the word "Glimmer" in this case. It would be quicker to use a program such as After Effects or Premiere to create this map, but I'm feeling creative today, and many of you won't have these apps, so I'm going to do it all in Studio and Photoshop.

Step One

First we have to create the map for the Glow. Open Photoshop and create a new document that is roughly twice as long as it is high. Draw two thick white lines horizontally and then apply **Gaussian Blur** to the image. The resulting image should look like the picture in Figure 12.7. Save the file as a .TIFF or .PICT and name it FLASH.

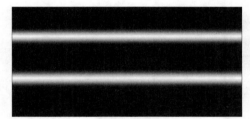

FIGURE *The mask for the Glimmer effect.*
12.7

Step Two

Create a new file in Ray Dream Studio. Insert a new Free Form object (**Insert>Free Form**). On the drawing plane, draw a shape that is the same proportions as your "Flash" Texture Map. Edit the **Extrusion path** so that the object is about a quarter of an inch thick on the screen. (See Figure 12.8.) Click **Done**.

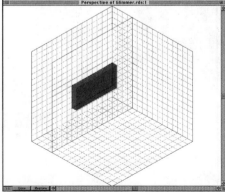

FIGURE *Create the object which will hold your*
12.8 *glimmer mask.*

Select the object and change your camera view to **Front** (**View>Preset Views>Front**). Select the object and then click on it with the **Eyedropper** tool to bring up the **Shader editor.** Change the color in the Color channel to **Black.** Now enter values of **zero** in the other channels until you get to the **Glow** channel. Insert a **Texture Map** component and place your Flash map into the **Glow** channel. Click **Apply.** Select **View>Better Preview**, and you should see something similar to Figure 12.9.

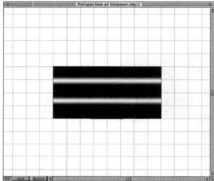

FIGURE **12.9** *Your glimmer mask object should look something like this.*

Step Three

Now we're going to create the "Glimmer" text by dragging the **Text** tool into the **Perspective** or **Hierarchy** windows and typing **Glimmer** into the text field. (See Figure 12.10.) Once you have the "Glimmer" text created, go back to the front view (if you ever left) and drag the production frame so that it encom-

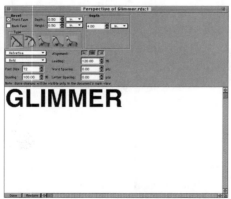

FIGURE **12.10** *Creating the object that will receive the flash/glimmer.*

FIGURE **12.11** *Resize the production frame to match the size of the Glimmer object.*

passes your "Glimmer" model exactly. (See Figure 12.11.) We're doing this so that our "Glimmer" Glow map movie is the proper size.

Now click on **Glimmer** and cloak it by opening the **Properties palette**, clicking on the **General** tab and checking **Cloak**, as in Figure 12.12.

FIGURE **12.12** *Cloaking the Glimmer object.*

Step Four

Now we set up and render the Flash movie for use in the Glow map.

With the Production Frame still in view, drag the **Flash** object to the left of the **Production Frame** and rotate it **60 degrees**. (See Figure 12.13.) We should be at frame 0:00 at this point. Now move to **frame 2:00** and shift-drag **Flash** to the other side of the Production Frame, as in Figure 12.14.

Reset the timeline and delete any lights in the scene. Then open the **Current Scene Settings** window, click on the **Effects** tab and drop the **Ambient** light setting to **0%** and make the **Background** or Backdrop **black**.

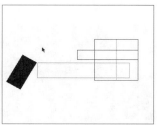

FIGURE **12.13** *Setting the scene up to render the initial flash-effect Movie map.*

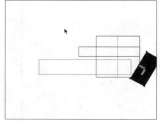

FIGURE **12.14** *Setting up the end of the flash mask object's path.*

Now click on the **Output** tab and expand the **Image Size** tab. Type **150** in the **DPI** field (this higher resolution should ensure a good-quality flash even when the final object is close to the camera). Now render the animation and save it as FLASH.MOV or FLASH.AVI. When you save the file, be sure to choose a compression scheme which allows you to save at 256 grays or grayscale. This will cut down on your file size considerably. For example, the original QuickTime was 24MB, but saving it with the Animation codec at 256 levels of gray reduced the file to 683K, and saving it with the Cinepak codec at 256 grays reduced it to 293K.

Step Five

Now uncloak and copy the **Glimmer** text object. Create a new file and paste the **Glimmer** object into it. Select the **Glimmer** object and then click on it with the **Eyedropper** tool to bring up the **Shader editor**. Put whatever you want in all of the channels except the Glow channel. In the Glow channel, select **Movie** under the **Insert** menu and open your **FLASH.XXX** movie. (See Figure 12.15.)

Render your animation. You should get something similar to Figure 12.16.

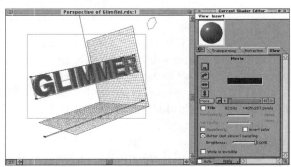

FIGURE *Adding the Flash movie to the Glimmer object.*
12.15

FIGURE *The final Glimmer animation effect.*
12.16

FIGURE
12.17
Using the Aura filter creates a great blown-out effect.

This Flash movie could also be placed into the Reflection, Highlight, or any other channel for varying effects. You can also use the Aura filter for an added bit of mood, as shown in Figure 12.17.

— *CRAIG LYN & JOHN W. SLEDD*

ANIMATING CROSS-SECTIONS

While this example is neither American Beauty nor Irish Rose, it takes on flowery attributes when duplicated and piled high. You will be creating all shapes in the cross-section plane and all points on the envelope and sweep path with the Time Controller set at 0.

Step One
With the **Timeline** set at 0, choose **Insert>Free Form**. From the **Geometry** menu choose **Extrusion Method>Pipeline**.

Step Two
In the drawing plane of cross-section 1, use the **Pen** tool to create several curved lines. You can make these as irregular as you like as long as they overlap as seen from the center. (See Figure 12.18.)

Step Three
Use the **Add Point** tool to create a cross-section between the end points of the **Sweep Path**. Select the **Sweep Path**'s right end point and choose **Create** from the **Sections** menu. (See Figure 12.19.)

Step Four
From the **Geometry** menu again, choose **Extrusion Envelope>Symmetric**. Move the left point of the envelope closer to the **Sweep Path**, and the midpoint farther away. (See Figure 12.20.)

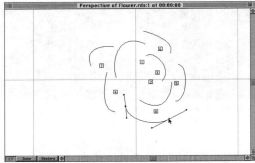

FIGURE *Create the shapes for your petals.*
12.18

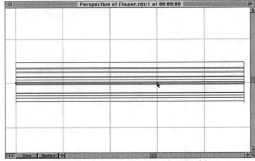

FIGURE *Create a new cross-section for the bloom.*
12.19

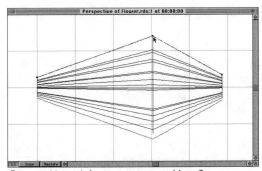

FIGURE *Now it's beginning to resemble a flower.*
12.20

Step Five

Next use the **Bezier** tool to smooth the curves into the lines of a closed flower. (See Figure 12.21.) When you've finished, go to the **Reference View**, click the **Better Preview** button, and apply a **Shader**. Admire your bud.

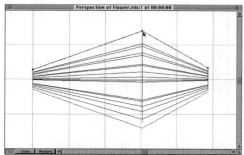

FIGURE *Sit back for a moment and admire your bud.*

12.21

Step Six

Use the **Add Key Event** tool to put a new **Key Event Marker** at the end of the flower's time track (at 2 seconds in this example). (See Figure 12.22.)

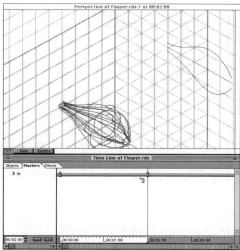

FIGURE *Adding a key event for the blooming action.*

12.22

Step Seven

Click the **Last Frame Button** in the **Time Controller** toolbar; this takes you to the end of your time track, where you'll open the flower. Select the left end point of the envelope and drag it close to the upper edge of the drawing plane; then select the midpoint and move it a little more than midway to the upper edge. (See Figure 12.23.) The right end point stays where it is. You can really spread the petals as this is the most your flower will ever bloom.

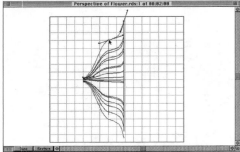

FIGURE **12.23**   *Spread the flower as much as you can because this will be as wide as your bloom will get.*

Step Eight

Go to cross-section 3 and use the **Selection** and **Bezier** tools to adjust the size of the curves for however much you want the petals to taper. (See Figure 12.24.) Move them around; play with them.

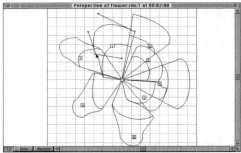

FIGURE **12.24**   *Taper the petals to make them soft and . . . well . . . flowery.*

If your flower looks more like a ragweed than a waterlily, you can fatten it up by duplicating and offsetting the second flower's event markers.

With the **Time Controller** set at **0**, select and duplicate the flower, and jump into the duplicate. (It will have the original object's name, followed by a **1**.)

Step Nine

With the **Masters** tab showing, select the first **Key Event Marker** and drag it holding down the **Option** key (Mac) or the **Alt** key (Windows) to the place on the timeline where you want your second flower to begin opening. (See Figure 12.25.)

You can repeat the duplication process until you run out of memory or patience. While at the **Masters** level you can change the Shaders, successively

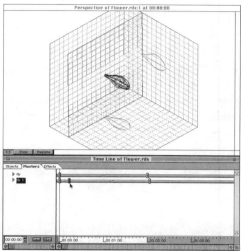

FIGURE **12.25** *Option-drag the Key Event Marker to determine the start of the bloom.*

lightening or darkening each duplicate; you can animate the Shaders; if you find you're looking at flower 10 you can apply **Cloaking** to each flower so that it becomes visible only when it starts to unfold. See Figure 12.26 for the duplicated flower.

— CECILIA ZIEMER

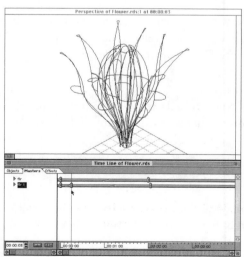

FIGURE **12.26** *Add duplicates of the flower to fatten it up if needed.*

BEAM ME UP

In this example we're going to create a teleporter-type special effect by animating the Transparency channel. I created the movie to be used in the transparency effect by applying a dissolve transition between a black and a white image in a video-editing program. This effect is standard in most video-editing packages, so you shouldn't have to look too far to find it. The finished transition movie is shown in Figure 12.27.

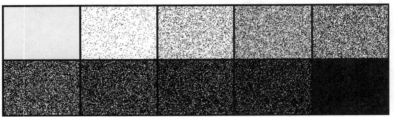

FIGURE
12.27   *Adding a dissolve transition movie to your Transparency channel can add some very interesting effects.*

Step One
Create a new scene in Ray Dream Studio by choosing **New** under the **File** menu. Choose **Sphere** from the **Insert** menu.

Step Two
Click on the sphere with the **Selection** tool and then click on it with the **Eyedropper** tool. Click on the **Transparency** tab in the **Shader editor** and choose **Movie** under the **Shader editor's Insert** menu.

Step Three
For this example, we want the sphere to fade out. The problem is that I created the dissolve transition so that it dissolves from white to black. This will cause the sphere to fade *in* instead of out. To fix this, check the **Invert Color** box. (See Figure 12.28.)

Step Four
Render the movie making sure that **Transparency** is checked in your **Scene Settings>Renderer** tab. Figure 12.29 illustrates the desired effect.

— JOHN W. SLEDD

FIGURE **12.28** *The dissolve movie in the Transparency channel.*

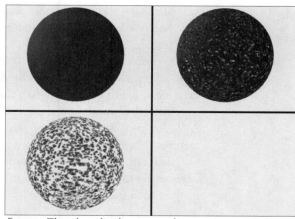

FIGURE **12.29** *The sphere dissolves into nothingness.*

USING MOVIES AS OBJECTS

For this example, I will show you how to use a movie to represent an object that would be very difficult to model and animate. This particular animation will be of a beaker full of bubbling liquid with a rotoscoped flame instead of a modeled one and rotoscoped bubbles in the beaker. (See Figure 12.30.)

FIGURE **12.30** *Animated flame and bubbles.*

Modeling the many bubbles in the liquid would be a very time-consuming task to say the least, not to mention attempting to do a realistic flame using traditional 3D methods.

It should be pointed out that very good flames can be done either with RDS's Fire primitive or with the Fire shader in Rayflect, Inc.'s Four Elements extension. Neither will look like this one though.

Instead of modeling these items, we will be using QuickTime movies (or AVIs for you Windows users out there) and Ray Dream Studio's rotoscoping features to simulate the effects.

Granted, I will be using some additional tools that many of you will not have access to, but countless sources provide stock QuickTime and AVI movies for just such uses.

Step One

First we start with the beaker and the bubbling fluid. I created the Bubbles movie in Figure 12.31 using MetaCreations' TextureScape 1.5 and saved it as a QuickTime movie. Using the inner wall of the beaker profile, I modeled a simple object to be used as the fluid. We will map the Bubbles movie to the Fluid object to get the bubbling action going.

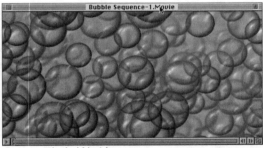

Figure **12.31**   *The bubblin' brew.*

With the Liquid open in the **Modeling** window and the **Better Preview** option selected, I imported the movie into the Shader's **Color channel** and applied it. (See Figures 12.32 and 12.33.) I prefer to work on objects in the Modeling window (as opposed to the **Perspective** window) when the mapping of the placed image or movie is critical. For instance, I wouldn't want my bubbles going from top to bottom, now would I? I find it easier to forecast the results of my Shader mapping options when I am looking at the object exactly as the Mapping feature is looking at it. The fewer reorientations I have to perform in my head, the better. Also, if you have the Modeling window open for the object in question, there's no chance of your shading the wrong object.

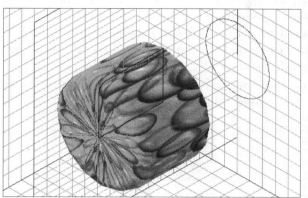

FIGURE
12.32 Shading objects at the Master level helps with both Shader mapping and Shader precision.

FIGURE
12.33 Using the movie as the Liquid object's Texture Map.

The default **Surface Mapping** option was sufficient for this one. I closed out the **Modeling** window and rendered a test animation just to make sure everything was pointing in the right direction.

Then I copied the information in the **Color** channel into the **Bump** channel to give the bubbles a little more "feel." (See Figure 12.34.) Still something wasn't quite right: What good is bubbling green liquid if it doesn't glow? To remedy this, I dragged the file into the **Glow** channel as well. I didn't want it to be too bright so I lowered the **Brightness** setting. (See Figure 12.35.)

FIGURE
12.34 Duplicating the map into the Glow channel to give the bubbles a little bit of feel.

FIGURE
12.35 The Brightness slider allows you to control the amount of glow.

Step Two

Now that I had the bubbling liquid, all I needed was a flame for the burner. This one proved to be a bit trickier. I created the flame in Adobe Illustrator and imported it into Adobe After Effects to add the flicker. Once done making the flame dance using the **Ripple** filter, I made two movies, one with the actual flame (See Figure 12.36) and one for the Alpha channel (mask) (See Figure 12.37) that I would use to mask out the inactive parts of the object that the flame would be projected onto.

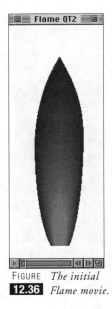

FIGURE *The initial*
12.36 *Flame movie.*

FIGURE *The Flame*
12.37 *Mask movie.*

I created a plane in the **Free Form Modeler** which was roughly the same size as the Flame movie. (See Figure 12.38.) Then, using the same method described in Step One, I imported the QuickTime of the flame into the Shader's Color channel. (See Figure 12.39.) Again, the default Mapping option worked fine.

This left me with a white plane with a blue flame in the middle of it (see Figure 12.40) — not a very convincing flame. I had to mask out the white outer edges of the move so that only the flame would show. This is where the Alpha channel I created in After Effects came into play. I imported the **Alpha** channel movie into the **Transparency** channel of the **Shader editor.** (See Figure 12.41.) This masked out every part of the object except the flame. Since the mask was created from the same movie as the flame, it moved in sync with the Flame movie in the Color channel. Once this was taken care of, I copied the movie information from the **Color** channel into the **Glow** channel to give the

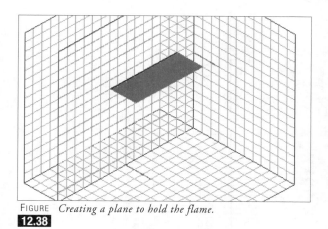

FIGURE
12.38 *Creating a plane to hold the flame.*

FIGURE
12.39 *Importing the Flame movie into the Color channel.*

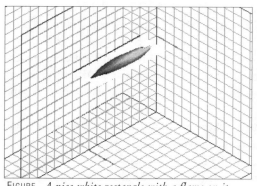

FIGURE
12.40 *A nice white rectangle with a flame on it . . . needs some work.*

FIGURE
12.41 *Masking out unwanted areas with the Alpha channel movie.*

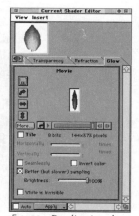

FIGURE
12.42 *Duplicating the flame to the Glow channel.*

flame its brightness. (See Figure 12.42.) I didn't need to use the Brightness slider for this one because the glow was just right as it was.

After all of this was taken care of, I moved the camera into the proper position (see Figure 12.43) and rendered the movie. Both of these objects took me a fraction of the time it would have taken had I attempted to model and animate equivalent objects, and with nary a key event created.

There are some important things to consider here. Either your movie must be as long or longer than your RDS animation from the start or it needs to be

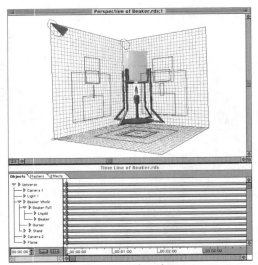

FIGURE *Set the scene up and render it.*
12.43

seamlessly loopable so you can loop it throughout your animation using the Oscillate tweener. The good news is that you don't need to worry about keyframes when using movies. RDS takes care of playing the movie in sync with your RDS animation. Other good news is that if your movie is too long (as the one in this sample was) you can simply drag the end keyframe for the movie to the end of the render area to compress the movie. Of course it will play faster this way, so if that's not what you want, just leave it alone or expand or compress it to taste.

One last note on this technique: if you are using the Glow channel, you may or may not need to use the same movie in the Color channel too. It depends on what you're after. This particular animation would have done fine with maps in only the Glow channels, but then we wouldn't have had as much fun, now would we? Experiment with different-colored Glow and Color channels for some interesting effects.

Also, if you're using glow to simulate a light source, it's a good idea to place a light of the same color in the area to illuminate the objects around it. Otherwise, something will be missing. You could get really creative and add the same Flame movie to the gel of your light for some very realistic effects.

Other uses for this technique include the use of QuickTime or AVI explosions, and smoke and fire effects such as the ones on the Pyrotechniques and Pyrotechniques2 CD-ROMs from Visual Concepts Engineering.

— JOHN W. SLEDD

CREATING A CAMERA CUT EFFECT WITHIN RDS

The question has come up several times as to whether or not you can animate the switching of cameras within RDS. Well, the answer is simple — no. But you can animate the same camera to achieve the same effect. You know by now that you can animate the motions of a camera. Typically this would be done to have the camera pan around the scene or perhaps to have it follow an object. The difference between animating the camera to pan around a scene versus animating it to film from point A and then abruptly switch to point B lies in the tweener. The following is a little tutorial example to give you an idea of how to implement this technique in your own animations.

Step One

Create a scene to be animated. Here we will create a few primitives just to give you a better idea of the different views we will be shooting. Create a **Sphere**, a **Cube**, and a **Cone** in your scene by choosing each from the **Insert** menu. Once you've inserted all three objects, drag them into a triangular shape, as in Figure 12.44. It might be a good idea at this point to change the color of each shape too, just so that they are easily recognizable.

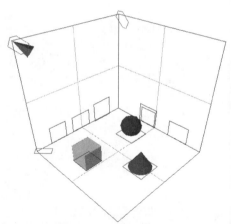

FIGURE *Configure the primitives into a triangle*
12.44 *shape and make them all a different color.*

Step Two

Here we are going to create the camera changes. With your camera still in the **Reference view**, select **Production Frame** from the **View** menu and, using the camera controls (**Windows>Camera Properties**), center your scene in the production frame. Move to **frame 1:00** in the Timeline window and choose **Preset**

Position>Top from the **View** menu. This action will change your camera from a **Conical** camera to an **Isometric** camera. In the **Camera Properties** palette, change it back to **Conical** using the **Type** pull-down menu. Center your scene in the production frame using the **Camera Properties** palette or the camera tools.

Now go back to the **Timeline** and move the **Current Time Indicator** to frame **2:00**. Now change your camera view again to the **Front** view by selecting **Preset Views>Front** from the **View** menu. Change the type of camera back to **Conical** again and center the scene in the production frame. Your scene should look similar to Figure 12.45 at frames 0:00, 1:00, and 2:00, respectively.

FIGURE　*You should see pretty much the same thing while view-*
12.45　*ing the scene at the specified points on the Timeline.*

⇨ **Note:** Don't move the production frame itself — the Production Frame is not animatable and will change the view in your entire animation if you move it in one frame.

Step Three

Now we're going to implement the Discreet tweener. Double-click on the camera's **time track** between frames 0:00 and 1:00. (See Figure 12.46.) You will get the **Transition Options** dialog box. Change the tweener from **Linear** to **Discrete** in the pull-down menu. Make sure the threshold is **100%** and click **OK.** (See Figure 12.47.)

Now render or preview your animation to view the Camera Cut Effect.

— JOHN W. SLEDD

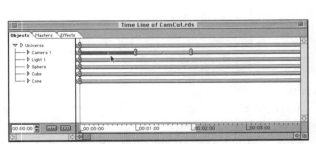

FIGURE　*There's magic in your tweener.*

FIGURE　*Setting up the*
12.47　*Discrete tweener.*

MOTION THROUGH ANIMATED BACKGROUND AND FOREGROUND ELEMENTS

In this tutorial, we're going to cover the illusion of motion through the movement of elements that would normally stay still during an animation. We're going to give the illusion of forward motion to the character in the scene by moving the scenery around him. This lets the camera and the character stay pretty much stationary while the foreground and background elements do all of the work. Furthermore, we're going to create the illusion of depth by moving our foreground at a higher rate of speed than our background. This is a technique often used by traditional cel animators but it's extremely useful in the area of digital animation as well. Of course, most traditional tricks and techniques have important places in the digital realm. Figure 12.48 shows a few frames from the resulting animation.

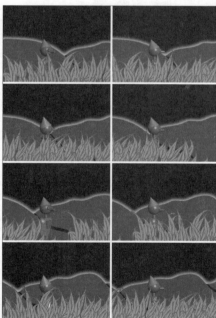

FIGURE 12.48   *The motion in this animation is mainly the movement of the foreground and background elements.*

Step One

Open the file called FOREBACK.RDS from the CD-ROM. (See Figure 12.49.) I've set almost everything up in this file, so I'll take a moment to tell you what I've done. We'll start from the front of the scene and work our way back. The first element in the scene is a Free Form object which has such a shallow extrusion that it is basically a plane. On this plane, I've mapped a Texture Map of leaves that I created with MetaCreations' Expression, saved as an Adobe Illustrator file, then opened up in Photoshop where I created a mask to use in the Transparency channel. Figure 12.50 shows the resulting maps.

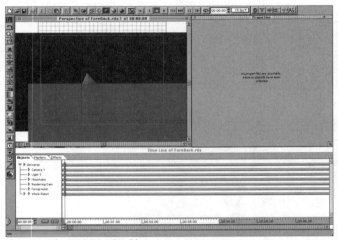

FIGURE *The FOREBACK file.*
12.49

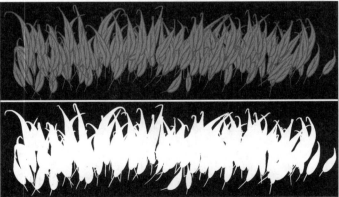

FIGURE *The two maps created from the Expression file. The first is the map*
12.50 *used in the Color channel and the second is the mask used in the Transparency channel to mask the areas not covered by the leaves.*

The second object in the scene is a little guy I've just named Bobby Bluebot (actually his RDS name is Whole Robot). He looks green in the animation but that's because there's a big yellow light shining on him. Bobby is wandering through a patch of dense foliage in search of his sister Barbara. Yep, I'm making this story up as I go along.

The other object in the scene is the background plane. I used the same object that I used for the foreground leaves, but this time I mapped an image of some distant mountains. Figure 12.51 shows the entire map for this object.

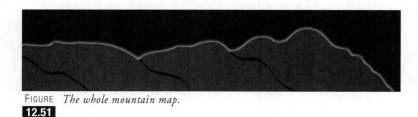

FIGURE *The whole mountain map.*
12.51

There is a distant light in the scene and, of course, two cameras — one for rendering and one for placement. The good news is that most of the work really needs to be done from the rendering camera, so you won't be bouncing around too much.

Now that you have an idea of how the scene is organized, let's move onto Step Two where we'll start animating things.

Step Two

Here we're going to start the animation by animating the foreground elements. The foreground plane really isn't large enough to cover the distance we need to cover in our animation. To fix this, change your view to **Camera 1** and select **Front** from the **Preset Views**. Select the foreground object, duplicate it and **Shift-drag** the duplicate to the right of the original so that the left side of the duplicate pretty much matches up to the right side of the original. Group the two foreground objects. (See Figure 12.52.) This will essentially create one long plane with a small gap in the middle. This repeating of a scenery element is commonplace where long running sequences appear in old Saturday morning cartoons — especially those whose creators' initials were H and B.

Now we're going to animate our newly extended foreground scenery. Go back to the **Rendering Cam** view and then move the **Current Time Bar** to **frame 4:00**. Now **Shift-drag** the foreground group to the left until only a little bit of it remains to the right of the production frame. (See Figure 12.53.)

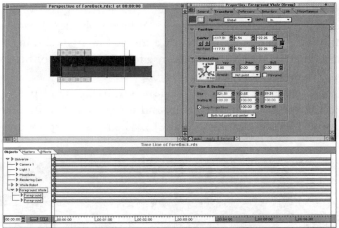

FIGURE
12.52 *Extending the foreground element by duplicating the original Free Form.*

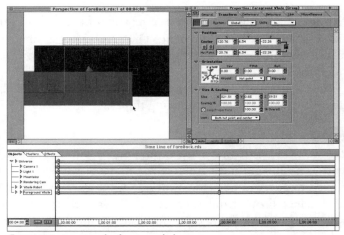

FIGURE
12.53 *Animating the foreground elements.*

While you're here, let's animate the background too. Click on the **Mountains** object and **Shift-drag** it just a little bit to the left. We don't want to drag this one too far because we want the background to move slower than the foreground to give a sense of depth. Just kind of eyeball it here. You can steal the information from the Properties palette if you like. (See Figure 12.54.)

Well, that's it for the foreground and background elements. Pretty easy, eh? If you'd like, you can render your animation now. I can tell you, though, that it's not going to be that good yet. In the next step, we're going to give little Bobby

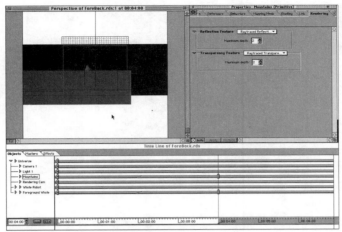

FIGURE   *Animating the background element.*

12.54

some action so that it actually looks as though he's moving about and looking for
his sister. We'll do this with a Bend and Twist deformer. Move on to Step Three.

Step Three

Here's where we give Bobby a little action of his own. Rewind the animation back
to **frame 0** and view your scene from **Camera 1**. Select **Preset Views>Top** and
zoom in on Bobby, as in Figure 12.55. Select **Bobby** and click on the **Behaviors**
tab in the **Properties palette**. Select **Bend and Twist** from the pull-down menu.

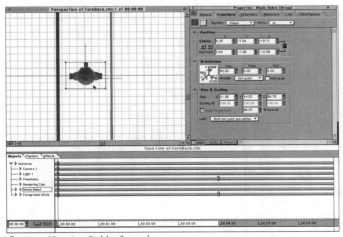

FIGURE   *Viewing Bobby from the top.*

12.55

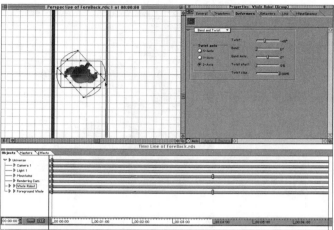

FIGURE   *Adding a Bend and Twist deformer.*
12.56

Enable the **Direct Manipulation** tool in the upper left-hand corner of the **Properties palette** and then, by clicking on the upper right-hand handle on Bobby, twist him so that he's looking off to the right. (See Figure 12.56.)

Now move the **Current Time Bar** to **frame 1:00** and give Bobby an equal twist in the opposite direction. (See Figure 12.57.) From here we want to duplicate that little twisty action throughout the rest of the animation, so send the **Current Time Bar** to **frame 2:00**. We want to mix the action up a bit; instead of just copying key events, let's just eyeball another Twist deformer and make Bobby look off to the right again. We're trying to mix things up, so don't worry about being precise.

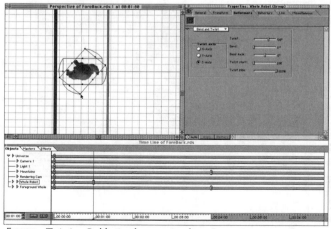

FIGURE   *Twisting Bobby in the opposite direction.*
12.57

(See Figure 12.58.) Repeat the following steps for frames 3:00 and 4:00. Your scene at these frames should look like Figures 12.59 and 12.60 respectively.

Well, now you've finished. Set up your scene to render with the settings in Figure 12.61. The reason Shadows are disabled is because otherwise shadows would be cast on your mountain object in the back, and that would look silly. Select your favorite file format for animations, and render away.

— JOHN W. SLEDD

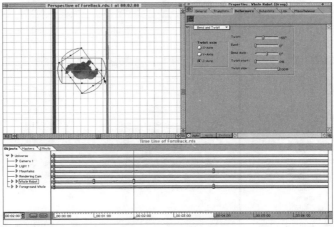

FIGURE *Second glance right.*
12.58

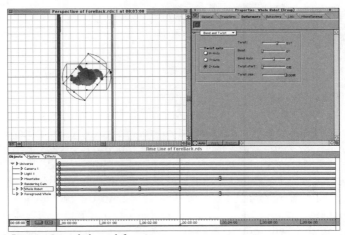

FIGURE *Second glance left.*
12.59

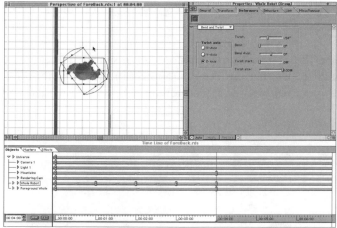

FIGURE
12.60
Third glance right.

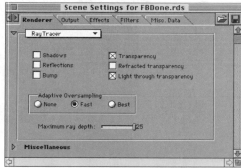

FIGURE
12.61
The final render settings.

FLYING LOGO TUTORIAL

Flying logos are the bread-and-butter assignments for many 3D animators. Some hate them, some love them, and lots of clients want them. In this tutorial, I'm going to take you through a basic, four-second, flying logo animation. I've created a file called LOGO.RDS for you to work with.

The key to flying logo work is to set up the scene the way you want the final shot to look, and then work backwards. Figure 12.62 shows what our closing shot will look like. From here, I'll instruct you on where to go to bring all of the pieces together. Figure 12.63 shows a few frames from the animation.

FIGURE *Our animation's closing shot.*
12.62

FIGURE *A few frames from the animation.*
12.63

Step One

Open **LOGO.RDS** from the Chapter 12 files on the CD. (See Figure 12.64.) As I mentioned above, the key to creating one of these animations is to set everything up the way you want before you start to animate. In this file, I've set up all of the lighting, arranged the models for the final shot, and created and set up a camera as your rendering camera. We'll be working mostly from Camera 1 because we want our rendering camera to remain untouched. In many instances, you might want to animate the camera too, but for this tutorial, it's gonna stay put. Just in case you forget though, I have saved the starting position for Rendering Cam. If you goof up and move it by accident, simply choose **Starting Position** from the **Position** pull-down menu in the **Camera Properties** window while viewing your scene through Rendering Cam. Take a moment to look around the scene and get acquainted with it before moving on to Step Two.

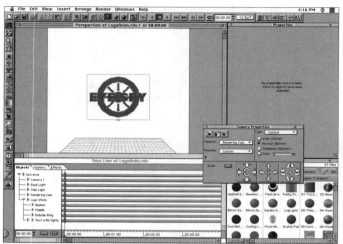

FIGURE *The file ready to be animated.*

12.64

Step Two

View your scene through Camera 1 (**View>Camera>Camera 1**). Now go to a top view (**View>Preset Position>Top**). This is a top view of your scene at frame 0. (See Figure 12.65.) Since we want this set up to be as the animation looks at the end, we need to duplicate some keyframes to ensure that's where we wind up.

Select the **Rendering Cam** and all of the objects in the logo group and **Option/Alt**-drag them to **frame 3:00**, as shown in Figure 12.66. This copies

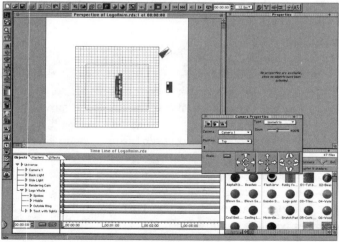

FIGURE *It's easiest to work from the top view in this particular scene.*

12.65

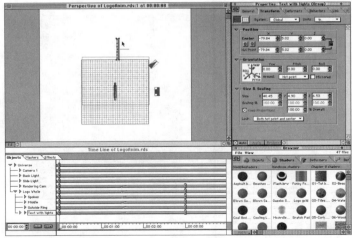

FIGURE *Copying the beginning keyframes to set the final positions.*
12.66

the locations and settings of all of these objects to frame 3:00 and sets everything up near the end of the animation just as we want it. From here, go back to the beginning of the animation, and let's start animatin' stuff.

Step Three

Here's where the fun starts. What we're going to do here is to set up all of the objects at their starting positions in the animation. Most of these positions will be off-screen as far as Render Cam is concerned, and that's exactly what we want and exactly why we're working from Camera 1. So first, let's take the Text with Lights object and drag it toward the top of the screen. See Figure 12.67 for positioning and notice that you can steal the exact position settings from the Properties palette if you like.

FIGURE *Dragging the Eye Spy text to its starting point.*
12.67

Now take the Middle object and drag it out toward the camera, as shown in Figure 12.68. It doesn't matter that this will be right in front of the rendering camera because, that's what we want — trust me.

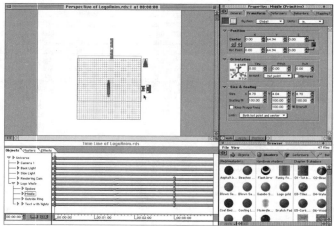

FIGURE
12.68   *Dragging the Middle object to its starting point.*

Now select the Spokes object and drag it to the back of the scene, as shown in Figure 12.69.

Now you have all of your objects in their starting points. What we've done here is to set up an animation where all of our objects start from a far-off point and meet exactly as we want them at the end of the animation. You might

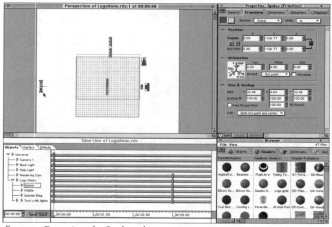

FIGURE
12.69   *Dragging the Spokes object to its starting point.*

want to play back the animation at this time to see what's going on. View it from both cameras and play it back from each one.

Step Four

Now we're going to add a little excitement by assigning Spin behaviors to a couple of the objects. Make sure you're viewing the scene from **Camera 1** and select the **Spokes** object again. Click on the **Behaviors** tab in the **Properties palette** and then click on the plus sign (+). Select **Spin** and click **OK**. Set the **Axis of Rotation** to the **Y axis**, make your **Cycles Per Second .5** and your **End Time 4.0**. (See Figure 12.70.) Now select the **Outside Ring** object and assign a **Spin** behavior to it in the same manner. This time, however, let's leave the **Axis of Rotation** on the **Z axis** and set the **Cycles Per Second** to .75. (See Figure 12.71.)

What we've done here is to set the Spokes object to spin around like an airplane propeller. Since we're essentially using this as a gobo (albeit a visible gobo) for a visible light in the background, this will add some great visual

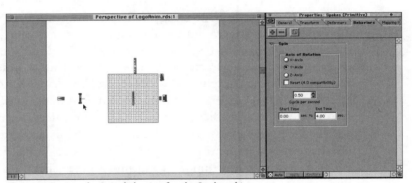

FIGURE   *Setting the Spin behavior for the Spokes object.*
12.70

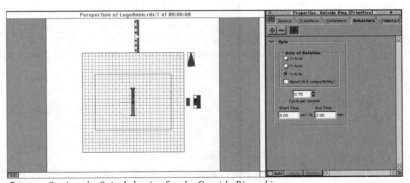

FIGURE   *Setting the Spin behavior for the Outside Ring object.*
12.71

impact to the final animation without being too busy. We've also added a Spin behavior to the outer ring of the logo, but it's spinning on a different axis from the Spokes object. This makes it spin like a top around the other elements of the logo and creates a secondary gobo effect with the visible lights. Preview your animation from both cameras to see what's going on.

Step Five

Now for one last punch before we wrap up the animation: when the Eye Spy text gets into place, we want it to flare brightly and then return to the normal soft glow. This is accomplished by using the Aura filter. I've already set up the Aura filter for most of the animation, but you'll want to add these next few steps. Go back to **frame 0** and click on the **Effects** tab in the **Hierarchy** window. Duplicate the **key event** to **frame 3:00**. (See Figure 12.72.) Now go to **frame 3:06**, open up the **Current Scene Settings**, and click on the **Filters** tab. Click on the **Edit** button and change the **Intensity** to **49%** and the **Range** to **16**. (See Figure 12.73.) Now click **OK**. You'll see a key event created on the Timeline. Now **Option/Alt-Drag** the **key event** at **3:00** to **4:00**. This will return the Aura settings to those at the beginning of the animation. (See Figure 12.74.) Just to make the flare nice and smooth, double-click on the time bars between each of the keyframes and change the tweener to **Bezier**. The default settings are fine. (See Figure 12.75.) Feel free to change all of your moving objects' tweeners to Beziers just to smooth out your transitions.

And that should do it. You can render your animation now. Make sure your rendering camera is set on **Render Cam**, and render away. Once you understand the basics, start playing around with your timing. Drag a key event here or there just to mix things up and smooth the action out. Animations are like songs and comedy: timing is everything.

— *JOHN W. SLEDD*

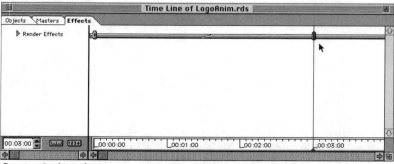

FIGURE *Locking the Aura settings until we're ready to change them.*
12.72

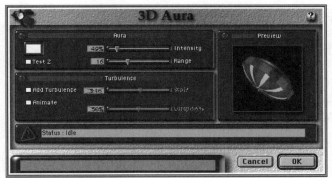

FIGURE The Aura's flare settings.
12.73

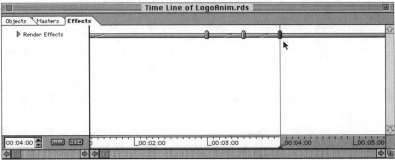

FIGURE Copying the original Aura settings to return it to its starting brilliance.
12.74

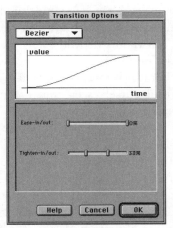

FIGURE Setting a Bezier tweener to
12.75 smooth out the Aura's flare.

LINKS AND INVERSE KINEMATICS TUTORIAL

Setting up linking constraints for use with Inverse Kinematics (IK) is a subject that confuses many new and even not-so-new 3Ders. It is a confusing subject, but if you approach your model building with linking in mind, it can become a much easier concept to grasp.

Many of us developed bad habits working in 3D before we started using linking, and these bad habits have to be broken if we want the quickest route to understanding this monster. Back in the good old days, when we built a model, we didn't really have to pay much attention to the orientation of the objects we used to construct it. We could create several free form objects and just rotate and arrange them simply so that they fit the way we wanted in our assembled model. This was fine before links became available or before we started using them, but problems began to rear their ugly heads when we started trying to link this stuff. Many of you might have tried to link a model you'd built, only to find that your links never came out as you expected. This was probably because you didn't really take into consideration the specific orientation of all of the pieces of your model. You may have rotated one object to the point where your Z axis was pointing left to right, your Y axis was pointing up and down, and your X axis was pointing front to back. Then in your next object, the orientation might be as it is for the Global Universe, which is Z up and down, Y front to back, and X left to right. And then your next object might be completely different from the two of those. As I've said, this didn't matter when we weren't assigning links and constraints, but when the time comes to assign these, this way of working makes for a virtual linking nightmare.

The reason for this is that you have to reorient your thinking for each and every object you're assigning constraints to. You have axes pointing in different directions, but your linking constraints depend solely on the orientation of the object to which you're assigning the constraints. Since we usually assign linking constraints to one object because we want it to behave a certain way in relation to another object, we find ourselves having to figure out how to assign a constraint on one object's Y axis so that it relates a certain way to another object's Z axis. Sometimes this is desirable, but in the case of a finger, this simply makes things much more difficult to understand. When you get to the point where linking and the understanding of X, Y, Z coordinates becomes second nature, you can afford to be sloppy, but I still wouldn't recommend this. Building your models with linking in mind and keeping it as clean as possible to that end is just good practice, and if any other poor unfortunate soul ever has to figure out one of your models, it'll help them tremendously if it's built properly.

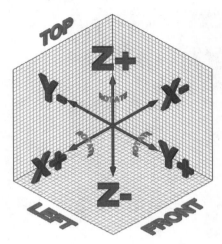

FIGURE **12.76** *Building your objects and models so their axis conform to the Global Universe's axis will make assigning link constraints much easier.*

The key here is to build your objects and models so that they share the same orientation as the Global Universe. (See Figure 12.76.) This will make it much easier to understand, because you're always working with the same orientations. If all your objects share the same Global Universe orientation, you never have to calculate for axis switching. This typically means that you build your objects and models from back to front and bottom to top. This is simply real-world working practice. You don't build a house starting with the roof and you don't build a bridge starting from the other side.

In the example for this tutorial, the hand is built from back to front. Sometimes, because of the way the Free Form modeler works, you can't really built an object top to bottom. That's fine, because you can still simplify the procedure by making sure all of your objects' axes point in the same direction — then you're well ahead of the game, even if those axes don't correspond to the Global Universe. If possible, however, use the Global Universe as your guide — at least until you get the hang of this. You can build your objects and models top to bottom but with a horizontal orientation, and then assign all of your links with it in the horizontal orientation. After you've finished, you can group the model and then rotate it to an up and down position.

The model for this tutorial is about as easy as it gets. It's built back to front and it's in an orientation that is easily understandable. As an added bonus, the orientation is that of the Global Universe.

Before we get started, I want to give you a few pointers on Links and how the Constraint controls see your object. Figure 12.77 shows the Custom Link

FIGURE   *The Custom link is essentially a combination of*
12.77   *many other link types.*

control panel. I'm choosing the Custom link because it essentially combines the Slider, Axis, Shaft and Lock links into one handy palette. In our tutorial, we'll be working only with the Rotate constraints, but I'll address the Slider links briefly.

The Slider links are like a train track. You have your X track, Y track and Z track, and the object is the train. When you enable the Y axis Slider link, you are essentially turning the Y axis for your object into its track. The object can travel only along that track. If you look at the middle of the Slider link, you'll see three little button doohickeys (they're really called "markers" but the artist in me likes to use high-tech terms like "doohickey" from time to time). The middle one represents your object (the train) and the ones to the left and right are the constraints (or rockslides) on the track. The train cannot go past the rockslides, as any good train robber with a box of dynamite knows. It can move freely anywhere between the rockslides but cannot go past them. You can slide the constraints up and down the track to expand or contract its range of motion.

The same analogy holds true for the Rotation links. To better understand these and how they relate to the axis they represent, think of the little circles as rings of track that circle around the corresponding axis arrows back in Figure 12.76. The rings of track would fit over the axis, and your object would ride around on the track just like the word "rotate" does in that illustration. The middle doohickey represents your object. The outside doohickeys represent the boundaries that your object cannot cross (more of those rockslides). Adjusting the middle doohickey will actually move your object, but adjusting the outside doohickeys simply limits the object's range of motion.

All these links and their constraints are based on your object's hot point being the center of rotation for the object, so imagine that your hot point resides directly in the middle of that little Rotation circle.

Let's get on with the tutorial and see how it goes.

Step One

Open the file **LINKS&IK.RDS** from the Chapter 12 folder on the CD. You should see what is shown in Figure 12.78. What we have here is a hand that's partially built. The reason that it's only partially built is because we can cut down on the amount of linking we need to do by creating one finger, assigning the link constraints and then duplicating and resizing it from there. This is a wonderful time-saver that can potentially destroy your project, so pay close attention to my warnings along the way. After we've finished, you might want to try duplicating your fingers and assigning links to them one at a time, because there will be times when you'll need to do this.

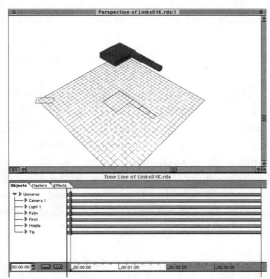

FIGURE *The starting file.*
12.78

Now that I have you trembling, let's move on. Click on the separate objects in this file and notice that all of the axis are oriented the same way as the Global Universe. Z is up and down, Y is front and back, and X is left and right. This will make this job a cinch.

Go to the top view of the files, and let's prepare this puppy for some constraints. If you click on each one of these objects now, you'll see that the hot points are all in the middle. Objects rotate around their hot point, so we need to change this before we assign the links. Zoom in on the model and drag each digit's hot point back to where the knuckle should be. (See Figure 12.79.) You can use the Shift key to make sure your path is straight. If you were going to link this palm to a wrist, you'd want to move the hot point on the palm too, but we're not going to do that in this tutorial, so you can leave it alone if you like.

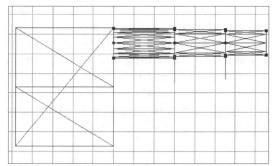

FIGURE
12.79
Defining the rotation point by moving the hot points.

Step Two

Now let's link the Digit objects to one another. In a model like this, the last object in line (the Fingertip, for example) needs to also be the last object in the chain. This is common sense, but it's still worth mentioning. So drag the **Middle** object onto the **First** object in the **Hierarchy** window and then drag the **Tip** object onto the **Middle** object. This will set up your hierarchy as in Figure 12.80. Make sure things are set up exactly the way you want them at this point. Once you start establishing links, you could run into trouble if you try to break hierarchies. Don't worry that we didn't link the **First** digit to the palm; we'll take care of that through grouping later.

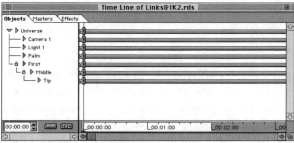

FIGURE
12.80
The hierarchy of the finger model.

Step Three

Now let's set some constraints. Click on the **Tip** object and go to the **Links** tab in the **Properties palette**. Choose **Axis** from the pull-down menu. (See Figure 12.81.) The reason we chose Axis is because, if you'll notice, the tip of your finger (your *real* finger) bends along only one axis. Go ahead and try it. Your whole finger will bend side to side but that's due to the last knuckle and has nothing to do with the tip. The tip has to go where the pieces higher up on the hierarchy tell it to go. So this little guy only has one axis to worry about.

FIGURE **12.81** *Assigning an Axis link to the Tip object.*

The problem we need to solve here is which axis to rotate it around. Well, this is exactly why, whenever possible, we want the axes of our objects to correspond to the axes of the Global Universe. If we left the Axis of Rotation on the Z axis, the tip would rotate from side to side because it would be rotating around the Z axis, which runs top to bottom. If we put it on the Y axis, it would spin around like a drill — cool for a sci fi piece but not for a regular old hand. The X axis is the axis we want, because that would make the finger bend like a real finger. An easy way to decide which axis use is to view your scene down the axis that will best allow you to rotate your object using the 2D rotation tool. Viewing the scene as-is would be the best way to view it if we wanted to rotate the object side to side, because when viewing from the top, we're looking down the Z axis as if it were the sight on a gun. This is another good way to look at the circle that shows your Rotation constraints. Think of it as a sight that parallels the axis in question. If we were viewing the scene from the front, we'd be looking down the Y axis, which would be how we'd want to view the object if we wanted to rotate it using the 2D rotation tool. If you change your view to **Preset Position>Left**, you'll see that this would be the best way to rotate our Tip as it should rotate and, since you're viewing the scene from the left, this means you're looking down the X axis, because it runs left to right. So choose **Preset Position>Left** (if you haven't already), click on the **X Axis of Rotation** in the **Axis link** control panel and chose **Limited** from the **Rotate** pull-down menu. (See Figure 12.82.)

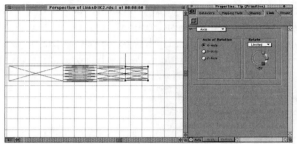

FIGURE   *Reorient your view to see which axis to use.*
12.82

Now here's where you'll see the relation to your object of the little button doohickeys in the **Rotate** control. Select the **2D Rotation tool** and rotate the tip of the finger. Notice how the middle button that represents your object is pointed forward, just like the tip of your finger, and notice also how it moves between the two constraint buttons but doesn't move past them. Your object will also stop rotating at these points. (See Figure 12.83.) When you've finished playing, reorient the tip so that it's pointing forward again.

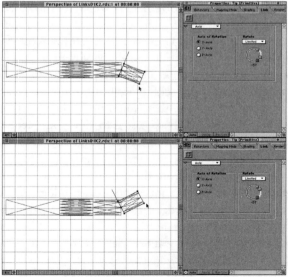

FIGURE   *Rotating your tip with the 2D Rotation tool shows you*
12.83   *the correspondence of the link control panel.*

Since very few people's fingertips actually bend backwards that much, the first thing you'll want to do is to select the **upper constraint** and move it down to meet the middle button. (See Figure 12.84.) A setting of **2** is pretty good, since the tip of your finger generally does have a slight backwards angle.

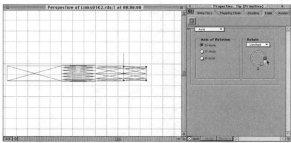

FIGURE *Setting the upper constraint.*
12.84

The lower constraint is pretty good but, if you curl your real finger up, you'll notice that it makes almost a perfect 90-degree angle with the middle section of your finger. So click on the **lower** doohickey and move it to a setting of **–90**. (See Figure 12.85.) Now if you go back and use the **2D Rotation tool**, you'll see that your finger tip bends pretty much as it should.

Congratulations! You've assigned your first link constraint. Let's do another, shall we?

FIGURE *Setting the lower*
12.85 *constraint.*

Step Four

Select the **Middle** object and repeat the last series of instructions. Assign it an **Axis** link. Select the **X axis** as your **Axis of Rotation**. Drag the **upper** limit down to between 1 and 5 and drag the **lower** limit to about –5 and drag the **lower** limit to about –92. Now play with that object using the **2D Rotation tool**. Notice how the Tip object follows the Middle object. This is the benefit of the link. Congratulations! You've assigned your second set of link constraints. (See Figure 12.86.) Make sure the finger is straightened back out, and move on to Step Five.

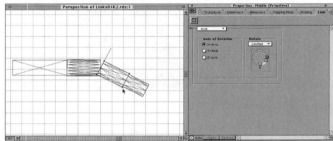

FIGURE   *The link constraints for the Middle object.*
12.86

Step Five

Now we're going to assign a link to the First object. This one will be a little trickier because, if you check out your own hand, you'll notice that not only does it bend around the X axis like the others, it also bends side to side around the Z axis. To accomplish this, select the **First** object and assign a **Custom** link to it in the **Links** tab of the **Properties palette**.

When using the Custom link, the most important thing you can do as a beginner is to assign constraints for only one axis at a time. We're in a good position to assign the constraints for the X axis, so let's go ahead and do that. Choose **Limited** from the **Rotate X** pull-down menu in the **Custom** control panel. Give it an **upper** limit of about 5 degrees and a **lower** limit of about –84. Now play around with it using the **2D Rotation tool**. (See Figure 12.87.) When you've finished playing, reset it to a straight position, and let's assign the Z axis constraints.

Now go to the top view of your scene, because we know we want the finger to go from side to side, which means that it would be rotating around the Z axis. Choose **Limited** from the **Rotate Z** pull-down menu, and set your own constraints based on how your own finger moves. Remember that you're looking down on your object, so your **Rotate Z** indicator is essentially assigning constraints for left and right motion. The upper constraint sets the limit for rotation to the left and the bottom constraint sets the limit for rotation to the right. An easy way to to this is to use the **2D Rotation tool** and rotate the

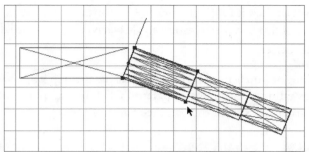

FIGURE
12.87
Setting the X axis for the First object.

object to where you think the limit should be. Then you can drag the constraint down until it stops, because constraints can't go past an object any more than the object can go past a constraint. (See Figures 12.88 and 12.89.)

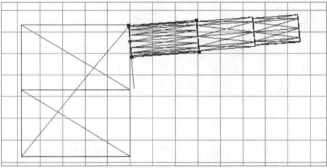

FIGURE
12.88
Set the constraint by rotating the object to where you think the constraint should be and then moving the constraint down until it stops because it runs into the object.

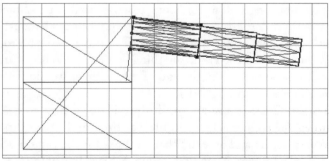

FIGURE
12.89
Do the same for the lower constraint, and you've finished.

Well, that does it for finger one and it's constraints. Now to get the real benefit from all of this work, we'll assign an IK behavior to the three digits in Step Six.

Step Six

Don't blink or you'll miss this one. Click on the **Tip** object then click on the **Behaviors** tab in the **Properties palette**. Click on the plus (+) sign and choose **Inverse Kinematics** from the list. (See Figure 12.90.)

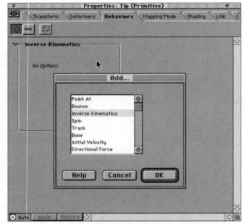

FIGURE   *Applying the Inverse Kinematics behavior.*
12.90

Now repeat the above steps for the other two sections of finger. Go to the **Left** view and drag the **Tip** object around with the **Selection tool** and see what happens. You've just assigned your first bunch of link constraints and IK. Congratulations again!

Step Seven

We have one finger done and four to go — well, three fingers and a thumb. The time has come for you to group your finger elements. Select the **First** object, which will automatically select the other two due to the linking, and group them. Name the group anything you like — I chose **Finger Whole.** Now drag the hot point back to the end of the group as we did with the separate finger objects. (See Figure 12.91.)

Duplicate the group and **Shift-drag** it down next to the first group. (See Figure 12.92.) Now select **Duplicate** three more times to create your two remaining fingers and an extra that we'll use for the thumb. (See Figure 12.93.) Select the last finger group and choose **Object Invisible** from the **View** menu. We'll come back to it later. Now let's resize the groups to make more accurately

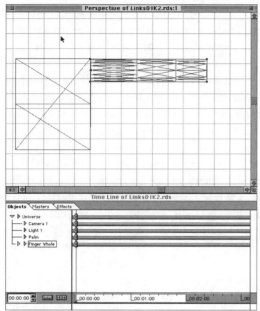

FIGURE *Grouping the linked objects.*
12.91

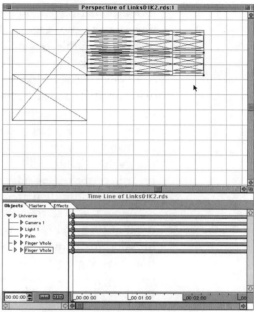

FIGURE *Duplicating the finger group.*
12.92

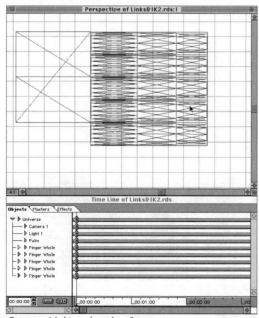

FIGURE *Making the other fingers.*
12.93

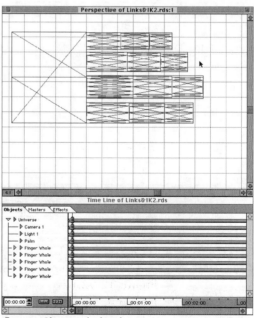

FIGURE *Shaping the hand.*
12.94

proportioned fingers. Let's make our first finger the pinky and work our way down to the end. Don't enlarge any of the groups; just reduce the fingers that aren't the middle finger. Reposition them if necessary, and you should have something like Figure 12.94.

Whatever you do, do not ungroup any of these groups. If you need to work on them for any reason, expand the group by clicking the arrow beside the group's name, or jump into it. The reason for this is that the links applied to the objects in these groups are now relying on the group coordinates for all of their information. If you ungroup any of them, they will go haywire, and not even an Undo will completely fix the problem. If you've saved, you can try it if you're feeling adventurous, but otherwise, always expand the group to move the individual items. This is what I was talking about earlier with grouping versus setting up individual objects and assigning linking constraints to all of them. This way is quicker and more organized, but the other way is a bit safer. Just remember to expand the groups to work on them, and you'll be fine. (See Figure 12.95.) In case you don't feel like finding this out on your own, Figure 12.96 shows what happened when I ungrouped the index finger. Figure 12.97 shows what happens when I tried to Undo the mistake. So just don't do it.

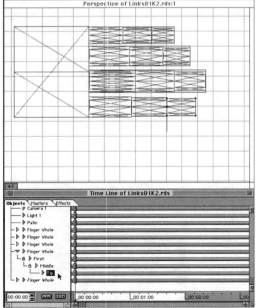

FIGURE **12.95** *Expand your groups to move the individual pieces. Ungrouping them will cause catastrophe that not even Undo can correct.*

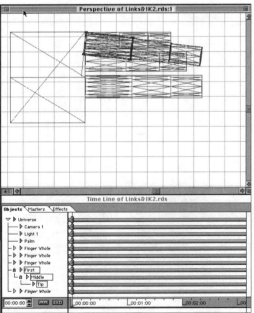

FIGURE **12.96** *This is an example of what can happen if you ungroup a duplicated and linked model.*

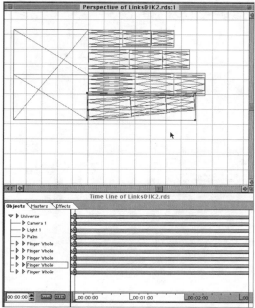

FIGURE
12.97
Not even an Undo can completely fix the problem.

Step Eight

This is the last step in this tutorial. Make the final Finger Whole object visible, and let's create our thumb. When you have the object visible, move it to where a thumb should be. (See Figure 12.98.)

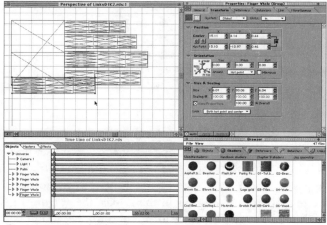

FIGURE
12.98
Position the thumb where a thumb should be.

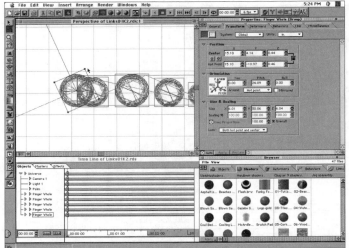

FIGURE   *Give the thumb a slight rotation around the Y axis.*
12.99

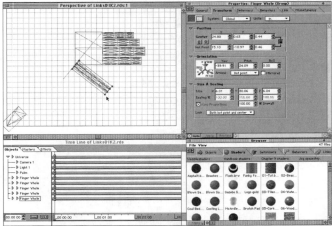

FIGURE   *Now rotate it a little more around the Z axis.*
12.100

The odd part about doing a thumb is how it is offset and rotated a little. The thumb itself doesn't really rotate, but the way it's set up makes it seem that it does. Go to the **Front** view of the scene and **rotate** the thumb group about **25 degrees** on the **Y axis**. (See Figure 12.99.) Now go back to the **Top** view and **rotate** it about **–40 degrees** in the **Z axis**. (See Figure 12.100.) You need to change the link constraints a bit for the thumb, because it has a larger range of

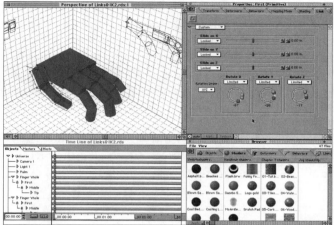

FIGURE *Your finished the linked and IKed hand.*
12.101

motion and that little rotating thing. You can leave the Tip and Middle objects the same, but the First object needs some tweaking. You might also want to resize it a bit. (See Figure 12.101.)

— *JOHN W. SLEDD*

USING AUTONOMOUS EFFECTS' HOTLIPS TO DO QUICK LIPSYNCING

If you want your animated character to speak, you'll need to have your character's mouth move synchronously with what it's saying. Conventional animators laboriously determine the exact sequence of phonemes in a sentence, craft a different mouth and tongue position for each phoneme, and then place these positions in the time line to match the audio exactly. Even the shortest utterance can take hours or days to lipsync.

Fortunately, Autonomous Effects (www.afx.com) offers the HotLips extension to Ray Dream Studio. In seconds, HotLips can generate a satisfying open-and-shut mouth animation exactly synchronized to your audio track. Although it isn't quite as believable as a careful hand animation with many phoneme positions, it's much, much, easier to do.

HotLips can also generate synchronized motions for characters playing musical instruments and other creative audiovisual effects, such as flashing disco lights.

Step One

Locate or generate a simple vocalization to use, of under five seconds in length. You can either record your own or use the example from the CD-ROM, POLITICO.WAV. You can use a program such as Creative WaveStudio, which comes with many PCs, to create a .WAV file, or SimpleSound on the Mac to create an .AIFF file. Just be sure not to select a compressed audio format.

Step Two

Get the lips object that we'll animate from the CD-ROM file HLTSTART.RDS. These lips were created using the Free Form modeler and consist of two circular cross-sections. (See Figure 12.102.)

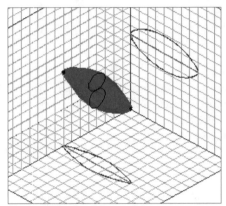

FIGURE   *The closed lips model.*
12.102

Step Three

You can now prepare for animation. Drag the **render start/stop time markers** to make the movie go from **0:00** to **5:00** (five seconds). Select **18 frames per second** on the Render toolbar. At lower frame rates, the lips would be moving too quickly to be shown clearly. You can also use the **Render Settings** dialog box to accomplish these steps, if you want.

Step Four

To model the open position of the lips, click on the **Last Frame** button on the toolbar or drag the red **Current time** marker there.

Double-click on the **Lips** object to edit it. Click on **Section>Next** to go to the middle cross-section, then ungroup it and move the top circle up and the bottom circle down. Select both, regroup them, click **Done**, and you've got the open lips. (See Figure 12.103.)

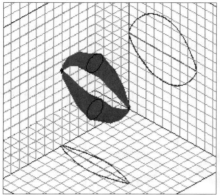

FIGURE *Lips open.*
12.103

Step Five

Add the HotLips tweener by clicking on the **Masters** tab in the **Timeline** then double-clicking on the **track** for the Lips. Select **HotLips** from the drop-down list of tweeners.

Give HotLips your audio file by clicking on **Browse** on its control panel. Then drag the **Gain** slider right until a bunch of the peaks of the preview curve are up at the dotted line at the top. It is fine if some peaks clip at the top.

Double-click the **Seconds** field of the **Timeline**, and enter **0.15**. This will make the lips precede the sound, giving the right cause-effect relationship. The Band controls let loud closed-mouth high-frequency phonemes such as S and F be suppressed, as well as low-frequency phonemes such as V and M. The defaults should be fine, so hit **OK**. (See Figure 12.104.)

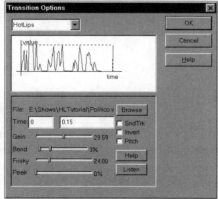

FIGURE *The HotLips tweener settings.*
12.104

Step Six

Click to **time zero** and the **Left** view (**Ctrl/Command-4**), then pull up the **Camera Properties** window. Select the **Conical** camera with a zoom of around **170**.

Render the movie, using the ray tracer with all special features disabled to save time. The default 216 by 144 image size will be fine. The final scene file can be found on the CD-ROM as HLTFINAL.RDS. Save the movie to disk using Cinepak compression. (See Figure 12.105.)

FIGURE   *A few frames from the HotLips animation.*
12.105

Step Seven

Add the audio track to the movie. On a PC, use the Talky program included with HotLips. On a Mac, use the MoviePlayer using the hidden **Add** command (pull down the **Edit** menu while holding down **Option**). For more detail, see the HotLips documentation. In any case, this step will just take a few seconds and little thought once you have the procedure. The final movie is on the CD-ROM as POLITICO.AVI.

Step Eight

Play your movie with the Media Player (PC) or MoviePlayer (Mac). For a real animation, you should use eye and head motions to enhance your character's believability — this will take some of the focus off the exact lip motion (you wouldn't look very believable with no eye or head motion, either!).

— RUSS ANDERSSON

FACIAL ANIMATION USING FACESHIFTER

You can animate meshes in Ray Dream Studio using the standard Mesh editor, by setting up different shapes at different times. Although this works well in simple applications where only a single portion of the mesh must be animated, the approach breaks down when you want different portions of the mesh to do different things — say, eyebrows raising or muscles flexing — independently of the grimace on a character's face. Using the Mesh editor, you must animate all possible combinations, which is tedious at best and downright impossible when different sections have different timing.

Instead, you can use the FaceShifter extension from Autonomous Effects Inc. (www.afx.com) to animate the mesh. FaceShifter morphs between a set of templates using sliders on a control panel to select the desired proportion of each template shape. It can even animate separate sections of the same mesh independently of each other.

To use FaceShifter, you must build your shapes from the initial reference shape, assemble all the shapes in a common group, and decorate them with various controls. Once you've done this, animation is easy — as you hop along the time line, you simply adjust the control sliders.

We'll illustrate FaceShifter with an example animation of a Poser 2 head. (See Figure 12.106.)

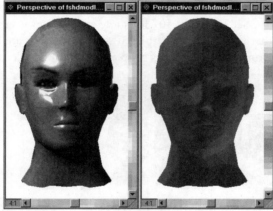

FIGURE   *This is the face we'll be shifting.*
12.106

Step One

The first step in any FaceShifter project is to create the model. This model must contain all the vertices, links and holes that you'll need in any of the final shapes, and must be a mesh-model.

For our example, you can find the model on the CD-ROM as FSHD-MODL.RDS. You can turn on Better Preview mode for a little while to see the (slightly mismatched) Texture Map for the object. During animation, you'll probably want only the Preview (fast) mode.

There's a small cube in the middle of the head to provide a background for the mouth when it's open. Otherwise we'd be looking at the inside back of the model's head when she opened her mouth.

Step Two

To create the shapes to use as your morph targets, do an **Edit>Duplicate** on the reference model, then repeat the duplication the required number of times for the different expressions you need. Give the duplicates original names (for example: Smiling, Open, Raised and Puffed). This duplicating procedure places the duplicates of your model directly on top of one another. Although this placement is not necessary for FaceShifter to work properly, it will keep your final bounding box a reasonable size.

Double-click on each duplicate in the **Hierarchy** window to jump into the Mesh Form modeler to adjust each shape according to what you named it. When you're presented with the option to Create New Master or Edit Master, choose the default **Create New Master**. When editing the model, you must only move vertices — by dragging them or using the Magnet tool, say. You cannot add vertices, fill, empty polygons, or so forth at this stage.

For this example, create shapes for smiling, open mouth, raised eyebrows, and puffed cheeks. See Figure 12.107 for some examples of what you might wind up with. Note that these objects are placed side by side but are done so for your viewing pleasure only. To keep things simple, keep your objects overlapped.

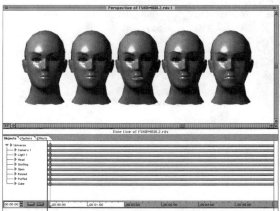

FIGURE   *These are some samples of what your faces might look like.*
12.107

Each duplicated shape should then be cloaked in the **Properties palette**'s **General** tab, but keep your original object uncloaked. Because you duplicated your object, you also duplicated the Texture Maps. You might want to go through your duplicated shapes and assign the default **Red** shader — there's no sense in their all being shaded with Texture Maps since they are cloaked. You can check out the the file FSPREX.RDS from the CD-ROM, which contains four example shapes: Head, Open, Raised, Puffed, Smiling.

Step Three

Put the initial reference shape and the four expressions into the same group (**Shift-select** them all, then **Arrange>Group**). (See Figure 12.108.)

Select each shape, excluding Head and Cube, and click on the **Behaviors** tab in the **Properties palette**, click on the large plus (+) sign, and select **Shape** from the list of behaviors. You don't need to alter any of the controls. (See Figure 12.109.)

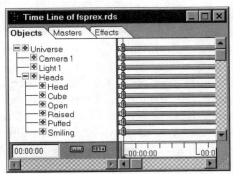

FIGURE **12.108** *Grouping the shapes with the Head object.*

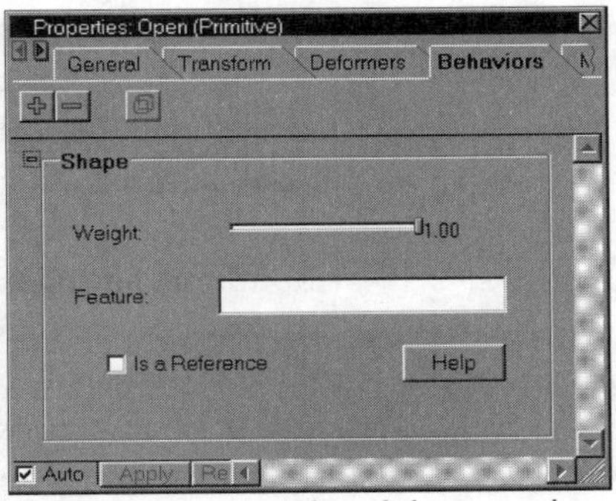

FIGURE **12.109** *Assigning a Shape behavior to the different expressions.*

Select the **Head** object, click on the **Deformers** tab, and select the **FaceShifter** deformer. Into the top four **Object** fields, carefully enter the names of the faces you created, **Open**, **Raised**, **Puffed**, and **Smiling**. (See Figure 12.110.)

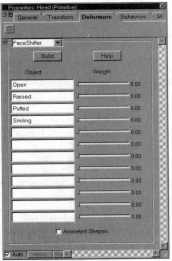

FIGURE **12.110** *Entering the four shapes.*

Step Four

Click on the **Head** object and its **Deformer** control panel. Slide each control one at a time up and down to see the basic shapes. If you have trouble, you can check out the completed scene file, FSFINAL.RDS, from the CD-ROM for comparison.

Now, with all controls at **zero**, bring **Smiling** up to **one**, then watch the mouth carefully when you bring the **Raised** control up to **one**. By default, the different shapes are averaged together and interact. Stay in the **Preview** (fast) mode to avoid the slow texture-mapped redraws.

Select the **Raised** shape and fill in the word **Eyebrows** into the **Feature** text field of the **Shape Behavior** control panel. For the **Puffed** shape, add the word **Cheeks** instead.

Now, if you try the same test, you'll see that the eyebrows, cheeks and mouth are all independent. The Smiling and Open mouth positions still interact, because they are telling the same vertices to move in different directions.

This is good, because now you can have smiles with different amounts of mouth opening, just by moving a control a little, without going near the Mesh editor. And of course all these settings are animatable.

Important Note

If you've made your model for FaceShifter directly in the Mesh editor, rather than using an existing model with Custom or intrinsic mapping, you need to do a couple of things to make sure it will work correctly: lock the UV values, and lock the **triangularization**. These stabilize your object so that it doesn't change around as you edit the copies to create the morph targets. The following steps will guide you through this procedure.

1. Jump into the **Mesh editor** on your reference object before you make the duplicates.
2. Select the entire object, and click on the **Mapping Mode** tab. If it is already set to **Custom**, just click on **Keep Current Value** for each coordinate, and skip to Step 5. If you are using the Spherical or Cylindrical mapping modes, continue on with Step 3.
3. Set the **Mapping Mode** to **Custom**, and click **Keep Current Value** for both **U** and **V** axes. This turns jams all the UV values to the same values. That's no good at all, so here comes the trick.
4. Set the **Mapping Mode** back to its original **Spherical** or **Cylindrical** setting, and then back to **Custom**. When you come back to Custom this second time, the panel will default to Keep Current Value, and the current values will be kept and will be different for each vertex as desired.
5. Lastly, with your entire object selected, do a **Selection>Triangulate**. RDS 5 will do this for you anyway — doing it here just makes sure that RDS 5 does it the same way each time for each of your targets.

That's it — complex mesh-form editing and animation made simple.

For more information about FaceShifter, consult its documentation, available online at the www.afx.com website.

— RUSS ANDERSSON

USING BONEBENDER

The BoneBender plug-in is available from Autonomous Effects (www.afx.com) and consists of the deformers and behaviors needed for placing a skeleton in a Mesh object that actually deforms the mesh as it moves. It is important to note that you must convert all objects to meshes before you begin. BoneBender, like all other skeletal animation systems, requires you to work from polygons.

So, without further interruption, here it goes.

Step One

Insert a **Free Form** object into your scene and name it **Legs & Hips**.

When the Free Form modeler opens, switch to the **drawing plane**, turn off previews, and draw a 4-inch by 4-inch circle in the center (Use the **Center** option under **Sections** if need be). (See Figure 12.111.)

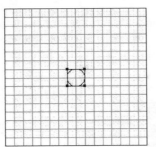

FIGURE *Starting the Legs & Hips.*
12.111

Switch to the **Top** view and set the **Extrusion Method** to **Pipeline**, as in Figure 12.112. Add some points to the end of the extrusion path using the **Pen** tool to create legs and hips, as in Figure 12.113, and set the **Envelope Type** to **Symmetrical**. Adjust the envelope so that it resembles Figure 12.114 and then set the **Surface Fidelity** all the way up to **400%**.

Click on **Doone** and then center the Free Form in the **Main** view, including the hot point. (See Figure 12.115.)

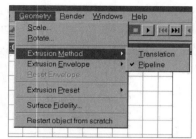

FIGURE **12.112** *Selecting the Pipeline Extrusion Method.*

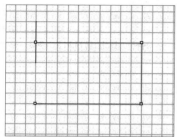

FIGURE **12.113** *Adding to the path to form the legs and hips.*

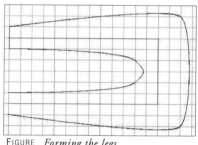

FIGURE **12.114** *Forming the legs and hips.*

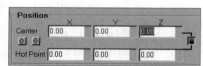

FIGURE **12.115** *Centering the Legs & Hips object and its hot point.*

Step Two

Now jump into the **Mesh Form modeler** and begin manipulating the model as a set of polygons. While the entire object is still highlighted, select **Weld** from the **Selection** menu and use the **Default Tolerance** to weld the parts together. (See Figure 12.116.)

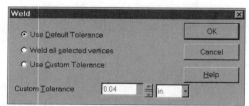

FIGURE **12.116** *Welding the object.*

Choose **Subdivide** twice from the **Selection** menu, and you should end up with around 3776 polygons. (See Figure 12.117.) When you've finished there, rotate the mesh so that the legs are pointing up into the air. (See Figure 12.118.)

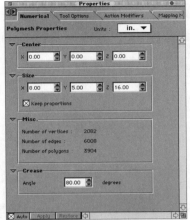

FIGURE **12.117** *Subdividing the object twice should leave you with about 3776 polygons.*

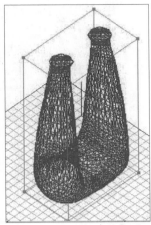

FIGURE **12.118** *Rotate the mesh so that the legs are pointing up.*

Now switch to the **Bottom** view, select the very **center vertex** and, using the **Magnet tool** set for **Bumpy** with a **Radius** of **3**, move that center point up about **.5 inches** to make an indent in the top of the hips. (See Figure 12.119.)

You might want to center the mesh now. It will come in handy later on if you set the size to even values — just a suggestion.

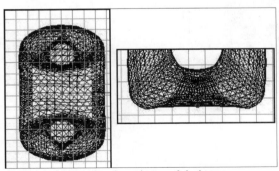

FIGURE **12.119** *Adding a dimple to the top of the hips.*

Step Three

Now center it, scale it **200%** and mirror it so that the legs are facing down once again. This gives us our Z axis flipped. (See Figure 12.120.)

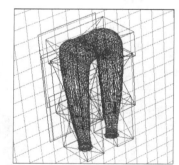

FIGURE *Mirroring the axis.*
12.120

Step Four

Now comes the fun part. We need to add bones to our mesh. We'll approach this in the same way as how all bipeds are built. Five bones will be used: one for the hips, one for each femur, and one for each ankle.

The bones in this project are nothing more than primitives to which we'll assign a Bone behavior. Figure 12.121 shows what your finished bone skeleton should look like. Our Legs & Hips object is inside the skeleton, as Figure 12.122 shows.

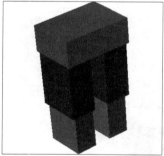

FIGURE *A view of the Bones from*
12.121 *the outside*

FIGURE *In wireframe mode, you*
12.122 *can see how the legs and hips object is aligned with the skeleton's objects.*

Although it's difficult to see in the gray image in front of you, these bones are colored. It's a very good idea to change the colors in the Shaders of your bones. Similar bones get similar colors for organizational purposes. This is simply a way to give you more visual feedback during animation and arranging your scene.

As you build and arrange your bones, make sure you check the **Mirrored** option in the **Orientation** section of the **Transform** tab in the **Properties palette**. This ensures the bones have the same orientation as your mesh. Also make sure that your bones overlap. This creates a virtual skin over your object, which makes all of the vertices behave. If there is no skin to overlap your bones, walking would cause your insides to leak out — not pleasant to watch. If a vertex escapes the influence of the bones, very strange things can happen.

Once you've finished with your skeleton, save your project.

Step Five

Now that you have your bones set up the way you want them, you need to relocate the hot points to the areas where the joints will be, and then link your skeleton. Figure 12.123 shows the hot point placement for the upper and lower bones. The waist bone's hot point is centered. Once you have that set up, it's time to assign your links and IK. We won't go into much depth about linking and IK because it's already been covered in a previous tutorial, but we will get you into the neighborhood. (See Figures 12.124, 12.125 and 12.126.) Once you get your links, constraints and IK set up, group your Legs & Hips object and your skeleton and name it **Lower Body.**

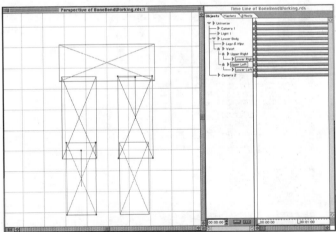

FIGURE *Hot point placement and link setup for your skeleton.*
12.123

Step Six

Now comes the time to assign the Bone behaviors to the bones themselves (this is, after all, what makes them bones) and assign the BoneBender deformer to the Legs & Hips object. This is rather straightforward. For the leg bones, click on a bone, click on the **Behavior** tab in the **Properties palette**, click on the Plus (+) sign and choose the **Bone** deformer. You should already have the IK behavior in there so the Bone behavior gets added underneath. Go ahead and drag it up to the top of the list so that it looks like Figure 12.127. These same

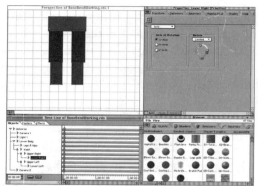

FIGURE **12.124** *Constraining the lower leg bone.*

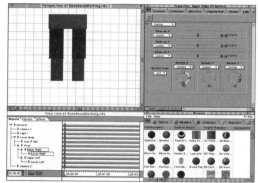

FIGURE **12.125** *Constraining the upper leg bone.*

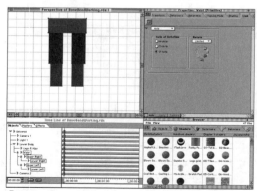

FIGURE **12.126** *Constraining the waist.*

settings apply for all of the bones in this project, so there's no need to give you more than one figure. They are the default Bone settings with one exception. The **Elbow Bender** is selected instead of No Special Bender.

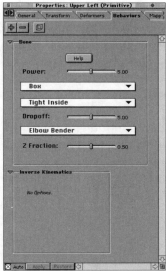

FIGURE **12.127** *What your Behaviors tab should look like once you've finished Boning and IKing.*

Now select the Legs & Hips object and assign a **BoneBender** deformer to it. (See Figure 12.128.) This is what allows your Legs & Hips object to be deformed by the bones.

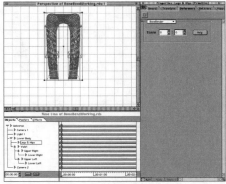

FIGURE **12.128** *Assigning the BoneBender deformer.*

Now you've pretty much finished setting up a boned object using BoneBender. You might wonder what good it is since you can't see your legs, but that's easily enough fixed. All you need to do is to cloak each bone to make it invisible. This is a great feature, because you can animate the skeleton while it's visible and then just cloak everything before rendering. This leaves only your Mesh object visible, but the influence of the bones remains.

All the bones are applied and links assigned at time=0sec. This is your setup state, which is the state from where BoneBender takes all of its beginning information. You don't have to start your animation here, but this is where everything must be put into place. If you want to play with your bones to make sure they work, you must move to another point in the time line — any old point will do — and bend a bone. You might want to cloak the bones so that you can see your mesh, but remember, even cloaked items have bounding boxes and projects that you can work with.

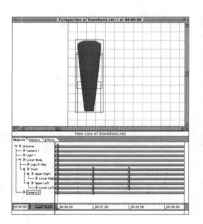
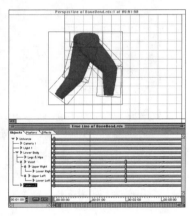
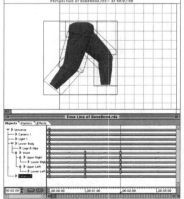
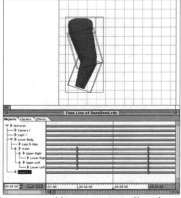
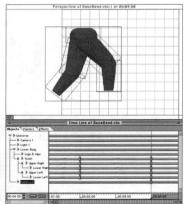

FIGURE
12.129   *Following this template will allow you quickly to set up a walk cycle.*

Step Seven

Now, let's put some motion into these legs. Figure 12.129 shows how your model should be set up at the various points in time. This is a pretty simple walk cycle, but by using this basic motion as a reference, you can quickly map out the basic cycle and embellish it with details later.

Step Eight

Once you get your legs and waist moving, you will also need to move your Lower Body section from left to right to provide the forward motion. To do this, you will need to key the specific frames that have to do with foot placement.

To help out with this, place a marker of some type that will easily identify where the feet are supposed to be placed. Use your imagination. A walk will have short distances between footsteps. Running will need longer paces. If you do a quick preview, you shouldn't see the infamous "skating feet" syndrome. Currently, BoneBender and Ray Dream Studio do not have any method of locking feet in place. Figure 12.130 shows an example of the Marker object with its motion path.

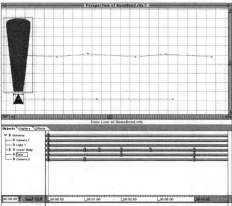

FIGURE **12.130** *Creating a Marker object will help you pace out the forward motion of your Lower Body.*

Step Nine

Now that we have our first BoneBender model set up, lets render it and see what it looks like. You should have something that looks like Figure 12.131.

Go ahead and experiment. Don't feel that what I have shown you is the only way to do it or the best you can expect. Remember, it took many animators and thousands of hours to make *Toy Story,* so try to have fun. As an additional resource, the original file has all the links and bones already set up for you to play with. (Note: You must have the AFX BoneBender plug-in for this to load.)

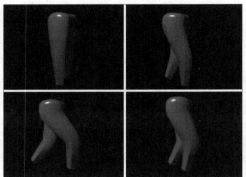

FIGURE 12.131 *A few frames from our BoneBender animation.*

Additional Notes: Polygon Count

I think I should probably say a few words about polygon/triangle count. As of version 5, Ray Dream Studio handles things more like polygons than splines — obviously, because Wireframe previews show not the cross-sections, but the polygon representations of them.

When dealing with polygon-based objects, it is important to remember to keep the number of triangles as low as possible. Some basic guidelines follow:

- Use no more than 512 triangles for spheres or cylinders unless they will be taking up 60% of the image at resolutions greater than 640 x 480. Cubes and rectilinear objects should be kept under 256 vertices as well. Think frugal.
- Unless you are doing a closeup of the hands or feet, keep the polygon count on those types of items low (less than 2048).
- Most of the models imported from Poser 2 will have a very sophisticated polygon mesh that is excellent for renderings, but hard to work with for preview. The Nude Detailed Female is over 16,000 triangles.
- Areas where there is bending should have as much as two or three times the polygon count as nonbending areas. Although this doesn't sound like a polygon-saving technique, having concentrations only at the joints rather than having the entire model made up of a fine mesh can save you tons of polys in the long run.
- Through testing, I have found that a single 1024-triangle-based object with just default mapping and lighting requires almost 1MB of memory to handle. With over 20,000 triangles in some of the models from data sets, it is no wonder that you are better off just duplicating something instead of trying to bring in many copies of it.

— *DWIGHT EVERS*

CHAPTER

13 Rendering Tips and Techniques

RENDER AT THE HIGHEST RESOLUTION POSSIBLE

Always render at the highest resolution that your system will allow — the amount of RAM and hard disk space are the determiners here — and save the file without lossy compression. You never know when that image might need to be output as an LVT or be blown up to poster size. What looked great as an 8 × 10 iris at 300 dpi might look like a pile of bricks when it's an LVT or blown up 200%.

— *TONY JONES*

RENDER EXTRA FOOTAGE FOR EDITING PURPOSES

When rendering animations that you plan on splicing together with other animations using a video editing package, be sure to include a couple of extra seconds at the end in case you want to use transitions such as fades or sweeps. After all, it's impossible to have too much footage and you've got to have something to fade out of, right?

— *JOHN W. SLEDD*

CLOAK OBSCURED ITEMS TO REDUCE RENDERING TIME

If it's not going to be seen, the Ray Tracer doesn't need to know it's there. The rays of the Ray Tracer bounce off everything in your scene, whether you can see it in the production frame or not. This adds rendering time.

To maximize your rendering efficiency, try cloaking items that are hidden behind other items in your scene or items that are outside the production frame due to the camera's position during an animation.

Don't cloak an object if it's important that the cloaked object's reflection be visible in your scene or if the object casts a crucial shadow on something within the production frame.

Practicing this technique during an animation can save you hours in the final rendering process.

— *STEVE MCARDLE*

USE THE BATCH RENDERING QUEUE

The batch rendering queue (see Figure 13.1) is one of Ray Dream Studio's most valuable features. The Batch Queue (accessible under the Render menu)

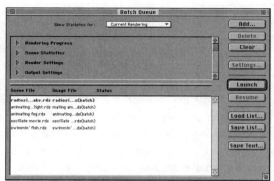

FIGURE *The Batch Queue is one of Studio's most valuable*
13.1 *features.*

allows you to set up several files to render, and takes care of opening each file, rendering it, and saving it. This means you can render several files while you are away from your computer.

The Batch Queue also allows you to pause renderings and then restart them at a later time. For instance, if you are rendering a long animation or high-resolution still but you have other things to do on your computer as well, you can set the Batch Queue up to render your file during times when you are not using your computer — when you are sleeping, at lunch or whatever else. This feature can also often save a file in the event of a crash. If your machine crashes during a regular render, you lose everything. But if it crashes while rendering through the Batch Queue, more often than not you can pick up from the last save.

The Batch Queue can also provide you with valuable information on each file, such as its render settings (which you can also change via the BQ) and the time it took to render. This last feature is particularly useful for those who bill for rendering time.

— STEVE MCARDLE

RENDER CLEAN, COMPRESS LATER

If you are planning on editing an animation or an image after you render it, it's always better to render it in a pure, uncompressed form, such as sequenced .TIFF or Photoshop files. You will probably wind up saving the final version in a compressed format of some sort or another, and double compression is never a good thing. Using this method, you don't lose any quality unnecessarily and you'll have a copy of completely clean footage to work with or use in other projects.

— TONY JONES

AT WHAT RESOLUTION DO I RENDER THIS?

Here is a quick guide to rendering resolutions needed for popular output formats.

CD-ROM

Typically the largest CD-ROM movies are 320 × 240 at 72 dpi. There are other considerations when developing video for CD-ROMs, such as how best to compress your animations to get the most out of the limitations of the CD-ROM throughput, as well as the market at which your specific CD-ROM project is targeted, and that market's system specifications. Will your animations be seen mostly on 2x CD-ROMs and 8-bit color monitors or on 6x CD-ROMs and 24-bit accelerated video cards? The latter would make up the ideal consumer, but sadly, many fall in the previous category.

Web

All Web graphics are screen resolution, which is typically 72 dpi. Some screens are 75 dpi, but 72 dpi is typically the standard for Web graphics.

Dye Sub

Most dye sub printers are 300 dpi, so render your image at 300 dpi. This spec does not hold true for other output devices, though. A 2540 dpi imagesetter does not require you to render your files as 2540 dpi. That's a whole different set of rules, because dye subs create final output, whereas imagesetters create output for use with offset printing, and offset printing has its own rulebook.

Film Output (Including Slides)

Film output is typically measured in pixels instead of inches, with a number of dots per inch. Actual resolutions vary, depending on the film recorder. My film output shop wants images which are at least 3000 to 4000 pixels wide for 4×5 transparencies and 1500 to 2000 pixels wide for 35mm slides. Consult with your output service provider for specifics on your film resolution and, if it's animation you're after, your frames per second.

Print

Print is another area where you should consult with the people actually doing the work. The number which determines your final resolution is the lines per inch in which the piece will be printed. The standard rule of thumb is that your dpi should be 1.5 to 2 times your lpi (over 2 times is wasted information and under 1.5 sometimes yields undesirable results). So if the project you are doing the illustration for will be printed at 175 lpi, then your illustration should be anywhere between 300 and 350 dpi. Standard line screens are 85, 120, 133, 150, and 175 lpi. You will encounter different lpi requests, but doubling that number is always a safe bet.

USING VERY LIGHT FOG FOR DEPTH CUES

This recreates a natural phenomenon called *aerial perspective*. In reality, light is scattered by moisture and pollution in the air. Depending on the time of day, it tends to scatter the blue light while letting other light pass through. Thus we see misty blue mountains in the distance instead of bright green.

In Hollywood visual effects, this is simulated in miniature with a misty fog, and the principle also applies to 3D graphics. You can also do this with Ray Dream Studio's Depth channel in Photoshop, and get greater control.

To do this with the rendering effects, go into your **Scene Settings** window, click on the **Effects** tab and choose **Distance Fog** from the **Atmosphere** pull-down menu. For aerial perspective, choose the **gray** color, and make it slightly bluer than it was previously.

You will see visibility distances for near and far. Set the beginning distance where you feel it is best for your scene, and then enter very large numbers in the second distance, where visibility will drop to complete fog. You will need to experiment with these settings, as each scene is different. However you should end up with a light haze. If you still see a heavy fog, try again.

In this case, a low-resolution test render is the best way to check the settings.

In the scene I created, I used clip models and arranged them in an RDS scene. If you compare the initial render (see Figure 13.2) with the one with depth cueing enabled (see Figure 13.3), you can see a vast improvement in the way the

FIGURE **13.2** *Initial render without the use of depth cueing.*

FIGURE   *The same rendering with the use of depth*
13.3   *cueing.*

image looks. The darker shadows tell your mind that the particular object is closer than others, and the slightly desaturated and bluer colors elsewhere tell you the opposite about everything else. This may still seem a bit heavy, but I was assuming a more humid environment. The cloud background was inserted in Photoshop.

Figure 13.4 is just too heavy, as if it were shot in a fog bank. This is useful for situations where you want fog, but not for aerial perspective.

FIGURE   *Don't add too much fog for this effect. It*
13.4   *will drown out your image and defeat*
the purpose.

You can create interesting effects with this technique by changing the color of your light and changing your fog to a similar color. By doing so, I quickly created the same location at sunset. (See Figure 13.5.) With a little Photoshop retouching using the rendered mask (see Figure 13.6) as a selector, I faded the sky to match the direction of the light.

This technique can also be used for interior scenes. Many professional photographers and motion filmmakers put a light haze of smoke in their interior scenes to give the light more character and to separate objects in depth.

FIGURE
13.5
Experiment with the fog and lighting colors.

FIGURE
13.6
The mask generated by Ray Dream Studio can be used to composite your image with a Photoshop or Painter generated sky.

FIGURE
13.7
You can use the distance channel to add your own depth cueing in your image editing application.

A more interactive method of doing this would be to use RDS's G-buffer: distance setting, and render an Alpha channel. (See Figure 13.7.) Using this channel, you can select your image based on depth, and apply filters or specific curves in Photoshop — no details here, just a tip for more fun!

— JOHNATHAN BANTA

Postproduction Tips and Techniques

BURNING OUT HIGHLIGHTS

Use the Dodge and Burn tools in your image-editing application to accent areas of highlight and shadow in your renders.

— *JOHNATHAN BANTA*

ADD MOTION BLUR TO STILL IMAGES

Still renderings of moving objects often lack a certain oomph that photographs always seem to capture. This is because the scene you rendered really isn't moving — it's lifeless. Add some motion blur in your favorite image-editing application to give your still images extra energy.

— *STEVE MCARDLE*

INSTANT MASKING

Use the Mask G-Buffer to create instant masks for your images. This will make compositing with other images much easier because all the work will have been done for you by the G-Buffer.

— *CECILIA ZIEMER*

COMPOSITE LIGHTING

At some time in your 3D career, you'll probably run into an occasion where you need to render an object to be composited into existing art or perhaps even a photograph. The image on the opening page of this chapter is a good example. Cecilia's castle was created and rendered in Ray Dream Studio and composited over a rendering done in MetaCreations' Bryce. The most integral parts to this piece are the lighting and the camera settings. If you don't match both of these in your render, things will look just plain funky (and I mean the bad funky, not the good Parliament and Funkadelic types).

If you're the one doing both pics, just in separate apps, this job is a little easier. You simply check your lighting and camera settings in one app and make sure they are similar in the other. If you're working to match a rendering to a photo or perhaps a piece of art from another artist, then you simply need to do an evaluation of the scene to determine how many light sources there are, where the light is coming from, and what color and how bright it is. You also need to determine the position and focal length of the camera. The keys to this information lie in the highlights and shadows of the existing art and in how the background and foreground elements relate to each other. (See Rick Greco's nuggets of knowledge on focal length in Chapter 7.) You may have to play around a bit, but if you do it enough, it'll become second nature.

— *JOHN W. SLEDD*

ADDING MOTION BLUR IN ADOBE PREMIERE

Here is a step-by-step tutorial describing how to create motion blur. (You will need RDS and Adobe Premiere to create the motion blur.)

Step One

Open RDS and either open an existing project or create a new one.

Set up your animation as you would normally, using whatever pixel resolution you want. (See Figure 14.1.)

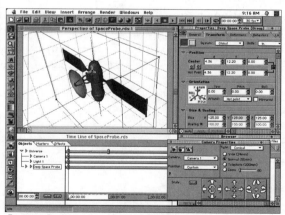

FIGURE *Setting up your RDS animation.*
14.1

Typically, for video 640 × 480 is used; 320 × 240 is also used for a lower resolution for video or possibly for testing your animations. But you can use whatever dimensions you want to. For this example we will use 320 × 240. In the **Current Scene Settings** window, click on the **Output** tab and click on the blue arrow next to **Image Size**, set the **Width** to **320 pts**, the **Height** to **240 pts** and the **Resolution** to **72 dpi**. (See Figure 14.2.)

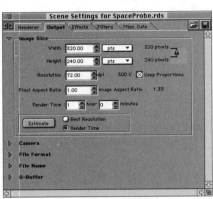

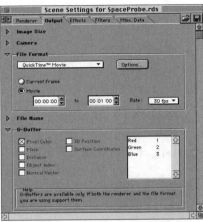

FIGURE *Pay attention to the Render settings.*
14.2

FIGURE *Choose the QuickTime file format.*
14.3

Also under the **Output** tab, click on the blue arrow next to **File Format**. Select the **Movie** radio button, set the **Format** to **QuickTime Movie**, and set the in and out times to the time area of your animation. (See Figure 14.3.)

Click on the **Options** button. You will need to set up your animation to render at **30 fps**. And you should either use no compression (this will eat up a lot of hard drive space) or if you must use some compression try a very high-quality JPEG compression. (See Figure 14.4.) Neither of these options will let

FIGURE *Compression settings.*
14.4

you view your animations in real-time, but that is not critical at this point. Right now it is most important to keep the animations as high-quality as we can. For this example, under **Compression** settings we will use the **Photo — JPEG** at **Best Depth**, with a quality of **90**, at **30 fps**.

After checking your animation using the **Time Controller** toolbar, you are all set to render your animation. Go to the **Render** menu and choose **Use Current Settings** to render your animation. When it is done, save your movie and your project, and then quit RDS.

Step Two

Open Adobe Premiere.

Go to the **Make>Presets** dialog box, click on the **Time Base** button, and click on the **30 fps** button. Click **OK**. (See Figure 14.5.)

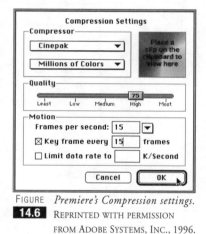

FIGURE *Premiere's presets.* REPRINTED WITH PERMISSION
14.5 FROM ADOBE SYSTEMS, INC., 1996.

FIGURE *Premiere's Compression settings.*
14.6 REPRINTED WITH PERMISSION
FROM ADOBE SYSTEMS, INC., 1996.

Click on the **Compression** button and pick the compression that you use either for viewing movies on your computer or for outputting movies to video. (See Figure 14.6.)

For this example, we will use **Cinepak** set to **Millions of Colors**, using a quality level of **75%** at **15 fps**, with a keyframe every **15 frames**. Click on **OK**.

Click on the **Output** options button. (See Figure 14.7.)

Set the **Output** to **Work Area** as **QuickTime Movie**. In the **Video Area**, set your size to the same size as the movie you rendered in RDS; in this case, **320 x 240**. It does not matter if you have the 4:3 Aspect box checked. Set the

FIGURE *Premiere's Project Output options.* REPRINTED
14.7 WITH PERMISSION FROM ADOBE SYSTEMS, INC., 1996.

Type to **Full Size Frame**. If you are not adding audio to your project (we won't be in this example), uncheck the **Audio** checkbox. Check the **Beep When Finished, Open Finished Movie, Optimize Stills** and **Show Samples** boxes, and uncheck the **Flatten** box. Click **OK**.

Click on the **Preview** option button. (See Figure 14.8.)

FIGURE *Setting Premiere's Preview options.* REPRINTED
14.8 WITH PERMISSION FROM ADOBE SYSTEMS, INC., 1996

Set the **Preview window** size to a comfortable size to preview your movie in Premiere. For this example, **320 × 240** is fine, since that is our target resolution. However, even if you were working on a movie that would be rendered at a higher resolution, like 640 × 480, you still might want to set your Preview window to 320 × 240 to keep as much screen real estate available for your floating palettes. Uncheck the **Center to Screen, Show Safe Areas**, and **Show Time Position** boxes. Unless you have audio in your movie, uncheck the **Audio** box. Check the **More Options** button, and then set the **Rate** to **15 fps**, set the **Mode** to **Effects to Disk**, and set the **Type** to **Full-Size Frame**. Check the **Process at:** box and set it to **320 × 240**. Check the **Video Filters** box. Click **OK**.

Click on the **Save** button. Name these settings **320 × 240 Motion Blur** and click **OK**. Click **OK** in the **Presets** window. (See Figure 14.9.)

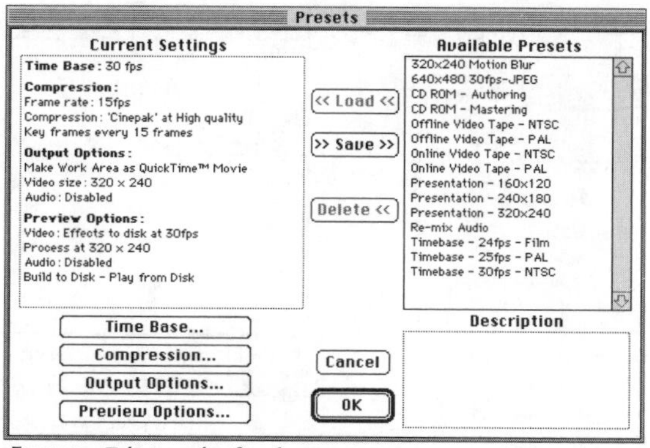

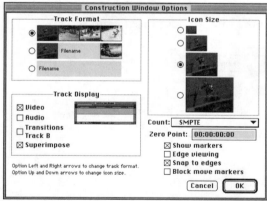

FIGURE **14.9** *Editing the final presets.* REPRINTED WITH PERMISSION FROM ADOBE SYSTEMS, INC., 1996.

Step Three

Go to **File>New>New Project**. Click on the **320 × 240 Motion Blur** settings and click **OK**. From now on, whenever you want to create motion blur all you have to do is start from here.

　　Go to **Window>Construction window** options. (See Figure 14.10.) In the **Track Display** area check the **Video** and **Superimpose** boxes and uncheck the **Audio** and the **Transitions Track B** boxes.

FIGURE **14.10** *The Construction Window options.* REPRINTED WITH PERMISSION FROM ADOBE SYSTEMS, INC., 1996

　　Set the **Count** to SMPTE, check the **Show Markers** and **Snap to Edges** boxes, and uncheck **Edge Viewing** and the **Block Move** markers. Click **OK**.

　　Go to **Project>Add/Delete Tracks**. (See Figure 14.11.) Set the **Total Video** tracks to 7, and set the **Total Audio** tracks to 3. Click **OK**.

FIGURE *The Add/Delete Tracks window.*
14.11 REPRINTED WITH PERMISSION
FROM ADOBE SYSTEMS, INC., 1996.

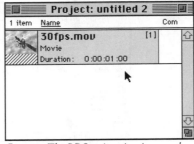

FIGURE *The RDS animation imported*
14.12 *into the Project window.*
REPRINTED WITH PERMISSION
FROM ADOBE SYSTEMS, INC., 1996.

Go to **File>Import>File** and select/open the animation you rendered in RDS. The animation should now appear in the Project window. (See Figure 14.12.)

Now is a good time to save the Adobe Premiere project. Go to **File>Save**, name and save the file.

Step Four

Click and drag the animation from the Project window and place it on the **Construction** window so that it is above track A. Then click and drag the animation in the **Construction** window so the starting point is at **0:00:01:00** (the 1-second mark). You can see what the starting and ending points of a movie are by looking at the Info window. (See Figure 14.13.)

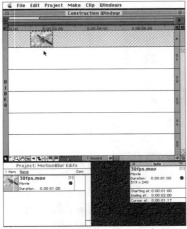

FIGURE *Dragging the clip into the*
14.13 *Construction window.*
REPRINTED WITH PERMISSION
FROM ADOBE SYSTEMS, INC., 1996.

Now click and drag the same movie from the **Project** window and place it at the **1-second** mark on **track S1**. It should now be directly below the first movie you placed. Continue to do this until there is a copy of the animation on every track (A, S1, S2, S3, S4, S5) at the 1-second mark. (See Figure 14.14.)

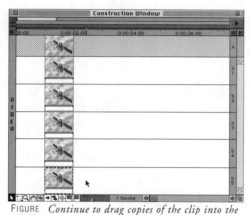

FIGURE **14.14** *Continue to drag copies of the clip into the Construction window.* REPRINTED WITH PERMISSION FROM ADOBE SYSTEMS, INC., 1996.

Now click on the animation on **track S1** and hit the left arrow key **once**. This will change the starting point to **0:00:00:29**.

Next, click on the animation on **track S2** and hit the left arrow key **twice**. This will change the starting point to **0:00:00:28**.

Next, click on the animation on **track S3** and hit the left arrow key **three times**. This will change the starting point to **0:00:00:27**.

Next, click on the animation on **track S4** and hit the left arrow key **four times**. This will change the starting point to **0:00:00:26**.

Next, click on the animation on **track S5** and hit the left arrow key **five times**. This will change the starting point to **0:00:00:25**. (See Figure 14.15.)

Under each of the animations on the Superimpose tracks (tracks starting with an "S"), there is a thin line that controls the Fade Level of that track.

If your put the cursor above any one of those lines and hold the Shift key down, you will be able to drag the whole line up and down. As you do this, the Info window will show you the percentage of the Fade Level.

All the Fade Levels will start at 100%; you will need to change the **Fade Levels** on each of the **Superimpose** tracks to the following settings: **S1=50%, S2=50%, S3=50%, S4=20%, S5=10%**. (See Figures 14.16 and 14.17.)

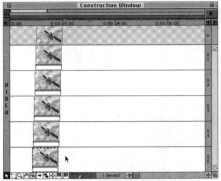

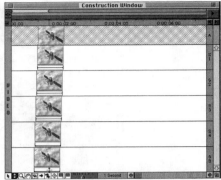

FIGURE *Offsetting all of the copies of the clip.*
14.15 REPRINTED WITH PERMISSION FROM
ADOBE SYSTEMS, INC., 1996.

FIGURE *Adjusting the Fade settings.* REPRINTED
14.16 WITH PERMISSION FROM ADOBE SYSTEMS,
INC., 1996.

Info	Info	Info
30fps.MooU [6]	**30fps.MooU** [5]	**30fps.MooU** [2]
Movie Duration: 0:00:01:00 320 × 240	Movie Duration: 0:00:01:00 320 × 240	Movie Duration: 0:00:01:00 320 × 240
Fade Level: 10%	Fade Level: 20%	Fade Level: 50%
Cursor at: 0:00:01:16	Cursor at: 0:00:01:14	Cursor at: 0:00:01:13

FIGURE *Adjusting the Fade settings on each track.* REPRINTED
14.17 WITH PERMISSION FROM ADOBE SYSTEMS, INC., 1996.

You will now have to set the start and end points for the Work Area Bar, which is the yellow line with the two red arrows at either end in the Construction window.

Click and drag the left red arrow to the starting point of the animation on **track A**, which should be 0:00:01:00. Then click and drag the right red arrow so that it is at the end of the animation on **track S5**. (See Figure 14.18.)

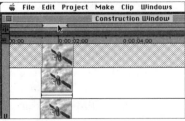

FIGURE *Changing the Work Area Bar.*
14.18 REPRINTED WITH PERMISSION FROM
ADOBE SYSTEMS, INC., 1996.

If you wish, you can hit the **Return** key to see a preview of the animation with motion blur. (See Figure 14.19.)

FIGURE 14.19 *Checking the preview.* REPRINTED WITH PERMISSION FROM ADOBE SYSTEMS, INC., 1996.

Now go to **Make>Movie**, type a name for the new animation with motion blur, and click **OK**. That's it. The movie you've just saved will now have motion blur.

— *JEFFRY GUGICK*

USING THE G-BUFFER FOR CLOUDS

By utilizing the G-Buffer channels in Ray Dream Studio, you can create custom masks for use in MetaCreations' Painter (version 5 supports Alpha channels) or other image-editing applications.

In this quick step-by-step tutorial, you will create an object in Ray Dream Studio, render it with a G-Buffer Distance channel, and then add clouds in Painter using the G-Buffer information to create the effect of your object emerging from the cloud bank.

Step One

Create a new scene in Ray Dream Studio by selecting **New** under the **File** menu. Create a text object by dragging the **Text** tool into the **Perspective** or **Hierarchy** window. Type in the word **G-Buffer**. You can apply a Shader of your choice or just leave the object with the default Red shader.

Step Two

Orient the object and camera as shown in Figure 14.20. Don't worry about being precise. We just need a general depth idea.

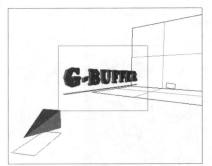

FIGURE *Positioning the camera.*
14.20

Step Three

Go to the **Render Settings** under the **Render** menu and click on the **File Format** tab. Set up your dialog box like the one shown in Figure 14.21. Now render the image and save it in the **Painter RIFF** format.

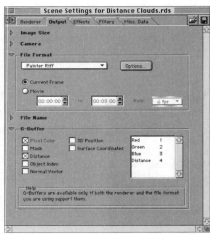

FIGURE *Checking the G-Buffer and File*
14.21 *Format info.*

Step Four

Open Painter and create a cloud image to be used as a clone source. To create the clouds, choose **Make Fractal Pattern** from the **Pattern** menu in the **Art Materials** palette. Choose a size and adjust the other parameters to get the particular cloud effect you're looking for. Figure 14.22 shows the settings used in the particular example. Your cloud image will open as an untitled document. (See Figure 14.23.)

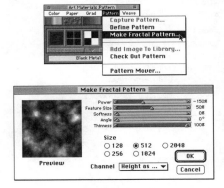

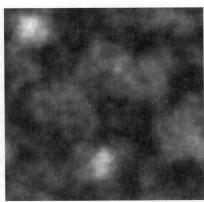

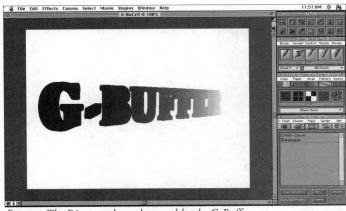

FIGURE **14.22** *Creating the cloud image in Painter to use as a clone source.*

FIGURE **14.23** *The fractal cloud pattern.*

Step Five

Open your render in Painter and take a look at the Distance channel by clicking on the **Mask** icon in Painter's **Objects** palette and then clicking on **Distance** in the list. (See Figure 14.24.) Now click back on the **RGB-Canvas** channel and load the Distance channel by clicking on the **Load Selection** button and choosing **Distance** from the **Load From** pull-down menu (see Figure 14.25). Invert the selection by choosing **Invert** from the **Select** menu. The original Distance channel defaulted to a selection of the foreground area of your image; by choosing Invert, you are now selecting the background areas of the image.

Under Painter's **File** menu, select from the **Clone Source** menu item the cloud fractal pattern image that you created. (See Figure 14.26.) Now click

FIGURE **14.24** *The Distance channel created by the G-Buffer.*

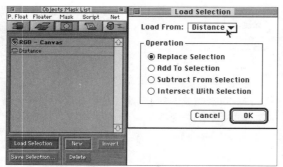

FIGURE
14.25
Loading the Distance channel.

FIGURE
14.26
Setting the Clone Source.

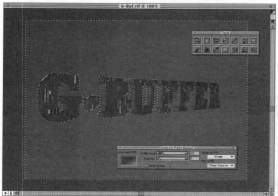

FIGURE
14.27
Using the Fill tool to fill your selection with clouds.

on the **Paint Bucket** Fill tool and choose **Clone Source** under the **Fill With** pull-down menu in the **Controls** palette. Click on your image in the area you want to fill with the Fill tool. (See Figure 14.27.) The Distance channel masked out the items that were closer to the camera and allowed a full cloud effect to encompass the rear of the scene. You can take this moment to adjust the **Brightness/Contrast** setting of your clouds as in Figure 14.28 — of course, you can do that on the original cloud file before filling your selection, too.

Figure 14.29 is the final result of our Distance channel cloud composite.

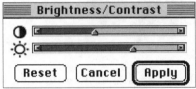

FIGURE *Setting the Brightness/Contrast.*
14.28

FIGURE *The finished piece.*
14.29

CREATING AN ANIMATED FOUNTAIN WITH AN RDS STILL IMAGE

One very important thing that a 3D animator must learn is that if it doesn't have to be 3D, it shouldn't be 3D. Now that may sound rather strange, but 3D rendering, as you know, can be very time-consuming. Your image or movie will wind up in 2D anyway, so if an effect of equal or surpassing quality can be achieved more quickly in a 2D app, that's the better choice.

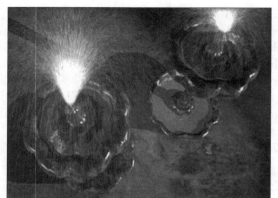

FIGURE
14.30
The underlying fountain is an RDS render, whereas the water is created by the Final Effects plug-in.

In this example, we will use the compositing program known as Adobe After Effects and MetaCreations' KPT Final Effects plug-in to create the water for the fountain in Figure 14.30. Not only would it have taken considerably longer to render this movie using RDS's Fountain primitive, Final Effects' particle system is more robust and offers a wider range of control.

Step One

Render your single-frame PICT (or whatever file format your compositing application supports) image at any size you want to serve as the background for your 2D animation. If you intend to incorporate the final animation into a multimedia presentation, the standard size for that is 320 × 240 pixels. The render used in this example is shown in Figure 14.31.

FIGURE
14.31
The actual RDS fountain background used for this animation.

Step Two

Launch After Effects. Go to the **Composition** menu and choose **New Composition**. The **Composition Settings** dialog box appears. In the **Composition Name**, type **Fountain**. Choose **320 x 240** pixels from the **Frame Size** pull-down menu. In the **Frame Rate** box type **15 fps.** Set the **Duration** to **2 seconds** and click **OK.** Your screen should look like Figure 14.32.

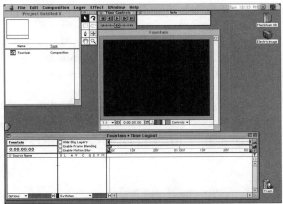

FIGURE *The beginning of your After Effects animation.*
14.32

Step Three

To import the RDS render into the composition, go to the **File** menu and choose **Import>Footage File.** Click on the **FOUNTAIN.PICT** and then click **Open.** Drag the FOUNTAIN.PICT to the **Fountain Composition** icon. (See Figure 14.33.)

FIGURE *Adding your background image to the*
14.33 *composition.*

Step Four

Before we apply the particle filter to the composition, the first thing we need to do is to create a new layer from which the fountain particle will be applied. Make sure the **Time Layout** is activated. To create a new layer, go to **Layer** menu and choose **New Solid**. The **Solid Setting** dialog box appears. Type **Particle** in the **Name** box. Make sure the size is set to **320 x 240** pixels. Click on the **Color** box and set it to **100% black**. Click **OK**.

Step Five

Make sure the **Particle** layer is still selected. Go to the **Effect** menu and choose **Particle>FE Particle System LE**. To align the Emitter to the top of the fountain, click on the plus (+) icon from the **Producer** submenu. Drag the mouse to the location and click on the point where you want the fountain to spread. (Figure 14.34). In the **Particle Animation System**, choose **Fountain** from the pull-down menu. Type the values as shown in the **Particle Value**. (See Figure 14.35.) Choose the color for **Birth** and **Death** as you like.

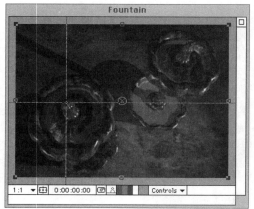

FIGURE **14.34** *Determining the origination point for the particles.*

FIGURE **14.35** *The settings for the particle generator.*

Step Six

Press the **Play** button to preview the animation. For a real-time screen redraw, After Effects provides several Preview options. These are located next to the RGB Channel box. Click on the **Resolution** box and choose **Quarter** from the pull-down menu. Preview the animation again.

Step Seven

As the animation is playing, the water begins to spread at the beginning of the animation. We need to change the timing so the fountain will begin to accelerate at frame 0 instead. From the **Fountain Time Layout** double-click on the **Particle** layer. The **Layers** window appears. Drag the **In** button to **01:00f**, as shown in Figure 14.36. Click the **In** button to set the In point. Close the window. Make sure the **Fountain Time Layout** is still activated and the **Fountain** layer is selected. Go to the **Layers** menu and choose **Time Stretch**. In the **New Duration** box, type **2:00 sec**. Go to the **Time Control** floating palette and press **Play** to preview the animation.

FIGURE   *Resetting the time when the fountain begins.*

14.36

Step Eight

To apply the particle animation in the second fountain, repeat Steps Four through Seven. At Step Five, position the Emitter accordingly. Set the **Turbulence** values to **0.7** and the **Producer** location to **264.0. 28.0**.

Step Nine

Save the project. Go to **File>Save Project**. Type **Animation**. Click **OK**.

Step Ten

If you choose to output the animation as a QuickTime movie, go to **Composition** and choose **Make Movie**. You will be prompted to save the **Movie As**. Type **Final**. Click **Save**. The **Render Queue** dialog box appears. Before you click the **Render** button, there are a couple of options that you will need to check. Go to the **Render** dialog box and click on the **Current Setting**. The **Render Setting** dialog box appears. In the **Quality** option choose **Current**

Setting from the pull-down menu. Go to the **Resolution** option and choose **Full** from the pull-down menu. Click **OK**. After Effects provides several output formats for your needs, but for this exercise we will use **QuickTime** as the final format. In the **Output Module** click on **Lossless**. The Output Module settings appear. In the **Composition Format** choose **QuickTime** from the pull-down menu. In the **Video Output** module click on the **Format Option**. Choose **None** from the pull-down menu and click **OK**. Click **Render** to render the animation.

— *SHARKAWI CHE DIN*

Special Effects Tips and Techniques

I know some of you probably turned directly to this chapter because special effects is what got you interested in 3D in the first place. You love to blow stuff up, zap things, and catch stuff on fire. Instead of calling a good counselor for you, as I probably should, I'm going to show you how to do all of these things and more.

Many of the tutorials in this section could have easily had places in the other chapters, but a dedicated SE chapter seemed like the way to show you several of the nifty tricks you might not have thought RDS was capable of. We'll cover explosions, shockwaves, lightning bolts, fires, smoke and more. Some of the techniques rely on other applications, and some can be done totally within RDS. Have fun going through these and, most importantly, start looking at every tool and features RDS offers from every angle you can think of. You might just be surprised at what you come up with.

TIPS

MOONING WITH FOUR ELEMENTS

Here are a few tips on how to grab the sun and moon in Rayflect's Four Elements extensions — and how not to get lost in your virtual world.

If you're in a Four Elements world and you choose a Front position from your camera, you're looking towards the west. Likewise, if you choose a Back position, you'll be facing east. The problem is that the Preview window in Wind is always facing West. So if you're setting up an animation where you want to see a sunrise or sunset, it's best to set up your camera with a Front view and do your previewing in the Four Elements: Wind Preview window.

Also, don't just use the Moon in Four Elements when doing a night scene. Clever positioning of the sun on the opposite side of your sky sphere (near the equator) can yield the most spectacular imagery. You don't have to use the illumination capabilities of the sun (that is, attach it to a light); just use it to color the sky.

— *JOHN W. SLEDD*

USE THE FOUR ELEMENTS SHADERS TO CREATE MOVIES FOR SUPERMESH

Many people think SuperMesh (Zenstar) and Four Elements (Rayflect) are competing products. They do have some similar features but in fact they are extremely complementary. You can use the Four Elements Shaders to create animated maps for use in a SuperMesh object for those times when Bump mapped water (or whatever) simply doesn't cut it. Do this by applying a Four Elements Shader component in the Color channel of a Shader and applying it to a flat surface. Render the animation from an Isometric perspective and then use the resulting movie as a source in a SuperMesh object.

Also, some of you might have noticed the absence of a way to paint meshes for SuperMesh within RDS. Well, if you have Four Elements, you have a way to paint within RDS and preview the mesh that will be created. Simply create a 4E terrain and use the Paint tools to create the map. Then, save the map from within the Earth dialog box and reopen in SuperMesh. It doesn't get any simpler.

— JOHN W. SLEDD

FOUR ELEMENTS FIRE SHADERS

If you've mapped a 4E Fire shader onto a plane and it's simply too flat, there are a few things you can do. If camera movement is your problem, as with when your camera moves around to the side of the fire plane, simply assign a Point At behavior to the fire to make sure that the flat side of the plane is always facing the camera.

If you simply want a larger or thicker fire than a plane with a Fire shader on it gives you, you can either mix Fire shader components in the plane's Shader or you can stack several fire planes one after another to give the fire more body and more action. Clicking the Shuffle button in the Fire control panel for each plane mixes things up nicely. Don't forget to copy the newly Shuffled Fire into all of the channels in your Shader editor to which you currently have Fire components assigned (usually the Color, Transparency and Glow); otherwise they won't match up.

TECHNIQUES

CREATING GLOWING ATMOSPHERES FOR YOUR HEAVENLY BODIES

This first technique is an extremely easy and quick way to add an atmosphere around planets in your space scenes. If you want to blow them up and catch them on fire afterwards, well, that's your prerogative, but for now, we're just going to give them atmospheres. Figure 15.1 shows a luscious forested moon with a nitrogen-rich atmosphere sitting beside the original, nonatmosphered version of the same planet. It's easy to see how this trick can add a great deal to those ever-so-popular space scenes.

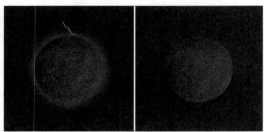

FIGURE   *Here's our planet with and without atmosphere.*
15.1

Step One

This particular file can't get any simpler. It consists of two lights, a sphere and a camera. One of the lights is the distant light and the other is responsible for the atmosphere. You can open the scene in the file ATMOS.RDS from the CD-ROM or you can just follow the pictures — it's that easy.

So for starters, let's create a new scene and insert a **sphere** for your planet. The planet should be **110.80 inches** in diameter and be placed in the exact center of the Global Universe. Apply whatever planetary shader you have on hand to finalize your planet. (See Figure 15.2.)

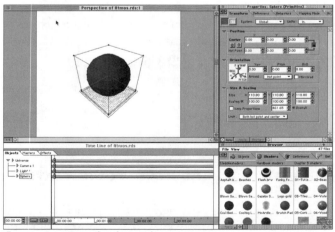

FIGURE   *Setting up the planet sphere.*
15.2

Step Two

Now, click on your **default spotlight** and change it to a **Bulb** light. Give the Bulb a light-blue color and leave the rest of the settings at **default**. Now send the light to the center of your Universe and give it a **0, 0, 0 orientation** (this isn't really necessary, but I like things to be tidy). (See Figure 15.3.)

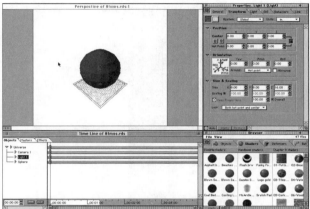

FIGURE *Setting up the atmosphere light.*
15.3

Step Three

Well, we need a sun here, so insert another light, make it a **Distant** light and give it the color and placement you'd like to see a good sun have. (See Figure 15.4.) Now render your animation to see a nice dead planet.

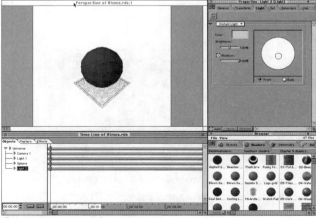

FIGURE *Here comes the sun.*
15.4

Step Four

Here's where we give the planet its atmosphere. As with so many other special effects, this one depends on one of the filters provided in RDS by those geniuses at Rayflect. This time we're going to use the 3D Light Sphere filter. You can find and insert this filter by opening the **Current Scene** settings for your file, clicking on the **Filters** tab then clicking on the little pink plus (+) sign. Choose **VL 3D Light Sphere** from the smorgasbord of choices. (See Figure 15.5.)

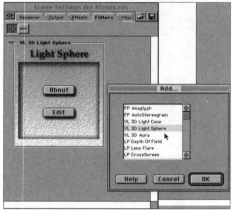

FIGURE *Selecting the 3D Light Sphere filter.*
15.5

Now click on the **Edit** box in the **3D Light Sphere** panel and set the parameters up to jive with Figure 15.6. This particular project won't be animated, but if you do decide to animate it, you might want to give the **Animate** checkbox a click. This can provide some interesting swirling cloud effects. Once you have everything set, click **OK**.

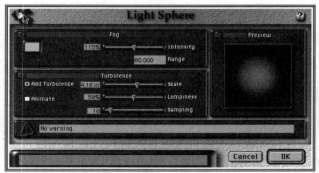

FIGURE *Setting up the 3D Light Sphere parameters.*
15.6

Step Five

Now all that's really left to do is to render your project.

An interesting aside to this project — at least I found it interesting when I first used this technique: the Bulb light inside your planet, which is responsible for your glowing atmosphere (thanks to the 3D Light Sphere filter), has its Shadows box checked. When I set my first atmosphere scene up, I figured I should uncheck this checkbox so that the light would escape the boundaries of my sphere and allow the glow. Well, that's not how it works. If you uncheck the Shadows checkbox, your 3D Light Sphere won't show up at all, so make sure it's checked in your future projects.

— JOHN W. SLEDD

SHOCKWAVES

Well, since we're out in space and all, we should certainly blow something up. Nowadays, nothing blows up in outer space without hurling a shockwave off into the great unknown. (See Figure 15.7.) Many thanks to Craig Lyn for providing the tutorial that led me through my first shockwave. This tutorial comes pretty much straight from his book *The Macintosh 3D Handbook*, which is also published by Charles River Media, so I can get away with stealing it and saying so. Although I didn't follow his steps exactly as laid out, they are very close. Sometimes, if you're looking for a certain effect from a tutorial, you need to improvise.

This is a relatively simple effect. It consists of creating your shockwave movie and then applying it to a plane in your scene. You use a grayscale version of the movie as your Transparency mask so that the plane becomes invisible where there is no shockwave and partially transparent in areas of the shockwave.

FIGURE *A shockwave created from an interstellar explosion.*
15.7

Step One

The first step is to create the shockwave movie that you'll map to your plane. You do this by painting three slightly different shockwave discs in a painting app. Figure 15.8 shows the three different maps. You want to create your maps at the highest resolution you think you'll need, based on how close the map gets to the camera. For this animation, the ending animation was going to be 320 x 240 pixels, so I created these files at 600 x 600 pixels. This gave me plenty of resolution to play with.

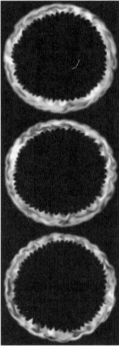

FIGURE *These are the three*
15.8 *maps used for the*
shockwave movie.

I then pulled these maps into an Adobe After Effects composition (a 4-second composition, to be precise) to create the spinning motion for the rings. In After Effects (most video-editing to 2D animation packages should be able to take care of these basics) I did three things. For starters, I assigned a different **Opacity** setting to each of the rings. I gave them each a **33% Opacity** at the start of the animation because I wanted to see bits and pieces of each ring through the other rings. I then duplicated that key event information to the **3-**

second mark and created a key event near the end of the animation where I set the rings' **Opacity** to **0**. This kept the rings a constant 33% up to the 3-second mark and then faded them out to the end of the animation. This was to give the impression of the rings dissipating.

I then rotated each ring differently throughout the animation. I rotated one ring **90 degrees**. I rotated another **-90 degrees** and then I rotated the third **180 degrees**. This, coupled with the Opacity, created a nice swirling motion within the rings, which now appear to be one moving ring instead of three separate rings.

Lastly, I created a **key event** at the beginning and end of the animation for each of the rings' scale setting. This locked the setting at **100%** for the entire animation. I then went back to the beginning keyframe of the animation and set the scale to **1%**. This caused the rings to expand over the course of the animation as if they are flying out from the source of the explosion. Figure 15.9 shows the finished After Effects project at the 2-second mark.

With the AE animation set up, I rendered out the movie to a QuickTime file to use in my Color and Glow channels. I also rendered out a grayscale version of the movie to use in the Transparency channel. For this particular project, I knew I wanted a light-blue ring for my shockwave, so that's what I created. To be honest, however, it would have been more efficient and more flexible (because I could then change the color of the ring on the fly) to just create the grayscale version of the movie and then use it as a mixer in the **Shader editor** but, oh well, live and learn. Figure 15.10 shows frames from the finished shockwave movie.

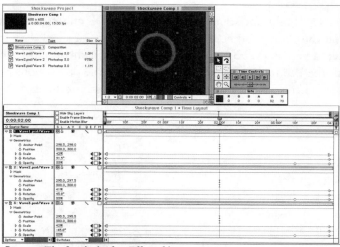

FIGURE *The finished After Effects file.*
15.9

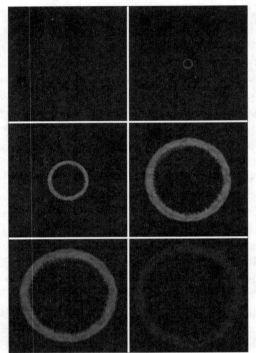

FIGURE *Frames from the finished shockwave movie.*
15.10

Step Two

Now let's build our scene in RDS. Open RDS and create a new file. The first thing you want to do here is make a plane for your shockwave movie to sit upon. Insert a **Free Form** object into your scene and name it **ShockObject**. Draw a line with the **Pen** tool on the drawing plane with the proportions as shown in Figure 15.11. Then view the object from the left and adjust the Extrusion Path to match

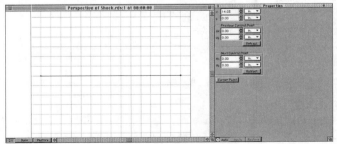

FIGURE *Drawing the side of the plane.*
15.11

the proportions of the line we drew in the cross-section. (See Figure 15.12.) Using the grid makes this easy and gives us a square plane to map our movie on.

FIGURE *Giving the extrusion the same proportions as the plane.*
15.12

Now go to the **Reference** view and let's shade the model. Insert a **Movie** component into your **Color** channel and open the **Shock** movie file you created. Now drag that movie into the **Glow** channel. Give your **Highlight** and **Shininess** channels values of **0** and leave the other channels at their default settings. Now click on the **Transparency** tab and insert another **Movie** component. Open the **Shockwave mask** movie and click on the **Invert Color** box. Now apply the **Shader** and click **Done**. Finally, click on the **Masters** tab, select the **ShockObject** and click on the **Mapping Mode** tab. Select the **Top** projection mode. (See Figure 15.13.)

FIGURE *Setting the Mapping mode.*
15.13

Step Three

Center the hot point of your ShockObject and center the object in the **Working** box. (See Figure 15.14.) You can also increase the scaling percentage of the ShockObject to **136.35%** in the **Transform** tab of the **Properties**

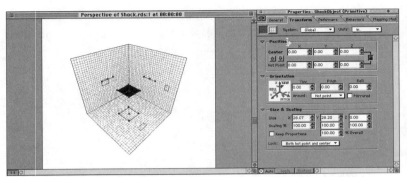

FIGURE *Centering the ShockObject's hot point.*
15.14

palette. This is not really necessary, but if you want the tutorial set up exactly like mine, you should do it.

Now we're going to need a way to frame the shockwave in our composition. We could use the **Better Preview** mode, but we really don't want to do that for two reasons. The first reason is that it's slow. The second reason is that even if we do turn on **Better Preview** mode, the animation starts out with no visible shockwave, so we still wouldn't know where it is until later on in the animation, and arranging your scene setup anywhere but at frame 0 is a bad habit to get into. You could disable animation for the your rendering camera when setup time came, but if you forget, you'll have to start all over. A better trick, which is faster than **Better Preview**, is to insert a **Sphere** into your scene, set its size to two or three inches and center it in the scene along with the

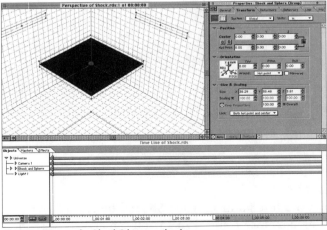

FIGURE *Group the ShockObject and sphere.*
15.15

plane. Since we know the shockwave will be coming from the center of the plane, we can use the sphere as a placeholder for how to set up the scene composition. The sphere will be cloaked before rendering. **Group** the ShockObject and the sphere and call the group **Shock and Sphere**. (See Figure 15.15.)

Step Four

Now let's set up a **Render Cam** and compose the scene. Insert a new camera, name it **Render Cam**, and click **OK** to accept the default settings. Now select the **Render Cam** in the **Hierarchy** and fill in its **Transform** tab in the **Properties palette** as in Figure 15.16. Now choose **Render Cam** from the **View>Camera** menu to view your scene through the rendering camera. By including our sphere as a guide, you can tell exactly from where your shockwave will come. (See Figure 15.17.)

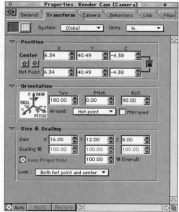

FIGURE *The Render Cam settings.*
15.16

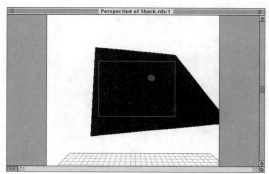

FIGURE *View from the Render Cam. Notice our sphere*
15.17 *marker.*

Step Five

Well, your shockwave is all set up to render, but we need an explosion to trigger the shockwave. Click on your **Light 1** and rename it **Explosion Light**. Give it a light-blue color, zero out its **Brightness**, give it a range of **42.00** inches and disable the **Shadows** box. (See Figure 15.18.) Now click on the **Transform** tab and set it up as in Figure 15.19. It will take a good bit of trial and error to set up the light correctly in your own original scenes, but I've already spent that time for this one, so I'm giving you the magic numbers. These magic numbers should place your light right in front of your Sphere object in your Render Cam view. (See Figure 15.20.)

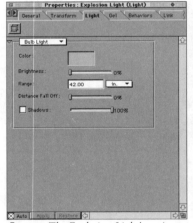

FIGURE **15.18** *The Explosion Light's settings.*

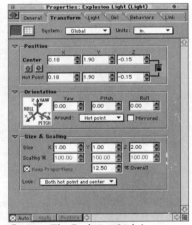

FIGURE **15.19** *The Explosion Light's coordinates.*

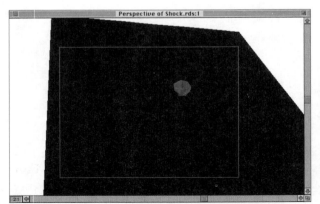

FIGURE **15.20** *The Explosion Light should be directly in the line of sight between our Render Cam and the Sphere marker.*

Now we want to animate the Explosion Light's **Brightness** settings. Set your animation up for **15** seconds and move your **Current Time Bar** to frame **00:04**. Set the light's **Brightness** to around **100%**. (See Figure 15.21.) Now **Command/Alt-Drag** the key event that you've just created to **frame 2:02**. This will hold the Brightness setting for just under a second. (See Figure 15.22.) Now move to **frame 3:10** and bring the **Brightness** setting back down to **0**. You can just **Command/Alt-Drag** the beginning key event to frame 3:10 if you like. This will fade the light out as the explosion dies.

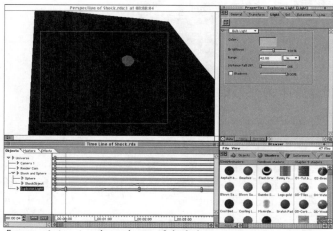

FIGURE **15.21** *Animating the explosion of the light.*

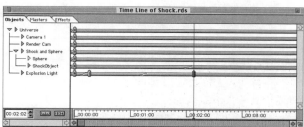

FIGURE **15.22** *Holding the brightness of the explosion by duplicating key events before fading it out towards the end.*

Step Six

Now we want to add the flare to the Explosion Light. Bring up the **Current Scene** settings and click on the **Filters** tab. Click on the plus (+) sign and select **LP Lens Flare**. When the LP Lens Flare box comes up, click on **Edit** and set your parameters up as in Figure 15.23. Since the Lens Flare uses the light's

Brightness settings for the strength of the flare, we don't need to animate anything here. You could do so if you wanted, and leave the light at a constant brightness, but it's much easier to animate the light than to have to navigate your way back to this control panel every time you want to add a key event.

FIGURE **15.23** *Setting up the Lens Flare parameters for the explosion.*

While you're here in the **Scene** settings, click on the **Effects** tab and put something in the **Background**. I chose a **Bi Gradient**, but you really don't see anything but the black areas in the final animation. If you have a big starfield lying around, you might want to pop it in there. If not, black will do. (See Figure 15.24.)

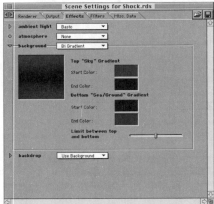

FIGURE **15.24** *Put something in the background. Otherwise the transparent areas of your shockwave plane will be white.*

Step Seven.

That's it. Now all you have to do is render the thing. Choose an appropriate **Image Size**, the **Render Cam** and a **Movie** file format, as in Figure 15.25, and

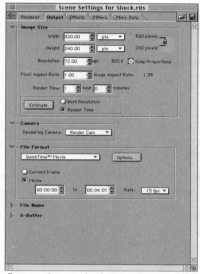

FIGURE 15.25 *Setting the Output options.*

FIGURE 15.26 *Setting the Renderer options.*

to speed things up, get rid of any Renderer options you don't need. (See Figure 15.26.) Now render away and watch your universe explode.

— JOHN W. SLEDD

LIGHTNING BOLTS

While writing this book, I received an email from Biographics Research/Hutchison Avenue Software Corporation (http://bgr.hasc.com/) about a new RDS extension they were developing for lightning generation called ThOr. Sadly I couldn't try it out because it was a PC-only thing at the time, but I hope this will have changed by the time you read this. ThOr is certainly worth checking out if you're interested in quick and easy lightning effects. If, however, you're interested in laborious, time-consuming techniques for creating lightning, continue on with this tutorial. Actually, it's really not that bad. It is more time-consuming than a lightning generator would be but it will also offer you a little more control over how the lightning looks, because you create the lightning yourself from the ground up.

There really is no mystery to this lightning technique. You draw the lightning, you map it to a plane and you've finished. The trick comes in when you want to animate it. Still, it's not difficult, but some methods can be better than

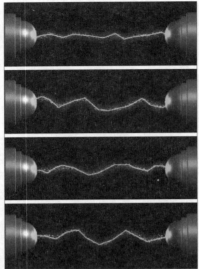

FIGURE
15.27 *A lighting technique comes in handy for your everyday mad-scientist work.*

others. For this tutorial, I'll use Painter 5's animation capabilities to create the electrical bolts seen in Figure 15.27.

Step One

Open Painter (you can use Painter 4 if you like, but I can't guarantee the steps will be the same — it's been a while since I used it) and create a new document. Set the **Canvas** size to **Width: 100**, **Height: 600** and **Resolution: 72** pixels per inch.

Finish off this dialog box by selecting **Movie** with **15 frames** as the file type, and click **OK**. (See Figure 15.28.) Select **2 Layers of Onion Skin** and **8-bit gray** on the next dialog, and click **OK**. (See Figure 15.29.) You should get a file similar to the one in Figure 15.30.

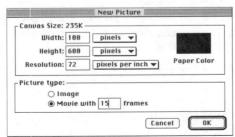

FIGURE *Setting up the Painter animation file.*
15.28

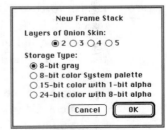

FIGURE *Selecting more options.*
15.29

FIGURE **15.30** *The resulting file.*

FIGURE **15.31** *Selecting the Scratchboard tool.*

Now select the **Scratchboard** tool from the **Pens** library (see Figure 15.31) and choose **White** as your foreground color. In the **Brush Controls>Size palette,** change the **Size** to **1.0** and the **± size** to **1.8.** (See Figure 15.32.) Now set the **Draw Style** to **Straight Lines** in the **Controls palette.** (See Figure 15.33.) Now we're ready to draw some lightnin'.

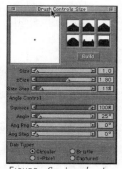

FIGURE **15.32** *Setting the size.*

FIGURE **15.33** *Setting the Draw Style to Straight Lines.*

Step Two

Draw your first lightning bolt starting at one end and working your way to the other. (See Figure 15.34.) Now turn on your **Tracing Paper** under the **Canvas** menu and then advance to the next frame using the **Frame Stacks palette.** (See

Figure 15.35.) This will give you an overlay of your last frame to use as a guide for this frame. The first thing you want to do is to choose the **Freehand Draw Style** and then go back to the **Straight Lines Draw Style** in the **Controls palette**. This resets the starting point for your brush. For this bolt, follow the first bolt closely — not too closely, just close enough. (See Figure 15.36.) When you've finished, advance to the next frame, select **Freehand** and then **Straight Line** again to reset the brush and draw another bolt. Make this one completely different from the first two. It's wise to keep the ends in the same general area because you'll need those to match up with your models on the ends, but the middle can get crazy if you like. (See Figure 15.37.)

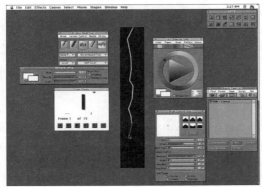

FIGURE
15.34 *The first lightning bolt.*

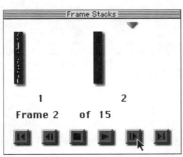

FIGURE
15.35 *Advancing the frame.*

FIGURE
15.36 *Creating the second bolt.*

FIGURE
15.37 *Drawing the third bolt.*

Now advance to the next frame and repeat the above process. This frame should follow the last frame pretty closely, but not too closely. See the pattern here? Every two bolts are similar but no two groups of bolts should be very similar. Keep repeating this pattern until the end of your 15 frames. Pay attention to what frame you're on, though, because Painter will just keep adding frames to the end if you keep clicking on that Advance button. You'll have an extra bolt at the end with no partner as 15 is an odd number, but that's OK.

When you've finished, you can play your animation to see your first batch of lightning in motion. When you've finished playing, rewind the animation and turn off the Tracing Paper because we ain't done yet.

Step Three

Now that you have your lightning going, let's add some sparks to the bolts. You can add these either at the ends only, or along the whole bolt if you like. Actually you can add them anywhere you damn well please, but I'm going to add mine along the entire bolt.

Adding these little sparks is a breeze, thanks to one of Painter's cool brushes. While still in the **Pens** library, select the **Pixel Dust** variant and then the **Freehand Drawing Style**. (See Figure 15.38.) I suppose you could go back to the Straight Line Drawing Style, but I did this one freehand. With the Pixel Dust brush selected, roughly trace the bolt in each frame, as in Figure 15.39. When you've finished, do a **Save As** and save the movie as **LIGHTNIN.MOV** or **LIGHTNIN.AVI**. Select your favorite compression scheme which has a 256 gray option. This will be your lightning mask movie.

FIGURE **15.38** *Use the Pixel Dust variant.*

FIGURE **15.39** *Tracing the bolt with the Pixel Dust to create sparks.*

Step Four

Open the **RECEPT.RDS** file from the CD-ROM and double-click on the **Lightning Plane** to jump into the Master object. Click on the object with the **Eyedropper** tool to bring up the **Shader editor**. In the **Color** channel, insert the color you want your lightning to be and place levels of **0** in the **Highlight** and **Shininess** channels. Insert a **Movie** component into your **Transparency** channel and check the **Invert Color** box. In the **Glow** channel, insert a **Mix** operator and place **Color** components in both sides. Insert a **Movie** component into the **Drop Function Here** box and open your movie. Figure 15.40 shows what your Glow channel should look like.

FIGURE **15.40** *The Glow channel tree.*

And that's it. The lights in the scene provide the actual light that would be coming from the bolts, and an Aura filter gives the bolt a little bit of glow. For a very interesting effect, you could animate the intensities of the lights so that the illumination quality would change on the receptacles to interact with the electricity motion. An animated gel would be a good way to do this.

Have fun zapping things from here on out.

— *JOHN W. SLEDD*

SMOKING WITH THE AURA FILTER

This last tutorial of the chapter is meant to really put your creative juices into overdrive. We'll cover just one effect — the smoke in Figure 15.41 — but several

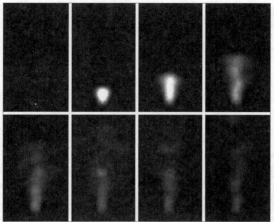

FIGURE **15.41** *This smoke movie would make an ideal Transparency mask.*

different effects are available based around the same idea. I got these ideas from Steve Yatson of MetaCreations and Antoine Clappier of Rayflect.

Although this smoke technique could be used as-is in the scene where you'd want the smoke, my choice would be to create the smoke in its own file, render a movie, and then apply the movie to a plane. This keeps the scene simple and avoids the unwanted "smoking" of other objects in your scene that might have Glows assigned to them.

Step One
The first step in this tutorial is to insert a **Fountain Primitive**. Give your fountain the same settings as in Figure 15.42. This will ensure that it will start from

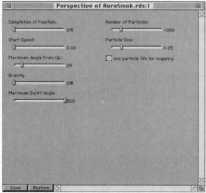

FIGURE **15.42** *The start point for the fountain.*

ground level and move upward. I've set up my animation as a two-second animation, but you can make yours any duration you like. When you have the length set up, skip to the end of the animation and change your Fountain settings to those in Figure 15.43 then return to frame 0.

FIGURE *The end point for the fountain.*

15.43

Step Two

Now it's time to shade the fountain. The fountain's shading never changes during the course of the animation, but it certainly could if you wanted a particular effect — red flames at the bottom blending to smoke, for instance.

Anyway, I shaded this one totally for smoke. I inserted a **Mix** operator in the **Color** channel and mixed two shades of gray with a **Gradient Pattern** function. I gave the Gradient a pretty high **Turbulence** which added some "billow" to the smoke. I then copied this tree into the **Glow** channel. (See Figure 15.44.)

Next, I set the **Transparency** channel to **96%**. (See Figure 15.45.) I also set the **Highlight** and **Shininess** channels to **zero**. This makes the smoke pretty much invisible until the Aura filter runs across it.

Step Three

The final step is to add the Aura filter and create a black background. Go into the **Current Scene** settings, click on the **Filters** tab and then click on the little Plus (+) sign. Select **VL 3D Aura** from the list and click **OK**. Set your **Aura** up as in Figure 15.46. Notice that I added a good bit of Turbulence here too. This, coupled with the Turbulence in the Gradient function creates a nice billowy effect. When you've finished there, click on the **Effects** tab and add a **Background** color of **black**.

Render the animation, and you'll get a great smoke movie that will fit anywhere in your animation you can fit a plane to map it to. Or if you're not using

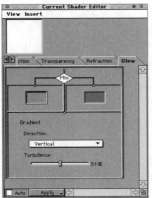

FIGURE **15.44** *The Color and Glow channel trees for the smoke. Notice the high Turbulence setting.*

FIGURE **15.45** *A high Transparency makes sure the smoke isn't visible until the Aura filter passes over it.*

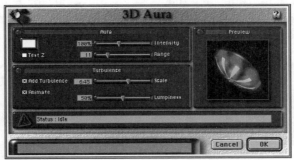

FIGURE **15.46** *The smoke's Aura settings.*

Glows on any of the other objects in your scene (which is unlikely, since where there's smoke there's fire), you can simply copy and paste this fountain anywhere you'd like to have smoke.

This technique can take on many forms, from rocket exhaust (just use oranges and reds instead of grays), to explosions, to what ever else you can dream up. You also aren't limited to the Aura filter. Figure 15.47 shows an explosion created totally in RDS using a variation of the above technique. The variation is that the fountain is pointed towards the camera, has a very low Transparency setting, and is colored with hot reds and oranges to simulate sparks and debris.

The main part of the explosion is created using several Bulb lights with gels (Gradient gels blending from orange to yellow) and the VL 3D Light Sphere fil-

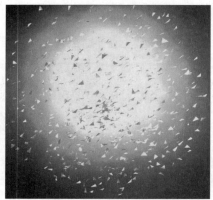

FIGURE
15.47
An explosion created in RDS using a technique very similar to the smoke technique.

ter enabled. Each light creates its own sphere so it's possible to make large rolling explosions. Animating these can get tricky, but the results are worth it. The trickiness of the animation is another reason I recommend creating files that are nothing but effects, and then mapping the resulting movies to planes.

FIGURE
15.48
A few frames from an explosion animation created in Painter and After Effects

Of course you can always build your effects in their own separate files and then copy and paste into your working files. The choice is up to you, and each project is different. If you do decide to use the invisible plane technique, remember that you can map any movie created anywhere onto these planes. Figure 15.48 is from a movie of an explosion I created in Painter 5 and After Effects in a very similar fashion to the Lightning and Shockwave tutorials. The possibilities are unlimited, and breaking an effect down into a little project of it's own can really help you when it comes to figuring out the next greatest special effect.

— *STEVE YATSON, ANTOINE CLAPPIER AND JOHN W. SLEDD*

Web, schmeb, who cares? Any 3D artist with any sense of what's hot, that's who! Aside from researching a book report, looking up stock reports, or digging up nasty personal tidbits about your Aunt Barbara on the Microsmarts search engines, the Web is a graphic lovers playground. Hey, where else can you publish your work practically for free?

As a creative owner of RDS, you have ability to take part in the fun not only by conjuring up your own nifty ol' 3D graphics, but also by putting together animated GIFS and RealVR scenes.

ANIMATED GIFs WITH A DASH OF TRANSPARENCY

So now you've got the coolest button the Web has ever seen rendered in RDS and you want to save it as a GIF to use on your home page.

Wait, this button is too cool though — you want to animate it so that it blinks and people really jump and down over it. Easy enough — check out the following steps to render one blinky button and place it on the Web.

First you need to create this cool button you're going to animate, render, and save as a Sequenced GIF.

Step One

Let's make the Button object. Take a look at Figure 16.1 and you'll understand where this first part is taking you.

The first thing is to insert two **spheres**; we'll use these to make the button. We're not entering this in a contest, so don't expect too much from this particular button.

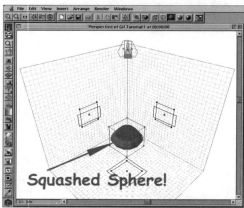

FIGURE
16.1   *Two spheres is all it takes to make a cyberbutton.*

Next, **select** one sphere and **resize** it down on the **Z axis**, squashing it. Not too much! Through the **Properties palette**, resize the squashed sphere, making it about **125%** larger, then name that object **collar** and name the unchanged sphere **dome**.

Reposition the two objects until the dome sits nicely within the collar. Ta da, instant button.

Now shade dome button and the collar to taste. Keep in mind that you'll want the dome part of the button to be blinking, so choose a nonglowing Shader that will be applied for the "off" stage of the blink. I chose a silvery reflective Shader for the collar, and a red semitransparent shader for the unlit dome.

Since my button's blink is based on the Glow channel, I set up a switch in the Glow channel for the dome's shader. I simply used a Multiply operator to multiply a reddish color with a Value slider. The Glow is off when the Value slider is set to 0% and is progressively increased as you raise the percentage of the Value slider towards 100%.

For frame 1, with no Glow, set the **Value** slider to **0%**. (See Figure 16.2.)

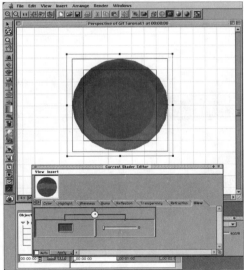

FIGURE *Creating a channel switch in the Glow*
16.2 *channel.*

Step Two

Now that you have a prop for the animation, it's time to ready the set for showtime.

Start by selecting the default light already in the arranging window and drag its **Z projection** along the **X axis** and nest it by the **X,Y,Z convergence**.

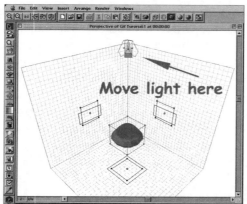

FIGURE **16.3** *Getting the lighting just right.*

(See Figure 16.3.) This will place it in the upper left of the production frame relative to where you're about to set your camera.

Now, select both the light and the dome of the button. Use the **Point At** command (**Command/Ctrl-M**) to aim the light at your button.

Change your camera view to Top and change your camera type back to **Conical** from **Isometric**. (See Figure 16.4.)

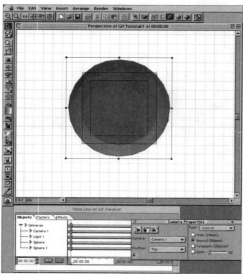

FIGURE **16.4** *Setting your camera view, camera type, and production frame.*

Ignore the Resize warning and resize your Production Frame to hug the edges of your button. Leave ten or so pixels on each side for the Transparency mask to wrap totally around the button.

I added a background to reflect off my button's reflective surfaces. If you're going to add a background, do it here at the beginning of your animation.

Under the **Effects** tab of the **Scene Settings palette** I chose **Background**, and loaded an image that was sitting on my hard drive. By chance it looked pretty cool when I later rendered it. (See Figure 16.5.)

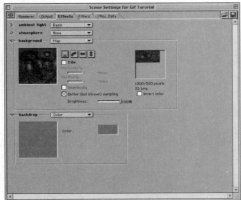

FIGURE *Adding a reflected background and choosing*
16.5 *a color for for your backdrop.*

Here is where you can choose the Transparency mask color via the Backdrop option. A mask tells a Web browser what areas of the GIF should be transparent or in other words, allows the Web browser's background color to show through. We want our button to look round, with no square border showing when viewed in a Web browser.

You can choose White or Black later on in RDS's Save option for a GIF, but choosing another color for the Backdrop in the Effects tab of the Scene Settings palette seems to override it. This is a powerful feature.

When you choose a Mask/Backdrop color, you'll want it to be a color that does not exist in the final rendered image. This way, when you save your image to GIF89A format, or as part of an animation, you can select only that color for the Transparency mask.

Every pixel that carries that mask color will allow the Web browser background to show through when viewed in a browser. If there are traces of that color in the rendered GIF image, those parts of the image will become transparent too, allowing the Web browser background to show through there as well.

Do not choose Use Background in your Backdrop options. You will place the Background image you've loaded behind your object when it renders, and ruin your attempt at a clean mask. If you're using a Background map, to avoid complications with the mask you must choose a color for the backdrop.

For a mask, I've had good luck using a very bright and nasty 100% pink. That color almost never makes it into an image at 100%.

I then added an Aura effect for the blinking dome of the button, courtesy of Rayflect's Aura filter set to Default settings. This comes into play for the second frame of the animation when we change the shader of the dome to make it glow. (See Figure 16.6.)

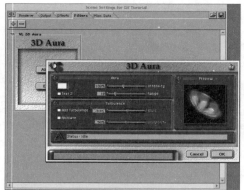

FIGURE   *Enhance the glow effect with the Aura filter.*
16.6

Step Three

You need to add the glow which is the blink for your button — a button without a blink is dull, boring and poor company. First set up your time line for one second of animation — it's set at two seconds by default, so you'll need to adjust it. After you've done that, drag and set your red event marker to 1 second. (See Figure 16.7.)

Now call up the **Shader editor** and select the dome object. The dome's Shader will load into the **Shader editor**. If it by chance doesn't, select the dome's Shader with the **Eyedropper** tool, being sure the dome itself is still selected in the arranging window. Then select the **Auto** mode in the **Shader editor** (if it's not already checked), and click into the **Glow** channel. In the **Glow** channel, drag the **Value** slider to **100%**. (See Figure 16.8.) This turns on the Glow for the second frame of the animation.

If we were doing more than two frames, we'd want to fiddle with a discrete tweener to control the Glow in the Shader over time, making sure the Glow

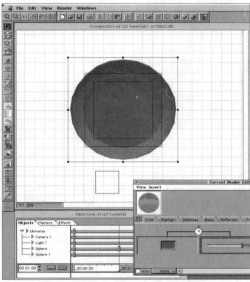

FIGURE
16.7
Adjusting your event marker for frame 2.

FIGURE
16.8
Turning on the Glow for frame 2.

turned on and off abruptly as opposed to fading in and out linearly. The same goes for the light settings you'll change in Step Five, but since there are only two frames, at time 0 and 1 second, there is nothing to "tween."

With the event marker still at 1 second, select the light. In the **Properties palette**, change the color of the light to a red, but be sure to keep the same lightness setting — we're changing only the hue and saturation, changing the lightness will unnecessarily affect the intensity of the light. The red hue of the light will suggest that the red glow of the button is illuminating the surface of the collar. It's a subtle trick, but it helps complete the effect of the button glowing realistically. (See Figure 16.9.)

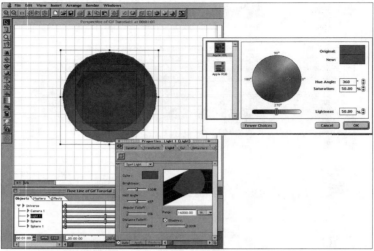

FIGURE   *Changing the color of the light.*
16.9

Step Four

Your Render settings are the all-important part of this tutorial, and depending on what software you own, your approach might be different from this.

Unfortunately, RDS does not produce a self-contained animated GIF, but it does output a sequence of GIFs from an animated scene.

If all you own is RDS and you have no ability to stitch together a couple of GIFs, say through GifBuilder or MS GIF Animator, you're stuck with rendering to QuickTime or AVI formats, which the major Web browsers with the appropriate plug-ins will recognize.

Since we're talking about GIFs here, we'll assume you can stitch together the GIFs output from RDS.

In the **Scene Settings palette**, choose the final dimensions of your render. Remember, it's for the Web, so render at **72dpi** (the average monitor screen resolution) and choose the dimensions.

Since this is such a wonderful button, go to the **File Size** option under the **Output** tab and set your dimensions to **144 pixels by 144 pixels**, or at **2 inches by 2 inches** screen size. This is huge for a button, but this is a very special button. (See Figure 16.10.)

Within **File Format** under the **Output** tab, we'll choose **Movie, 0 to 1 second/2 frames per second/Sequenced Gif**. This gives us two rendered frames of the button — one Off frame and one On/Button Lit frame. Now skip down to the **G-Buffer** and enable the **Mask** via the checkbox. (See Figure 16.11.)

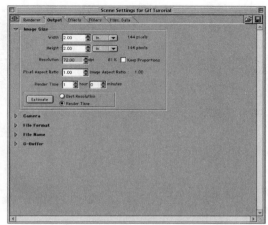

FIGURE *Setting your Render size.*
16.10

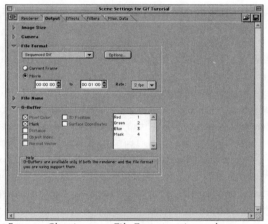

FIGURE *Choosing your File Format setting and*
16.11 *enabling your Mask.*

You must enable the G-Buffer before you move into your Sequenced GIF options, or you won't be able to choose a mask from the Transparency options, which will be grayed out.

If you've chosen a color for the Backdrop, remember, that color overrides the Plug-In transparency setting for the Sequenced GIF.

Now click on the **Options** button under the **Sequenced Gif** area, leave the **Numbering** format at **default**, as shown in Figure 16.12, and dive right into the **Plug-In** options. (See Figure 16.13.)

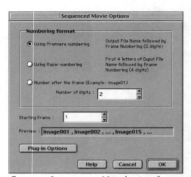

FIGURE   *Leave your Numbering format*
16.12   *at Default.*

FIGURE   *Choose your GIF options.*
16.13

Here you'll choose **Gif89A** (which is the GIF format that recognizes transparency), **Palette/Optimal**, **No Dither** (dithering is just plain ugly for this button), and **Transparency/Black**.

To digress for a moment: in the current version of RDS (5.0), I've tried to produce a GIF that will load into a browser with Transparency enabled, and no matter what settings I use, all I get is a solid color mask that must be enabled through another program or software plug-in.

There's a documented bug in the current release of RDS that does not enable the Transparency of the G-Buffer mask generated during your render. This makes the use of the GIF89A Transparency option in RDS's current release useless. I suggest you just choose a good Backdrop color in the Effects tab, and go with that. You can choose straight white or black, but from my experience, they are two tricky colors to use for GIF mask, often enabling Transparency within the render image proper.

I recommend skipping the whole Sequenced GIF format, and suggest choosing a format like Sequenced Photoshop, Sequenced PICT, Sequenced TIFF, or any other format that will save an Alpha channel. These formats can be read by most programs that will host plug-ins that can read the Alpha channel mask describing the Transparency. Also, you'll have control over the color space conversion from 24-bit RGB, giving you a chance to produce a higher quality 8-bit image when converting to GIF.

To render, use the Batch Queue. Simply load the file from your hard disk into the Queue and launch. The result will be two GIF files — one with the button off, one with it glowing on. As I've been saying, you'll need to take these files into another program to stitch them together as one file — a file that a Web browser will recognize as a GIF animation.

Step Five

If by the time you read this, RDS is still not able to output a GIF89A with transparency, follow try this variation on the previous steps under Render Settings. Refer to that section while observing these changes.

Choose Sequenced Photoshop/TIFF/PICT format for your render and enable the G-Buffer mask. Next, launch the render and save the file(s) to your hard disk if you haven't used the Batch Queue. Then import the two files into Photoshop, and, one by one, change their color mode to Index Color. (See Figure 16.14.) Note that after this step you are left with two channels in each image — one for Index Color, and one for the G-Buffer mask.

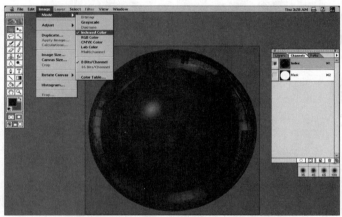

FIGURE *Converting to Index Color in Photoshop.*
16.14

Export the images one by one via the GIF89A Export module. Within the **Export** module dialogue, from the **Transparency From** pop-up menu choose **Mask**. See Figure 16.15.

The resulting file(s) can be opened inside a Web browser and, lo and behold, you finally have Transparency in the areas described by the trusty mask channel. The edges should be very clean, much cleaner than if you had described the transparent areas by other means.

Now you are able to import the GIFS you've just created into a GIF animator program. Depending on the program you're using, the mask you've just enabled may or may not be read.

In GifBuilder the mask is not read in as Transparency. Instead you'll end up with a solid color where the transparent areas should be — usually gray, as exported by default from the Photoshop GIF89A Export module.

In GifBuilder, simply choose **Transparency** as **Based on First Pixel** (see Figure 16.16.) for each imported frame, and save the file.

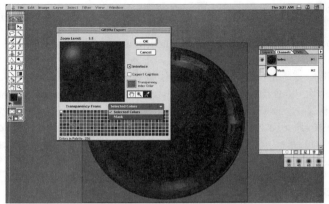

FIGURE
16.15   *Enable your channel mask during export from Photoshop.*

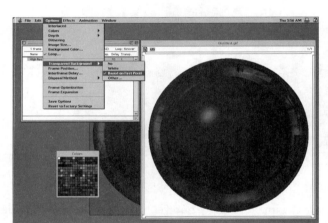

FIGURE
16.16   *Select **Transparency** in GifBuilder.*

FIGURE
16.17   *Sit back for a moment and admire your button.*

Your animation is ready to be uploaded to your Web server from your hard drive. To preview it directly from your hard drive, open it from inside your Web browser to see if it's working properly. (See Figure 16.17.).

Putting the GIF on Your Web Site

This is as simple as putting the knitted Sequenced GIFS, patched together in GifBuilder or another app, into the right directory on your server. Browsers look at animated GIFS as the same as regular GIFs, even though they display the images in sequence as a form of animation.

Once the animated GIF is uploaded and on your server, simply link to it in the same way as you would with another graphic image, and you're done. Then, crack a soda, sit back for a moment, and admire your button.

— RICK GRECO

CREATING A RealVR SCENE

Putting together a RealVR scene is a joy, and RDS makes it as simple as putting an IVRM camera into your scene and rendering your file through the Batch Queue feature. The result is two files, one a JPEG, and an accompanying text file that the RealVR Viewer and the RealVR browser plug-ins require to project the rendered scene onto your computer screen.

The JPEG is basically mapped onto the inside of a virtual sphere by RealVR, and you can control your view using your mouse in combination with the Control and Shift keys. The mouse is used by clicking, holding, then dragging within the view of the image frame. As you drag, the virtual sphere spins around you, though from your perspective it seems as though you're moving your head or turning around in a circle. Dragging left or right allows you to "look" in those directions. The same applies if you drag up or down — then you're looking towards the floor or ceiling, the ground or the sky. The arrow keys also work, and I find them the simplest way to navigate around.

If you press the Shift key, you'll zoom into your scene, and the Control keys will zoom you out. RealVR zooms not by actually walking you forward and backward into the scene, but simply by increasing the level of magnification for the view. So in order to get good-quality close-ups of your scenes, it's best to render at pretty high resolutions.

The difference between creating a standard 3D scene and a RealVR scene lies mostly in the conception. The IVRM spherical camera reveals 360 degrees in all planes, so the world you produce must be complete for all sides facing the camera. This requires a bit more time to create all the models and virtual sets, but other than that, it's all common sense, and Ray Dream Studio does the rest.

Here's a step-by-step example of a simple scene composed of primitives and simple Shaders. You can open up and look at a completed version of this RDS file, along with the rendered files, on the *Ray Dream Handbook*'s CD-ROM. What you'll find there is more complete than the one you'll be doing here, but all I did was replace the primitives with groups of primitives and some more interesting shading.

Step One

First create the IVRM spherical camera. (See Figure 16.18.) Place the camera at coordinates **0,0,0**, because this is the point around which to build your scene. (See Figure 16.19.)

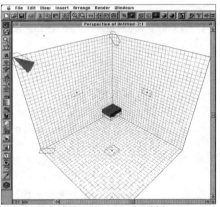

FIGURE *Insert an IVRM camera.*
16.18

FIGURE *The IVRM camera should be at 0,0,0.*
16.19

Now insert a flat surface to be used as your floor and duplicate that five times. These will be used as wall and ceiling surfaces. (See Figure 16.20.)

Arrange the surfaces to form an exploded cube as in Figure 16.21. The space inside the cube is where we'll insert and arrange objects for the scene. Before you start arranging, you need to know what is up and what is down in the final render. The ground plane and ceiling planes are perpendicular to the Z axis, and the walls are parallel to it.

You may want to make the other planes invisible while working from this point up to the final steps, just to make it easier to arrange your scene. (See Figure 16.22.)

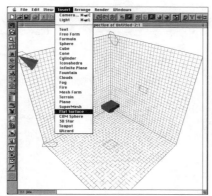

FIGURE **16.20** *Insert a flat surface.*

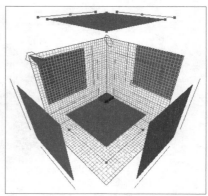

FIGURE **16.21** *Arranging the walls and ceiling.*

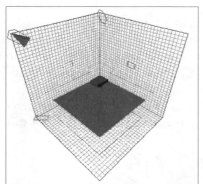

FIGURE **16.22** *Making the walls invisible makes working in the scene easier.*

Step Two

Let's insert some objects. I'm using primitives here, to keep it simple, and shading them each with a color specific to each. (See Figure 16.23.) After you've applied your Shaders and adjusted the objects, you'll add a Bulb light to light the room you're creating.

Now you can make your other planes visible, arranging them to make the room, and shading them with individual colors so you can tell them apart.

Step Three

In the **Current Scene** settings palette's **Output** tab, you'll need to set the **Image Size** aspect ratio of width to height as **2:1**. This is imperative for the scene to render properly for RealVR.

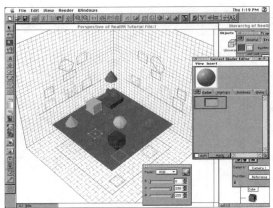

FIGURE   *Inserting and coloring your primitives.*
16.23

I use settings of **1000 Width** by **500 Height** in pixels. (See Figure 16.24.) There are no limits to the size though, and if you just want to render for resolution's sake, then your only considerations are how many megs your RealVR viewer can handle, and RDS's 16,000 by 16,000 pixel limit (or, in the case of RealVR's 2 to 1 aspect ratio, 16,000x 8,000).

I have run across problems using the Adaptive renderer with RealVR, so you might want to change your renderer to Ray Tracer at this point.

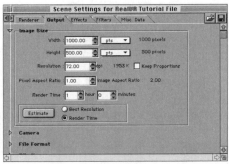

FIGURE   *Setting the Image Size.*
16.24

Now choose the camera you've designated as IVRM spherical, and save the RDS file. Close the file and add it to your **Batch Queue** list. (See Figure 16.25.) You must render RealVR files via the Batch Queue to generate the .IVR file that accompanies it.

Launch the Queue and chow on a coffee cake — be careful not to get any crumbs in the keyboard, though.

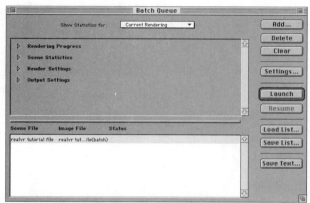

FIGURE   *Adding the file to the Batch Queue.*
16.25

When RDS has finished rendering the scene, you can open up the file in the RealVR viewer that is supplied on the Ray Dream Studio CD-ROM. You can also view it right off your hard drive through a browser with the RealVR plug-in installed as well. Figure 16.26 shows the final render.

FIGURE   *Our final RealVR JPEG.*
16.26

RealVR to QuickTime VR

Adapting a RealVR image for QuickTime VR couldn't get much simpler. All you need to do is to take the RealVR rendering from RDS and rotate it 90 degrees counterclockwise in a paint program, then run the image file through the RealVR-to-QuickTime-VR file conversion utility that can be found at the Apple Computer Web site.

—*RICK GRECO*

CHAPTER

17 Artist Profiles

N ow that your 3D toolbox is packed with tips, techniques, and thought processes, take a moment to sit back and see how three *Ray Dream* pros put it all together to plan and create a project.

On the next few pages you'll have a chance to go behind the scenes with John Crane, Rick Greco and Steve McArdle to see how they build an award-winning image. You'll find that these artists use many of the techniques covered throughout this book. What this means is you shouldn't feel intimidated by these images since, if you're on the last chapter, you've obviously read the rest of the book and already have all of this knowledge locked away . . . right? Well, OK, so perhaps I'm dreaming here but even if you haven't read through the entire book just yet, hopefully these images will inspire you to suck up as much of the knowledge in here as possible and you'll be creating your own masterpieces in no time.

John Crane: Ant Acid

John Crane's *Ant Acid* is an amazing testament to what can be accomplished with Ray Dream Studio, good planning and a pocket full of patience.

Rick Greco: BJ Progressive Counter

Rick Greco will show you how to put together a professional editorial illustration by breaking down his creation of the *BJ Progressive Counter.*

Steve McArdle: Meta-Hog

Many of you have been clamoring for a writeup of this masterpiece for a long time. Well, Steve finally did it and now you have it.

JOHN CRANE: ANT ACID

The Birth of Ant Acid

Precision modeling, lots of RAM and a lot of patience gave birth to "Ant Acid." She was born on a Power Macintosh with 132 MB RAM using Ray Dream Studio for everything but the decals. Ant Acid represents over 200 hours of modeling, sizing, aligning and fitting, and is a good example of what Ray Dream is capable of these days with a little planning. (See Figure 17.1.)

In the Beginning

For accurate reference, I began by photographing heavy machinery at a nearby construction site, paying special attention to linkages and hydraulics in the arms. The main model consists of nearly 1,000 objects, many of them duplicated masters, "jumped-in" to and re-instanced. The final model size, including 16-bit decals created in Photoshop, was 2.2 MB. Four lights, two with shadows

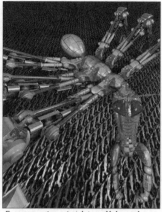

FIGURE *Ant Acid in all her glory.*
17.1

disabled, were positioned around the model. Twelve different cameras were established to point at specific joints, then made invisible . One more camera I named "move around" could be freely positioned without disrupting the others.

If you look closely at the model, you'll note that it's really just a collection of rather simple shapes, all fitted together. In my opinion, this is one of Ray Dream's real strengths; aligning and positioning objects.

The Legs

The master leg was precision-modeled using the **free-form modeler**, the **Properties palette** and the **Alignment palette**. Each leg is composed of 136 objects set to maximum **Surface Fidelity**. (See Figure 17.2.) Many of those

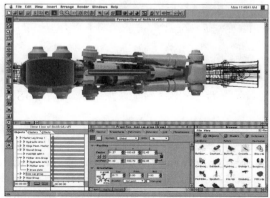

FIGURE *Each leg was composed of 132 objects.*
17.2

objects, such as the teeth in the shovel, are duplicated masters. Bolts, end-caps, brackets, hoses and hydraulics were all designed and modeled such that, were Ant Acid ever to come to life, she would actually work.

Because the final poly count was so high, I worked in bounding box mode as much as possible to speed things up. Switching to shaded preview to see results of a move and spot-rendering critical junctions helped make sure everything was aligned properly.

For the master leg, two hydraulic groups were created; one for the double-set on her femur, and one for the master pull arms on the tibia and fibula. The chrome-rod-sliders were inserted with plenty of adjusting room to later aid in animation. Items such as hoses leading into the body were created and extended with plenty of grace room, just in case things got messy down the road. The same applied to the bracket that would attach the group to the spherical body. As the first group was being built, I added its pieces to the objects browser for easy retrieval.

The chrome knee cap was important because there had to be enough room on either side for both leg sections to freely rotate within. A large pin anchors each leg's endpoint through the knee. The hot point of the leg group was positioned on the pin so the leg would accurately revolve around it. Doorways on either side of the knee cap were made large enough to accommodate some movement.

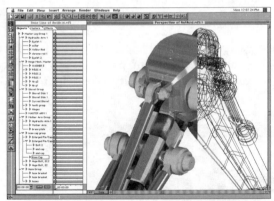

FIGURE 17.3   *The chrome knee cap was designed with motion in mind.*

The Head

The head was probably the most important part. (See Figure 17.4.) It's composed of 109 objects, again, many of them duplicated masters. Chrome balls running along the length of her head are duplicated sphere primitives. The hair is a rotated free-form duplicate, and the plates on the snout are duplicated free forms re-sized and angled up in specific increments with a simple spot bump applied from *Ray Dream's* stock shaders. Eyes were critical in defining her personality. Each eye is free-formed, then extruded with a **Free** envelope and pinched at the ends. The shader allows for a semi-transparent look, highly reflective and very "machine-like." **Reflection:** 24, **Shininess** and **Highlight:** 100, **Transparency:** 29, **Refraction:** 30.

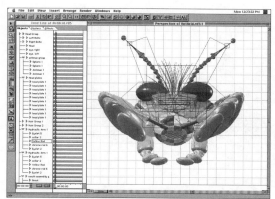

FIGURE *The head is composed of 109 objects.*
17.4

Her jaws began as the jaws from a Dream Model termite. I deleted the right side of the group, then enlarged the set and applied the same yellow chrome shader I'd established for the body. The shader is a procedural created in *Ray Dream's* shader editor and applied consistently to the main body pieces. Industrial yellow with a paneled **Bump** channel, which was created using the **Checkers** and **Wires** function, formed her steel plated skin. (See Figure 17.5.) **Highlight** and **Shininess** were set to 85 and **Reflections** to 30. Decals were created in *Photoshop* with specific aspect ratios, then applied as rectangular paint shapes. I applied each decal in better preview mode then duplicated the group

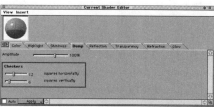

FIGURE *Ant Acid's metal plate shader.*
17.5

with symmetry and adjusted the decals accordingly. I find that applying decals as rectangular paint shapes small, then dragging larger helps in this sometimes frustrating process.

The Body

The body is composed of 4 free form objects and two primitives. (See Figure 17.6.) The hot point of the back bulb was moved to the intersection of the chrome universal joint to allow proper rotation, then rotated 30¡ up.

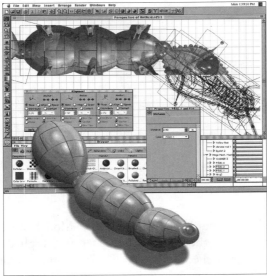

FIGURE *The body is composed of two free form objects and*
17.6 *two sphere primitives.*

Final Assembly

Once the individual pieces were completed, a new scene file was opened and final assembly began. Everything was built around the body. I had to make sure the hoses and arm brackets protruding from each assembly lined up properly with the under-side of her spherical body and didn't pierce the skin on top or bottom. (See Figure 17.7.) Extra cameras and multiple views made this easy. (See Figure 17.8.) Her head was angled down about 20¡ to show a bit of attitude.

During the course of construction I rendered many low-res previews and stored them as reference. When doing so, all of the enablers were turned off, surface fidelity was set to its minimum setting, and adaptive oversampling was turned off. This allowed a relatively fast preview of the concerned area.

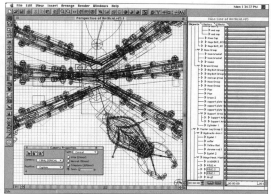

FIGURE **17.7** *Assembly of Ant Acid as a whole.*

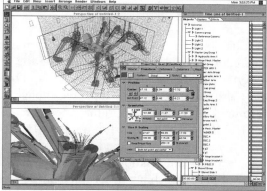

FIGURE **17.8** *Setting up multiple views helped with the construction.*

Rendering

The main model took three days to ray trace. The settings and effects were established as follows: Image size was 4,200 by 2,447 pixels. All enablers were used with a maximum ray depth of 12 (I had to interject a little reason in this project somewhere). **Silhouette quality** was set to 200% and **adaptive over-sampling** was set to Best. The **mask** and **distance** channels were set in the **G-Buffer**. (See Figure 17.9.) In the rendering/effects dialog, I set the **Backdrop** to black, and the reflected background to map, importing a medium-resolution Bryce landscape I'd rendered as a panorama to add interesting reflections. The panorama rendering eliminated that nasty pinch at the top and bottom of rounded shapes. Ambient light was set to 65%.

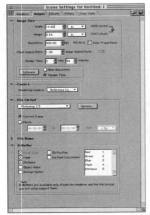

FIGURE   *The Render Settings.*
17.9

Use System Memory is always checked in my RDS preferences so before a long rendering, I usually restart the computer with a custom extension set and launch a fresh version of the application. I set her up in the **Batch Queue** specifying a directory on a remote hard disk and asked Ray Dream to please save every 30 minutes. I also made certain I had a large enough scratch disk designated. If time permits, I'll also usually optimize the scratch disk. I relaunched Ray Dream with 110 MB's RAM allocated to it, opened the batch queue, double-checked my settings, hit launch and then took a short vacation.

Ant Acid's whereabouts are unknown. If seen, please dial 911 and lock your doors. Do not try to approach her or feed her. She is considered hydraulically-armed and extremely dangerous. (See Figure 17.10.)

An earlier version of this article first appeared in 3D Artist magazine, Issue #27. For more information about 3D Artist visit **http:/www.3dartist.com** or call (505) 424-8945.

FIGURE   *Ant Acid. hydraulically-armed and extremely*
17.10   *dangerous.*

RICK GRECO: BJ PROGRESSIVE COUNTER

It starts with a meeting of the senior art and editorial staff members. You're at the round table, trying to determine how to turn these barren landscapes of text you've been given into something called a magazine. It's not an easy job, but it's one you've come to know well; and every month, at about this time, you have the pleasure of making it your business of telling everyone your big ideas on how to bring these articles to life.

Whereas the Art Director generally creates and shapes the design that makes your magazine look as fantastic as it does, he/she still needs the all powerful illustration to do the job. Whether it be a photograph or an illustration, you and your team need to draw from the content of the stories and compliment them with the sweetest eye candy you can conjure up on a deadline that is always sooner than you feel comfortable with.

The piece in Figure 17.11 was created for an article appearing in Casino Player Magazine, one of the many gambling publications our publishing company produces every month. On the table was a story about progressive betting in Blackjack — essentially a methodical way to hedge your chances of winning more hands more often. We've covered this material before, as often happens in publications such as ours. The secret was to brew up a new image with a unique statement that didn't appear too trite, yet created visual excitement and tied back into the story somehow. Like I said, its not an easy job.

I got lucky the day this article was up for peppering (my own term for spicing up an article with illos). "... counting ... counting ... hmmm ... counting ... aha! — that little red thing mom used to bring to the store to add up the prices of the items she had in her shopping basket," I thought.

FIGURE *The Blackjack Progressive Counter.*
17.11

Why that occurred to me I have no clue, but that's the way these things happen. So after a brief discussion and a small leap of faith on my Art Director and Editor-in-Chief's part, I was on my way to bringing mom's little red plastic counter into the world of casino blackjack.

Hit Me!

I started by modeling and shading the body of the counter. (See Figure 17.12.) This was a happy effort, as it took very little time, and it required a shader that a ray tracer seems to excel at rendering realistically and quickly — plastic.

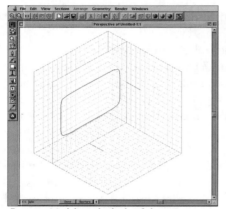

FIGURE **17.12** *Modeling the body of the counter.*

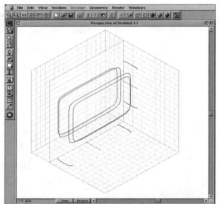

FIGURE **17.13** *Rounding the edges of the body using the scaling envelopes.*

I started with a simple set of cross sections, and using the scaling envelope formed the rounded front edges. (See Figure 17.13.) Rounded edges are generally something that RDS's **Free Form modeler** allows you to do very intuitively, and until you've tried modeling in other 3D software, it's easy to take this for granted. Anyway, this part took about three minutes.

Next I had to figure a way to "knock out" the area where the numbers would show through. I thought about this briefly, and came up with a solution that would both save time and look great — a paint shape.

In *Macromedia Freehand* I created two sets of maps, one for bump, and one for transparency. (See Figure 17.14.)

The bump map would solve the need for a bevel in the numbers "window", whereas the transparency map would actually do the knocking out that created the window through which the numbers would show.

In the **Shader Editor** I brought the transparency map into the **Transparency** channel, the bump map into the **Bump** channel, and left the

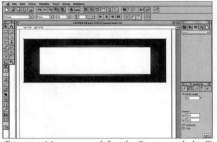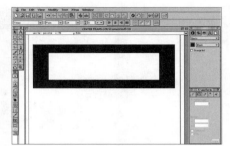

FIGURE *Maps created for the Bump and the Transparency channels of the counter to form the*
17.14 *window.*

other channels empty, so as not to allow the other channels to override the underlying shader beneath the paint shape I was using to apply these two maps.

A test render showed this worked better than anticipated. I could have done this through a Boolean operation with a proper object to Boolean out the window, but I did it without changing any actual geometry — always a plus if it can be done.

The next step required that I create the letters "HIT!", and also to create the reels the letters would be painted on to. (See Figure 17.15.) This solution came along with the initial idea of how to create the knock out and the bevel. I realized that actually modeling reels would introduce a lighting issue I had no desire to deal with. I knew this could be a problem from previous experience from modeling a photorealistic slot machine some months before. The reels were a lighting nightmare, requiring that I experiment with way too many work-around solutions to justify the apparent simplicity of that part of the project.

The answer here, once again, was *Freehand.* I simply created the letters, and used gradients to produce the illusion of reels. I mapped this to a flat object,

FIGURE *The reels for the inside of the counter.*
17.15

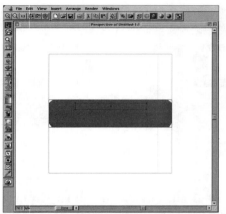 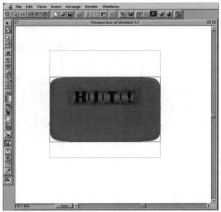

FIGURE   *Positioning the "reels" so they would show through the transparent window.*
17.16

placed it within the body of the counter I'd already modeled and mapped with the "window" cut out, and used the Preview Tool to help me position the "reels" properly within the frame of the window. (See Figure 17.16.)

At this point I had to dig into my childhood memory and try to recall the way the buttons looked on this gadget of motherly thrift. Flat head, white, sticking into the body. Home run. Another minute-long modeling process.

Using cross sections in the **free form modeler**, a button took shape. (See Figure 17.17.) I duplicated the initial button object four times, arranged them with the body, and moved on to place the "Blackjack Progressive Counter" text onto the front of the grouped counter object.

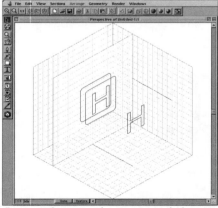

FIGURE   *The counter button was made from a*
17.17   *single free form object.*

The text along with an accompanying clipping map was created in *Freehand*, and simply mapped to the front of the body object via a paint shape. A test render showed it all worked, and I was ready for the next step.

The Chips are Down

Mom's shopping counter was the inspiration for this graphic, yet, slapping appropriate new words onto the front of the counter model simply wasn't enough to create a convincing illustration. Naturally it belonged near blackjack table, and since this graphic was illustrating a story on techniques to win at blackjack, it needed to be among casino chips — lots of them, and of high denomination. I thought about using playing cards in the image too, but at this point, the image I was seeking was fairly clear in my head; and cards just weren't part of the hand I was playing here (pun intended).

Modeling the chips was as easy as creating a circle onto the **drawing plane** in the **free form modeler**, using the scaling envelope to create the slight internal bevel, and scaling it to the approximate thickness for a casino chip. (See Figure 17.18.)

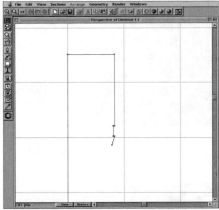 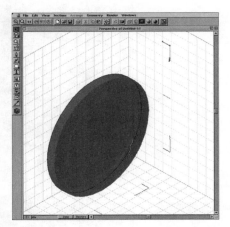

FIGURE *The chip models are simple free forms.*
17.18

I would've liked to have mixed a few chip denominations in the chip columns, but as usual, with most of what I do, I had limited time to spend designing them and didn't have the time to create the extra texture maps. As often happens when faced a deadline, I was forced into a simple solution, and luckily (no pun intended) this solution precluded options that I think would have complicated the graphic visually. I dropped the idea of multiple denomination chips, therefore saving me the process of creating maps for them and arranging the various color chips to balance the graphic properly.

My luck appeared dressed in black. Generally (although there are exceptions), a black chip means means $100 or more — definitely a high-enough denomination to indicate that the user of my Blackjack Progressive Counter was a winner. Black would also compliment the other dominant colors in the image well — the green felt of the blackjack table, and the red of the Blackjack Progressive Counter.

The shader for the master chip object would be what would give it all of it's character, so I referenced the chips I keep around my Atlantic City office while designing the texture maps for mine in Photoshop. The first map (See Figure 17.19) was applied using **projection mapping** and the center map (See Figure 17.20) was applied with a paint shape. Also, a slight amount of bump was applied to the upper surface of the chip with a texture map in the bump channel.

Arranging the chips and the chip stacks so they would look natural was not as hard as it could have been, but it did take a bit of time to get the right

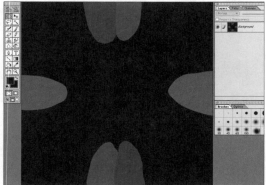

FIGURE
17.19 *This is the map that creates the little dabs of color around the outside of the chip.*

FIGURE
17.20 *This is the map for the text on the chip.*

feel. By grouping and ungrouping sets of them, and using the **Transform** tab in the **Properties Palette** to change their positions and orientations, it went much easier and quicker than if I had tried drag them around by hand.

Belly Up!

The blackjack table was comprised of two grouped free form objects. (See Figure 17.21.) I kept the shaders for the table felt and armrest cushion very simple. Shader complexity for these objects would add to the time required to finish and render the scene, while not adding any significant interest to the final illustration.

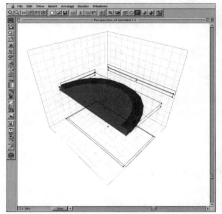

FIGURE **17.21** *The table was made from two free form objects and shaded simply.*

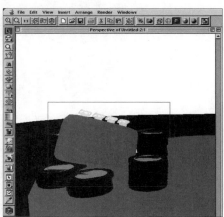

FIGURE **17.22** *The composition of the final scene.*

Can We Make Some Kind of Arrangement?

Previsualization is a skill I've acquired after many years as a photographer. In my mind's eye, I am able to view a location, a collection of props and/or people, along with some ideas of the lighting, and come up with a direction that I can follow when all these elements are be in front of me.

Essentially working backwards from the fairly vivid image I'd described to my colleagues earlier, I arranged and framed all my objects as a still life of sorts. (See Figure 17.22.)

Those Vegas Lights

I used two "feathered" spotlights at high angles, one to the front right and right rear, both set at 75% intensity. A bulb light set to 33% intensity was added in the very front of the scene towards the left side of the Blackjack Counter just off the table.

No Smoking Please

The last element was the photographic Backdrop image. (See Figure 17.23.) This was not hard to find, as I have many casino shots in my archives to choose from, but I must admit the image I chose worked out very well (quite by accident), as the graphic lines it provided in the background seemed intentional.

FIGURE *The image I chose as my background was perfect in*
17.23 *many ways.*

Everything is Getting Blurry . . .

Before committing this image to a render I checked the **Distance Mask G-Buffer** under the **Render options**. I used this mask in post production to create a gradual blur (a simulated depth of field effect) towards the **Backdrop**. I could have used Rayflect's Depth of Field filter to do so instead, but I come from the old *Ray Dream* days, before *RDS* and before *Rayflect's* wonderful array of filters and effects, so my tendency is to want to create some effects by "hand" via *Photoshop*.

To do this, I prefer to use the straight blur found in *KPT Convolver*. Reason being that using the **Gaussian blur** native to *Photoshop* will slightly blur a few pixels outside the mask area, creating a haze in the image at the mask's edge. *Convolver* allows you to apply a large amount of controlled standard blur easily and in one pass, whereas with *Photoshop's* **Blur** or **Blur More** filters you'd have to apply them many times to achieve the same effect without any of the feedback and control available from *Convolver*.

Render Me Silly

I rendered this image high resolution for print, and was happy to see it, in our magazine's matchproofs, taking up more than the half page I had rendered it for. Though I wasn't so happy at first when I realized it had been sized it up in

QuarkXpress instead of actually being rendered for that resolution, but it looked great in the proofs and when printed.

Super-Add-A-Matic

Strangely enough, during this write-up, I'd also been unpacking from my recent move to Las Vegas and from one of my packed boxes emerged none other than Mom's "Super-Add-A-Matic" counter that inspired this image. (See Figure 17.24.) It was red, the buttons were white, but that's where the similarities to my Progressive Blackjack Counter ended. No matter, I could still use it to help save a few of the bucks this illustration put into my pocket — it would be *especially* nice though if it worked in the blackjack parlors all around my new home!

FIGURE **17.24** *Mom's original Super-Add-A-Matic counter that inspired the whole illustration, which was discovered months after the image was published!*

STEVE MCARDLE: META-HOG

Meta-Hog started as a back-up plan for a 3D contest I was submitting work to. (See Figure 17.25.) Before I go any further, let me just say that back-up plans are "good things", because my primary image basically fell apart, and Meta-Hog (originally called Wheels) quickly became my prime focus.

I was struggling to find subject matter for my 3D scene and took a break by going down to the corner store to grab a Slurpee (hey it was the middle of August!). While I was there, I flipped through some magazines. While flipping, I saw a magazine that had a new motorcycle on the cover and was talking about the revival of the cruiser bike and let's just say I had an inspiration. I bought the magazine and went back home to try to create something worthwhile.

Unfortunately I only had 2 images in the magazine to use as source for this bike — a front and a side. It looked like I was going to have to fudge a lot of the model, but hey that's the fun of it isn't it?

FIGURE *Meta-Hog started out as a secondary piece...believe it*
17.25 *or not.*

I had to start thinking about how I was going to create this highly detailed model without totally killing myself, and my system. It quickly became apparent that I would have to focus on individual components of the bike instead of worrying about putting them all together until later because the whole job would be too much to worry about at once.

Stage I

I like to do a lot of my figuring out while I'm working, so I generally don't do any drawings, I just start modeling once I have my references set up (in this case those 2 photos). I chose the wheels as my starting point and began with the tires. I created a profile of a cut through a tire, and used the **Torus** preset in the **free form modeler** to create the shape. I also modeled a few grooves where the tread should go to help get some bumping, however I always had the intention of using a bump map to get a more realistic and accurate effect in the end. Once the tire was done, I created the rim of the wheel basically in the same way, with a freeform and torus preset applied to it. I then moved onto the spokes. Here I basically created a single pair of interlocking spokes and gave them a hot point in the center of the wheel. This would allow me to duplicate children objects of the master around the center of the wheel with the same offset, as well as saving me a lot of time. Next came the axle (which was actually just a cylinder primitive), then a couple of brake pads made in the **free form** modeler, and then some end caps for the axle. Pretty quickly I had a not-too-bad-looking wheel built. (See Figure 17.26.)

To give the tire a more realistic look, I went into detail by adding custom bump maps to it. I added embossed text to the walls of the tire by applying **Paint Shapes** with texture maps in the **Bump** channel. Then I applied an overall

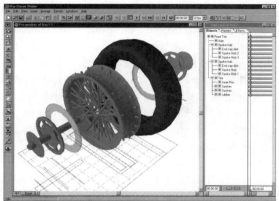

FIGURE
17.26
An exploded view of one of Meta-Hog's wheels.

bump map image to the tire to form the treads. By changing the **Mapping Mode** of the tire to **Cylindrical**, I could easily control the bump mapping to make sure that the treads were only applied to the face of the tire, and not the walls. I applied the appropriate shaders to the wheel objects (mostly reflection values), and it was now done. With a quick duplication and little tweaking of the object's width and size, I created the rear wheel.

I now had the foundation for my bike. I knew it was going to get trickier from here.

Stage II

I proceeded up from the front wheel and started building the forks that connected the wheel to the handlebars and rest of the bike. These were basically extruded free form cylinders with slight variations along their extrusion. I created connectors so that they weren't floating in mid-air, and started modeling in some detail such as bolt and nut heads. Once I had the forks established in place, I started modeling the handlebars/headlight section as a completely separate component. I opened a new document and started working on the handlebars first. I created a circle in the free form modeler, extruded it with pipeline method enabled and no extrusion envelope, and manipulated it until I got the handlebar shape. I then built the grips and the brake lever components and placed them onto the handlebars. I added the instrument panels; connected them to the handlebars and proceeded to build the headlight. At first I wasn't sure how I was going to get the headlight to work the way I wanted, but played with it until I figured a few things out. First off, after making the headlight casing shape, I put a reflector objected inside the headlight. It was much like an open ended cone. The reason for this is that I wanted to put a bulb light inside the headlight to simulate the bulb in a real headlight, but at the time, Ray Dream didn't support visible lights. The reflector inside the headlight would reflect the light from the bulb light and make it look like a visible light if I had the highlight settings high enough on the shader I was applying to the reflector. I then placed a transparent sphere into the headlight to simulate the glass covering, and shaded it with high transparency, some refraction, and a **Wire** function in the **Bump** channel to give the appearance of molded glass. All these elements together led to very satisfying results in the final rendered image, which, to this day, people still ask me how I did it.

I proceeded to build the indicator lights using some of the same principles, and added the wiring to the brakes and levers. The steering component of the bike was now done, and things were looking up. (See Figure 17.27.)

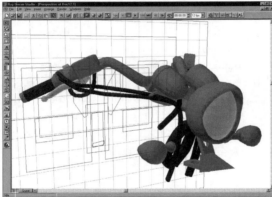

FIGURE *The assembled handlebars and Lights.*
17.27

Stage III

The engine was the next part I needed to build, seeing I had the framework around it ready. Again, I started working on the engine components of the bike as a separate file. My goal here was not necessarily to model an actual engine, I don't envy the task of replicating an engine in 3D exactly. I was more concerned with creating a model of an engine that was believable, but not necessarily exact. Even still, the resulting engine consisted of over 150 modeled objects. All the objects were modeled in the free form modeler, and thankfully, the engine is relatively symmetrical, so I could duplicate a decent amount of the objects and flip them. This allowed me to model one side of the engine and flip many of it's components and use the on the other side. (See Figure 17.28.)

I think this is a good place to say that, while Meta-Hog was only viewed from one side, it is a fully realized model in 360 degrees, because I planned

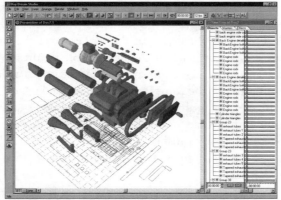

FIGURE **17.28** *The disassembled engine.*

(and still do) to use it in other contexts, and am considering it's inclusion in an animated sequence.

Once the engine was completed, it was quite easy to add the exhaust system, (which is really part of this engine construction anyway). I shaded the components (again mostly with various reflective values) and tweaked any positioning I thought was necessary. At this point I could finally sit back and take a rest because I was nearly there.

Bringing it All Together

At this stage I thought I would bring together the 3 parts I had worked on so far. With a bit of scaling and positioning, they fit together quite nicely. I could now work on building the connectors between the components, such as the brake cables, an actual braking device on the wheel, and a gas tank to help bring the engine and handlebars parts together. (See Figure 17.29.)

I proceeded to build the storage compartment, seat, structural tubing, and connectors. Finally I went ahead and built the rear suspension and drive train

FIGURE **17.29** *Meta-Hog begins to take form.*

with free form objects. The shocks, for example, were really a series of cylinders surrounded by a large spring that was modeled with the spiral extrusion preset in the free form modeler. Finally I put the fenders over the tires, and attached any appropriate connectors such as the brake cable fixtures to the fenders. On the rear fender I put the rear light and rear indicators (which were actually scaled down duplicates of the front indicators). I added a kick stand to the bike since it was going to be standing still and needed some visual support.

At this point I finally had a chance to sit back and take a breath. The modeling of the bike was finally finished. (See Figure 17.30.) I did, however, think one last touch was necessary to really make it my own . . . (See Figure 17.31.)

FIGURE *The finished model.*
17.30

FIGURE *That personal touch.*
17.31

Composing

I now started playing with the camera in different angles and positions trying to get the most appropriate viewing angle of the bike to show it off as best I could — and give it as much presence as possible. After much tinkering, repositioning, adjusting the rotation of the handlebars and front wheel and several test renders I finally found my position. (See Figure 17.32.)

FIGURE *Setting the shot.*
17.32

I then started building my environment, which was going to be a landscape, with the then newly released *SuperMesh* extension. I created the height map in *Photoshop*, and brought it into *SuperMesh* for height field extrusion. After messing around with the resolution of the resulting mesh, I placed it behind the bike and laid it into its final position. Because the bike had a lot of reflection in it's components I needed to create a duplicate of landscape object and place it behind the camera, so you could see the reflection of it in the bike. I then needed to make a sky, so I opened some cloud images I had on PhotoCD in *Photoshop* and colour-corrected them to give them a sunset looking feel. I made sure that I designed the clouds so the sun in the image would look as if it was sitting just over the landscape. I wanted this for dramatic effect, and because I wanted to utilize the then Beta version of *Rayflect's Pro Lens Pack* to create the flare of the sun.

After I had settled on the background sunset I was using, I placed it into the scene via the **Background** tab under the **Rendering> Effects** tab. I also copied this file into the **Reflected Background** tab so that the clouds would reflect in the bike and not just sit behind it. I then did some test renders of the scene so that I could see exactly where the sun was sitting on the background bitmap in relation to the scene. Once I could see where it was sitting I could place my light sources in the scene accordingly so it would look as if the sun was giving off the light. I did this through some carefully placed spot lights. (See Figure 17.33.) I then placed my final light exactly where the sun would be so that I could set it up for the lens flare effect from the *Rayflect Pro Lens Pack*. (See Figure 17.34.) I did another test render to make sure it was positioned right, and to make sure there weren't any inappropriate cast shadows from the other lights.

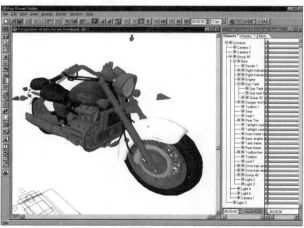

FIGURE *Setting up the lights.*
17.33

FIGURE **17.34** *Adding the lens flare.*

Up until this point I was rendering my scenes with the ray tracer, but with Reflections, Transparency, Refractions, Bumps and Shadows disabled This speeds up the ray tracer considerably for proofing, while still giving you decent results for detail checking. It was at this stage I did a small test render, with the all the ray tracing options enabled, to see how the reflections of the metals and the transparency/refraction of the headlight would look. Everything looked pretty good to me, so I made a few adjustments to the ground to give it a wet look, like after a rainfall. Finally I went into the render settings and set the file up for 8 × 10" at 250dpi, crossed my fingers and hit the render button.

I think the hard work was worth it, as Meta-Hog came to be a pretty satisfying image for me, and has generated a lot of excitement for 3D in those who have seen it, which is really pretty satisfying in itself.

APPENDIX

Software Company Index

In case you are interested in any of the products mentioned in this book (and some not mentioned), here is your contact information.

COMMERCIAL

Adobe Systems Inc.

Photoshop
2D image manipulation and creation application.

Premiere
Nonlinear video editing application.

Illustrator
2D PostScript creation application.

After Effects
2D video animation and special effects application.
1585 Charleston Road
Mountain View, CA 94039
V: 415.961.4400
F: 415.961.3769
www.adobe.com

Artbeats

Animated clips, tilable textures, and backgrounds on CD-ROM.
P.O. Box 709
Myrtle Creek, Oregon 97457
V: 800.444.9392
V: 503.863.4429
F: 503.863.4547
www.artbeats.com

Autonomous Effects, Inc.

Ray Dream extensions (BoneBender, FaceShifter, HotLips, PoserImporter, TV Tweaker and more in the queue).
www.afx.com

Corel

CorelDraw
2D vector art creation application.

Corel Building
1600 Carling Avenue
Ottawa, Ontario,
K1Z 8R7
CANADA
V: 800.772.6735
F: 613.761.9176
www.corel.com

Form & Function

Wraptures Volume One and Two
Tilable texture maps and backgrounds on
CD-ROM.
3394 Southeast Woodward Street
Portland, OR 97202
V: 800.779.5474
www.wraptures.com/wow/

Macromedia, Inc.

Freehand
2D PostScript drawing application.
600 Townsend Street
San Francisco, CA 94103
V: 800.945.4601
F: 415.442.0190
www.macromedia.com

MetaCreations Corporation

Ray Dream Studio and Ray Dream 3D
Well, you know what these do.

Bryce 3D
3D landscape generating and rendering package.

Detailer
3D Paint application.

Infini-D
3D modeling, rendering and animation application.

Poser
Humanoid figure modeling application.

Painter
2D paint application.

Expression
Vector-based 2D drawing/paint application

JAG
Anti-aliasing application.

Kai's Power Tools
2D image processing filters.

Final Effects and Studio Effects
2D video processing filters for Adobe
Premiere and After Effects.

Goo
Image warping and manipulating application.
6303 Carpinteria Avenue
Carpinteria, CA 93013
V: 805.566.6296
F: 805.566.6385
www.metacreations.com

RAYflect, Inc.

Ray Dream extensions and training products
(Four Elements, Fun Pack, Pro Lens Pack,
Visible Light Pack, CD Training materials, and
at least one other VERY cool extension that
I'm not allowed to talk about right now but
should be available by the time you read this).
9, rue Duphot
75001 — Paris
France
http://www.imaginet.fr/rayflect/

Viewpoint Datalabs

3D Models
870 West Center
Orem, UT 84057
V: 801.224.2222
F: 801.224.2272
www.viewpoint.com

VCE — Visual Concepts Engineering

The Pyromania Series
Collections of fire and explosions on CD-ROM.
P.O. Box 921226
Sylmar, CA 91392
V: 800.242.9627
F: 818.367.9187
vceinc@earthlink.net

Zenstar Software

Ray Dream Extensions
(SuperMesh, CloneIt and more on the way).
www.zenstar.com

You can probably find these programs on your favorite on-line services such as America Online or CompuServe. You can also find them at www.shareware.com.

SHAREWARE/FREEWARE

Sculptor

Mike Clifton
1013 Thistle Court
Sunnyvale, CA 94086
clifton@cse.ucsc.edu

Mechanisto

Mike Clifton
1013 Thistle Court
Sunnyvale, CA 94086
clifton@cse.ucsc.edu

Terrainman/TerrainMaker

Joe Ashear
505 Court St. #10B
Brooklyn, NY 11231
AOL: Renderer
Internet: artoffact1@aol.com

PatchDance

Paul Sexton
PatchDance@aol.com

B

Contributor Directory

This book is an expression of the cumulative experience of dozens of *Ray Dream Studio* artists, each of whom has been gracious enough to share this experience with you, the reader. In the next few pages you'll have an opportunity to learn more about each artist and his or her background, and find out how to get in touch with them if you'd like to comment on their contributions to the book, find out more about their work, or trade additional tips and techniques. (This book is by no means exhaustive!)

LISA ABKE

Lisa Abke is a freelance graphic artist residing in the Detroit Metropolitan area of Michigan. She has been working in the graphics industry for the past 10 years but only recently made the transition into the 3D arena. She is currently working on expanding her knowledge and focusing her efforts on 3D graphics for print, multimedia and the Internet. Lisa can be reached at **wtabke@concentric.net** or you can visit her website at **http://www.concentric.net/~Wtabke** which features additional samples of her work.

RUSS ANDERSSON

Russ Andersson is Director of Vision Effects at Autonomous Effects, where he has written the BoneBender, FaceShifter, HotLips, etc. extensions for *Ray Dream Studio 5.0*. He brings a strong background in robotics and real-time computer vision to 3-D graphics. Earlier projects have included a sophisticated robot ping-pong player (which was the subject of his Ph.D. dissertation), specialized real-time computers, and a real-time computer vision system embedded in several attractions at Disney's EPCOT. He has written one book, contributed to several others, and done a bunch of other techie stuff. Russ hopes some of his demo pieces have some artistic merit, but mainly tries to make sure that people laugh hard enough that it doesn't matter. You can judge for yourself at **http://www.afx.com**.

STEPHANIE ARVIZU

Stephanie Arvizu is the former Product Manager for *Ray Dream Studio*. A 15-year veteran of the computer industry, she is currently on sabbatical raising her daughter, Tallulah. She retains her keen interest in 3D and keeps up with changes in *Ray Dream Studio* and other products through independent projects. You can reach Stephanie at **stephanie@nerds.com**.

LONNIE BAILEY

Lonnie Bailey is a digital media artist in Silicon Valley who is best know for dramatic organic imagery with a strong emphasis in lighting and texturing. You can find his images on the Internet, in most of the big galleries, as well as in print materials. Lonnie's images have been used in many different types of works such as convention displays, mail order catalogs and web designs. Coming from a traditional art background gained at Art Center Pasadena, Lonnie has extensively studied fine art, illustration, and design over the past 10 years. Although he has studied art for many years, Lonnie says he has studied the environment around him since he was a small child. I guess it shows in his works since he says " I rarely ever need to rely on reference material anymore." You can view some of Lonnie's images at his web site which, in itself, has received a lot of acclaim in the past year. The URL is **http://www.baileygraphics.com**. I think you will enjoy it.

JOHNATHAN BANTA

Johnathan Banta grew up in Wyoming, where he fell in love with the movies (particularly *Star Wars*) and comic books. Throughout his life Banta has worked in print, television, theatre, fine art, sculpture, FX makeup, visual FX, and CGI. In 1982 he extended his passions to computers and began to program Apple II computers with his friends in an attempt to recreate the best movie-based video games.

Banta's company, Agrapha Productions, recently moved its operations to Los Angeles from its two-year home in Mountain View, CA. Banta currently works as a digital matte painter for BOSS Film Studios and can be contacted at **http://members.aol.com/agrapha**.

RICHARD BUCCI

Richard Bucci began working with computer graphics in 1984 while studying for his B.A. in studio art at the University of Rhode Island. His present work includes technical illustrations and art for publications, artist-concept over-heads and short animations. He also does independent projects and occasional competitive art shows, and his work has been featured in such magazines as Computer Artist, Computer Graphics World, and Design Graphics, as well as on various websites and bookcovers.

You can contact Bucci at **rab222@aol.com** or view samples of his work at his website at **http://members.aol.com/rbucci1**.

DEREK CARLIN

Derek Carlin is the Senior Art Director at MC2 (pronounced M C squared) Advertising and Design in Austin, Tx. A contributing editor for Corel Magazine, he also heads up his own design shop working in traditional illustration, 3-D illustration and animation, interactive design, and all areas of print-based media. You can reach Derek at rhodess@mail.utexas.edu. Contact him at this address for a disc portfolio (serious inquires only).

SHARKAWI CHE DIN

Sharkawi Che Din is from Malaysia, and is currently pursuing his MFA degree in Computer Art at the Savannah College of Art and Design. After graduating from New Zealand as a Computer Graphics major, he taught Graphic Design at the Universiti Malaysia Sarawak for about a year before pursuing his master degrees in the USA. About two years ago he began to work in 3D on both Macintosh and Silicon Graphics workstations and has recently had his 3D work published in DV magazine, Computer Artist, Computer Graphics World, Electronic Publishing and In-FormZ magazines. His animation called the Time Passage won the second prize in the Animation category for MetaCreation's 1997 "Beyond The Canvas"

International Art and Design Contest. Sharkawi can be reached at: sharkawi@earthlink.net or by snail mail at **Faculty Of Applied and Creative Art, Universiti Malaysia Sarawak, 94300 Kota Samarahan, Sarawak, Malaysia.**

ANTOINE CLAPPIER

Antoine Clappier is CEO of RAYflect,SA a Paris, France, based company dedicated to 2D and 3D add-ons development. After 10 years of research and teaching in Computer Graphics, he has developed several products: 3D Fun Pack, Pro Lens Pack, 3D Light Pack and Four Elements. All these products are available for Ray Dream Studio 5.0 and Ray Dream 3D. For more information, check out: **http://www.imaginet.fr/rayflect/.**

JOHN CRANE

As well as being a professional illustrator, John Crane owns and operates Sandhill Studios, an illustration and animation source in Santa Fe, New Mexico. Prior to working on the computer, John was a traditional illustrator using, amongst other medium, airbrush and gouache. His experience includes work with publishing, print, multi-media and video. His illustrations have won numerous awards including the Modern Masters of 3D "Characters of Your Imagination" First place for Ant Acid and has been shown in the New York Society of Illustrators "Digital Salon." As an assistant editor for 3D Artist magazine, he writes how-to articles using Ray Dream Studio as well as other Macintosh 3D applications, covering the state of the 3D art on the Mac. He also teaches Photoshop at Santa Fe Community College and has established a 3D curriculum at the prestigious Santa Fe Digital Media Workshop. You can see more of John's work at **http://www.sandstudios.com.** You may reach him by e-mailing **jbcrane@sandstudios.com.** At this writing, John and his wife Annie are anxiously awaiting the birth of their first child, no doubt destined to be a creative computer wiz.

BÅRD EDLUND

Bård Edlund hails from Oslo, Norway, and is currently attending the Maryland Institute, College of Art. He has been using computers to create visual art all his life, blending elements such as drawings, 3D renderings, photography and digital illustrations. His work has been featured in several magazines and web galleries, including Soulflare at **http://www.soulflare.com/**. Check out his imaginative illustration portfolio as well as an eclectic collection of other artwork at **http://www.edlundart.com/**. For more information, feel free to email Bård at **edlund@edlundart.com**.

DWIGHT M. EVERS

Growing up with a garage full of every type of mechanical system (some working, some not), I fell in love with mechanical systems. When I went to college, I studied as a Mechanical Engineer and got my degree — at the same time picking up a Computer Science minor with an emphasis on visualazation. The progression from CAD/CAE to Illustration/Graphic Design was sped up by the influences of my soon to be wife. Dwight can be reached at **dmevers@bitstream.net** and you can see more of his work at **http://www2.bitstream.net/~dmevers**.

RICK GRECO

Rick has been working in the publishing industry for eleven years. He started out as a news photographer and then branched into magazine photography. For the last 8 years, he's been an integrated member of the editorial staff at Casino Journal Publishing Group where his skills as photographer, illustrator, image editor, creative consultant, Apple tech, and sometimes wise-guy are required for the group's many publication. "... with a relatively small staff it's important to maintain a mild level of insanity at all times," Says Rick.

Rick formed Ripix Studios in support of his freelance interests which include application of the above skills, as well as freelance writing for publications such as 3D Artist where he is currently acting as a contributing editor.

Rick can be reached via email at Ripix@aol.com and you can view more of his work at **http://members.aol.com/ripix**.

D. R. GREENLAW

D.R. Greenlaw has been creating fantasy artwork with Ray Dream since 1994, but he actually started working in 3D back in the seventies. As a kid he dreamed of making the next 'Sinbad' epic in his backyard using modeling clay and his dad's 8mm film camera.

"The 'epic' wound up looking like *The Seventh Voyage of Gumby*, but thankfully, my work as shown some improvement since those early days."

Greenlaw currently works as an artist and animator in the Los Angeles area. He can be reached by e-mail at **dgreenlaw@aol.com**. To see more of his artwork, visit his web gallery at **http://members.aol.com/dgreenlaw**.

JEFFRY GUGICK

Jeffry Gugick is a digital artist who spends the majority of his time on his Mac working on illustrations, animations, rotoscoping, and photo retouching. Most of his work is done for major corporations who find his talent to be, according to Gugick, "beyond reproach." He can be reached on the Internet at **jeffrysg@aol.com**, and is always in search of new clients who can utilize his many talents. Feel free to visit his Web site and sample his wares at **http://members.aol.com/jeffrysg/main.html**.

CARL HENNIG

Carl Hennig works as an administrator and computer consultant for the University of Waterloo in Canada. He considers himself a "private" artist, since most of his work is done for personal pleasure, but he does submit images to shows on occasion. His work is almost always subjective and abstract in nature, and he likes "free-form, nonstructured objects that have no relevant meaning to my or anyone else's life." Most of his work is designed for large format color printers or 35mm slide output. You can reach him at **carl@uwaterloo.ca**.

RANDY HOLLINGSWORTH

Randy Hollingsworth is a Software Quality Assurance Engineer with MetaCreations. He has been involved with *Ray Dream Designer 3 , Ray Dream Designer and Studio 4, Ray Dream Studio 5, and Ray Dream 3D*. His involvement spans the development of Ray Dream by Ray Dream Inc., Fractal Design Corp., and now MetaCreations. He has also performed QA work for The Learning Company and Electronic Arts. Randy's background as an animation and special effects buff helps him bring the 3-D user's perspective to the products he works on. Says Randy, "My job is very much like working at a movie camera factory. Once the product is out there, people are bringing their imaginations to life with it and telling stories. Seeing what people do with these tools is very rewarding!" Randy can be reached at **randyh@metacreations.com**.

MARK JENKINS

Mark is a senior designer at Rucker Design Group in San Mateo, CA. His award-winning artwork has been exhibited internationally and has been featured in several books and magazines about digital art. Considering himself a "jack of all trades" designer, his experience spans a broad range of areas, including illustration, corporate identity, packaging, and multimedia. Although he enjoys the experimental freedom of the Macintosh, Mark was trained traditionally and maintains high standards for typography and production. Mark is an expert user of Adobe Photoshop, Illustrator, Fractal Design Painter and Fractal Design Studio and has been a featured speaker at seminars on the subject of how to combine the most powerful features of those applications. Email him at **mark@rucker.com** for more details.

TONY JONES

Richard Anthony (Tony) Jones has a background in fashion and advertising photography along with water and oil painting. He is cofounder and partner in a new media company, Sun Dog Ltd., which specializes in photographic image manipulation, 3D animation and illustration, interactive CD-ROMs, and Web sites. Their clients include CitiBank, Master Card, Readers Digest, Blockbuster, and Exxon. You can see more of Jones' work at Sun Dog's Web site at **http://www.sundogltd.com/**.

ROBERT LOMINSKI

Hailing from an architectural background, Robert Lominski currently works in a firm that sells and supports CAD and multimedia products. When not working on the computer at his job, Lominski can be found behind the keyboard of his home computer creating freelance rendering and animation work. On rare occasions his wife Ana and their Dalmatian, Tika, lure him away from the computer to go biking or hiking in the beautiful area of New York's Hudson Valley where they live. You can reach Lominski at **ral@mhv.net**.

CRAIG LYN

Craig Lyn is the author of the *Macintosh 3D Handbook*, Second edition, a definitive guide to 3D on the Mac that offers the reader an inside tour of all of the tips and tricks used by professional 3D artists. (Several of these tips and tricks appear in this book.) Originally driven to the culinary profession by his love of food, Lyn made a radical career switch to 3D computer graphics in 1993 and cofounded Meshworks, a 3D design studio based in San Francisco. He currently works for a prominent film special effects company in San Rafael, CA.

Lyn is also a frequent contributor to both *MacWeek* and *Digital Video Magazine* and can be reached at craiglyn@aol.com.

STEVE McARDLE

Steve McArdle is an award winning 3d designer/illustrator who currently holds the position of Creative Director of 3d imaging and Digital Illustration at Amoeba Corp., a creative house in Toronto, Canada. He regularly writes articles for magazines on 3d illustration, as well as contributes to various publications in the field of digital graphics. His work has appeared everywhere from books to magazine covers, to international ad campaigns. More of his work can be seen at his personal web site **web.idirect.com/~gig** or at Amoeba Corp.'s web site **www.amoebacorp.com**. He can be contacted at **gig@idirect.com** or **iguana@amoebacorp.com**. Amoeba Corp can be reached at **(416)-599-2699** or through email at **info@amoebacorp.com**.

BRIAN MURRAY

Since starting to work in comics in 1984, Brian Murray has worked with all the major comic publishers (including writing, drawing, and coloring *Supreme* for Image Comics) and his covers have appeared on such titles as *Leonard Nimoy's Primortals*, *Gene Roddenberry's Lost Universe*, and *Star Trek: Deep Space 9*. He has also worked on animation for *Transformers* and *The Real Ghostbusters*, advertising for such clients as Coca-Cola and Mercedes Benz, and storyboards and visual conception for *Star Trek* at Paramount, Landmark films, an upcoming *Terminator* project, and a projected colony on the moon for Fluor Daniels and NASA.

Murray is currently producing 3D graphics for his latest comic book creation, *Skyraker*, from his studio in Southern California, where he resides with his wife Kathy and their son, Cameron. You can email him at **skyraker@cris.com**.

CHRISTIAN NAKATA

Christian Nakata graduated from The Columbus College of Art & Design as an illustration major with a minor in advertising design, doing most of his work with an airbrush and acrylic paints. Presently working at American Greetings as a graphic designer, he now almost exclusively uses the computer to create art. According to Nakata, "the computer has freed up the possibilities in my work and I tend to experiment a lot more than I used to." You can reach Nakata at **crnakata@aol.com**.

MICHAEL POGUE

Michael Pogue has been working on 3D hardware and software design for more than 15 years and has two patents in the field. He recently founded Zenstar Software to help bring high-end modeling and animation features to the Ray Dream suite of programs. (Zenstar is the publisher of the *SuperMesh* plug-in for *Ray Dream Studio*.) In his spare time, when he's not having fun with his wife (MG) and two kids (Kevin and Kate), Pogue is also an artist, working in acrylics. He can be reached through his Web site at **http://www.zenstar.com**.

AARON PUTNAM

Since Aaron Putnam is only 17 as of this writing, he hasn't had much experience in the professional graphic arts field. His purchase and use of *Ray Dream Designer*, however, has given him enough experience to produce professional quality images. The root of his artwork comes from the physical world, where he likes painting and drawing, but he enjoys creating 3D images because of the rewarding variety of skills and techniques that are involved. You can see more of his work at his Web site at **http://inferno.asap.um.maine.edu/emp/aaronp**.

JAY ROGERS

Jay Rogers lives and works in Austin, Texas, as a computer illustrator and designer, having only recently escaped from the foodservice industry. He began programming text adventures on personal computers in 1981 with a 16K Radio Shack TRS-80. *Myst* was the breakthrough 3D experience for him and led to the acquisition of a Power Macintosh, thousands of dollars in computer books and software, and a strange aching feeling in his wrists..

MARK SIEGEL

Mark Siegel is a freelance 3D artist working in the Los Angeles area and has a traditional background in graphic design and illustration. He has been using

Ray Dream Designer as part of his 3D arsenal since 1993 and has had two first place winning entries in Ray Dream's "Modern Masters of 3D Contest." His award-winning 3D work has also been featured in many national magazines, including *Popular Photography, Step-by-Step Electronic Design,* and the *NADTP Journal.* You can reach Siegel via email at **marksiegel@aol.com** or through his Web site at **http://www.earthlink.net/~msiegel**

JOHN SLEDD

John Sledd is a freelance illustrator residing deep in the mountains of northeastern Virginia (Front Royal to be exact), where he enjoys throwing dirt clods and hunting the elusive snipe (for those of you unfamiliar with snipe hunting, don't worry — nobody gets hurt). His work, both 2D and 3D, has appeared on many an outhouse wall and can also be found in more appropriate communication vessels such as *Painting with Computers* by Mario Henri Chakkour and *Fractal Design Painter 4* by Dawn Erdos. Sledd can be reached by email at **john@sledd.com** and you can view more of his work at **http://www.sledd.com.**

JOHN STEPHENS

John Stephens lives in rural Vermont. As an artist/painter, he first became interested in 3D modeling as a tool to envision perspective lighting and reflections on some of the objects and scenes he painted. He now divides his time between painting acrylic paintings for an agent in California and doing commercial computer artwork for book publishers in New York. You can reach him via email at **elecpi@aol.com.**

VIEWPOINT DATALABS INTERNATIONAL, INC.

Founded in 1988, Viewpoint Datalabs International is the pioneer and worldwide leader in 3D core-content creation and publishing. The company's library and custom services, widely recognized as the industry standard for high-quality 3D models, are used by content creators to develop 3D animation, designs, and graphics for a variety of markets, including film and video, games, interactive media, and desktop graphics. Viewpoint also distributes 3D models developed by third parties, creating new market opportunities for modelers and their creations.

You can visit Viewpoint's Web site at **http://www.viewpoint.com** to search, view, browse, and manipulate individual 3D models from Viewpoint and search, view, and download free 3D models from the Avalon public archive.

VICTOR WONG

In 1995 Victor Wong set out to see just what he could accomplish with a Macintosh LC575, a 160-megabyte hard drive, and a copy of *Ray Dream Designer*. The result was one of the winners in Ray Dream's Modern Master's competition that year. Wong says it proved to him that it's not the machine that creates art, it's the person, and he hopes it will inspire anyone with an "underpowered" computer to still set their sights high.

Wong is currently a third-year student in molecular biology and genetics at the University of Guelph, Ontario, but still finds time to do copious amounts of quality illustration work on his LC575. He can be reached via email at **vwong@uoguelph.ca**.

STEVE YATSON

Steve Yatson has been working with 3d software for the past 5 years. The last 2 have been spent with *Ray Dream*. His other interests include surfing and music. One of Metacreations resident "Dead-Heads" he made his way from Ohio to Silicon valley pursuing a career in computer graphics early in 1989. "My first job as a graphic artist was creating adds for a local caterer in between serving food! Fortunately I've come a long way since then." He now resides in the Santa Cruz area and is the proud father of a 5 month old son. Steve can be reached at **syatson@metacreations.com**.

CECILIA ZIEMER

Cecilia Ziemer is a nonobjective painter and fantasy artist who has also done science museum work and pecan tree grafting. About four years ago she began working on the Macintosh in both 2D and 3D and has recently had her computer artwork appear in *3D Artist*, *New Media*, and *Computer Graphics World* magazines, and in the book *Looking Good in Color* (Gary W. Priester). Ziemer lives in Sunnyvale, CA, and can be reached via email at **Ziemer@aol.com**.

Web Information Resources

This is a list of several on-line resources for Ray Dream Studio. Some contain tutorials, some texture maps, some just general good 3D information. An HTML file of these links is included on the CD-ROM.

http://www.lightlink.com/dreamers/

This is the address for the infamous Ray Dream List-serv hosted by the wonderful John T. Chapman. You'll find lots of goodies here, as well as the sign-up instructions for the list.

http://www.worldnet.net/~jedi/

This is Ray Dream Online. Hosted by the mysterious Patryk.

http://samadhi.jpl.nasa.gov/txmp/

This is a excellent source of texture maps for space scenes.

http://www.baileygraphics.com

Lonnie Baily has a pretty clever site with many tips on how he does his magic.

http://www.diardsoftware.com

This is the address for Diard Software. They are the makers of an application called Universe. This application creates 2D images of space settings which are ideal for use as backgrounds and texture maps for your RDS work.

http://www.yup.com/chesser/

Preston Chesser's website has tons of cool stuff for fellow Ray Dreamers and art lovers alike.

http://www.ruku.com

The PixArt on-line computer art mag is filled to the rim with computer art techniques covering Ray Dream and many other applications.

http://www.dram.org/rd/

The Ray Dream Users Group hosted by David Ramirez.

http://www.afx.com/html/tutor.htm

Of course, Autonomous Effects has tutorials too

http://web.idirect.com/~gig/

For those of you who really appreciated Steve McArdle's contributions to this book, he has a lot more cool info and great pics at his site. Check it out.

http://www.primenet.com/~tonylane/tutorial.htm

Tony Lane has several good tidbits and tutorials for using RDS and other MetaCreations goodies.

http://www.3Dark.com/

General all around good 3D information.

http://www.3dcafe.com/

Lots of free models.

http://www.3dsite.com/3dsite/

More general 3D Goodies.

http://www.3dartist.com/3dartist.htm

3D Artist Magazine on-line.

http://www.3d-design.com/

3D Design magazine on-line.

http://www.dv.com/

This is Digital Video Magazines on-line version called DV Live. This is a fantastic resource for all things digital.

Index